Fall 2007
Miami

Blackface Cuba, 1840–1895

RETHINKING THE AMERICAS

A complete list of books in the series is available from the publisher.

Blackface Cuba, 1840–1895

Jill Lane

PENN

University of Pennsylvania Press
Philadelphia

Printed in the United States of America on acid-free paper

10 9 8 7 6 5 4 3 2 1

Published by
University of Pennsylvania Press
Philadelphia, Pennsylvania 19104-4112

Library of Congress Cataloging-in-Publication Data

Lane, Jill, 1967–
Blackface Cuba, 1840–1895 / Jill Lane.
p. cm. — (Rethinking the Americas)
Includes bibliographical references and index.
ISBN 0-8122-3867-2 (cloth : alk. paper)
1. Cuban literature—19th century—History and criticism. 2. Race in literature. 3. Blacks in literature. 4. Theater—Cuba—History—19th century. 5. Blackface entertainers—Cuba. I. Title. II. Series.

PQ7377.L36 2005
860.9'3552—dc22

2004065105

For my teachers

Contents

Preface
On the Translation of Race

The representation of race in writing is one of the principal concerns of this book: throughout, I lend attention to the relation between writing, blackface performance, and racialized national identities in nineteenth century Cuban vernacular culture. As a result, the pressures on my own translations of these representations from Spanish into English are particularly acute. In response to those pressures, I have made several strong translation choices of which readers should be aware.

Frequently, nineteenth century Cuban blackface writing (in plays, fiction, or press commentary) presented the speech of African or black figures through phonetic transcription of "distinct" speech patterns, accent, or inflection. Through such elaborate "transcriptions," African or black speech is emphatically marked as an incorrect, improper, and often comic performance of Castilian Spanish. The disfigurement of the written language is thus crucial to the ways these texts represent race and participate in broader processes of racialization. Yet I chose not to attempt to translate these distortions in the English translations I offer throughout the text. This racially marked language resists translation, and not only because it involves nonexistent words, or an array of misspellings and misuses of Spanish that have no English equivalent. The only model that might guide a hypothetical translation is the language of U.S. blackface minstrelsy. I have been reluctant to engage in such minstrelizing in the process of translation, and I have little confidence that minstrelsy actually is an appropriate model for such translation. Consider one minor example: in blackface Cuban performance, frequently the article "the" (*el*) is dropped, misconjugated, or offered in the wrong gender (becoming "*e*," "*la*," or "*lo*"); in comparable parodies in U.S. blackface minstrelsy, the word "the" often becomes "de" or "duh." In what way is "de" an accurate translation of "lo"? None, other than that both engage in racialized, and frequently racist, transcriptions of ostensibly "black" speech. Even more, to evoke the language and quality of U.S. minstrelsy would confuse rather than clarify the particular investments of Cuban blackface because readers of English would be tempted to hear false historical parallels between them. With all this in mind, I have chosen to offer literal translations of these texts throughout, and have only occasionally tried to evoke their effects.

In cases beyond these (mis)representations of "black" speech, my translations continue to be more often literal—event bluntly so—than not. Because I frequently engage in close readings of specific word choices and turns of phrase, my translations tend to honor the literal meanings and connotations of the Spanish, rather than attempt to reproduce the overall effect—aesthetic, political, or otherwise—of the original. Instead, I try to describe and engage those effects in my analysis. A case in point: some Cubans might object to my translation of the very widely used diminutive "-ito" into "little," especially in the keyword *negrito*, the name of Cuba's most famous blackface stage character, and a common racialized epithet in Cuban vernacular, both then and now. Throughout, I have translated negrito as "little black." While the diminutive "-ito" does in fact mean "little," it frequently carries the connotation of a term of endearment, the way one might use a diminutive with children or loved ones, as when "doll" becomes "dolly," or when "Tom" becomes "Tommy." Thus, "negrito" could be translated along the lines of "blacky" or better, "my blacky." However, even if the term can be (and today, often is) used as a vernacular term of endearment between white and especially black Cubans, its meaning—especially in the nineteenth century—is never free of the infantilizing, patronizing connotation that "little" carries when applied to an adult black male. A perfect translation would, of course, carry both connotations: the experience of deeply demeaning love encapsulates a century-long relationship between audiences and the popular stage figure of the negrito. Because the meanings of this word in particular become so overdetermined, I have often chosen not to translate it at all.

Throughout this text I have also used the Spanish term *criollo*, in reference to people born in Cuba, rather than an English equivalent, "Creole." In doing so, I hope only to underscore the specificity of the Cuban criollo experience, and temporarily set aside the immediate Anglophone and French Caribbean associations with the term "Creole." A future project could do the opposite, and intentionally explore the connections and shared historical experiences of all American-born, "Creole," colonial subjects in the Caribbean basin with reference to race, representation, and anticolonial sentiment.

Cuba was famous in the nineteenth century for its carefully calibrated distinctions regarding race: words such as *negro/a*, *pardo*, *moreno*, and *mulato* each designated a specific interracial combination. There are no English equivalents for these terms, for historical rather than philological reasons:

racial terminology in English emerges from a related but different history of white supremacy and racial identity in the United States, and has thus generated a different way of thinking and talking about racial categories. Within Cuba's racial matrix, key distinctions were made about place of birth, so that *negro de nación*, for example, refers to a black born in Africa, while *negro criollo* refers to a black born in Cuba. Further, as the century progressed, notions of a *raza de color* (literally, "race of color") were mobilized in antiracist and racist discourse to evoke sameness or solidarity between these different racial identities. Thus the available English terms such as "black," "mulatto," and "people of color" prove inadequate to the task. I invite the English reader to keep this complexity in mind when reading those words. For related reasons, I have seen no reason not to use the Spanish terms *mulato* and *mulata* throughout, rather than "translate" them into Anglicized spellings of these same Spanish terms (mulatto, mulatta). Unless clearly marked, I have not used the term "Afrocuban" to refer to black *criollos*, since the term *Afrocubano* postdates the history of racialized national identities told here, and its use remains controversial in Cuba even today.

In general, I have tried to listen carefully to the performances, texts, choreography, and music I have analyzed. As I rule, I've offered ample citations from archival sources, so that other readers might hear the resonance and meaning of the original. I do so in part because the materials are little known in both English- and Spanish-speaking performance studies, and are particularly inaccessible to U.S. students and scholars, housed as most are in archives in Cuba. (I ask Spanish readers to be aware, too, that I have usually transcribed texts faithfully, even when the original does not use now standard spelling, grammar, or accentuation.) Ultimately, however, I am wary of acting as a mediator or translator between Anglo and Hispanic languages and cultural forms: not only is a great deal of the meaning of these texts lost in translation, but the texts very often consciously resist being known or captured by English. English was already the language of the threatening neocolonial neighbor to the north in nineteenth century Cuba; any translation between the two contexts drags the language across the painful social, political, and cultural divide that separates life on either side of the Florida Straits.

Finally, all translations are mine unless otherwise noted.

Introduction
ImpersoNation in Our America

El teatro es el alma del pueblo
—José Martí

"The theatre is the soul of the people," claims the epigraph on a publicity poster for a performance of the *bufo cubano* at Havana's Teatro Martí in the late 1950s. Such claims on behalf of the theatre are common, draped as mantles over national-populist theatres throughout Europe and its many postcolonies wherever theatre and national sentiment have converged. Attributed to the great Cuban patriot-intellectual José Martí, the leader and ultimately victim of the final anticolonial war against Spain, this particular claim is striking: invoked on behalf of the theatre that bears Martí's name, the performance is headlined by Carlos Pous, blacked up as the bufo cubano's beloved *negrito* or "little black." The combination of Martí and the negrito quite perfectly encapsulates a relation between blackface performance, national sentiment, and populist theatre in Cuba, actively cultivated for over a century in playhouses across the island. If theatre is the soul of the people, blackface theatre was the soul of the Cuban Teatro Martí.

In late nineteenth century Havana, the Teatro Martí was named the Teatro Irijoa and was one of the homes for *teatro bufo* companies, performing comic revue-style musical and theatrical entertainments, for whom blackface was a signature. That the Irijoa was renamed in 1902 in honor of José Martí is both startling and fitting. The Irijoa was certainly not Havana's most prestigious theatre—far from it. That status belonged to the majestic Teatro Tacón located on Havana's central boulevard, and named after the Spanish colonial Governor General Tacón, under whose administration the theatre had been built in 1838 to rival European opera houses. The Tacón was also renamed during the time of the republic, becoming the Teatro García Lorca, after the Spanish playwright, but the revered name "Martí" was reserved for the Irijoa. Several blocks away from the central promenade, the Irijoa was a far more modest commercial playhouse, built by an otherwise failed theatre impresario in 1884. Never housing a resident company, nor committing itself to any particular genre other than profit, the Irijoa was hardly an obvious candidate to carry the name of Cuba's greatest patriot in the early days of the new republic. Yet, as this book will demonstrate, the teatro bufo had from the outset claimed a special relation to national sentiment; installing the bufo cubano as the primary fare of a newly named Teatro Martí was a culmination and vindication of an anticolonial theatre practice that had long promised to elaborate and—however ironically—"save" Cuba's national "soul."

Paramount in that nationalist discourse is the figure of the negrito, Cuba's most popular stage character in the nineteenth century and well into the twentieth. We find him on the poster, as always, played by a white actor in blackface, with star billing over the "real" performer of color below him. Trading in virtual currencies of race, nation, and social longing, the negrito was a key site for the development and articulation of a recognizably national affect and style throughout the anticolonial period. That he remained the star, even as Cuba turned toward a new revolution with a new revolutionary hero in 1959, attests to the social weight this racialized national figure carried for so long.

This book traces a critical genealogy of the negrito as it developed throughout the nineteenth century. That genealogy, in turn, offers a critical history of the relation between racial impersonation, popular culture, and the development of an anticolonial public sphere. The teatro bufo was a primary expressive venue in the emerging public culture of the period, arguably the only cultural form created expressly by and for self-fashioned Cubans. Throughout this book, my analysis lends attention to the special role played by performance in general and racial impersonation in particular in Cuba's national discourse. Ultimately, I attempt to answer questions raised by the insistent presence of all those laughing negritos, like Carlos Pous at the Teatro Martí: what made blackface Cuban? Why and how was Cubanness imagined through blackface? How did blackface insinuate itself into the very center of Cuba's national "soul"?

Mestizaje and Nation

"There are no little blacks or little whites, only Cubans," or so claimed the mulato revolutionary Antonio Maceo in 1870. This much quoted statement—"No hay negritos o blanquitos, solo Cubanos"—encapsulates the complex relation between race and national sentiment for many Cubans, both black and white, in the period of anticolonial wars from 1868 to 1898 (Ibarra 1967, 52). The statement is a utopian call for the end of racial division in the service of a new, unifying national identity; at the same time, its admonishing tone reveals that such racial divisions prevail despite the promise of national unity. The phrase, and the imagination it conjures, is caught in a deconstructive double bind: in order to pronounce the end of race as a meaningful category, Maceo is forced to invent the diminutive racial term "blanquitos" or "little whites" to match the ubiquitous racist term "negritos." Acknowledging the persistence rather than the end of racism, this linguistic maneuver also suggests that racial equality must in fact precede the emergence of the nation that was meant to cure racism in the first place. This intricate relation between race and nation—mutually exclusive *and* mutually formative—characterizes the discursive terrain of race relations, nationalism, and anticolonial sentiment in Cuba for much of the nineteenth century.

Not coincidentally, Maceo's axiom—there are no negritos or blanquitos, only Cubanos—is an apposite entry into the history of the popular theatre in the anticolonial era as well. The transformation of the blackface "negrito" into a beloved and palpably "Cuban" figure is, in brief, the story of nineteenth century theatre in Cuba. The popularity of the teatro bufo with white, Cuban criollos coincided with Cuba's protracted struggle for independence from Spain, from the beginning of the first war of independence in 1868 to the beginning of the last in 1895.[1] From beginning to end, the teatro bufo belied fascination with "black" and "African" cultures in Cuba, and became famous for developing music and dance that ostensibly combined Spanish and "African" rhythms and choreography, as in the famed *guaracha* and the *danzón*. The teatro bufo also developed a repertoire of stock blackface characters, from the negrito to the mulata. What these elements shared was a pleasurable indulgence on the part of actors and audiences in distinctly racialized forms and images. However, their publicity, reviews, and the plays themselves typically characterized them not as racialized (not black, not mulata) but national (Cuban): the danzón and the negrito were first and foremost imagined as *Cuban*. The teatro bufo's protagonist, the "negrito," harbors the same disjuncture that haunts Maceo's axiom: the negrito is a manifestly racist caricature of black people by white actors; yet, over time, it came to stand in for a national sentiment whose primary attribute was a celebrated racial diversity. In short: blackface performance was a central vehicle for the expression of *mestizaje* as a national ideology.

The pages that follow take up the contradictions, implications, and significance of such a development. As such, this study of mestizaje and national discourse sits in eager dialogue with cognate projects in American studies, comparative ethnic studies, and Latin American cultural studies that—from different disciplinary sites—have explored the intricate relationship between racialization, citizenship, and national formation in the Americas. George Lipsitz (1988), Vera Kutzinski (1993),[2] and Roger Bartra (1992), writing about the Dominican Republic, Cuba, and Mexico respectively, provide compelling arguments that historic celebrations of mestizaje in nationalist or official state discourse have been deeply ambivalent: they promote hegemonic unity for an elite class, while masking the material exclusion and suffering of indigenous and *mestizo* citizens themselves. As a carefully cultivated national discourse, mestizaje throughout the Americas provided grounds for emergent American nations to articulate their difference from Europe, while gaining control—discursively, juridically, politically—over the relation between race and national belonging. Celebrations of mestizaje by American-born Europeans—those criollos Angel Rama has dubbed America's *letrados* or "lettered people"—allowed them to stake claims as "legitimate" heirs not only to European culture, but also to indigenous American heritage and land. Thus, nationalist discourses of mestizaje often ensured and enabled the continued expropriation of indigenous land and labor and the oppression of the very indigenous or black peoples whose cultures it purported to celebrate (Rama 1984, 1996).

Racializing Our América

"Cubano es más que blanco, más que mulato, más que negro" (Cuban is more that white, more than mulatto, more than black), wrote José Martí at the beginning of the final war of independence in 1895 (Ortiz 1953, 30). Like Maceo twenty years earlier, Martí believed that the project of antiracism was crucial to the success of the insurgency, and he argued for the equality of whites and blacks in the shared project of Cuban independence. The racially integrated insurgency of the Ten Years' War (1868–1878) set the model for this solidarity. Evoking an image of black and white revolutionary soldiers fighting side by side, Martí wrote, "juntos, rodilla a rodilla, echamos un mundo entero abajo[. . . .] A los disparos gemelos de los fusiles anunciamos, con el fuego creador, el alumbramiento de la libertad" (together, knee to knee, we brought down an entire world[. . .]. To the sound of twin rifle shots we announced, with creative fire, the birth of liberty [Ortiz 1953, 31]). Yet Martí, like Maceo, returns to notions of race (and frequently racial division) to articulate this new national unity: "Cuban" is always "more" than white, mulatto, or black, and it is also *unimaginable* without them.

This racial logic underwrites Martí's famous 1891 essay, "Nuestra

América" (Our America), his eloquent rallying cry for a pan-American nationalism—a nationalism built from and for "our" America, that would eschew derivative national models forcibly imposed or imported from colonial Europe or by the neocolonial American neighbor to the north. In a striking metaphor, he writes that the contradictions of colonialism have produced a particular national body in the Americas whose feet, head, and body are shaped by contrasting cultural and racial experiences: "Con los pies en el rosario, la cabeza blanca, y el cuerpo pinto de indio y criollo venimos, denodados, al mundo de las naciones" (With our feet in [guided by] the rosary, our head white, and our body marked by the Indian and the Creole, we arrive, boldly, to the world of nations).[3] From this estranged figure—with Christian feet, a white head, and brown body—emerges what Martí evocatively calls the "mestizo autóctono" or the "indigenous mestizo" (16). This creative oxymoron rewrites the usual discourse of mestizaje. Rather than reading the mestizo as the quintessential emblem of colonial contact, conquest, and violence—the mixed-race offspring of a native American and European conqueror—Martí casts the mestizo into the place of the native or "original" American itself. The "mestizo autóctono" both incorporates and elides the history of colonial violence that made mestizaje a reality: the "mestizo autóctono" is a false, but necessary, originary figure for a productive nationalism in what Martí famously called "nuestra América mestiza" or "our mestizo America."

If Martí's evocation of the mestizo seems to celebrate racial hybridity, this is soon complicated by his bald assertion in the concluding remarks of the essay: "no hay odio de razas, porque no hay razas" (there is no racial hatred, because there are no races [24]). For Martí, only feeble-minded thinkers ("pensadores canijos") insist on rehashing what he calls useless "bookshelf races" ("razas de librería") for armchair social theorists who will serve no purpose in the new América. Race, he says, is a cynical social invention that offends the manifest truth of "nature" herself (24). His writing seems, then, to turn on that same seeming contradiction that haunted Maceo: there is no race hatred, because there are no races; yet nuestra América mestiza will gain its strength not in spite but because of its mixed race experience.

Martí's thinking may well betray a disjuncture here, but we should first consider the possibility that "Nuestra América" harbors no contradiction at all. If we take him at his word—that race does not exist and mestizaje is the originary condition of a new American nationalism—then his mestizaje is a far more radical, utopian project than we might have previously imagined. Mestizaje is no longer the outcome (or offspring) of the mixing of the races, but a necessary response to effects of colonialism and racism in history. Mestizaje is not the biological outcome of racial difference, but a socially constructed cure to racial division. From this utopian horizon, mestizaje does not describe racial mixing as much as racial transcendence. Forcibly produced by racist social formations (colonialism, slavery, white supremacy, institutional racism), the mestizo can claim to be "autóctono" because he or she marks the origin of a *postracial* formation, existing beyond the discourse of race as we know it.

Martí was not alone in invoking "Our America" as the watchword for alternate imaginaries of social and racial solidarity in the hemisphere. A generation earlier, the U.S. abolitionist and author Martin Delany embraced from the north the America that Martí later claimed as "ours." Unlike U.S. speculators surveying Cuba, Texas, and northern Mexico for the expansion of U.S. slaveholding territories in the 1840s and 1850s, Delany cast his eyes south and saw a vast untapped possibility for the radical refusal of white empire and its systems of racial domination (what Delany calls "the American system-politic"). "Where shall we go?" asks Delany of black peoples in the United States in the early 1850s. His response was to advocate black immigration to Central and South America and the West Indies: black North Americans would find interracial solidarity with "a vast colored population"—he estimated over 21 million—that far outnumbered white Europeans. Paul Gilroy enlisted Delany's novel, *Blake, or the Huts of America* (1859–1862) whose black hero travels from the U.S. south, across Cuba, to Africa and back, as he plans a slave insurrection, as an early and important articulation of the "black Atlantic" as the geographical imaginary of black experience. Delany's writings lend themselves equally, if not more, to hemispheric imaginings: for Delany, moving south, rather than east ("back") to Africa, was the "political destiny of the colored race," as he argued in an 1854 book of that title. Delany's radical conception of a black Latin America recalibrated coordinates of race, language, and citizenship then the norm for ruling parties in both North and South America. He imagined Latin America as the site of self-determination and future hope for all colored people: "blacks and colored people are the stars which must ever most conspicuously twinkle in the firmament of this division of the Western Hemisphere." Like the later Martí, Delany imagines a new form of racial identity as the basis for the new structure of American belonging: the "colored race" intentionally elides differences between indigenous and African Americans. And like the later Martí, Delany saw a version of America that could and should be "ours." To give that America a common language that could transcend the historical divisions between "colored" peoples imposed by empire, Delany entreats all colored persons to learn Spanish: "no foreign language will be of such *import* to colored people, in a very short time, as Spanish. Mexico, Central and South America, importune us to speak their language" (Delany 2003, 160, 206–7, 255–58, 267).

Listening carefully to the struggle of black Americans, Delany writes, "if nothing else, the silent indications of Cuba, urge us to learn the Spanish tongue." Both silent and articulate, Cuba is the epicenter of Delany's black America. The fate of Cuba, in the immediate aftermath of war with Mexico, and the annexation of Texas, held the fate of slavery and thus of black peoples in the Americas. Either Cuba would be subsumed into the American "system-politic," or—in Delany's vision—Cuba's large black population would rise up, like Haiti's before it, to claim its freedom. "At the instant of the annexation of Cuba to the United States," wrote Delany, "it should be the signal for simultaneous rebellion of all the slaves of the Southern states and on that island." Such a rebellion would signal the founding a new kind of colored race, a new revolutionary struggle, and a new America. Not for the last time was Cuba the key site of such hegemonic struggle, the ground on which discourses of empire and revolution, of America and América, were violently staged.

Clearly, neither Delany's nor Martí's hemispheric postracial utopias have yet come to pass—not in "our," "their," or in any America. However, their radical promise is what makes their work relevant to projects of postcolonial and hemispheric solidarity, and to their use and analysis in the academy today. Among those that have heeded the call of Martí, we find the recent (if belated) interest in American studies toward a transnational model, drawing on a pluralistic frame—*Americas*—to understand the history and social scope of life in America. In this changing disciplinary formation, the dividing line is not quite nuestra América (Luso-hispanic, mestizo, *autóctono*, or "colored") against "their" America (Anglo, white, hegemonic, and neocolonial). Rather, the effort seeks to develop approaches to multiple Americas that can account for a long history of struggle over land, language, resources, and power that created and continue to maintain such divisions in the first place. This approach to the study of the Americas, produced both in and outside the United States, promises to do more than simply extend the boundary of American studies "south of the border"; it promises first to take account of the disciplinary complicity of American institutions—scholarly, political, and otherwise—in the making and maintenance of such divisions across the hemisphere. As Delany knew long ago, this orientation toward the south will require engaging new ways of knowing, and speaking in new languages. As we rise to that challenge, we bear in mind that, in an era of NAFTA's circulation of transnational capital, in which U.S.-owned or -funded *maquilas* mushroom across border zones of Mexico and the Hispanic and Francophone Caribbean and instantiate the "Latinization" of labor and poverty, in which the borderlands have been militarized to an extent greater than ever before, we are no closer now to realizing *nuestra América* than were Martí or Delany a century and more ago.

A hemispheric approach to the study of performance in the Americas, then, illuminates the different tropes, genealogies, and cultural forms in the respective cultures of imperialism and their different enactments of national longing and anticolonial imagination. A growing body of scholarship has illustrated the relevance of transnational approaches to cultural production—particularly embodied culture—in the Americas. Paul Gilroy persuasively introduced the notion of the "Black Atlantic" as the more relevant geographic paradigm for understanding African diasporic practice from the West Indies to contemporary Britain, while Joseph Roach proposed a similar paradigm, the "circum-Atlantic," to theorize the complex routes of social, cultural, and economic circulation, exchange, and substitution that gave shape to the colonial world. For both theorists, performance is central to the making of America because performance was already central to the native American and African cultural practices that were forcibly engaged in the story of European colonization. Even further, they argue, the situation of American conquest, colonization, slavery, and its aftermath produced historically unprecedented social circumstances that required the complex cultural processes of public memory, surrogation, and self-invention that performance makes possible (Roach 1996, Gilroy 1993).

Cuban novelist and ethnomusicologist Alejo Carpentier, in turn, long ago understood that cultural production in the Americas, particularly African diasporic cultural forms, requires transnational regional perspectives. His own study of Cuban music, *La música en Cuba,* written in the 1940s, situates the development of Cuban music in what Roach would later call a "genealogical" frame: "mucho tendrá que hacer todavía la musicografía americana, cuando emprenda el estudio de la música del continente no por *regiones o países,* sino por zonas geográficas sometidas a las mismas influencias de tipo étnico, a las mismas intermigraciones de ritmos y de tradiciones orales" (there is much that American musicology stands to gain in studying the music of the continent by *geographic zones* subject to the same ethnic influences, to the same migrations of rhythms and oral traditions, rather *than by region or country* [1946, 13]).[4] Carpentier charts a geography of music that traces both the origins and travels of music practiced in Cuba or imagined as "Cuban," tracing through music the histories of social dislocation and migration that in part shape our sense of region, nation, and hemisphere in the first place. The innovations of American colonial music and performance, like other "arts of the contact zones," to borrow Mary Louise Pratt's phrase, are products and negotiations of such unprecedented configurations of power and knowledge (1999).

A perspective attentive to the interrelationship of race, colonialism, and performance in our America reveals, for one, what Coco Fusco has named "the other history of intercultural performance": a history of the display and enforced performance of nonwhite peoples—in the work fields of slavery, on the auction block, in freak shows, in world's fairs—to serve and please a white colonial gaze (Fusco 1995, 37–63). From the indigenous "actors" in New Spain forced by Franciscan friars to enact dramas that depicted their own defeat, in what Richard Trexler calls a consummate "theatre of humiliation," to the long history of black performance across the diaspora created by American slavery, a history Fred Moten has trenchantly cast as the radical "resistance of the object," we find that the history of American theatres does not simply trace a teleology of the growth of "national" expression in the United States, Brazil, Cuba, or any other new American nation: it is first a history of the struggle over performance as a site of power itself (Trexler 1984, 189–227; Moten 2003).

ImpersoNation

In his essay "DissemiNation," Homi Bhabha suggests that the nation functions as a "liminal signifying space that is internally marked by the discourses of minorities, the heterogenous histories of contending peoples, antagonistic authorities and tense locations of cultural difference." That liminality is enacted through what he calls a "double time" of signification, split between the so-called pedagogical and performative address of the nation: pedagogical insofar as the "people" are the "historical 'objects' of a nationalist pedagogy"; performative insofar as the "people" are conjured and constituted by this very narration. Any claims to legitimacy, authority, and authenticity are enacted through a negotiation of the tension between the doubled and often contradictory modes of the pedagogical and the performative. This "double-time" of the narrative address of nation accounts both for its formidable power in the process of consolidating national values, and for its inherent ambivalence with respect to internal national difference (Bhabha 1990a, 297). Performance in general, and racial impersonation in particular, can be imagined as the embodied correlative to the split address of the Nation: double skinned, overlayered and overdetermined with claims and forms of national discipline. Through impersoNation, the "double-time" of the nation's address refracts into more intricate processes of simultaneous evocation, erasure, and performative enactment.

The problematic of imitation and impersonation concerned José Martí immensely in "Nuestra América." Martí believed that the one thing that American (qua Cuban) nationalism would *not* do is dress itself in the image of others. Metaphors of masking, dissembling, and impersonation organize his critique of what he calls the "criollo exótico" (the exotic criollo), whom he contrasts with his celebrated "mestizo autóctono" (indigenous mestizo). What separates them is precisely the former's imitation of all things European, down to his very clothes and bodily attitude. Martí has no kindness for these American dissemblers, calling them weak and cowardly "sietemesinos" or prematurely born infants (14), and labeling them "effeminate": they cannot reach the high tree of American righteousness because "No les alcanza al árbol difícil el brazo canijo, el brazo de uñas pintadas y pulsera, el brazo de Madrid o de París (The weak arm cannot reach the difficult branch, the arm with painted fingernails and bracelets, the arm of Madrid or Paris). He continues: "¡Estos nacidos en América, que se avergüenzan, porque llevan delantal indio, de la madre que les crió . . ." (Those born in America, that are ashamed, because they wear an Indian apron [front], from the mother that raised them . . . [14]). The frontal Indian "apron" evokes the visible marking of Indian or mestizo race that these American *poseurs* try to hide under European clothes and customs. "Exotic" in their foreign plumage, these criollos will be vanquished, claims Martí, by the "natural man" (16).

In contrast to the vital and "natural" (and distinctly male) body of the "mestizo autóctono," Martí depicts the "criollo exótico" as nothing more than a heap of borrowed clothes. Before his transformation into the new mestizo, the criollo was nothing more than layer upon layer of colonial costume, each body part covered, claimed, and colonized by a different foreign invader—a simulacra of European fashion whose "real" body has been reduced to a colonial phantom. His description is worth quoting in full:

Éramos una máscara, con los calzones de Inglaterra, el chaleco parisiense, el chaquetón de Norte-América y la montera de España. El Indio, mudo, nos daba vueltas

> alrededor, y se iba al monte, a la cumbre del monte, a bautizar sus hijos. El negro, oteado, cantaba en la noche la música de su corazón, solo y desconocido, entre las olas y las fieras. El campesino, el creador, se revolvía, ciego de indignación, contra la ciudad desdeñosa. Éramos charreteras y togas en países que venían al mundo con la alpargata en los pies y la vincha en la cabeza. (21)

> (We were a mask, with trousers from England, a vest from Paris, an overcoat from North America, and a cap from Spain. The Indian, mute, circled around us, and left for the mountain, to the top of the mountain, to baptize his children. The black man, watching, sang music from his heart in the night, alone and unknown, between the waves and the beasts. The peasant, the creator, turned, blind with indignation, against the scornful city. We were epaulettes and togas in countries that came into the world with sandals on their feet and a bandana on their heads.)

Martí's description is striking on several counts. The communal "we" implied in the title of the essay "Our America" suddenly takes on a more precise racial, ethnic, and class status through this description—indeed one that troubles Martí's commitment to a transracial national body. Separating out the behaviors of Indians, blacks, and peasants, that "we" seems to exclude those "others" from the speaking subject and fastens instead only on European (white) settlers in the Americas. Martí unwittingly privileges the perspective, if not the experience, of these European settlers and their criollo offspring: because of his qualifications, the term "we" only interpellates them. Martí implies, however, that no sense of real agency or authenticity will come from "us": "we" are just a mask and so much mismatched clothing; "they," in turn, sing full in the night, care for their children, and rise up against colonial offenses. "We" apparently need "them" in order to transform ourselves from the exotic criollo to the autochthonous mestizo.

Equally striking is Martí's reliance on a vocabulary of dissembling and costuming to describe this colonial impostor. Martí comes very close to stating outright that the colonial counterfeit persona is nothing better than an actor: his or her culture, fashion, self-presentation are all false because they are borrowed, because they refigure (and potentially disfigure) his or her "natural" body. The concern for theatrical imitation is not surprising: Martí is making a case for the authenticity of the new American mestizo, and does so by claiming its "naturalness," with all the notions of essential purity that this connotes. Here (as in every essentialist discourse) theatricality implies everything that the new mestizo is not: copied, costumed, inauthentic. The fact that it is the mestizo—paragon of racial mixing—to whom Martí appeals for this purity puts even greater pressure on its claims to national authenticity. If there is one thing the mestizo is *not* (he says, again and again) it is a costumed pretender, francophone *poseur*, effeminate dissembler—and certainly not a blackface actor.

The problem staged in Martí's writing haunts any revolutionary desire, act, or writing: how does historical change come about? How do we get from this ragged, tainted, socially mired present to that utopian future, without dragging all our heavy historical baggage along with us? How can Martí arrive at his postracial Cuba, if he must reinstate the discourse of race every time he attempts to leave it; how can he leave Maceo's paradox? Homi Bhabha might state the problem more simply, as the question of "how newness enters the world" at all (Bhabha 1994, 212). How does a nation really enter the world; how could transracial unity enter the world and remake our America? How did a Cuban national community enter the world? Not by the singular invocation or sacrifice of one man, not through the strategies and sacrifices of a rebel army, alone. The work of a national imagination is infinitely more complex and dispersed over a range of cultural practices, as the studies of nationalism by Benedict Anderson, Homi Bhabha, and others have amply demonstrated.

Martí too said as much in his appeal to General Máximo Gómez in 1884: "A nation is not founded as a military camp is set up. The preparatory work for a revolution is more delicate and complex than any other" (Martí 1999, 201). Martí would have understood what Homi Bhabha means when he says that "the scraps, patches and rags of daily life must be repeatedly turned into the signs of a coherent national culture, while the very act of narrative performance interpellates a growing circle of national subjects" (Bhabha 1994, 145). "Nuestra América" is Martí's finest act of narrating the nation, and its primary mode (as Bhabha's work invites us to see) is fundamentally performative—in the important sense initially lent to the term by J. L. Austin, as that which enacts what it enunciates (Austin 1962). Martí knows full well that he contradicts the palpable experience of Cuba's racially conflicted reality in 1891 when he announces, *tout court*, that "there can be no racial hatred because there are no races" (24): he hopes that, in the fullness of national time, saying will make it so.

No wonder Martí rejects the theatrical criollo: it is not just that the exotic criollo evokes a series of cultural identifications that Martí rejects, but that the logic of the criollo's performance is a travesty of the very kind of cultural performance in which Martí himself is engaged. The problem with the exotic criollo is that he is too close to, rather than too distant from, the mestizo Martí's patriotism calls forth. Indeed, he implies elsewhere that the mestizo is still wearing the wrong costume: "Las levitas son todavía de Francia, pero el pensamiento empieza a ser de América" (The frocks are still from France, but the thinking is beginning to be American [21–22]). Even though he uses the language of essential identity, Martí knows that the "mestizo autóctono" is fundamentally performed—right down to its impossible, performative name. Martí puts it this way: the young men of America "entienden que se imita demasiado, y que la salvación está en crear. Crear, esa es la palabra de pase de esta generación" (understand that there is too much imitation, and that salvation lies in creating. Creation, that is the password for this generation [22]). But the difference between imitation and creation, however fundamental, is actually quite small and can rest simply on the success or failure of performance. Indeed that difference can be understood as difference between what we call performance and performativity itself—between the really made up and the made up real. Both the criollo and the mestizo are colonial subjects "playing at" their identities in public culture; both present themselves in a complex bid for cultural capital, place, and meaning—both, in other words, make a serious bid to enter the real. The exotic criollo is only theatrical because his performance failed: he was "all mask," all costume; his "epaulettes and togas" chaffed in the tropical heat; his performance failed to enact what it enunciated, to be what it claimed.

Or, did it? Enter the *negros catedráticos*, the "black professors" of the teatro bufo. The time: any summer night in 1868 at the packed Villanueva theatre on the far side of central Havana's nightlife. Against the pretenses of European opera at the imposing Teatro Tacón in the city center, against the random, sensational entertainments—acrobats, contortionists, dancing pigs, bullfights—at the pavilion outside of town, the newly popular teatro bufo offered an array of especially "Cuban" performances: original, lively guarachas, and a flood of new plays that claimed to represent "typical" "Cuban" mores, humor, and figures of everyday life. The protagonist of this entire scene was the negro catedrático, who dominated the stage like no other in the year the first war of independence began. The negro catedrático was mock professor or aristocrat, a sham literati, a pretend duke or duchess, and foremost a species of Cuban malaprop, spouting no end of learned prose in a most questionable performance of intelligence or social wit. Strutting about in a tattered rendition of fine coat tails, top hat, and pointed European shoes, consumed with race, class, and colonial envy, pontificating in faux Latin or French on any useless subject, or stiffly dancing a pompous minuet, this mock-pious blackface figure is nothing if not "all mask." While he is ostensibly an urban, free, Cuban-born, semi-educated black character, everything about the catedrático's self-presentation is ill-fitted and put on: his oversized clothes, his belabored speech, his bad dancing, his presumption of European aristocratic manners, and, not least, his racial mask. This blackface figure is a striking example of Martí's "exotic criollo": literally and figuratively, he is "epaulettes and togas" in the Cuban heat of sandals and bandanas.

Yet, in direct contrast to Martí, the teatro bufo hailed this "exotic criollo" as being specially Cuban: the catedrático somehow captured a structure of feeling that felt specially Cuban to the audiences who delighted to the extreme in his pratfalls, antics, and linguistic humors. It was this same audience and these same actors that expressed support for the Cuban insurgents, both on stage and in the gallery at the Villanueva. Celebrated between Cuban flags and calls for Cuba Libre, that negrito on the Villanueva stage somehow provoked the approval, support, and sense of distinctly nationalist pleasure that Martí ascribed to his mestizo.

One simple way to reconcile this apparent contradiction and explain why the catedrático was hailed as specially "Cuban" despite the fact that he, like Martí's exotic criollo, seems to embody everything the ideal Cuban is not, is to say that it is not the catedrático himself that is invested with this sense of *cubanía*, but the communal laughter that he provokes. His comic performance implicitly mocks colonial culture and authority, and provides the space for newly patriotic, newly revolutionary Cubans to affirm their shared values, their anticolonial sentiments, and reiterate their shared sense of national belonging. The catedrático was the counterfeit criollo that demonstrated the boundaries of what would and would not count as "Cuban." Like Martí's essay, his work is primarily performative: he instantiates the newly forming boundaries of Cuban identity even as he repeatedly performs their (failed) crossing. At a time when the very meaning of "Cuba" as a nation is the grounds for anticolonial war, shared laughter at the pretenses of the catedrático is a means to perform the "delicate preparatory work" required to make—or performatively conjure—a new nation and its constitutive differences.

We might even say that the catedrático is an early version of Martí's critique of the exotic criollo: both give voice to a nationalist disdain for colonialist presumption; both provide a model against which a newly forming criollo class can further define itself. Chronology supports us here as well, since the catedrático precedes Martí's "Nuestra América" by over twenty years. If the teatro bufo does not portray a positive model of Cuban identity, one that would match Martí's "mestizo autóctono," it is because colonial censorship would not tolerate such a development, certainly not in the highly visible public space of the theatre, as the 1869 Villanueva massacre readily attests. Further, in 1868, at the dawn of the insurgent movement, the nationalist imagination is still embryonic, searching for forms and structures through which to express or embody itself. As the foremost spokesman for Cuban nationalism, Martí begins to answer that need, with the wisdom garnered from the long decade of anticolonial war and in studied anticipation of the next.

While the basic outline of this story is fair, even persuasive, it is troubled by one important fact: the catedrático is in blackface. This blackface is neither generous nor gratuitous: while we can sense an implicit critique of colonial values through the catedrático's antics, the actual critique is directed squarely at the urban, free, socially mobile blacks the figure also represents. Some apologists for the genre have speculated that the blackface was a simple cover, designed to bypass colonial censors; blackface does not reflect a racist view on the part of the actors, but is rather the disfiguring mark of colonial censorship. However, given that the economy of Cuba was still organized around slavery in 1868 and that the insurgency's purported commitment to abolition was the source of extraordinary racial panic in white Cuba, it is entirely unlikely that white criollo enthusiasm for this inept black figure was in any way benign. The very existence of blacks in Cuba had been viewed for decades as the primary obstacle to the development of Cuban nationalism: blacks adulterated the potential unity of the body politic (it was said) and slaves posed the threat of race war—a terrifying prospect even to liberal white criollos. When pro-Cuban actors use a racist black figure to mock colonial values, his function is as much to assuage that racial panic as it is to enable the anticolonial critique. This blackface humor works discursively at two levels: it controls and limits the otherwise menacing significance of blackness at the same time that it renegotiates the meanings of whiteness in a colonial hierarchy that privileged Spanish *peninsulares* (literally, "peninsulars," those born on the Iberian peninsula) over white criollos.

However, the persistence of the negrito in various forms throughout the entire anticolonial era, well past abolition and the threat of slave uprising, well past the real impact of colonial censors—indeed well into the twentieth century—suggests that the negrito performed a more complex cultural operation than this cursory discussion implies. The negrito does embody a racist desire to control the representation of black people and blackness in the new Cuban imaginary. And his persistence in public culture no doubt belies the persistence of racism as well. But what is striking is the fact that this Cuban imaginary cannot *stop* imagining the negrito. He appears, time and again in the theatre, in otherwise celebratory invocations of Cuban life and customs; he is offered up, time and again in the rhetoric of the press and the plays themselves, as a distinctly Cuban figure. In other words, far from being the foreign "exotic" criollo, he is consistently presented as an "authentic" expression of Cubanness itself. The blackface negrito is "more" than black, "more" than white, and instead combines these to produce the "Cuban." In doing so, the negrito suddenly begins to resemble Martí's "mestizo autóctono" with his white head and brown-marked body: both are invented cross-racial figures that mark a moment of national origin, a desire for transracial culture, a site of authenticity forcibly wrested from the colonial landscape of violent contact and collusion of cultures and races. The negrito functioned as a counterfeit currency that enabled criollos to forge—in both senses, to make and to fake—a national community in the anticolonial era. The negrito is not a colonial impostor who contrasts with Martí's lofty invocation of a new "authentic" mestizo as the rightful heir to Our America. Rather, the negrito and his practices of impersoNation are what made Martí's invocations of mestizaje and authenticity possible in the first place.

While not the focus of the present study, similar, although historically distinct, phenomena of "ImpersoNation" appear across the hemisphere: from U.S. blackface minstrelsy and acts of "playing Indian," to Argentine negritos in nineteenth century carnival, we find performances that link racial and gender impersonation to the development of racialized national discourses (see Saxton 1990, Lott 1993, Mahar 1999, Rogin 1996, Deloria 1998, Tchen 1999, Siegel 2000, Ybarra 2002). These figures of transracial impersonation do not serve as "symbols" in any simple sense within national imaginaries. What is at stake in cultural critiques of red, black, or yellowface is not the use of the image or the "correctness" of the representation of indigenous, African, or other diasporic cultures in the Americas. Rather, what matters is that such figures and formations are defined as available sites for white occupation, as sites of sanctioned racial "play" for white actors (see Hartman 1997). Through such performances, white actors step into the social skin of others and instantiate the assumed separation of body and subjectivity for nonwhite subjects, a separation fundamental to slavery and to military conquest, enabling the continued production and maintenance of racial difference itself.

Theatre History and Forgetting

"Ha llegado ya el caso de relegar á la historia hasta el recuerdo de semejantes comparsas" (The time has come to relegate to history even the memory of such *comparsas*), wrote J. M. Villergas in 1880 under the pen name "Don Circunstancias" (Mr. Circumstance) in the newspaper of the same name. He was referring to the black dance groups associated with African ethnic mutual aid societies and their boisterous performances on the streets of Havana, particularly on January 6, Three Kings' Day, on which slaves were allowed to dance with their comparsas in city-wide celebration. For Don Circunstancias such performances were nothing more than a "horrendous" social disturbance. It was not enough that the comparsas should cease to move through Havana's streets; rather, he wished that history should inter *even the memory* of them. Most striking about this genocidal wish is how casually it was registered. The wish formed part of no social or political treatise, nor even an editorial about race and culture in Cuba; rather, it was written as part of a regular column on theatre and entertainment in Havana, one otherwise replete with persnickety and grousing comments on the relative merits of this Italian soprano or that French tenor or this Cuban actor. But on this day, Don Circunstancias wished the complete erasure of black Cuban cultural performance. It is likely that on the day he made his wish it seemed to him in vain: he was, after all, complaining about the way the comparsas filled the streets with dancing bodies, drumming, and a rhythmic sound that could penetrate well into the shuttered rooms of unnerved wealthy white families along the way.

But we know that such wishes carry great consequence for our social memory: held by countless such reviewers, authors, archivists then and now, such wishes shape myriad choices of description, narration, illustration, and collection that in turn shape that discursive body so inadequately named "the historical record." Such wishes eventually impair our ability to recall those bodies, dances, and rhythms, leaving later scholars no choice but to become salvage historians, straining against the limits of the historical record to remember what was willfully forgotten. The pages that follow cannot promise a recovery of the realities that writers such as Don Circunstancias wanted to forget. Instead we must explore the very process of incomplete forgetting and strategic remembering that informed the making of Cuban national imaginaries during the anticolonial period, when there were not yet Cubans—but only blacks and whites.

Chapter 1
Blackface Costumbrismo, *1840–1860*

In 1836 the writer Félix Tanco y Bosmeniel expressed his hope that Cuba would soon produce a new literary aesthetic that could give voice to the social and political realities of life on the island. Inspired on the one hand by the literary activist Domingo del Monte's calls for a new realism in Cuban writing, and on the other by the romantic movement of European prose, Tanco declaimed, "Nazca pues nuestro Victor Hugo, y sepamos de una vez lo que somos, pintados con la verdad de poesía, ya que conocemos por los números y el análysis filosófico la triste miseria en que vivimos" (Then let our Victor Hugo be born and let us know once and for all what we are, described with the truth of poetry, since we already know through numbers and philosophic analysis the misery in which we live [*Centón epistolario* 7, 51]). Victor Hugo interests Tanco less for his poetry or drama than for a lesser-known novel, *Bug-Jargal*, which describes conditions of slavery and slave uprisings on Cuba's neighboring island of Haiti. "Por el estilo de esta novelita quisiera yo que se escribiese entre nosotros" (I would want that among us a novel be written in the same style as that one [51]), writes Tanco to Domingo del Monte. Most striking to Tanco was Hugo's careful attention to black life on the French Caribbean island. "Piensalo bien" (think about it), says Tanco in a most remarkable sentence: "Los negros en la isla de Cuba son nuestra poesía" (blacks on the island of Cuba are our poetry [51]). Yet Tanco's interest does not settle on blacks alone, but rather on the burgeoning mestizaje—the racial and cultural mixing between black and white, between African and Spanish—which he sees as central to a new Cuban reality: "pero no los negros solos, sino los negros con los blancos, todos revueltos, y formar luego cuadros, las escenas, que a la fuerza han de ser infernales y diabólicas; ¡pero ciertas, evidentes! (but not the blacks alone, rather the blacks with the whites, all mixed, and form pictures, scenes, that by necessity will have to be infernal and diabolical, but truthful and evident! [51]).

The by now legendary group of young writers associated with del Monte's *tertulia* or salon in the late 1830s and early 1840s wrote what are considered Cuba's first novels and did so precisely by giving voice to Cuba's "diabolical" but "truthful" world of slavery. Domingo del Monte commissioned a number of writings on the subject of Cuban slavery in his efforts to end the continued illegal slave trade in Cuba; those writings were delivered to the British abolitionist Robert Madden to be published abroad. Through this largely political venture, del Monte occasioned the beginnings of Cuban narrative, including such important novels as Cirilio Villaverde's *Cecilia Valdés*, whose first version was completed in 1839; Anselmo Suárez y Romero's *Francisco: el ingenio o las delicias del campo* (Francisco: The plantation or the delights of the country) first composed in 1839; Félix Tanco y Bosmeniel's *Escenas de la vida privada en la isla de Cuba* (Scenes from the private life of the island of Cuba) written in 1837; and, not least, the *Autobiografía de un esclavo* (Autobiography of a slave) written by the then-slave Juan Francisco Manzano in 1835, which is the only extant slave narrative in Spanish America. The *delmontinos*, as they have come to be known, were part of Cuba's growing criollo or Cuban-born educated class; they favored greater representative rights and freedom of the press for criollos, and were protonationalist and abolitionist in their persuasions. Although virtually none of these writings was allowed to be published in Cuba for decades, these intellectuals set a new agenda for Cuban expression—one that distinguished itself from the Spanish or European, and that, in so doing, took stock of the enormous impact the institution of slavery and the introduction of thousands of Africans had had on the island's cultural development.

Despite their lofty aims and considerable literary output, this agenda was not, finally, implemented by the delmontinos in mid-century Cuba. Their controversial ideas on the slave trade and on representative government invited the repressive wrath of Spanish authorities, who rigorously censored their writings and drove most to exile in the United States or Europe. As a result, their potential role as Cuban literati was in part usurped and eclipsed in the popular arena by an unlikely candidate: the poet and playwright Bartolomé José Crespo y Borbón. Crespo y Borbón was a poor Galician immigrant who made a spectacular career of impersonating and popularizing the figure of the *bozal* (African-born slave) in literature, in the press, and on the popular stage. As a writer, he took on several aliases over the course of his career, which began in 1838 with the publication of his first play; among his aliases we find the Caricato Habanero (The Havana comic), La sirena Cubana (The Cuban siren), and El Anfibio (The Amphibian), under which he published the collection of poetry *El látigo del anfibio* (The amphibian's whip) in 1840. By far his most popular, enduring, and complex pseudonym was that of Creto Gangá, so-called "escritor bozal" or African writer, an African-born slave persona whom Crespo debuted as the supposed author of the 1845 verse novel *Laborintos y trifucas de canavá* (Labyrinths and ruckus [trifulcas] of carnival). After his success with *Laborintos*, "Creto" managed to land a job in 1848 as an entertainment and cultural critic for Havana's leading newspaper, *La prensa*. Creto—or rather, Crespo-as-Creto—offered weekly satirical social commentary and accounts of so-called "African" life in Cuba throughout the late 1840s and 1850s from his own "African" point of view and in his markedly distorted "African" prose. In addition, Creto published several more verse novels, and authored several plays, among them the ground-breaking plantation comedy, *Un ajiaco, o la boda de Pancha Jutía y Canuto Raspadura* (A stew, or the wedding of Pancha Jutía and Canuto Raspadura [1847]). Thus "Creto's" writings appeared in weekly papers, circulars, small-press volumes, and on the popular stage from the 1840s through the 1860s, providing a discourse of race and Cuban culture that paralleled that imagined by Tanco, del Monte, and the other literary activists of their generation.

While "Creto Gangá's" comic and often racist writings may seem far removed from the antislavery narratives of the delmontinos, this chapter aims to show the degree to which both elaborated narrative practices of racial impersonation— "discursive blackface"—in giving voice to Cuban life and experience; both made recourse to practices and tropes of blackface to organize and bolster claims for an "authentic" and "new" Cuban voice. To do so, both projects drew heavily upon the techniques of the then-emerging aesthetic of costumbrismo. Between the strident blackface satires of Creto, the realist detail of Anselmo y Suárez's *Francisco*, and especially Manzano's *Autobiografía* lies the expressive range available for and about black peoples in Cuba at mid-century. Analyzing Crespo's blackface *costumbrismo* further provides an opportunity to explore how and why the impulse toward early ethnographic representation of nonwhite people oscillated between realism and parody, between documentation and discursive containment.

Costumbrismo in the Americas

Before and during the years of anticolonial struggle in Latin America, popular arts from lithography to print media frequently engaged the representational economy of what would later coalesce into the new discipline of ethnography. Plays, both performed and published, along with visual and narrative portraits printed in the press, appealed to "authentic" representation of social, ethnic, and national "types," deploying realist descriptive detail, along with tropes of witnessing and testimony. They elaborated social and racial taxonomies of the population, disseminating and naturalizing criteria of inclusion and exclusion in the body politic. We can imagine these practices as forms of "popular ethnography," linked to comparable practices elsewhere (see Ziter 2003; Kirshenblatt-Gimblett 1998 and 1990; Goodall 2002); throughout the Hispanic Atlantic world, such popular ethnography was accomplished through the naturalist style known as costumbrismo. Costumbrista arts in literature, lithography, and theatre paid keen attention to documenting and elaborating scenes of local life, and creating catalogues of so-called "typical" figures and social types that made up the special character of the given locale. Costumbrismo is often pejoratively dismissed as a kind of premodern parochialism that merits little serious cultural analysis. But costumbrista arts in Latin America and especially in Cuba offered an explicit means to undermine the "imperial gaze" of Spain and its proprietary claims: *precisely because* of their taste for displaying and elaborating local types and topical concerns, costumbrista arts provided one forum in which urban criollo classes imagined and articulated viable national communities, in the rich sense that Benedict Anderson has lent to the phrase.

In its broadest definition, costumbrismo is conceived as any description—literary, visual, or embodied—of a particular social or cultural custom that gives attention to realist detail. A more narrow definition isolates a minor literary genre composed of short *cuadros de costumbres*: short essays or, more accurately, "sketches" of social life. While critics disagree on whether to analyze costumbrismo as a style or a genre, most agree that the emergence of costumbrismo as an independent genre was consonant with the rise of the print press in Spain in the late eighteenth and early nineteenth centuries, which published cuadros de costumbres as part of its offerings (Montesinos [1959] 1983, 12; Upton 1987, 63–68; Bueno 1985, ix; Zanetti 1973, 7). Costumbrismo was not a Spanish phenomenon alone; throughout Europe a costumbrista aesthetic shaped the emergent public cultures enabled by an active press. Richard Steele's and Joseph Addison's early gazette *The Tatler,* along with the Frenchman Víctor-Joseph Étienne, better known as Du Juoy, in *La gazette de France,* served as precursors to a writing style that indulged self-reflective portraits of daily life. These ultimately resulted in the publication of numerous book-length collections of these sketches, culminating in Spain with the publication in 1843 of Ramón de Mesonero Romanos's *Los españoles pintados por sí mismos* (The Spanish painted by themselves), itself modeled on the publication in England of the collection *Head of the People, or Portraits of the English* in 1840–41, as well as the French publication of *Les français peints par eux mêmes* (The French painted by themselves) in 1842. In Cuba, in turn, we find that Crespo y Borbón published an early response to the Spanish Mesonero Romanos in his satirical *Las habaneras pintadas por sí mismas, en miniatura* (Havana women painted by themselves, in miniature),[1] which was followed in 1852 by the multiply authored collection *Los cubanos pintados por sí mismos* (Cubans painted by themselves).

Costumbrista writings on either side of the Atlantic shared certain key features. As the painterly term "cuadro" (painting/portrait) suggests, an interest in descriptive elements always outweighed story; the cuadros often lack dramatic tension, character development, and storyline, depending on the author. The genre tried to balance its commitment to representing aspects of contemporary life in true-life detail with its desire to draw out and underscore the typical or generic aspects of the subject. José María Cárdenas Rodriguez described his creative process thus: "Elegida la víctima, debe uno vestirla y disfrazarla de tal manera y con tal arte, que ella se desconozca enteramente y la reconozcan los demás, y ya se ve si para esto se requiere cacumen y meollo" (Once the victim is chosen, one must dress and disguise her in such a manner and with such art, that she cannot recognize herself entirely but everyone else can recognize her, and you can see that requires acumen and intelligence [Bueno 1985, xviii]). The usual "victims" were well-defined social practices, current fads, or particular "types" of people. In Spain, these might have included a bullfight, the lottery, a coquette, a functionary, and so forth; in Havana, costumbrismo elaborated a new collection of "victims" as Antonio Bachiller y Morales described:

> los negros que conducían al amanecer los cuadrúpedos al baño de mar, atropellando cuanto encontraban; desde los arrieros que esperaban al cañonazo del Ave María en las puertas de la ciudad para penetrar en la plaza del mercado, desde las damas en sus retirados aposentos, cubriéndose el rostro con albayalde y cascarilla, desde los ricos en la holganza e en el juego, hasta los laboriosos artesanos en sus talleres, y todos los demás tipos sociales. (Bueno 1985, xxii–xiii)

> (the blacks that drove their animals at dawn to their ocean bath, trampling all they encountered; from the muleteers waiting at the gates of the city for the cannon shot from the Ave María [church] to penetrate the plaza market, to the ladies in their secluded chambers, covering their faces with white lead powder and powder eggshell masque, to the wealthy in their indolence and games, to the laboring artisans in their workshops, and all the other social types.)

It is in this sense that the genre initially developed its ethnographic pretensions: documenting real social life as witnessed on any street corner, in any *mesón*, or in any lady's boudoir, while simultaneously drawing out the behavioral rule that lends such behaviors cultural coherence.

While some cuadros emphasized little more than their picturesque content, many were undertaken with a didactic agenda, whether they adopted a humorous, satirical, or moralizing tone. Cuba's first newspaper regularly to promote costumbrista writings, *Papel periódico de la Havana* [sic], made its moralizing agenda clear, as evident in a 1792 statement of purpose written by one of the editors:

> Atacar los usos y costumbres que son perjudiciales en común y en particular; corregir los vicios pintándolos con sus propios colores, para que mirados con horror se detesten, y retratar en contraposición el apreciable atractivo de las virtudes, serían en mi concepto unos asuntos muy adecuados al objeto del *Periódico*. (Bueno 1985, xi–xii)
>
> (Attack uses and customs that are prejudicial in common and in particular; correct vices, by painting them in their own colors so that when seen, with horror, they will be detested; and provide in contraposition portraits of the appreciable attractions of virtue: these are to my mind issues very adequate to the objective of the *Periódico*.)

Costumbrismo carried different social meaning depending on its context. In Spain, the advent of costumbrismo, like the rise of the popular press, was generally associated with the rise of the bourgeoisie and the consolidation of the middle class and its values, and in time with the development of the broader sphere of public action, communication, and negotiation that Jürgen Habermas names the "bourgeois public sphere" (1991). Sketches of contemporary local life provided an entertaining while efficient way to articulate the boundaries of a newly developing urban civility and to police middle-class values in a public arena. In Latin America, in turn, the popular press and its penchant for costumbrista detail took on explicitly nationalist rhetoric. Benedict Anderson demonstrates how, before and after the wars of independence in the Americas, the burgeoning production of small-press newspapers—gazettes or circulars, called both *revistas* and *periódicos*—were instrumental in the formation of American national communities. These gazettes, as Anderson points out, usually began as appendages to the governing institutions and the market economies of each administrative unit of the Spanish empire; over time, they began to shape specific communities of readers, precursors to the "imagined communities" that shaped the nation

(Anderson 1991, 62). As these newspapers began to incorporate costumbrista essays as part of their offerings, they capitalized on the pleasure derived from recognizing and further imagining oneself in relation to one's "own" community in print. Costumbrismo in Latin American popular press reached its peak in the 1830s, in the decade after the wars of independence; as such, the phenomenon can be seen as part of a larger cultural movement toward consolidating these new national communities, and elaborating the new hegemonic values of the criollo classes who had waged and won the anticolonial wars. It was in this same period that costumbrismo became a foundational feature of much Latin American fiction—which usually appeared in serial form in the same newspapers that published costumbrista cuadros—and became a palpable element of the visual and performing arts as well. The purpose of costumbrismo, as Doris Sommer argues, was to "promote communal imaginings primarily through the middle stratum of writers and readers who constituted the most authentic expression of national feeling" (Sommer 1991, 14).

Costumbrismo informed early theatrical production in the Americas as well, particularly through the *sainete,* a costumbrista genre of one-act comedies of social manners popular in both Spain and Latin America in the late eighteenth century, and again in late nineteenth. In its Spanish incarnation, the sainete featured picturesque "local color" from the back streets of Madrid or Sevilla. Usually without significant plot, these theatrical portraits accentuated the picaresque humor of its typically lower-class and marginal settings. Capitalizing on its eminently translatable formula, across the Atlantic the sainete instead paraded local "American" color from the streets of Buenos Aires to those of Mexico City, or in Cuban actor Francisco Covarrubias's case, the local denizens of Havana. Often bringing local types to the stage for the first time, the sainete was the prototype for national dramatic genres across Latin America. Like narrative costumbrista writings, the sainete and related forms in the Americas enabled the circulation of a popular self-ethnography, one means through which urban criollos imagined and took pleasurable stock of their particularity as a social group, and later, as a national community.

Costumbrismo's function in each of these genres was as much prescriptive as descriptive. The consistent amassing of descriptive details of contemporary social life progressively articulated a prescription for model citizen behavior in the new American states. In other words, costumbrismo performed both the pedagogical and performative function that Homi Bhabha ascribes to the narrative address of the nation: it is pedagogical insofar as the "people"—as audience for and content of the costumbrista narratives—are the "historical 'objects' of a nationalist pedagogy, giving the discourse an authority that is based on the pre-given or constituted historical origin or event"; it is simultaneously performative insofar as the "people" are conjured and constituted by this very narration (Bhabha 1990a, 297). This "double-time" of the narrative address of nation belies its extraordinary power to interpellate disparate people into a singular social body, as well as serves as the inherent mark of internal difference such a process repeats and regulates.

The development of costumbrismo followed a different trajectory in Cuba than on the continent, reaching its peak later and becoming allied with anticolonial sentiment rather than with postcolonial, national consolidation. Precisely because of the loss of the vast majority of its American possessions, the Spanish crown was more careful in its control of Cuba—its purportedly "ever-faithful isle"—and imposed staunch repression of all political discourse, especially as it appeared in print. Captain-General Miguel Tacón, who presided over Cuba from 1834 to 1838, brought to the island an atmosphere of uncompromising official vigilance. In addition to building and supporting Cuba's premiere theatre and opera house (El Teatro Tacón opened in 1838 in Havana), Tacón was famous for his rigid enforcement of censorship laws: prospective publication items had to pass the censorship of two lawyers before reaching the military censor, and in some cases had to gain the approval of the Captain-General himself, resulting in the rejection of most petitions for new periódicos, and a state of near-silence from the once active popular press (Jensen 1988, 112–14).[2]

For example, controversies arose around the local Sociedad Económica de Amigos del País (Economic Society of Friends of the Country) from early in the century, as Spanish loyalists vied to control more liberal sectors who sought to use the Sociedad as a base for republican ideals and, at times, anticolonial activism; among those associated with the Sociedad were such activists as Father Félix Varela, and, later the highly influential José Antonio Saco and Domingo del Monte. Efforts within the Sociedad to create and support Cuban arts or letters were eventually repressed for their anticolonial implications. Del Monte, who headed the education section of the Sociedad from 1830 to 1834 and later ran its Comisión de Literatura (Literature Commission), became committed to the improvement of standards of education and of Cuban letters, but his efforts were consistently stymied. In 1830, his petition for the establishment of a public chair in the humanities was denied. He and Saco collaborated as editors of the Comisión's new *Revista* in 1831. Originally titled *Revista y repertorio bimestre de la isla de Cuba* (Bi-monthly magazine and repertoire of the Island of Cuba), it was renamed in its second issue, *Revista bimestre cubana* (Bi-monthly Cuban magazine), purportedly in order to bring greater emphasis to its explicitly Cuban context and interests (Jensen 1988, 105; Paquette 1988, 87; Luis 1990, 28). While well reviewed and commercially successful, the magazine finally succumbed to loyalist pressures in 1834.

Both del Monte and Saco were also involved in the Comisión's attempts in 1833 to establish itself as an independent Academia Cubana de Literatura (Cuban Academy of Literature), which sought to teach and promote literature. While the Comisión was originally granted permission from the newly installed Spanish regent María Cristina, staunch loyalist elements in the Sociedad itself felt the Academía Cubana was an anticolonial provocation and refused to grant their permission; on his arrival, Captain-General Tacón suppressed the venture entirely (Luis 1990, 29). Del Monte summarized his experience thus:

> Desde que llegué de New York en 1829, no he cesado, en compañía de los demas jóvenes patriotas amigos mios, de promover en lo que podia en mis cortos recursos pecuniarios é intelectuales, todo lo que juzgaba conveniente en pro de la Isla, y principalmente no empleábamos en ilustrar la opinión pública, ya por medio de la imprenta, ya en conversaciones privadas, en reuniones académicas, en los paseos, en las tertulias, en los teatros; pero nuestros esfuerzos han sido en vano, porque la acción poderosísima y absoluta del sistema que nos regia y nos rige, neutralizaba nuestras pacíficas y pasivas conquistas, á manera de una bestia feroz, que con un movimiento imperceptible de su cola brutal, barre y destroza el frágil y trabajado edificio de un insecto laborioso. (Williams 1994, 17, translation hers; also *Centón epistolario* 2, 65)
>
> (Ever since I returned from New York in 1829, I, along with my other young patriotic friends, have not stopped promoting as best as I could with my limited financial and intellectual resources everything that I thought appropriate for the island's benefit. We were mostly engaged in enlightening public opinion, whether through the press, or in private conversations, in scholarly meetings, on outings, in social gatherings, in the theatres. But our efforts have been in vain, because the very powerful and absolute system that has governed and still governs us has neutralized our peaceful, passive achievements in the mode of a ferocious beast, which with an imperceptible movement of its brutal tail, sweeps away and destroys the fragile and labored building of an industrious insect.)

In this politicized atmosphere, costumbrista writings could easily risk being associated with subversive nationalist or anticolonial ventures. The mere interest in documenting the details of contemporary culture in Cuba could be construed as actively promoting the Cuban in tacit opposition to the

Spanish or peninsular. Writer Jacinto Milanés phrased it to del Monte, "buscaba yo un modo de escribir artículos de costumbres sobre nuestro país, resuelto por los consejos de V. á pintar nuestras cosas cubanas y dejar las peninsulares" (I was searching for a way to write articles on the customs of our country, determined, on your advice, to depict our Cuban matters and leave behind Peninsular ones [*Centón epistolario* 4, 188]).

Finding ways to publish "Cuban matters" was no simple challenge. Félix Tanco complained bitterly to del Monte in 1836 of the "tiranía que hoy se egerce en la Isla de Cuba contra la publicación y el comerico de ideas en letra de molde" (tyranny exercised in the Island of Cuba against publication and the marketplace of ideas in capital letters).

> Si algo se permite escribir y publicar; ó han de ser elogios á los que mandan, ó han de ser paparruchas idénticas al padrenuestro, ó al bendito. Cualquiera *idea cubana* por inocente que sea, si la has de dar a luz, tienes que vestirla a la española, tienes que sepultarla, que ahogarla entre mil palabras *peninsulares, metropolitanas, eminentemente transatlánticas*: tienes en fin que ponerle el *escudo* de *fidelidad* decorado con sus tres castillos y su llave. (*Centón epistolario* 7, 80–81, italics in the original)
>
> (If anything is allowed to be written and published, they must either be tributes to those in power, or be nonsense identical to the "Our Father" or the liturgy. To give birth to any *cuban idea*, no matter how innocent, you must dress it up in Spanish style, you must bury it, drown it in a thousand *peninsular, metropolitan, eminently transatlantic* words: in short, you must put on it the shield of *loyalty*, decorated with its three castles and its key [the royal coat of arms].)

Only ideas "dressed up in Spanish" would make it past the censors. Tanco went on to describe the particular aesthetic deployed by Cuban authors and readers that extended this strategy of colonial masquerade:

> Para discernir, para columbrar la intension sana y patriótica del que escribe, para desentrañar esa *idea cubana* oprimida por un diluvio de vocablos de plata-forma, es necesario ser un lince de entendimiento, y muy práctico por percibir el verdadero rumbo que lleva la idea entre esa balumba de palabras exóticas. No es muy agradable, ni todos saben escribir de este modo. ¿Y poseen los leyentes esta perspicuidad, esta táctica, este escalpelo colonial? No. (*Centón epistolario* 7, 81, italics in the original)
>
> (To discern, to begin to see the healthy and patriotic intention of the one who writes, to unravel that *Cuban idea*, oppressed by a torrent of platform words, it is necessary to be a lynx of understanding, and very practical to perceive the true direction taken by the idea under that heap of exotic words. It is not very pleasant, and not everyone knows how to write this way. And do readers have this perspicacity, that tactic, that colonial scalpel? No.)

Tanco advocated a particular form of anticolonial writing and reading, one that wielded a "colonial scalpel" to follow furtive ideas as they moved through and beneath an elaborate interplay of peninsular disguise. "Cuban ideas" in essays on slavery and political economy by Saco or del Monte, although occasionally published abroad, were not published in Cuba. Properly "disguised" Cuban ideas in costumbrista portraits of street life or carnival stood a far greater chance of being published, and as a result, these comprised the better part of criollo-authored literature published during this period.

Cuban costumbrismo, then, provided an important representational technology for national imagining: although eschewing specific patriotic language, costumbrista portraiture provided a relatively transparent platform for the representation of "Cuban" ideas and experience. When the anthology of Cuban costumbrista writings *Los cubanos pintados por sí mismos* (Cubans painted by themselves) appeared in 1852, its editor, Blas San Millán, cast the importance of the project in these terms:

> Los cubanos tienen que conocerse para pintarse con verdad, tienen que estimarse en lo que son y por lo que son; no aspirarían a la empresa de trazar tales cuadros si hubieran de retratar unos originales sin fisonomía propia que los distinguiera de lo extraño [. . .] bajo este concepto la obra que presentan es de mucho más trascendencia de lo que parece a primera vista, y su desempeño un verdadero servicio al país y las letras. (San Millán 1852, 5)
>
> (Cubans must know themselves to portray themselves truthfully, they must respect themselves in and for what they are; they [the authors] would not aspire to this task of sketching such portraits [in the present volume] if they had been required to depict originals without a physiognomy of their own to distinguish them from what is foreign [. . .] with this in mind, the work they present is much more transcendent than it appears at first glance, and their performance a true service to the nation and to letters.)

Costumbrismo offered the "colonial scalpel" by which the local could be differentiated from the foreign, modeling forms of self-definition and self-recognition through which emerging Cubans were hailed and interpellated as such.

Throughout this period, debates on the status and future of the colony were inextricably linked to questions of racial hierarchy and slavery, as they had been since the beginning of the successful slave revolution on the neighboring island of Saint-Domingue (later Haiti) in 1791—a cataclysmic event that haunted white peninsulares and criollos alike for decades to follow. Cuba's sugar industry had benefited greatly from the slave revolution in Haiti, taking Haiti's place as the leading producer of sugar in the Caribbean; that success prompted the plantocracy to import slaves in even greater numbers, in turn prompting increasing fears of a similar slave rebellion in Cuba. This fear, known generally as "the Africanization scare," grew steadily into race panic throughout the period, especially after the census of 1841 (later thought to be inaccurate) showed that the black population had finally exceeded that of the white. Liberal-minded criollos realized that as long as slavery existed, Spain could continue its repressive regime under the pretext of maintaining this racial regime. Although few publicly advocated an immediate end to slavery, many—like members of the del Monte tertulia—strongly opposed the continued illegal import of African slaves, which had theoretically been abolished since the 1820 treaty with the British.

Race became the central issue in the poetics and politics of costumbrismo and its anticolonial affiliations. In the theatre, race—and racial impersonation—were central to costumbrista performance from the outset. The purported originator of Cuban theatre, actor-playwright Francisco Covarrubias, not only wrote the first costumbrista dramas about life on the island, but also debuted Cuba's first blackface stage character in 1812: the negrito. He first performed the negrito in a "dialogue between negritos" during which, according to the publicity, they "sang and danced in the style of their nation." In 1815, the press noted that Covarrubias performed in a *tonadilla* named *El desengaño feliz o el negrito* (The happy realization or the little black). He continued to perform the role over his fifty-year career; his reported use of some form of bozal "dialect" was one of his most enduring "gifts" to Cuban popular culture and to the stage (Leal 1980, 31).

Although no extant source indicates how Covarrubias and his audiences understood his representation of the slave negrito (did he copy particular African dance or song? how did he develop these performances?), we have ample indication that the delmontinos pursued research and first-hand study to create their portraits of Cuban slavery. Anselmo Suárez y Romero, for one, whom del Monte commissioned to write a novel about slavery, relocated to the sugar plantation named Surinam to study life and customs there. In a letter to his patron, Suárez suggested that he began to be enticed by the aesthetic possibilities of his ethnographic experience and documentation:

> En todas partes hay esclavos y señores, en todas partes hay mayorales, q^e^. es lo mismo q^e^. decir—que donde quiera jime una raza de hombres desgraciados bajo el poder de otra raza mas feliz que se aprovecha, inhumana, de sus afanes y sudores. Sin embargo, desde q^e^. V. me encargó una novela donde los sucesos fueran entre blancos y negros y desde q^e^. la comencé, me ha entrado tal afición á observar los

escesos de aquellos y los padecimientos de los segundos, tal gusto por estudiar las costumbres que nacen de la esclavitud, costumbres raras y variadas á lo infinito qe. no me pesa, ántes me agrada mi estancia aqui para acopiar noticias y tela, con que poder escribir algun día otra novela por el estilo del "Injenio, ó las Delicias del campo." (Cabrera Saqui 1969, 23)

(Everywhere there are slaves and gentlemen, everywhere there are overseers, which is to say, wherever [you look] a race of unfortunate men live under the power of a happier race that takes advantage, inhumanly, of its labor and sweat. However, ever since you charged me with writing a novel in which the events transpired between whites and blacks, and since I began it, I have been filled with such an enthusiasm to observe the excesses of the former and the suffering of the latter, such pleasure in studying the customs born from slavery, customs rare and infinitely varied, that it does not weigh on me, rather I am pleased by my stay here so that I can collect notes and material from which I will be able someday to write another novel along the style of *The sugar plantation, or the pleasures of the country.*)

Suárez confessed pleasure at the documentation of the culture of slavery, as it enabled him to imagine and create a uniquely Cuban narrative. Suárez revealed the underlying racial logic of early "Cuban" expression, a logic common to both this abolitionist literature and a wider range of costumbrista performance and narrative: although he initially abhored the cruelty of slavery, he became "enthusiastic" in his notation of the peculiar cultural forms such systematic cruelty enabled. What had been the suffering of the slave was "extracted" by the popular ethnographer to be "refined" into national "customs," valuable for their rarity and variety, stored for use as the "pleasures of the country." In the fullness of time, his wish would come true: the novel *Francisco, el ingenio o las delicias del campo* was celebrated by Cubans as a fascinating portrait of slavery that revealed peculiar, varied, and rare truths of Cuban life, in spite or perhaps because of the suffering it captured and relayed.[3]

In their own time, however, these writings circulated only clandestinely. All of the writings on slavery commissioned by del Monte were censored: not one was published in Cuba before the abolition of slavery in 1886. In the 1840s, when a series of large-scale slave revolts were interpreted as the initial stages of an island-wide conspiracy—known as La Escalera—the violent repression that followed resulted in the execution of hundreds of slave and free blacks in 1844, including the execution of the mulato poet Plácido, the imprisonment of Juan Francisco Manzano, and the forced exile of most of the members of del Monte's circle, including Anselmo Suárez y Romero, Cirilio Villaverde, and del Monte himself. The effects on antislavery activism were devastating, as was the effect on the development of Cuban culture and letters. As Villaverde wrote to del Monte in 1844, "Tal desaliento y tal pavor se han difundido entre los pocos que cultivan las letras después de la salida de Ud. y de los sangrientos sucesos de Matanzas, que ni por su casualidad se reúnen dos para hablar, ni tratar de literatura" (Such discouragement and terror have spread among the few left to cultivate letters after your departure and the bloody events in Matanzas, that not even by chance do they meet to talk or deal with literature [Benítez Rojo 1986, 113]).

This is the racially charged context in which we should place the development of blackface performance, and the emergence of the writer José Crespo y Borbón and his decades-long impersonation of the slave-writer Creto. Crespo began his career during the watershed years of Cuban narrative, 1838 to 1840, when Suárez, Villaverde, and Manzano were composing their antislavery novels. Occupying the space forcibly vacated by the delmontinos in the aftermath of La Escalera, Creto's position on the literary scene is profoundly ambivalent: this figure signals a new mode of representing slave life in Cuba, at the same time that it signals the impossibility of any such honest representation at all. Creto's popularity represents a newly energized interest in African or black expression, at the same time that, as an entirely fictive "African" author, he signals the censure of any such expression written by Africans, free or slave, at all. In Crespo/Creto's writing, Cuba's "African" self is both conjured and disavowed; Cuba's particular "African" identity in the colonial era is constituted *through* its disavowal.

Creto Gangá

Like his immediate predecessors, Crespo used the representation of slavery to evoke a developing sense of cubanía with its attending anticolonial connotations, but did so through a new medium: discursive blackface. The shift toward caricature suggests that the committed realism of the costumbristas was a less viable alternative in an atmosphere of vigilant censorship. In truth, however, Crespo's use of blackface, while not fundamentally altering the realist logic of costumbrismo, underscored an existing tension between the descriptive and performative functions of costumbrista writing in general, opening the contradictory space between the coherent Cuba that it performatively conjured and the socially contested reality to which it referred. Preexisting social contradictions haunted the emergence of a national perspective, and the nation narrated not only its ideal body but unwittingly its repressed others as well. Crespo formulated the figure of the comic bozal—the nonacculturated African in Cuba—through the same costumbrista techniques regularly used by his contemporaries, drawing on tropes of witnessing, ethnographic attention to behavioral customs, and a careful, painterly amassing of realist detail. These very techniques are what allowed Crespo not to represent bozal expression, but to *invent* bozal as a written discourse.

The discursive blackface for which Crespo became famous was initiated in the third installment of *El látigo del anfibio, o sea, colección de sus poesías satíricas dedicadas a los estravagantes* (The whip of the amphibian, or collection of his satirical poems dedicated to extravagants [1839]), a collection that anthologized his early poems. The bozal made his entrance in a poem entitled "La serenata del negro Pascual a Francisca, en un ingenio" (The serenade of the negro Pascual to Francisca, on a sugar plantation). He appears not as a Cuban "type" per se, but as a salient costumbrista detail in a panoramic Cuban landscape. Narrated by a Spanish "caballero" on horseback, the poem begins with a survey of a plantation:

Los preciosos cafetales,
con sus fragantes cafetos,
mil tesoros, mil objetos
de placer y admiración.
El alma me engenaba
tantos dones hechiceros:
máquinas, hatos, potreros,
vegas, frutos, fruta y flor.
En un Eden me creía,
de gozar no me cansaba. (67)

(The precious coffee plantations
with their fragrant coffee trees,
a thousand treasures, a thousand objects
of pleasure and admiration.
My soul was enraptured
by so many enchanting gifts:
machines, cattle herds, pastures,
tobacco fields, fruit trees, fruit and flower.
I thought I was in an Eden,
and did not tire of taking pleasure.)

This idyllic landscape (not unlike the Surinam, which produced comparable "country pleasures" for Anselmo Suárez) and the lyrical prose that describes it, are interrupted suddenly by the sound of an alien voice: "Cuando a mi oído un accento / hirió de lánguido canto; me paro, escucho y en llanto / me sumergió esa canción; [que] un triste etiope entonaba" (When my ear was wounded by the accent of a languid chant; I stop, listen, I was submerged in the cry of the song [that] a sad Ethiopian sang [67–68]). The beauty and tranquility of the plantation is disrupted—"herido," wounded and offended—by the sound of a black man singing. As the sad "Ethiopian" serenades his unrequited love, Francisca, the quality of the prose shifts radically:

"Yo sabé que ño Rafé
son guardiero tu bují,
que tá namorá de tí,
y tú le correspondé."
[. . .]
"Frasica mio, chinito,
siguió el cuitado diciendo,
¿Po qué así tú tá jasiendo
sufrí tu probre nengrito?
Cuera bien qu tú mimito
chapiando cañavera,
disiba 'tuya, Pascua,
na ma son mi corasó.'
¡Batante me cuera yo!
tú solo que lo vida. . . .(68)

("I know that Mr. Rafé [Rafael]
is the guardian of your hut [bohío]
that he's in love with you
and you with him."
[. . .]
"My Frasica [Francisca], *chinito*,"[4]
continued the anxious one, saying,
"Why do you make your poor
negrito suffer like this?
Remember well that you yourself,
clearing the reeds,
said, 'for you, Pascua [Pascual]
and nothing else is my heart.'
I certainly remember!
Only you forget. . . .)

Framed as an arresting detail in the plantation landscape rather than as a subject in his own right, Pascual hardly seems a viable hero for his own sad tale—which ends in his tragic death at the hands of a jealous "ño Rafé" (Mr. Rafael). This irony is reaffirmed by the juxtaposition of the Spanish caballero's formal verse and the African's heavily accented bozal—a jarring difference that is redoubled by appearing in writing, where Pascual's distorted jargon is deciphered at times only with considerable effort on the part of the reader.

The bozal verse provides the poem's comic value. The poem manages to disguise the outright parody of the African's inability to speak Spanish "properly" by appealing to the truth-value of costumbrista representational techniques. Couching the appearance of the African character in a familiar costumbrista description, that descriptive detail in turn lends credibility to the written representation of spoken bozal. Pascual's odd speech pattern is presented as simply a true record of what the gentleman-author happened to hear (the sad accent that "wounded" the aural landscape) while indulging the fragrant pleasures of the countryside. The reader is prompted to recognize the sound and accent of the African-born speaker as a "true" feature of life on a sugar plantation, and find in that obviously distorted prose the same kind of costumbrista pleasure she or he would in recognizing other salient features of daily life in Cuba.

Crespo's innovation in Cuban costumbrismo was precisely this ability to capture an aural environment through his writing, developing an "aural costumbrismo." His work increasingly drew on the theatrical potential of the written word to conjure the many speech patterns, accents, and mannerisms of Cuba's different social and cultural populations. Crespo increasingly offered detailed linguistic portraits of his subjects, playing with phonetic spellings and orthographic representation to evoke precise variations of vocal intonations. His first play (published in 1838, although likely written earlier), a one-act romantic comedy of errors set in his native Ferrol, in Spain's northern province of Galicia, entitled *El chasco, o vale por mil gallegos el que llega a despuntar* (The trick, or he who stands out is worth a thousand Galicians [1838]) illustrates his talents for linguistic mimicry. The plot follows a well-worn comic formula: a wealthy, elderly widow is wooed by a young rogue pretending to be of Spanish noble birth; his greedy plot is thwarted by the clever efforts of the widow's two servants. The play's interest lies in Crespo's ability to capture and communicate the social quality and class of each character through his or her distinct accent and vocal inflection: the educated Galician señora, the rogue suitor with his faux Castilian formality, the two servants with their heavily accented Galician-brogue, and so on. It is worth noting that the play was published and never produced; a contemporary critic and costumbrismo enthusiast, José María Andueza, went so far in his review to insist that it was unnecessary to produce the play, since its costumbrista pleasures were specially enjoyable to the *reader*, who would enjoy deciphering the phonetic play of familiar speech patters (Cruz 1974, 42).

Crespo's focus on the aural aspects of the culture eventually embraced musical forms retroactively associated with specifically "Cuban" expression. Crespo was one of the first to write extensively in the poetic form of the *décima*, as in the "serenade" just quoted. A ten-line stanza, the *décima* had been common in Spanish literature of the Golden Age. Falling out of favor on the peninsula, it gained new popularity in the eighteenth century through the primarily oral culture of Cuba's rural countryside; in Cuba, décimas often became lyrics sung to the textual-melodic form called *punto guajiro* (see López Lemus 1995; Linares 1991, 87–114). Choosing to write in the *décima* form, then, Crespo added another *costumbrista* dimension to his work, bringing this "Cuban" popular rural form to a wide urban readership. Throughout the nineteenth century—precisely through efforts like those of Crespo—the *décima* took on increasingly nationalist overtones, as evident in this later popular verse:

Décima es caña y banano,
es palma, ceiba y anón.
Décima es tabaco y ron,
café de encendido grano.
Décima es techo de guano,
es clave, guitarra y tres.
Es taburete en dos pies
y es Cuba de cuerpo entero,
porque ella nació primero
y nuestro pueblo después. (López Lemus 1995, 4)

(Décima is sugar cane and banana,
palm tree, ceiba and *anón*.
Décima is tobacco and rum,
coffee of the finest roast.
Décima is a roof of palm,
clave, guitar and *tres* [musical instruments].
[Décima] is a stool on two feet
and is Cuba's whole body,
because she was born first
and our country after.)

Mary Cruz notes the irony that it was the less serious Crespo who adopted the more "Cuban" décima form, while his literary counterparts in the del Monte tertulia turned to European—mostly French—romanticism as a model in their efforts to find a Cuban voice and distinguish themselves from Castilian letters (Cruz 1974, 58).

Crespo also wrote a number of guarachas, another rural-based musical form similarly invested with an especially Cuban quality, purportedly originating from the unique combination of traditional Spanish dance with African rhythms. Although the teatro bufo is usually credited with popularizing the guaracha in 1868, we find that Crespo began writing guarachas as early as 1839 (Cruz 1974, 29). For these reasons, Crespo is often credited with participating in the development of Afro-Cuban music, and with anticipating the influence of that music on Cuban and Afro-Cuban poetry.

Blackface became the signature feature of Crespo's work in 1845, with the publication of *Laborintos y trifucas de canavá,* when he changed his pseudonym to Creto Gangá, and began writing first-person verse narratives from this supposed "African" subject position. The success of *Laborintos* led to a contractual partnership with *La Prensa,* whereby "Creto" was hired to write frequent social and cultural commentary for this leading Havana newspaper, soon making him Cuba's foremost "African" costumbrista author. This blackface costumbrismo redoubled the usual pleasures of costumbrista writing by combining highly topical subject matter with the curious and compelling aural universe of bozal. Among his favored subjects were letters written in verse to his "sifunta mugé Frasica"; that is, his deceased wife, Francisca, for whom he chronicled the most interesting happenings in Havana.

Among them we find a series of letters, later anthologized into a single volume, describing the visit of a Chinese doctor, whose nontraditional medicines and cures attracted the curiosity of many Havana residents. Creto chronicled this "laño de la brujerí" (year of witchcraft) when "La Bana" became a "tiera siáticu" (Asiatic land), and over a period of weeks he offered "Nutisia [. . .] de la milagra que jasé / y trufica que tené / cun méricu y buticario" (News [. . .] of the miracles that happened, and ruckus that we had, with the medic and pharmacist [rev. in *La Prensa* 8 September 1847]). That year did in fact mark Cuba's first as "Asiatic land," when the first of many ships carrying indentured Chinese laborers docked in the port of Havana. Over the next twenty-six years, some 125,000 such laborers would enter Cuba, many abducted or forced into labor from Macao, to live lives in Cuba almost identical to that of African slaves with whom they labored on plantations, and whom they were meant in theory to supplement or, later, replace as a work force. Those twenty-six years were marked for Chinese laborers, as they were for enslaved Africans, with much desperation, rebellion, sickness, and a suicide rate higher, they say, than anywhere in the world (see Baltar Rodriguez 1997; Álvarez Ríos 1995). Popular press accounts of "Chinese" peoples and practices, like Crespo's very early costumbrista portrait of the traveling Chinese herbalist, served to limit and shape the representational contours of Asian Cuba from its inception.

Another favored subject were "Creto's" many visits to the theatre: he carefully chronicled the development of the opera season in 1848, as in his article "Cosa que yo lo ve la Jópera cun mi suamo siño Geromo Suribamba" (Things I saw at the opera with my master Geromo Suribamba [Cruz 128, 116]). Crespo cast Creto as one of the many slaves that accompanied white masters and mistresses to the theatres, described by the U.S. traveler Samuel Hazard as: "dandified showily dressed little negro pages, most of them bright-eyed, sharp little fellows, who, in most 'gorgeous array,' stand outside the boxes of their beautiful mistresses, ready to obey and mandate or execute any commission they may entrust to them—such as carrying messages from one box to another, or slipping a card or note into the hand of some gentleman admirer" (Pérez 1992, 236–37). The opera enabled reiteration and performance of the colonial slave economy for the assembled audience: men displayed their fashionably dressed women as tokens of wealth and status, just as masters and mistresses displayed their slaves as tokens of their power. The many opera theatres built between 1838 and 1868 were monuments to the spoils of the slave economy: as Manuel Moreno Fraginals put it, "although it may seem strange, in every city there is a theatre endowed by a major slave owner" (Fraginals 1984, 74). Given Cuba's relatively modest population, the number of new theatres was striking: in Havana, El Tacón (1838); in Trinidad, the Brunet (1840); in Santiago, the Reina (1850); in Puerto Principe, the Principal (1850) and Fénix (1851); in Cienfuegos, the Avellaneda (1860); and in Matanzas, the Estéban (1863). As a literate and clever "dandified slave," the character of Creto may have seemed to transgress the colonial slave order that such theatres and their operas represented. Creto even went to lengths to explain how he managed to secure permissions from his master to attend other forms of theatre (for example, he went to see "La corobata la Sico banero" [The acrobats of the Havana Circus]), or to find his way alone to the Chinese herbalist. Such elaborate explanatory detail, however, only served to indulge the elaborate fiction of the slave-author without seriously disturbing the edifice of the "slavocracy" at all.

The Cuban *Ajiaco*

Creto "himself" was the author of Cuba's most influential play—one that, over the course of time, set the model for a decidedly anticolonial and Cuban popular theatre: the successful *Un ajiaco, o la boda de Pancha Jutía y Canuto Raspadura* (A Cuban stew, or the wedding of Pancha Jutía and Canuto Raspadura) which launched his career as a playwright in 1847. Set on a sugar plantation, the wedding celebration provides the excuse for numerous guarachas, and the clownish antics of two invited slaves, Rafael Manca and Lucas Macao—stage bozal roles, or *bozalones*, as they were called—provide a string of comic gags.[5] The surprise ending finds the master awarding Pancha and Canuto their freedom in overdue gratitude for having once saved his life. Despite the abolitionist gesture, *Un ajiaco* offers an equivocal view of slavery: the master blames not the institution of slavery, but the "ingratitude" of slave-owners for the injustices of slavery; Pancha and Canuto, in turn, accept their freedom by thanking that institution for bringing them from Africa.

Un ajiaco is central to any discussion of nineteenth century Cuban performance, race, and culture because it was among the first to articulate a notion of mestizaje as the foundation for a Cuban imaginary and was the first to rely on both blackface and popular music to do so. Ajiaco was the term later put forth and favored by the Cuban ethnologist Fernando Ortiz as an appropriate culinary metaphor to describe the ethnic, racial, and social diversity that has characterized Cuba's cultural development. In an important essay from 1940, "Los factores humanos de la cubanidad" ("Human factors of Cubanness"), Ortiz argued that this eminently Cuban stew offered a better metaphorical image for the distinctiveness of *cubanidad* than the otherwise clichéd and non-Cuban image of the *crisol* or melting pot (Ortiz [1940] 1991, 10–30). Ortiz baptized Cuba's particular process of cultural development with his own Cuban neologism, *transculturación* or "transculturation," which he felt best described the "extremely complex transmutations of culture that have taken place here," characterized by the progressive reinvention of the culture through the continual introduction of different cultural groups: "since the sixteenth century all [Cuba's] classes, races and cultures, coming in by will or by force, have all been exogenous and have all been torn from their places of origin, suffering the shock of this first uprooting and a harsh transplanting" (Ortiz 1995, 100). Ortiz rejected the then prevalent notion of acculturation to analyze this process of "harsh transplanting" as it describes only a transition of one culture to another, an acquisition of

one culture in place of the other. Transculturation, in contrast, embraces a notion of both the culture at large and its distinct demographic groups in continual and mutual transformation through a dynamic process of change and reinvention.

Originally an Amerindian dish, ajiaco is prepared by combining the day's available vegetables, fish, or meat—from corn to tuna to iguana meat—and seasoning them with the chili pepper *ají*. Unlike the notion of a melting pot, in the ajiaco the flavor of each ingredient ostensibly remains distinct while changing the composition of the whole. Some ajiaco is typically left over after each meal and is reused as the base for the following day's ajiaco. The stew thus illustrates not only Cuba's racial/ethnic diversity but also its ongoing process of change:

> Lo característico de Cuba es que, siendo ajiaco, su pueblo no es un guiso hecho sino una constante cocedura. . . . siempre en la olla de Cuba es un renovado entrar de raíces, frutos y carnes exógenas, un incesante borbor de heterogéneas sustancias. De ahí que su composición cambie y la cubanidad tenga sabor y consistencia dinstintos según sea catado en lo profundo o en la panza de la olla o en su boca, donde las viandas aún están crudas y burbujea el caldo claro. (Ortiz 1991, 16)

> (What is characteristic of Cuba is that, being an ajiaco, its people are not a prepared meal but rather a constant preparation. . . . In the cooking pot of Cuba there has always been a continual addition of exogenous roots, fruits, and meats, an incessant simmering of heterogeneous substances. It follows then that its composition changes, and that *cubanidad* will have a different flavor and consistency depending on whether it is tasted from the bottom, the belly of the bowl, or from the top, where the vegetables are still raw and the clear broth bubbles.)

As Gustavo Pérez Firmat affirms, Ortiz's substitution of ajiaco for the Anglo-American notion of a melting pot is "a political and rhetorical stratagem as much as a scholarly or scientific one. [. . .] Ortiz's implicit claim is that Cuban phenomena are best explained by Cuban words, that Cuba can speak for itself" (Pérez Firmat 1990, 26–27).

Although we have no indication that Ortiz was familiar with Crespo y Borbón's nineteenth century play, there is little question that Crespo's *Un ajiaco* prefigures Ortiz's major claims about the usefulness of the ajiaco as a rich and appropriate metaphor for an emerging cubanidad. The ajiaco of the play's title ostensibly refers to the special meal that Catana Huesitos has prepared for the occasion of the wedding festivities of her two slaves, Pancha and Canuto. The slaves Lucas Macao and Rafael Manca-perros anxiously await the meal, longing to eat the "jiaco cun cane y cun vianda" (ajiaco with meat and vegetables), which for them is tantamount to "toitico cosa güena / que lo come gente branca" (everything good that white people eat). Catana's husband Geromo warns the audience that the play will consist of no more than an ajiaco: "alviertan / que hoy aquí no hay más comía / que un ajiaco (beware that here today there's no more food than an ajiaco [Crespo y Borbón (1847) 1975, 72]). Yet the promised culinary ajiaco does not arrive over the course of the play; instead the audience is treated to a metaphorical ajiaco of the racially and culturally varied guests in attendance, whose particularities are expressed through poetry, music, dance, and other entertaining behaviors during the festivities. When, at the close of the play, Geromo invites the audience to join the table and take part in the flavorful ajiaco to be served, the metaphor is complete; he entreats the audience itself to participate in the rich diversity of the Cuban stew already assembled.

If his characters are read as forming a distinct Cuban ajiaco, then Creto/Crespo has, as it were, skimmed from the top of the broth, favoring those relatively "uncooked" and "exogenous" members recently added to the Cuban stew. The blacks in the play are all bozal slaves, whose speech and behavior is clearly marked as that of negros de nación, or African-born slaves. When Rafael and Lucas greet the groom they do so with "gestos y ademanes muy propios en los negros de su clase, como el tomarse la mano, y hacer sonar los dedos gruesos y pulgar" (gestures and manners appropriate to blacks of their class, such as shaking hands, and snapping their fingers [60]), as the stage directions indicate. Likewise, the speech patterns of all of the bozales are emphatically marked as those of an African speaker; the labored communication between Lucas and Rafael is central to the play's interest and humor. The central white characters, the slave owners, are also recent arrivals to Cuba: Geromo and Catana have migrated from the Canary Islands, one of the most common places of origin for white immigrants. Lucas comments on Canuto's fortune to have "ileño" (islanders) for masters, since they are reputed to be "güeno cun lo ningrito" (good with blacks). For their part, the Canary Islanders' peculiarities of behavior and speech are no less underscored. Geromo and Catana speak in heavily accented Spanish, which provides both variety and humor in the play, as illustrated by Catana's entrance: "Geromo, saca selvesa, / paque esta gente arremoje / la palabra y tome fuelsas" (Geromo, go get beer so these people can loosen their tongues and regain strength [71]). The rest of the play is populated by *guajiros*, an emerging Cuban "type" that would soon attract great attention in popular costumbrista literature, especially in the vernacular theatre. The guajiro is a white peasant, usually uneducated and not well spoken, whose less than refined manners and rough mode of speech are also a source of curiosity and amusement.[6] The play's interest in exploring the veritable ajiaco of linguistic aberration of the Cuban plantation countryside is well illustrated through the fate of the character of Alfonso, the house-slave, whose very name is progressively distorted by all of the other characters into other mutations of the name; neither the Canary Islanders, nor the guajiros, nor the bozales can pronounce the name, and over the course of the play it becomes Idelfonso, Alifonso, Lifonso, and so forth—with no one, including Alfonso himself, ever quite getting the name right.

All the characters are presented as part of a communal Cuban ajiaco, but the African element plays a special role: over the course of the play, the ajiaco is progressively "Africanized," until even Geromo punctuates the close of the play with a whooping Africanism, "*Quiquiribú!*" (93). This process of "Africanization" is acted out through a musical exchange—almost a duel—between the rural music of the guajiros and the so-called African music of the attending slaves. When the guajiro musicians first enter the scene, they are described as "varios guajiros de ambos sexos: algunos vendrán tocando en bandurrias o tiples, y cantando alguna tonada del país" (various guajiros of both sexes; some will enter playing *bandurrias* [like mandolins] or *tiples* [like guitars], and singing some *tonada* [melody] from the country [70]). Crespo's musical choices display costumbrista interest in rural musical cultures. The bandurria and tiple are both Spanish-derived string instruments that were developed and used enthusiastically in the rural music tradition. The tonada is a song sung in what is now known as punto, the musical setting for the rural verse form, décima. This tonada is followed by another longer tonada, dedicated to a "bella virgen guajira" (beautiful peasant virgin). The assembled guests respond with calls of "¡Qué canto tan bello!" (What a beautiful song!), and Alfonso/Idelfonso provides the "African" review of the performance: "¡Jah! Branco sí que lo sabe / cantá como ruiseñó" (Jah! Whites sure do know how to sing like nightingales [75–76]).

If Crespo's first innovation was to introduce music associated with white plantation culture to Havana's popular theatre in the late 1840s, his inclusion of "African" or slave music is all the more remarkable on the urban vernacular stage, especially since the latter is allowed to eclipse the former. The African-born bride and groom, Pancha and Canuto, are so pleased to have been awarded their freedom as a wedding gift from their master that they ask permission to offer their own musical entertainment by way of thanks. According to the stage directions, their music "debe imitar a la de los negros de nación" (must imitate that of African-born blacks); soon all of the black characters begin to dance and sing "a una voz" (in one voice [90]). Here too Crespo taps the costumbrista enthusiasm for rehearsing "authentic" features of plantation life, only in this case he inaccurately classifies the great range of African musical styles and traditions brought to Cuba by slaves as a singular and uniform type of music, that of "negros de nación." The wedding guests are so taken with the "African" music, they ask for several encores, displacing the guajiro musicians altogether; as Geromo says, "Mira el diablo de los negritos / que bien lo han jecho. . . ." (By devil, look how well those negritos have done it [92]).

By the time Canuto invites everyone assembled, including the audience, to partake in their cultural ajiaco, it appears that the Africans are included as equally important players; not only have two been awarded their freedom, but the whites seem to have embraced them and their music fully. Yet this tale of racial harmony masks a deeply compromised racial agenda. The Africans do bring an important measure of diversity to this Cuban ajiaco, but they do so at an extraordinary price—not least of which is their literal absence from the stage. Represented through blackface proxy, their own cultural or musical diversity is progressively simplified and homogenized as they are "added" to the Cuban mix. Furthermore, even as the play gives itself over to the musical pleasures of the African guests, the song that the Africans sing turns out to serve the white regime far more than the black slaves. Although the music is carefully specified as that of "negros de nación," the lyrics are a highly improbable sample of that music. The song ironically becomes a paean not to freedom, but to slavery itself and the white culture it serves:

Nengrito ma futuná
no lo salí lan Guinea.
¡Jah! Bindita hora que branco
me lo traé nete tierra.
[. . .]
La tierra branco son groria
cuando se jalla amo güeno,
¡Jah! la mío son critiano
y como súcara memo. (90–91)

(No black more fortunate
has ever left Guinea.
Jah! Blessed hour that the white man
brought me to this country.
[. . .]
White county is a glory

if you have a good master,
Jah! mine are Christians
and like sugar itself.)

In other words, although the metaphorical ajiaco includes blacks, it is, as Lucas Macao aptly put it, still something "que lo come gente branca" (that white people eat [54]). Crespo's *Un ajiaco* strategically uses "Africanization" as a way to outline and celebrate the contours of (white) "Cubanness," carefully controlling the degree to which Africans actually participate in the developing Cuban stew.

Un ajiaco forms part of Crespo's extended blackface performance insofar as the play *itself* is in blackface. The cast list is written in Creto's bozal, featuring, for example, "Señá Catana Huesitos" and "Señó Geromo Pachato." Creto offers a lengthy dedication to "la Cabayera Siño Don Santiago Gurea" (the Gentleman Mister Sir Santiago Gurea) and an "adivitisió a la letó" (a notice to the reader) in which he even goes so far as to explain his use of "lengua gente branca" (language of white people) in the stage directions. These were written by none other than his friend Crespo, "que lo sabe catillano como yo gangá" (who knows Castilian as well as I know gangá [51]). A great measure of the popular appeal of the play is the labyrinthine fiction of its "black" author.

Other writers were frequently enlisted in this fanciful project of building the plausibility of the otherwise improbable "African" slave-author. Reviewing Creto's works, or addressing Creto Gangá directly in editorials in the press, other writers participated in the ever more complex pretense of Creto's literary career, to the growing delight of readers. The following exchange between Crespo-as-Creto in *La Prensa* and a literary critic from *Diario de la Marina* is typical. Wary of Creto's success with his first novel, the *Diario* commentator addresses the judges of Havana's recently established literary prize; invoking Homer, Virgil, and Cicero in his defense of "literary verse," he admonishes the judges not to forsake the "dulce versos de Meléndez o Zorrilla" (the sweet verses of Meléndez or Zorrilla) in favor of Creto's curious but mangled verse. In his lengthy response, published the next day in *La Prensa*, Creto apologizes for not recognizing the names of those authors mentioned, and quips, "¿Cómo va sabé diese cosa si son uno bosá que nunca lo ha jecho ma que sembrá caña, chapiá lingenio. . .?" (How would I know about that as a bozal who's never done more than plant and cut sugarcane on the plantation?) Creto wonders whether the writer might offer a lesson in Latin in exchange for lessons in Gangá so they might come to an understanding (see Cruz 1974, 55–56). Creto engaged in similar debates, some lasting for months, with various interlocutors, many of whom disapproved of and debated the very idea of a slave turned reporter. In later cases, Crespo went so far as to impersonate his own critics and commentators, creating ever more intricate rivalries for his Creto in the pages of the popular press.

This kind of exchange offers insight into the popularity of Creto's writings, and its role in larger discourses of race and racism at mid-century. Although often clever in his turns of phrase, Creto was consistently presented as a naive "bosá," offering a comforting and roundly patronizing image of slaves to counter the recent memory of slave insurrections. Who but an ignorant slave would imagine that the *Diario de la Marina* critic would find lessons in the African "language" Gangá an adequate exchange for access to Latin? Crespo's blackface performance functions as a form of sociopolitical containment: he takes on the persona of the black slave and through his discursive enactments he progressively masters, controls, and circumscribes that persona's behaviors and possible intervention in a wider public sphere. The purportedly descriptive function of costumbrismo masks its prescriptive and proscriptive agenda. Crespo offers Creto as a "typical"portrait of a Cuban slave; the character's profound humility, naiveté, and ignorance can likewise be recuperated as mere descriptive details belonging to the social "type" under scrutiny, rather than gross limitations set on the persona by the author.

In this mode of artistic containment of black peoples, Crespo was followed by a range of other costumbrista artists of the period, particularly in the newly popular field of lithography, best exemplified in Eduardo Laplante's picturesque lithographs of Cuban plantations, published in the lavishly illustrated text *Los ingenios de Cuba* (The sugar plantations of Cuba) in 1857, and especially by Víctor Patricio Landaluze's enormously popular illustrations of Cuban life, published in that paradigmatic text of Cuban costumbrismo, *Los cubanos pintados por sí mismos. Colección de tipos Cubanos* (Cubans painted by themselves: A collection of Cuban types [1852]). Laplante, Landaluze, and other costumbrista artists favored scenes of urban or rural servitude, featuring placid slaves at steady work, smartly dressed manservants, beautiful languishing mulatas, or joyful black musicians in tranquil repose. Like Creto Gangá, these portraits of black life in Cuba typically staged the artists' own paternalistic projections about black peoples, ascribing to them a marked humility and docility that were less realistic descriptions than painterly containments of the threat they might otherwise pose.[7]

Yet even as discursive blackface accommodated racist panic, its strategy allowed for a certain—if timid—engagement with otherwise repressed oppositional discourse regarding Cuba's participation in the illegal slave trade, and against slavery in general. Creto's defensive remark that he, as a slave, could hardly be expected to be familiar with Homer or Virgil was of course a plausible and "true" representation of the state of illiteracy to which slaves were rigorously subject; his quip could be read as a tacit critique of that practice. Here, Crespo's use of costumbrista detail aligned itself with the realist project of the earlier writer Anselmo Suárez y Romero in his abolitionist novel *Francisco*. As Suárez y Romero's friend and critic José Zacarías González del Valle wrote of the novel,

> el novelista no debe poner arengas en boca de sus personajes, y menos siendo inverosímiles; [. . .] por lo mismo que la novela tuya sirve para ir corregiendo nuestras costumbres, ha de salir verdadera, cubana y tan provista de hechos indisputibles que no haya más que ver el retrato a abominarlo. (Cabrera Saqui 1969, 32)

> (the novelist should not put sermons in the mouths of his characters, much less improbable ones; [. . .] insofar as your novel serves to start correcting our customs, it must come out truthful, Cuban, and so well supplied with indisputable facts that one needs only to see the portrait in order to abominate it.)

For Suárez y Romero, drawing the eminently truthful, "Cuban," and self-evidently abominable portrait of slavery relied precisely on the amassing of one credible detail after another in densely choreographed descriptive passages that delivered the narrative action. As an author, he made no qualitative distinction between, say, his lengthy and meticulous discussion of the rites, festivities, and songs through which different plantations honor religious and other holidays, and his equally meticulous description of exactly when, how, and with how much suffering resistant slaves were subjected to whippings, including a vivid account of the salt applied to their bleeding wounds (Suárez y Romero 1969, 64, 81). Disinterested narrative description became the vehicle for a gruesome portrait of the horrors of slavery. Couched in far more palatable and humorous terms, Crespo's representation of the difficulties of slave life followed the same logic: the naïve quality of Creto's accounts of the "facts" of his life could momentarily harbor a serious critique.

Between these seemingly contradictory readings of his work—curtailing and containing black power while condemning the system of slavery that underwrote such containment—Crespo's use of blackface also lent itself to readings beyond the "race question" (the "cuestión social" as it was then euphemistically called). Crespo's ludicrous adventures in Havana's social and artistic scene, along with his lively linguistic duels with educated white rivals, can also be seen to satirize the social pretensions of Castilian culture. When Creto defended his verse against such venerable Spanish writers as Meléndez or Zorrilla, the joke was that Creto's mangled Spanish hardly compared to the mastery of these learned poets; at the same time, the degree to which the *Prensa*'s readership enjoyed Creto's impertinent challenge to the Spanish poets was also the degree to which the joke was on the arrogance of the poets themselves. The blackface persona, in other words, allowed for the expression of broad anticolonial sentiment. One of his better-known poems, "¡Que cuntentura pa mi! ¡Y que rabia pa lo sabio!" (What happiness for me! And what fury for the experts!), captured this satirical operation in full:

Yo lo sabe dimasiá
que nelle icribe bunito,
y que no se pué compará:
poque yo icribe en gangá,
y nelle en güeno epañó,
la dielle instruye, la mia . . .
disi nelle, y disi yo,
que son uno puquiria. . . .
Ma llena yo mi acansía
lo demá son bobería
¡Y que güeno bobería!
[. . .]
Viene a suncribise aprisa
vieja, fea, tueto y cojo,
pa dalo a lo sabia en lo sojo
y a mi muchisimo risa. [. . .] (Crespo y Borbón 1965, 150–53)

(I know only too well
that they write beautifully
and we can't compare
because I write in Gangá
and they in good Spanish,
theirs instructs, and mine . . .
they say, and I say,
is a load of garbage. . . .
But I fill my piggy bank
and the rest is nonsense
and what good nonsense!
[. . .]
Come subscribe quickly
old, ugly, one-eyed or lame,
to give it to the wise ones in the eye
and give me a great big laugh. [. . .])

Urging his many readers to continue subscribing in profitable numbers to his writings, Creto jockeyed to have the last laugh on the critics. His poem not only delighted in infuriating the guardians of high culture, but also invited an alliance with other dispossessed peoples (the old, ugly, disabled) in order to strengthen his offensive. Although this critique of Spanish culture may seem relatively innocuous, recall that virtually all avenues for expression of anticolonial sentiment were censured rigorously throughout this period; some of Creto's popularity was owed to his consistent ability to smuggle social criticism past the noses of the censors in the guise of a harmless, jovial "African."

Crespo's capricious moves across the ideological checkerboard—from racial containment to anticolonial critique—are owed to a precise use of discursive blackface, the written representation of racially marked expression. Crespo's literal and careful "translation" of spoken bozal into written Spanish is the ground on which it claims to be credible. His representation of bozal speech was, over the course of his long publishing career, remarkably systematic and consistent, so much so that his bozal writing appears to follow its own rules of grammar, conjugation, declension, and orthography. These were made all the more "authentic" by the frequent interjection of African terms and sayings, and—as we have seen—by the use of verse and song structures already associated with African presence in rural Cuba. After several other "African" writers appeared in rival newspapers in 1849, Creto remarked wryly in an editorial in *La Prensa* that the public would benefit from a standardized guide to bozal:

> toví lo tiene iperansa de véselo salí po la mundo tanto scritore de la vitol y mena mío, que va sé prisiso jaselo uno garamático y uno disionaria de luenga mío, pa que toro lo jabra como mosotro lo prieto. (*La Prensa*, 23 January 1849)[8]

> (I still hold the hope of seeing arise in the world so many writers of my appearance and mien that it will be necessary to write a grammar and a dictionary in my language, so everyone can speak like us colored people.)

Creto proposed his linguistic project in the selfsame disfigured speech he hoped to standardize, underscoring its comic contradiction. In her attempt to determine whether the rival African writers may have been inventions of Crespo himself, critic Mary Cruz operated on the rather remarkable assumption that Crespo/Creto's writing was organized according to existing, fixed grammatical patterns; she attended to minor variations in the orthography and grammar typically used by Creto to conclude that Creto's rivals in the popular press had therefore to be the creations of other authors (Cruz 1974, 158).[9] Crespo's performance of bozal speech was so consistent and credible, in fact, that some later critics were persuaded that Creto's writings could and should be appreciated as valuable historical documents of bozal speech in mid-century Cuba. For José Antonio Portuondo, Creto Gangá "nos dejó el filón mas rico para el estudio [. . .] de una de las más interesantes hablas criollas de nuestro continente mestizo, el bozal" (left us the richest thread for the study [. . .] of one of the most interesting criollo speech forms from our mestizo continent, bozal [Portuondo 1974, 9]).

If bozal is one of Crespo's gifts to either Cuban ethnography or letters, let the receiver beware. Even as bozal appeared to ground his writing in a kind of realist linguistic portraiture, that bozal harbored an even deeper fiction. Crespo highlighted his "African" pseudonym ("Gangá" was one of many ethnonyms used by whites and slaves alike roughly to identify different African ethnicities) and wrote "in" bozal—as though bozal were a dialect, and not a derogatory term for the poorly spoken Spanish of recently arrived slaves. Through these strategies, Crespo effectively *created* bozal as a written language of "African-Spanish" (or "congo-español" as one reviewer put it) where no such system of writing had otherwise existed. Bozal is a cultural performative, conjured into existence through repeated performances like those of Creto Gangá. The point is not whether there were "real" slaves who might have "really" spoken this way; there is little doubt that one could undertake a study of comparative linguistic development of African slave populations in the new world and find that in fact slaves in Cuba learned and spoke Spanish in similar or significant ways, and that insofar as they might bear systemic traits, these speech patterns might be usefully analyzed alone or in relation to the ongoing development of Creole languages elsewhere. That one can undertake such a study in no way alters the fact that the moment that this slave speech was transliterated into Crespo's writing it ceased to be a "record" of speech and became a travesty of writing.

Before Crespo/Creto's body of writings may be read as an evidentiary "document," it must be read first as an unsympathetic record of error catalogued for uses against the very interests of the alleged speakers. Several critics have referred to Crespo's work as "caricature costumbrismo"; the line between realist portraiture and parody becomes very thin where the representation of nonwhite people is concerned (see Kutzinski 1993, 34; Cruz 1974, 75). Crespo's attention to "realist" detail—the careful and consistent collection of orthographic error—was precisely what lent the parody a certain plausibility, giving credence to the underlying (and spurious) cultural assumption that the writing of a black African slave (itself a highly unlikely occurrence) could only be accomplished through recourse to mistake, error, and linguistic misuse. The very idea of the slave as writer was necessarily pushed toward tropes of parody. In other words, Crespo not only parodied black speech, but—far more troubling—also presented that speech as an inherent parody.

Juan Francisco Manzano

Creto Gangá was the lie that told a truth about the deeply compromised state of black expression in Cuba, especially written expression by slaves, throughout this period. For confirmation, we need only to compare him to the poet-slave Juan Francisco Manzano. Born in the late 1790s, Manzano became an urban house servant. He escaped the harsh treatment of his mistress and began publishing poetry as early as 1821. In 1830 Domingo del Monte took an interest in him, publishing several of his poems in his journal *La moda,* and undertook the project of raising money to secure Manzano's freedom, which he did in 1836. Prior to Manzano's manumission, del Monte commissioned him to write about his life as a slave. Del Monte gave the resulting two-part *Autobiografía* (of which only the first part survives), completed in 1835, to the British abolitionist diplomat Robert R. Madden, who published part of the text in English in 1840 along with several of Manzano's poems under the title *Poems by a Slave in the Island of Cuba, Recently Liberated.* In the same year, V. Schoelcher translated part of the *Autobiografía* into French. During the same years that Crespo was beginning his blackface publishing career with *El látigo,* Manzano's autobiographical text of the events that shaped his young life as a slave—although not published in Cuba until 1937—was circulating widely among members of the del Monte tertulia and the intellectuals associated with it.

Not unlike the fictional Creto, Manzano aspired to write what he called a "truly Cuban novel" based on his own experiences. But unlike Creto, for Manzano the institutional, social reality of slavery compelled him to wait until such a day as he was no longer a slave to produce what he hoped would be his best work. Agreeing to write the story of his early life as a slave, he told del Monte that he had nonetheless reserved "los mas interesantes susesos de ella p[a] mi si algún dia me alle sentado en un rincon de mi patria, tranquilo, asegurada mi suerte y susistensia" (the most interesting events of it for myself so that if some day I find myself sitting in a corner of my country, calm, assured of my fate and sustenance), he could then write "una nobela propiamente cubana" (a properly Cuban novel [Manzano 1937, 85]). As far as Manzano was concerned, his horrific tale of slavery should not qualify as a good Cuban novel, and he was anxious to protect some part of his experience and his talent from the degradations of slavery. His letters to del Monte indicated a constant anxiety that he would not be worthy as a writer until he could leave behind the stigma of slavery: "Temo demereser en su apresio un siento por siento," he wrote, "pero acuerdese smd. cuando lea q^{e} yo soy esclavo y q^{e} el esclavo es un ser muerto ante su señor, y no pierda en su apresio lo q^{e} he ganado" (I fear losing your esteem a hundred percent, but remember Your Grace when you read this that I am a slave and that a slave is a dead being before his master, and do not lose sight of what I have gained [84]). Although this may well have been the strategic humility of a slave writing for his freedom, a trope of shame haunted his letters and the autobiography which confessed his mortification at every turn, and the narrative frequently tried and failed to fasten on those other aspects of his life that brought him pleasure and a sense of dignity.

Writing an autobiography, Manzano presumably could rely on the authority of his firsthand experience to give credence and moral suasion to his detailed story of slave life in Havana; it was of course precisely the special authority of his personal experience that interested del Monte, Madden, and his other readers to this day. Suárez y Romero, for one, marveled at the power of the facts that Manzano could assemble: "¡Qué escenas tan domésticas, tan propias de nuestra vida privada! cómo corrige Manzano solo con la fuerza de los hechos la tiranía de los amos!" (What domestic scenes, so true to our private lives! how Manzano corrects the tyranny of masters with the force of facts alone! [*Centón epistolario* 4, 81]). However, Manzano did not share Suárez y Romero's confidence; unlike the authority that Crespo or Suárez y Romero claimed for the "indisputable facts" that punctuated and organized their fictions, Manzano claimed to wrestle for narrative control over the facts of his life. The facts themselves tormented and agitated the author, halting his writing or refusing to be heard:

> he estado mas de cuatro ocaciones p^{r} no seguirla, un cuadro de tantas calamidades, no parese sino un abultado protocolo de embusterias, y mas desde tan tierna edad los crueles azotes me asian conoser mi umilde condision; me abochorno el contarlo, y no se como demostrar los hechos, dejando la parte mas terrible en el tintero, y ojala tubiera otros hechos con q^{e} llenar la historia de mi vida. (Manzano 1937, 83–84)

> (On more than four occasions I nearly decided to leave it unfinished, a portrait of so many calamities seems nothing more than a bulky chronicle of lies, all the more so since from such a young age cruel lashings made me understand my humble condition; I am mortified to tell it, and I do not know how to demonstrate the facts, leaving the worst part in the inkwell, and I wish I had other facts with which to fill the story of my life.)

The text was haunted by these moments of silence, as when he recounted the time he was subjected to such a thorough whipping that he was "a pique de perder la vida" (about to lose his life); rather than complete the tale, he wrote, "pasemos en silencio el resto de esta exena dolorosa pasado este tiempo con otra multitud de sufrimientos semejantes pasamos a la Habana . . ." (let us pass over the rest of this painful scene in silence after this period with another multitude of similar sufferings we moved to Havana . . . [45]). Here as elsewhere Manzano's narrative trailed awkwardly away from and around the spaces of trauma and suffering, making the narrative as much a document of his necessary silence as of the compelling "facts" of slavery.

Manzano knew from experience what Creto Gangá's popularity confirmed: an educated, literate slave necessarily became a spectacle in the public sphere. The simple fact of being articulate turned the slave into a most curious object open for amazed scrutiny: he was a potential legal scandal (as it was not, in fact, legal for slaves to be fully literate or published); he was a social spectacle (as a wondrous exception to the "rule" that slaves ostensibly lack the capacity to write); and he was simultaneously a special cultural artifact suitable for display (as a "representative" of a whole class of social beings about which some Cubans might have been curious). Manzano recounted that, at a young age, as a result of time spent with his mistress at church and at the opera, he was capable of reciting sermons, *loas* (short plays), *entremeses* (theatrical interludes), passages in dramatic theory, and discussions of stage sets; he delighted his mistress's guests by performing recitations in return for tips, which his parents were able to add to their savings to buy their own manumission some years later (35). As he grew older, his new mistress found his literary talents threatening and inappropriate for a slave, and he was ordered to cease the story telling and poetry recitations. As a result, his literary talent took on an even more theatricalized—if dysfunctional—dimension:

> como p^{a} estudiar mis cosas q^{e} yo componia p^{r} careser de escritura ablaba solo asiendo gestos y afeciones segun la naturaleza de la composisión desian q^{e} era tal el flujo de ablar q^{e} tenia q^{e} p^{r} ablar ablaba con la mesa con el cuadro con la pared. . . ." (41)

(In order to study what I was composing since I lacked writing skills I talked out loud to myself affecting gestures and emotions according to the nature of the composition it was said that my facility for expression was such that just to talk I would talk with the table with the picture with the wall.)

By the time Manzano had learned to write and had published several poems, he was keenly aware that he was no less curious or on display than he had been as a child. He noted in a letter to del Monte that Don Dionisio, a potential publisher of his work, had assured him of his "interéz de q^{e} biesen en Europa algunos q^{e} tenia razon de ablar de un siervo de su casa, poeta, cuyos versos resitaba de memoria y algunos dudaban q^{e} fuesen de una sin estudios" (interest that some in Europe see that he was right to speak of a house servant, a poet, who recited poems from memory and some doubted that they were written by one without education [85]). Manzano could not escape writing or being read "as a slave," try as he repeatedly did; his status as a literate slave relegated him to the position of a special exhibit, a spectacle of marvelous social contradiction.

One of the most salient aspects of Manzano's *Autobiografía*, as with Creto's writing, was his controversial relation to "proper" written Spanish. As the previous quotations amply demonstrate, Manzano's writing was disfigured in similar ways to that of Creto: awkward in its syntax, fraught with misspellings, replete with odd, inaccurate, or missing punctuation. However,  Manzano's text was substantially less consistent in its (mis)use of Spanish than Creto's. Manzano's erratic, unpunctuated writing reads as poor Spanish, while Creto's far more consistent text can be and was recuperated as a kind of new dialect of "African" Spanish. Although Manzano's "poor" writing was not therefore received as inherently comic, the errors that marked his writing have been considered similarly integral to his mode of expression. That is, despite the fact that Manzano's text surely could have been edited for correct grammar or punctuation—as editors and publishers virtually always do for any authors' text—Manzano's editors and critics seemed to find his writing more compelling and credible precisely *because* of its numerous errors. This is certainly true for a number of recent critics, who interpret his syntactical errors as symptomatic of his oppression under slavery; Cinto Vitier, for one, believes that Manzano's "errors are not really mistakes but appear in the text like the scars on his body." For these readers, these discursive "scars" poignantly dramatized his condition as a slave and told a tale as compelling and "true" as the events they narrated (Vitier 1973, 19).

Even for Manzano's contemporary critics, his peculiar discursive style not only lent emotional power to the narrative, but was also instrumental in persuading readers of its authenticity. Anselmo Suárez y Romero, whom del Monte chose to edit the version of the *Autobiografía* sent to Madden, felt that the text's "sloppiness" was what guaranteed that readers would find the story believable, and thus he chose not to alter it substantially. Although he did edit some sentences for syntax and punctuation, he left all other aspects of style virtually unchanged:

> Por lo que dice al estilo he variado muy poco el orijinal á fin de dejarle la melancolia con que fué escrito, y la sencillez, naturalidad y aun desaliño que le dan para mí mucho mérito alejando toda sospecha de los sucesos referidos sean mentira y mentira que un pobre chino nos lo contase para nuestra vergüenza. (*Centón epistolario* 4:81)

> (With respect to style I have changed the original very little in order to retain the melancholy with which it was written, the simplicity, naturalness, and even sloppiness that give it, in my view, much merit by removing all suspicion that the events related are lies, and lies told by a poor mulato [*chino*] to put us to shame.)

Regardless of Manzano's actual abilities or desires as a writer, his story requires discursive "simplicity, naturalness," and "sloppiness" if it is to be palatable to readers. In other words, it requires precisely what Creto Gangá's blackface writing delivers with ease and without apology: a sense of native ignorance whose good intentions and innocence are made credible through a visible discursive struggle with standard Spanish.

Manzano is trapped in the grammatical double bind on which Creto thrives: if Manzano's writing is marked or defined by error, he cannot escape being read "as" a slave, rather than the individual "properly Cuban" poet he wishes to be; but if he does not write with this "simplicity" and good-natured "sloppiness," he risks not being read or heard at all. Crespo's blackface persona is defined through this contradiction, which he manipulates to suit the shifting social and political address of his writing. Manzano, however, is trapped in this contradiction, which leaves him with only one, compromised avenue toward expression, leaving all others to the inkwell. For Manzano, his discursive "scars" are at one and the same time the markers of his veracity, offering the moments of greatest poignancy and truth in his writing, but also the markers of his falsehood, signaling the degree to which he cannot write or be read "as" himself, but only "as" a slave.

Put in slightly different terms, we can say that the slave Manzano is no less required to write in blackface than the fictional slave Creto. "Blackface" here entails embodying the normative and limiting expectations of a white readership, which understands certain discursive conventions (grammatical error, nonstandard syntax) as the markers of a "black" and "slave" author. To contend that Manzano writes "in blackface" is not in any way to undermine the seriousness of his struggle in composing the *Autobiografía*, its significance in the history of slavery in Cuba or in the Americas, or even the sincerity or veracity of Manzano's narrative such as it is. To the contrary, charting the deeply racialized conventions of writing and reading allows us to gauge the extraordinary degree to which the authorial credibility or "authenticity" of black authors was viciously undermined in the Cuban context of slavery. To remember that these racialized conventions are historically situated cultural conventions will disabuse us of the temptation to read either Manzano's errors or Creto's bozal as simply the "natural" and "true" expression of slaves in mid-century Cuba without first carefully examining how the "natural" and the "true" are defined, for whom, and to what ends.

Both Manzano and Creto Gangá participate, wittingly or not, in the performance of a particular discursive blackness, which contradictorily defines blackness precisely as lacking a credible discursive center, or stable authorial "I." If Creto Gangá gains popular appeal where Manzano can not, it is not, strictly speaking, because he is the parody (or copy) of Manzano's original, or that he is the "fake" to Manzano's "real" slave. Rather, Creto is more successful than Manzano at enacting and playing into the very "real" conventions of race, writing, and reading in this period; it is the "real" Manzano, rather than the fictional Creto, whose work risks being read as a "chronicle of lies."

Manzano is similarly compromised by the inherent racial logic of costumbrismo through which Crespo/Creto gains his popularity. Commissioned by del Monte, Manzano's *Autobiografía* was meant to keep company with the other new, innovative costumbrista novels of the tertulia—including Suárez y Romero's *Francisco*, Tanco's *Escenas de la vida privada en la isla de Cuba* (Scenes in the private life of Cuba) or Cirilio Villaverde's travel narrative *Excursión a Vuelta Abajo* (Excursion to Vuelta Abajo)—each of which sought to document through fiction the complex social norms and customs that the authors had experienced or witnessed. Yet Manzano was the only one commissioned to write an autobiography, rather than a story based on personal experience. Although Manzano's remarkable status as a poet-slave easily warrants del Monte's insistence that he tell his life story, it is nonetheless clear from the outset that Manzano himself is the object of costumbrista interest, rather than the author of it. Ironically, by writing an autobiography rather than the "truly Cuban novel" he originally hoped to write, Manzano

progressively loses his individual authorial voice: the more personal his story becomes, the more "representative" of slave experience it is seen to be. When del Monte sent the autobiography along with other authors' writings to Robert Madden for possible publication abroad, del Monte made the curious choice to suppress all the authors' names but Manzano's. His cover letter explains:

> Acompaño á usted las adjuntas "Muestras ineditas" de nuestra naciente y desmerada literatura provincial. [. . .] Notará usted que excepto las de Manzano, no llevan el nombre de sus autores las demás composiciones de la colección. Como casi todas ellas hacen alusiones á asuntos prohibidos por nuestro Gobierno, no he querido que, si por cualquier evento, fuese a parar á otros manos que las de usted ese cuaderno, peligrasen por mi culpa esos inofensivos poetas. . . . (Williams 1994, 19–20; translation hers)

> (I am sending you the attached "Unpublished samples" of our growing and weak provincial literature. [. . .] You will notice that, excepting Manzano's, the other compositions in the collection do not bear the authors' names. Since nearly all of them allude to subjects forbidden by our Government, I did not wish that, if by chance the album ended up in other hands than yours, those inoffensive writers would be endangered through my fault. . . .)

His choice to retain Manzano's name is striking, given that Manzano would benefit no less from the protection extended to his white colleagues. Manzano had in an earlier correspondence confessed his fear of just such retribution to del Monte: "[soy] vuestro afectisimo siervo qe fiádo en la prudensia q^{e} os caracteriza se atreve a chistar una palabra sobre esta materia, y mas cuando vive quien me ha dado tan largo qe genir" ([I am] your devoted servant, who, trusting in your characteristic prudence, dares to breathe a word about this subject, especially since the one responsible for my grief is still alive [Manzano 1937, 84]). Despite this, del Monte chose to keep Manzano's name public. We can speculate that he may have felt that the autobiography would not seem credible to a skeptical European audience without providing ample evidence of the actual existence of the slave-author, including his name.

Whatever the case, Madden was not in agreement: when he did finally translate and publish the autobiography, he dropped Manzano's name completely, and published a substantially edited version of the autobiography under the subtitle "the History of the Early Life of a Negro Poet, written by himself."[10] "His name, for obvious reasons, I think it advisable not to publish," Madden wrote in the preface, but to leave no doubt as to "the authenticity of these poems," he filed copies of the originals with the British and Foreign Anti-Slavery Society (Mullen 1981, 38). Although the intention may have been sincere, critic Sylvia Molloy is likely correct in finding it not so; Madden does not, after all, hesitate to reproduce extensive details about the anonymous poet's life, which would have made him easily identifiable in Cuba, especially given that he was the only known poet who had been a slave in Cuba at the time. Far more likely is that Madden felt he should "make the text anonymous in order to heighten what he considered its representativeness"; he hoped the text would offer not the story of one slave's life, but—in his words—"the most perfect picture of Cuban slavery that ever has been given to the world" (Mullen 1981, 39) Molloy rightly underscores the "burden of representativeness" under which this text, like others written by minority subjects, operated. In such cases, she writes, "neither the autobiographies, nor the personas they create, are easily accepted individually by a reading community which much prefers to perceive difference *en bloc*" (Molloy 1991, 44–45).

To bolster Manzano's text, Madden added a number of poems to the published dossier, along with a lengthy preface, historical appendix, and other explanatory material—all authored by himself. Madden slipped easily into the subject position of the slave: despite enthusiasm for the rare and compelling "evidence" that Manzano's autobiography provided, ultimately Madden relied on the logic by which a figure like Creto, rather than Manzano, would stake claims for authenticity and truth: blackface. Madden saw no contradiction between his own blackface poems and those by Manzano, because Madden—it appears—considered the subjectivity of the slave available for occupation and use by any willing author. An apologist might object that surely Madden's discursive intrusions were staged in the service of the abolitionist cause; surely Madden—as a white British abolitionist—could critique slavery more freely than a black Cuban in bondage. Maybe so. But this representational logic—in which white men speak the truth of black experience better than blacks themselves, and summarily do so against the will of the black speakers—compounds rather than contests the representational logic of slavery. The burden of representation that already organized the logic of costumbrismo was redoubled for the black author: the injunction to be representative overwhelmed the unique authorial voice to the point that the writer could not even retain a stable authorial "I" from which to tell his tale.

Manzano's letters to del Monte indicated his profound belief that, after securing his manumission and finding new employment, he would eventually be able to take his full place at the table of white authors, leaving behind the stigma of slavery. But this was not to be. The fact that Cuba's social, economic, and cultural life was still vigorously organized around slavery ensured that Manzano would always be seen "as" a slave, and that his writings would be thus "representative." For these reasons and despite his greatest hopes, Manzano never could write the novel composed of those valued, secret portions of his life he had reserved and protected from slavery. Ironically, however, his manipulated, mediated, and troubled *Autobiografía* turned out to be a more "truly Cuban" novel than Manzano could have imagined, dramatizing through its discursive conventions and its multiply edited versions the limits and logic of race and discursive representation in slave-holding Cuba of the nineteenth century.

When Crespo decided to innovate on the usual costumbrista formula in 1845 by introducing a first-person narrative voice for his Creto Gangá, his innovation was implicit in the racialized logic of the genre and of the historical moment. Rather than provide a dispassionate, "objective," third-person description, it seems almost logical that the costumbrista slave should speak in the first person. This is not because the slave was granted a special authority as a speaker, but the contrary: because the slave was already definitionaly situated as one of many features of the Cuban landscape, he or she was always already one of the objects to be described rather than the author who would depict them. As such, the *manner* in which the slave spoke—or even more, the mere *fact* that the slave spoke—was thus as revealing and interesting as anything the slave might actually say. Everything the slave said, then, was recuperated as descriptive of what all slaves did. Crespo played into precisely this costumbrista logic, gleefully presenting his fictional Creto as a representative "type." Taking on the ethnonym "Gangá" as his personal surname, he announced Creto as representative of an African ethnicity in Cuba, one of many "negros bosales" (black bozales) whose habits, behaviors, and customs he offered for inspection. The fact that many of Creto's behaviors and customs were, of course, far from those of a real slave, who would be unlikely to pass leisure time at the opera, the circus, or commenting on contemporary fashion, only made the same point: the prime costumbrista value of his writing was found not in its content, but in the discursive bozal through which it was delivered.

Back in 1836, Félix Tanco y Bosmeniel sensed that, for better and worse, slavery was at the heart of Cuba's unique identity. He, like others in the del Monte circle, strongly condemned those who claimed it was "un mal necesario tener hombres en clase de propiedad para hacer azucar" (a necessary evil to have men in the category of property in order to produce sugar [*Centón epistolario* 7, 53]), and advocated an enlightenment conception of the universal equality of humans. Even so, when he looked at Cuba, he saw slavery as the source of a new social poetry: "no hay mas poesía entre nosotros," he elaborated to del Monte, "que los esclavos: poesía que esta derramando por todas partes, por campos y poblaciones, y que solo no la ven los inhumanos y los estúpidos (there is no greater poetry among us than the slaves: poetry that is sprouting everywhere, from the country to the towns, and only the inhuman and stupid cannot see it). In a curious turn of phrase, Tanco made an ambiguous joke at the expense of "the inhuman and the stupid":

> advierte que al paso que se vaya civilizando aunque lentamente la clase blanca todavia muy bozalona, la esclavitud de los negros se levantará en la misma proporción, como una sombra deforme, mutilada, horrorosa; pero poetica y bella, y capaz de producir ingenios tan vigorosas y originales como el de Byron y Victor Hugo—¡Quien sabe cuantos esclavos deberan un dia su libertad a los poetas! (*Centón Epistolario* 7, 81)

> (be warned that to the extent that the white class, still very *bozalona* [unacculturated, wild] slowly becomes civilized, the slavery of the blacks will rise in the same proportion, like a deformed shadow, mutilated, horrifying; but poetic and beautiful, and capable of producing genius as vigorous and original as that of Byron or Victor Hugo—Who knows how many slaves will someday owe their freedom to the poets!)

Crespo y Borbón turned out to be precisely one of those *white* "bozalones" for whom the attachment to slavery impeded the slow progress of white "civilization"—a "civilization" destined to be haunted by the horrible shadow of those whose lives it so deformed. Yet Crespo understood Tanco's sensibility entirely: for Crespo, as for his fans, the new poetry of Cuba would be found in the imagined sound and rhythm produced by the culture of slavery. When Tanco pleaded with del Monte to account more fully for the impact slaves were having on language in Cuba, it was Crespo who heeded the call. As Tanco worried that the Spanish in Cuba had become a repository for "una infinidad de palabras y locuciones inhumanas y bárbaras" (an infinity of inhuman and barbarous words and locutions [86]), Crespo reveled in the linguistic mestizaje around him, nowhere more than in the "barbarous" linguistic practices of bozal slaves. To be sure, not one slave would owe his or her freedom to Crespo's bozal writings; on the contrary, Crespo's satirical presentation of slave life illustrated the ways in which a celebration of "the poetry of slavery" could be entirely consonant with its rationalization and continuation.

Crespo's blackface writing did acknowledge the Cuban "poetry" othe wise invisible to the "inhuman and the stupid," providing an extended fli tation with the possible linguistic pleasures of Cuba's "Africanization." Yet the abuse of proper Spanish produced a defamiliarizing operation, not on the fictional African writing, but on very real Spanish writing itself. Creto's fictional costumbrista ethnographies offer us a peculiar instance of colonial mimicry: defamiliarizing Spanish through the distortions of the so-called "African" make audible a "new" or an "other" Spanish—one that was later recuperated as, precisely, "Cuban." Creto's abuse of Spanish was so fully enjoyed by its white Cuban audience that countless of his "African" "aberrations" were subsequently embraced and introduced into a wider vernacular. Today, without reference to Creto, they are commonly known as "cubanisms." Creto Gangá would, in the fullness of Cuba's national time, be remembered as one of the first to write—not in bozal—but in "cubano."

Chapter 2
Anticolonial Blackface, 1868

On the thirtieth of May 1868, the newly formed theatre company Bufos Habaneros debuted in Havana at the Teatro Villanueva. The actors were for the most part young men and women with little or no professional stage experience. Theatre history remembers (and romanticizes) them as "Cubans without slaves, poor artists who knew how to capture popular taste, wise observers of the country's domestic reality, men and women who lived in constant contact with free blacks and artisans, destructive critics of the romantic, operatic atmosphere of the great salons" (Leal 1982, 31). Their performances, which combined original short plays—most comic, some sentimental—and original songs, called guarachas, projected an aura of genuine originality, which was immediately registered by the press. The Bufos Habaneros captured a style, a rhythm, a particular affect that was experienced by audiences as entirely new and yet utterly familiar. Both scholarly and popular theatre histories record the "birth" of the teatro bufo as a turning point: it marks the moment in which audiences recognized themselves on stage, and in that moment of recognition, in that mutual gaze from audience to stage and back, recognized themselves as *Cuban.*

The success of the Habaneros' new form of entertainment can be measured by the quantity of imitators: by midsummer, they were rivaled by the Caricatos, whose popular cross-dressing actor, José Candiani, presented the Habaneros with their strongest competition. By the fall, the two leading companies had been joined by the Bufos Minstrels Cubanos, Bufos Madrileños (a Spanish rival company), Los Bufos Cantantes (the Bufos Singers), Las Bufas (an all-female troupe, known for their performance of the guaracha entitled "La negra mala" or "The bad black woman"),[1] the Compañía Bufo-Arlequinista, Los Cubanos, and the Bufos Torbellinos, self-promoted as a "compañía cubana dramática, bufo-minstrélica, lírica, coreográfica y mímica" (Cuban, dramatic, bufo-minstrel, lyric, choreographic, and mime company), all working in Havana at the same time.[2] One critic in the *Diario de la Marina* complained about the city's "bufomania" in August. By November,

El País claimed that "no hay ciudad de alguna importancia en el interior que no tenga su compañía bufa" (no city of importance in the interior is without a bufo company).[3] In the provinces the Bufos Matanceros, Tipos de Cuba (Types of Cuba), the Bufos Vuelta Abajo, the Caricatos Provinciales, and the Bufos Cardenenses (from Cárdenas) claimed audiences of their own. Over the course of the season, the companies developed furious competition, producing countless new one-act plays, new blackface humor, and new guarachas.

Many elements of bufo performances were not, in fact, new at all. Much of their debt was to José Crespo y Borbón, to a generation of playwrights that emerged in the 1860s, and to visiting theatre companies from Spain and from the United States. But their performances transformed their source materials and set the ground for a recognizable Cuban aesthetic that gained new relevance in the context of anticolonial resistance, emerging in the same year as the first war for independence. What came to be known as the Ten Year's War—Cuba's first and unsuccessful bid for independence from Spanish colonial rule—brought this first bufo season to a premature close in late January 1869: the same Teatro Villanueva that housed the first bufo performance was, nine months later, the site of one of the so-called Sucesos de la Villanueva (Happenings at the Villanueva), which erupted during a performance by the Bufos Caricatos.[4] By the explosive year of 1868, then, blackface operated as a significant counterfeit currency whose entertainment "value" helped to forge (in both senses, to make and to fake) an "authentic" Cuban national community during the era of anticolonial struggle.

Cuba as Anticolony

The transition marked by the 1860s in Cuba is not one from colony to national community, but rather a smaller but dramatic transition from colony to *anticolony*. Partha Chatterjee argues that *anticolonial* nationalism "creates its own domain of sovereignty within colonial society well before its political battle with the imperial power" (Chatterjee 1993, 6). The moment in which "anticolonialism" comes to be—to be persuasive, to be at all—is long and complex, and its transitions marked out and negotiated through a range of social, cultural, and imaginative structures in motion over time. We can imagine this process in Brechtian theatrical terms: the colonial world is defamiliarized, and loses its veneer of naturalness, normalcy; the social and cultural mechanisms that inform the colonial scene are suddenly more bare, the arbitrariness of their logic now open to greater scrutiny. Knowledge and experience of the colonial world is turned against itself—becoming *anti*colonial—allowing for the imagination of other social worlds, and their other possible futures.

The anthropologist Victor Turner might refer to this historical moment as the "limen" between Cuba's colonial history and its subsequent struggle for nationhood, as he does of a roughly comparable moment, the Hidalgo Insurrection, in Mexican history (Turner 1974, 99). Describing a change in the social imagination of a wide population, this transition cannot be explained as the direct cause of one or several social or political factors, or as the conscious "plot" of "revolutionaries." Borrowing language from social psychology, Turner names a liminal social moment a "primary process": one that "erupts from the cumulative experience of whole peoples whose deepest material and spiritual needs and wants have for long been denied any legitimate expression" (100–111). The 1860s in general and 1868 in particular in Cuba witnessed such a "primary process" insofar as the concatenation of disparate elements that comprise "cumulative social experience" began to reveal alternate coherences, alternate forms of meaningful composition.

Cuban anticolonial sentiment cannot be reduced to a simple or single ideological attitude on the part of the colonized toward independence or toward the metropole. In the case of Cuba, the metropole itself was undergoing major social upheaval in the 1860s, shaped by the ongoing contest between "liberals" who supported constitutional rule, and royal absolutists; the conflict between such liberal and absolutist parties had, in part, fueled the multiple "Carlist wars" beginning in 1833. The year 1868, so important to Cuba as the beginning of its struggle for independence, was dramatically marked in Spain by its own successful uprising against the Bourbon monarchy in September 1868, which deposed Queen Isabel II and installed a constitutional monarchy with universal male suffrage in her place. Thus ardent cries for "revolution" or for "liberty, equality, and fraternity" were the clarion calls of vastly different ideological struggles in Spain and Cuba. In Cuba, "liberty" was the purported goal for those on either side of the struggle for independence, from those seeking total "liberty" *from* Spain, to those advocating instead complete "liberty" *within* Spain, favoring equal application of the constitution and electoral laws in the colonies as on the peninsula. The term "liberty" and its correlatives (liberal, liberalism) function as major keywords, in Raymond William's sense (1985), insofar as the term *liberty* anchored competing social struggles; struggles over its meaning played themselves out in material arenas, from the battleground to the theatre.

"Anticolonialism," then, names a broad range of social behaviors and political critique that began to disarticulate the colonial status quo, more than coalesce into a single alternative. To think of Cuba as an anticolony allows us to further understand the nature of social and political change, and to consider popular imagination as an important site in which a polity might begin to posit and rehearse alternate social realities.

Debates over race and representation were central to any critique or defense of Cuban colonialism. The colonial state argued that the presence of a large slave population made Cuba a poor candidate for nationhood. As Ada Ferrer writes, the colonial state "asserted that to risk expelling Spain was to invite a more horrible fate. Cuba, they said, would be Spanish or it would be African. It would be Spanish or it would be another Haiti" (Ferrer 1999, 2). Although the 1862 census demonstrated that the white population had regained majority numbers, then constituting 57 percent of the total population, the illegal slave trade continued with little and irregular enforcement from Spanish authorities. Between 1856 and 1860, by one count, Cuba imported ninety-thousand slaves, one of the highest rates for any five-year period in its history. Thus, although the white population had kept pace, primarily through large-scale immigration of white laborers, the continued presence of an enslaved black population kept the threat of race war present for some who might otherwise have sought independence from Spain (Pérez 1995, 111, 116–19; Scott 1985, 10–13).

The future of slavery was a primary factor attenuating explicit white anticolonial activism throughout the decade. The criollo elite—plantation owners and those in businesses invested in the success of the sugar industry—felt ill-served by Spain's self-interested control of tariffs and commercial policy, but their reliance on slave labor limited their options for social and political action. Spain could and did periodically threaten to enforce the ban on the slave trade whenever Cuba's planters expressed their dissatisfaction too openly; not surprisingly, it was these wealthier, slave-owning criollos who had in the 1850s seriously considered annexation to the United States as a solution. When annexation ceased to be a viable option after the Emancipation Proclamation in the United States in 1863, Cuban planters were caught in a double bind. The elites' interest in being released from Spanish control was stymied by the very system of slavery on which they relied; as historian Louis Pérez puts it, "Creole elites could not plot to end Spanish sovereignty as a way of defending slavery without provoking Spain into ending slavery as a way to defend sovereignty" (Pérez 1995, 112). As a result, the elites did little more than pursue reformist policies, and came to support a notion of very "gradual" and indemnified emancipation (see Scott 1985). Among their chief demands were a reform of the tariff system, Cuban representation in the Spanish parliament, and legal equality with peninsulares. Their reformist approach was, however, largely ineffective: the few liberal reforms instated in 1865 were soon dismantled by the newly ascendant conservative government in Madrid, and replaced with even more restrictive measures controlling Cuban politics, press, and self-representation. Thus, when the small, radicalized sector of criollos decided that armed insurrection was the only remaining alternative, they chose to end slavery along with Spanish rule. When Manuel de Céspedes began the insurgency in October 1868, emancipation was one of its first rallying cries.

In the decade leading up to this so-called *Grito de Yara* (Cry from Yara), the inevitability of abolition prompted a return of concern over the potential dangers of future "Africanization" when the black population—many of first-generation African descent—would join white society. From the 1860s, concerns about "Africanization" stood in euphemistically for an ever widening range of social, cultural, and sexual relations between black and white in the Cuban social imagination. Race fear inspired a spate of new legal reforms aimed at promoting segregation and restricting miscegenation. Social anthropologist Verena Martinez-Alier has documented, for example, the rigidly enforced ban on interracial marriage from 1864 through the mid-1870s, in which time not one interracial marriage license was granted (Martinez-Alier 1989, 31–32). If the discourse of "Africanization" implied that the country was firmly divided between white and black, its inhabitants were in fact categorized according to a far more nuanced system of social and racial classification. Social status was measured in reference to a complex matrix of race, class, and power, which marked one's relative position between Spanish and African, white and black, rich and poor, foreign born and native born, slave and free, nobility and commoner, and so forth (Martinez-Alier 1989, 22). Despite the seeming precision of these racial and social categories, by the 1860s white criollos found themselves trapped between inadequate social markers: being *white* did not grant them the social and legal privileges of the peninsulares, and being criollo did not offer clear differentiation from criollos of color—blacks, mulatos, or other people of color—from whom many wished to be distanced clearly.

This anxiety on the part of white criollos was made explicit as the war progressed. Consider, for example, the exchange between the newspaper *La Verdad* (the truth) and its adversary, *La Mentira* (the lie). *La Verdad* had argued that the principles of liberty, fraternity, and equality should be applied equally to all subjects under Spanish rule; as a province of Spain, Cuba should enjoy rights and privileges identical to any other province on the Iberian Peninsula. *La Mentira* took issue with the assumption that all men are equal without consideration of what was then euphemistically called one's "class and condition"—that is, one's social status and race. In a front-page editorial, *La Mentira* made its argument satirically, adopting and exaggerating the ideological position of *La Verdad* in order to reveal the implicit (and, in *La Mentira*'s view, presumably intolerable) consequences of this view. "Libertad para *todos,* libertad para *todas* las razas, libertad para los nacidos bajo *todos* los cielos, quiere decir que el negro, el mulato, y el blanco son y deben ser desde hoy enteramente iguales en nuestra afortunada isla" (Liberty for *everyone,* liberty for *all* races, liberty for those born under *every* sky, means that the black, the mulato, and the white are and should be from this day forward equal on our fortunate island [italics in the original]). The editorial continued, "si es cierto que los habitantes blancos tienen justicia bastante en quejarse, justicia sobrada asiste á la gente de color para atronar al mundo con sus gritos" (if it is true that the white inhabitants have ample reason to complain, overwhelming reason informs people of color to deafen the world with their shouts). The logic here is, needless to say, flawless: both white criollos and all people of color in Cuba had ample reason to critique the existing power structure. However, *La Mentira* assumed that the very suggestion that whites, blacks, and mulatos were equal would illustrate the absurdity of white criollos' claims. The writer went on to advocate reforms to laws governing racial segregation, and painted an increasingly satirical picture of interracial harmony:

> Entre el negro, entre el mulato, en los lugares preferentes, si estan dispuestos á abonar su importe: entren con toda confianza y siéntense al lado del redactor de *La Verdad,* al lado del redactor de *La Mentira,* al lado de nuestras madres, al lado de nuestras hermanas, al lado de nuestras esposas, al lado de nuestras hijas. ¿Teneis dinero para comprar un palco en el teatro? Pues ocupadlo con vuestras familias, sean negras ó cobrizas. Las nuestras se considerarán muy felices en poder hablar con ellas al paño: las nuestras nos bendecirán por haberles proporcionado una union por la que tanto suspiraban: las nuestras no cesarán de celebrar los principios de *La Verdad,* la lógica de *La Mentira* y el brillante bienestar que á pasos agigantados ha de traernos la libertad, la igualdad, la fraternidad. (22 January 1869)
>
> (Let the black enter, and the mulato, into those preferential spaces, if they are prepared to underwrite the cost: enter with complete confidence, and take a seat next to the correspondent from *La Verdad,* and next to the correspondent from *La Mentira,* next to our mothers, next to our sisters, next to our wives, next to our daughters. Do

> you have money to purchase a box at the theatre? Well then, occupy it with your family, whether black or bronze. Our families will be very happy to be able to speak with them behind their handkerchiefs: ours will bless us for having enabled this union for which they so yearned: ours will not cease to celebrate the principles of *La Verdad*, the logic of *La Mentira*, and the brilliant well-being that, in giant steps, liberty, equality, and fraternity would bring us.)

Racial segregation in the theatre acts as prime emblem of white "preferential" space, the arena where white men display and protect the racial and sexual purity of "their" women. The right to such equality, the writer went on to say, had to be guaranteed by force: why not arm all the blacks and mulatos, so they can ultimately ensure compliance with their new social privileges? Finally, he suggested, Cuba would have to reconsider its global position, given its new liberal orientation: it would no longer be European Cuba, since "en Europa hay mucho Rey, mucho Emperador y mucho absolutismo" (in Europe there's too much King, too much Emperor, and too much absolutism); nor would it be North American, since the United States had "mucha fuerza de absorción y de un sorbo pueden tragar nuestra raza" (great power of absorption and in one gulp could swallow our race). Since Cuba had no credible relation to Asia, despite the presence of Chinese laborers, or Oceania, he concluded, "Pues, señor, no queda mas que el Africa: volvamos á ella de todo corazón los ojos, proclamémosla nuestra madre adoptiva y llamemos y consigamos que sea este hermoso país *Cuba africana*" (Well, sir, there is nothing left but Africa: let us turn our eyes to her with open hearts, let us proclaim her our adoptive mother, and let us name and register this beautiful country as *African Cuba* [italics in original]). Although the language of liberty, equality, and fraternity would, in two short decades, shape the discourse of black civil rights, in the early months of anticolonial insurrection, the pictures the writer drew were scandalous, delineating a future that whites in Cuba would abhor. Again the lines were drawn: either Cuba would be Spanish, or doomed to be African; either Cubans would accept their place in the social order of Spanish rule, or they would cast their fate with blacks and mulatos, those people of color whom—the editorial implied—would threaten the racial and social purity of white women and who might use force to turn Cuba into *Cuba africana.*

Imagine, then, how highly charged the practice of blackface and celebration of "African" music might have been in the white "preferential" space of the theatre at this moment. The potential meanings of blackface, like anticolonial sentiment, were broad and often contradictory. Blackface could function as a sign of racial division, marking and reinforcing the difference between white and black; at the same time, it could function as a sign of racial contact, where black met white to form some new "mestizo" entity. Finally, it could function as a sign of a racial mutability, guarding a site in which racial identity for black or white might be a changeable and negotiable social status. Through blackface, the teatro bufo negotiated not only the racial boundaries of black and white in a social economy still structured by slavery, but also the meaning of *whiteness* in the colonial hierarchy that privileged white peninsulares over white criollos. More precisely, this blackface comedy engaged and successfully mediated these competing visions of an Africanized or mestizo Cuba. In schematic terms, the shift in the theatre from the bozal to the new figure of the catedrático firmly entrenched the appeal and use of blackface as a popular means to imagine—or welcome—a future Cuba that would no longer be Spanish, but also never quite African.

Anticolonial Costumbrismo

The teatro bufo's sudden recourse to fiercely parodic blackface costumbrismo revealed growing complexity in the forms and styles of theatrical costumbrismo, which began to articulate itself in sharp contrast to peninsular culture. Three major new authors of the genre emerged in the 1860s whose works were enthusiastically revived by bufo companies in 1868: José Socorro de León, Juan José Guerrero, and Antonio Enrique de Zafra. Juan José Guerrero was to the rural guajiro what Crespo had been to the black bozal. Like Crespo, Guerrero invented an authorial persona, Alfonso (who also went by the variations Alifonso, Idelfonso, and so on), a bumbling not quite literate guajiro who chronicled events of his (fictional) life in a series of one-act plays, written in the late 1850s, published in 1864, and repeatedly performed by the Bufos Caricatos in 1868: *Un guateque en la taberna un martes de carnaval* (A party in the tavern one carnival Tuesday), *La suegra futura* (The future mother-in-law), *Un tarde en Nazareno* (An afternoon in Nazareno), and *Las boas de Petronilla* (Petronilla's weddings). Like Creto, Alfonso provided entertaining prefaces to each play, in which his guajiro speech was carefully transliterated. *Un guateque*, for example, was prefaced by a letter to one "Señol Don Pedro Maltín" in "La Bana" (Mister Sir Pedro Martín, in Havana) whom Alifonso beseeches on behalf of their mutual friend "ño Policarpio," who wants to host a *guateque*, Mr. Policarpio "sia empeñao . . . colmigo paque yo mempeñe conusté, paquiusté sempeñe conel Capitán paque no empía el Guateque" (has interceded with me so I'll intercede with you so you'll intercede with the Captain to not impede the *guateque* [97]).[5] Guerrero's rural characters speak "in" the pseudo dialect of *campesino* much as Creto spoke "in" the fictional dialect of bozal. The entire plot of *La suegra futura* (1864), for instance, revolves around the gross linguistic misdeeds of a *campesina* mother as they threaten to compromise her daughter's engagement to her well-heeled urban suitor.

While *La suegra futura* was revived to enormous success by the Bufos Caricatos in 1868 (and again in 1879) as a vehicle for the cross-dressed actor José Candiani, who played the role of the crass mother-in-law, *Un guateque* more clearly engages the heated linguistic play and comic costumbrismo of the teatro bufo. The play leaves it intentionally unclear whether the labored speech of the servant Emetrio is due to his Galician background or a speech impediment; he summarizes the central conflict of the play thus: "Eeeél paaae qui . . . quiere queeel hiiijo seeea taaaberneero, y eeel hiiijo quieeeere seeeer meeeedico" (The father wants his son to work at the tavern, and the son wants to be a doctor, [100]; a more evocative translation would reproduce the speech distortion: "Theee faaaather wa . . . waaaants hiiiis sooooon" and so forth). The aspiring doctor Nemesio, like the later black catedráticos, struggles with mispronounced medical jargon:

Nemesio: Cuando el cuelpo se incogestiona a causa de la parótidas que se coagulan enel esófafo, el cólon se prolonga, y se contrai too el tegío beltebral: he aquí, pol que la laringe de dilata, [. . .] ¿Tú compriendes? (106)

Nemesio: When the body is congested due to the glands that coagulate in the esophagus, the colon is elongated and everything contracts in the vertebral ceiling: here then, because the larynx gets dilated, [. . .] Do you understand?

Nemesio's sister Trinidad is engaged in a generational struggle of her own, focused on her desire to skip the traditional *zapateo* at the tavern to attend a local *danza*. The conflict between mother and daughter carries anticolonial overtones, as Trinidad characterizes zapateo as a ponderous (Spanish) tradition, and danza as an invigorating new (Cuban) style instead: "¿Quién baila eso [zapateo] ya, habiendo dansa enel mundo? (Who dances [zapateo] now that danza is in the world? [114]). Because of their sharp comic delineation of popular Cuban culture, all of Guerrero's plays were revived and performed during the 1868 season by bufo companies, especially the Bufos Caricatos.

The leading Cuban playwright of serious dramas, Antonio Enrique de Zafra, also wrote comedies that became important to the bufos, particularly his one-act play, *La fiesta del mayoral* (The overseer's fiesta), debuted by the Bufos Habaneros in July of 1868. Zafra's few comedies included blackface performance and the musical costumbrismo for which the teatro bufo later became famous. For example, Zafra's plantation comedy *Tres para dos* (Three for two [1865]), which premiered at the Tacón in February 1865, opens with an original guaracha sung by a chorus of bozal slaves. The lead character, the slave José, sings,

Yo só nengrito
Que caña mete
Yo vá pa campo
Caña tumbá
Camina lito,
suena nan fuete.
Guaté no é chicha
ni limoná
Fuá! fuá! fuá!
Lan nero cravo no vale ná. (n.p.)

(I am a negrito
who deals with cane
I go to the fields
cut down cane
walk ready,
sound so loud.
Guaté is neither
fish nor foul
Fuá! fuá! fuá!
Black slaves ain't worth a thing.)

Although the chorus reiterates this last assertion that black slaves aren't worth anything, the play shows keen interest in the value of "slave" music, which punctuates this otherwise conventional love plot, alternating with "guajiro" ballads. As with *Un ajiaco* several decades earlier, the final wedding festivity unites not only the estranged bride and groom, but "black" and "white" rural music as well. However, black and white Cubans are not therefore brought together: to the contrary, a satirical scene in which the slaves "play" at being the plantation owners makes clear that black and white people are rigidly segregated, even if their music is not.

The emergence of the teatro bufo in 1868 benefited from one further related influence. In 1867, a Spanish comedy troupe, the Bufos Madrileños, directed by Francisco Arderíus, toured Havana with the musical comedy *El joven Telemaco* (The young Telemachus). Describing their work as "zarzuela-bufa," they introduced comic *opera bufa* to Cuba. *Opera bufa* (from the French, *opéra bouffe*) refers to musical performance in which spoken verse alternates with singing, as opposed to grand opera, in which all parts are sung. The Bufos Madrileños not only left behind their name to the Cuban bufos (the Habaneros explicitly named them as a source), but, more importantly, shared their penchant for parody. The Madrileños were known in Spain for their parodies of operas and *zarzuelas*, such as their 1864 production of *Los dioses del Olimpo* (The gods of Olympus), a comic adaptation of Offenbach's *Orphé aux enfers* (Orpheus in hell). *El joven Telemaco* parodied classical Greek drama, and, as Rine Leal points out, introduced the nonsense term "suripanta" to Cuban theatre. "Suripanta" was among the Bufos Madrileños' fake Greek words they used to parody the droning, ponderous Greek chorus: "Suripanta la suripanta / macatranqui de somatén / sumfáriben sunfaridon / melitónimen sonpén." The expression "suripanta" was later used as a derogatory term to refer to the "chorus" of women who followed the anticolonial rebels to the warfront (Leal 1982, 22–23).

Very much in the style of the Bufos Madrileños, the Cuban bufos frequently performed comic adaptations of contemporary operas. In Cuba, however, these parodies took on a distinct anticolonial tenor. Performing in popular theatres like the Villanueva and Torecillas, usually home to revue and circus entertainments, the bufos often featured burlesque versions of the current operas or zarzuelas at El Tacón—thereby ridiculing, in part, the taste of the ruling colonial set who were its primary patrons.[6] Parodies comprised a fair part of the bufo repertory in 1868, including such works as *Matea la lavandera* (Matea the washerwoman), a parody of Legouvé's *Medea*; a bufo version of *El trovador*, called *El trovador africano*, featuring the romantic travails of young African slaves; *El que hace un cesto hace un ciento* (He who makes one basket makes a hundred) based on *Flor de un día* by Camprodón; and the blackface adaptation *De hombre a hombre* (Man to man) of *De potencia a potencia* by Tomás Rodríguez Rubí. There was even a "Cubanized" blackface version of Arderíus's parody *Los dioses del Olimpo* called *Los dioses del Manglar*, set in Manglar, the black neighborhood just outside of Havana's city limits and featuring a "black" *brujo* or African witch doctor. In these parodies, operatic scores were usually replaced by guarachas. Press reviewers relished these new "Cuban" operas, favoring them over their Italian counterparts:

> La compañía de bufos [the Bufos Habaneros], nos consta, tiene un extenso repertorio de sandungerísimas guarachas, con las que podrían contentar mucho al público que le favorece, mejor que con los cantos italianos, que sólo suenan bien con su letra propia, y en boca de quienes los entienden. (*Diario de la Marina* 9 June 1868)
>
> ([The Bufos Habaneros], it appears, have an extensive repertoire of charming guarachas, with which they could please their public, far more than with Italian songs, which only sound right in their own language, in the mouths of those that understand them.)

The simple fact of singing in Spanish to rural melodies and using local instruments (such as the tiple) lent to these musical parodies a "Cuban" appeal.

Catedracismo: From the Bozal to the Catedrático

The protonationalist dimension of the costumbrista plays suggests that the Cuban "bufomania" of 1868 was not directly caused by the Spanish imports, by touring U.S. minstrels waiting out the U.S. Civil War,[7] or even by the periodic publication of Cuban costumbrista plays. Nor was the bufo craze a simple matter of poking fun at highbrow theatre offerings at the Tacón. Much more than a sum of these parts, the bufos brought an important new coherence to the revue stage, lending thematic and stylistic consistency to its different genres of music, plays, and dances. When Crespo/Creto's *Un ajiaco* made its debut at the Teatro Circo (later renamed Villanueva) in 1847, it did so on an evening that included such varied entertainments as a "grand Roman fight," a contortionist exhibition, and a trapeze act, along with interludes of sentimental songs and comic monologues (Cruz 1974, 69). The teatro bufo's debut on the same Villanueva stage in 1868 featured an evening of similarly varied songs and dances: the blackface comedy *Los negros catedráticos*, the new guaracha "Que te vaya bien, chinita" (Hope things go well, Chinita); a dance sequence called "Los bufos habaneros"; a parody of Rigoletto's "La donna e movile" entitled "El aguador"; a satire of the serious dramatist Isaac Carrillo y O'Farrill; and the opera parody *El que hace un cesto hace un ciento*. Each of the performances shared a consistent interest in things supposedly "Cuban." Far from "exotic" circus and revue acts, the bufo entertainments celebrated the specially *Cuban*, in form, content, and publicity.

While blackface was not new to the Cuban stage, it was central to this new "Cuban" coherence: one can well argue that in the bufo performances of 1868, blackface was *the* consistent style and thematic through which the

"Cuban" explicitly emerged on stage at all. All of the plays—whether costumbrista sainetes, parodies, or catedrático comedies—made continual recourse to black or African characters and themes. The protagonist of the 1868 theatre season was, however, the so-called negro catedratico or black professor, who debuted in Francisco Fernández's play *Los negros catedráticos* on that first night of bufo performance in May, 1868. Here the term refers not to a professor but instead to an urban, free black character with comic pretension toward erudition. The play was so popular that Francisco Fernández composed a sequel within a matter of weeks entitled *El bautizo* (The baptism), followed by a third installment, *El negro cheche, o veinte años despues* (The black *cheche,* or twenty years later), the next month. "Catedrático" plays formed a major part of the bufo repertory throughout the season, including Alfredo Toroella's *Un minué* (A minuet) and *El ensayo de Don Juan Tenorio* (The rehearsal of Don Juan Tenorio), along with such titles (most no longer extant) as *Una boda catedrática* (A catedrático wedding), *De la tribuna al tango o de teado en teado* (From the tribune to the tango), *El trovador africano* (The African troubadour), *Los medicos de Haiti* (the doctors from Haiti, set to music), *El gato prieto* (The black "cat"), *Los negros retóricos* (The black rhetoricians), *Los negros ilustrados* (The black erudites), *Un día de reyes en la Habana* (One Three Kings' Day in Havana, which reportedly featured an African *cabildo,* or mutual aid organization), *Lo que vá de ayer á hoy, ó el destronamiento de una reina de cabildo* (From yesterday to today, or the dethroning of a queen of a cabildo), *De catedrático a catedrático* (From one catedrático to another), and *El negro por la fuerza* (The negro by force).[8]

Most remarkable about the figure of the catedrático is the degree to which the figure was couched in the familiar terms of popular costumbrismo, replete with its protoethnographic claim to represent "real" local types. Unlike the slave bozal, the catedrático appears to have had no real-world referent in Cuba's demographics. Eric Lott defines the realm of such counterfeits this way: "contradictory popular constructions that were not so much true or false as more or less pleasurable or politically efficacious in the culture that braced them" (Lott 1993, 110). What kind of counterfeit was the catedrático? As with counterfeit money, we can ask whether the fake "coin" passed undetected, and whether and for what it could be traded. There were no loquacious verse-spouting catedráticos populating free black neighborhoods of Havana, yet audience members—and even some later critics, including Fernando Ortiz—believed that Havana's neighborhoods were, indeed, partly populated by black catedráticos. The pleasure and efficaciousness of the image was thus "purchased" through the particular fiction that was advanced as truth. The catedrático proved to be a special counterfeit whose currency lent credibility and power to the idea of the "Cuban" in the first place.

This complex operation of the counterfeit is well illustrated in the play that launched the catedrático to fame, *Los negros catedráticos*, and its two sequels, *El bautizo* and *El negro cheche, o veinte años despues*.[9] Notably absent from the trilogy are any white characters and any reference to the world of slavery, as there would have been in the costumbrista plays of Crespo, Guerrero, or Zafra. The scene has shifted definitively from the plantation to urban Havana, from slavery to the world of free blacks. The stage directions stipulate that, in the opening scene, the characters' home is poor, but their actions and behavior aspire to a wealthier, educated class.

In typical costumbrista fashion, the lists of dramatis personae for the three plays walk a fine line between a proto-ethnographic social taxonomy of racial types and its caricature. They include two negros criollos (Cuban-born blacks) and one *negro congo* (African-born black), one mulata, and several *negros curros* (black, urban, free youths)—all descriptive terms one might well have used to describe the demographic and racial makeup of the urban black population. Here the play acts on the costumbrista penchant for popularizing taxonomies of "real" social types. However, the leading and most popular racial "type" of the play, and of the whole bufo phenomenon in 1868—the negro catedrático—made no appeal to authoritative demographic description: the catedrático was fierce caricature. Populating the same stage world as negros criollos and negros de nación, the catedrático likely served as the fictional, parodic frame of reference by which to understand the other types, just as the teatro bufo as a whole served as a parodic frame by which to catalogue and portray divisive and politically charged social realities on the eve of anticolonial war.

The first scenes establish the contrast and competition between the catedrático and the bozal—here called "congo"—as the central problematic of the play. The first act opens onto a "session of state" between two catedrático patriarchs, Crispín and Ancieto, negotiating the potential marriage of their son and daughter. Despite the difficult parental responsibility of choosing suitable matches for their children, Crispín notes gratefully that they, at least, are better off than "esos desgraciados seres de los extranjeros climas de Africa" (those pitiful beings in the foreign climes of Africa). Ancieto concurs: "¡No hablemos de esos ignorantes individuos! Lástima me da su incultura y el grado de brutología en que se encuentran en *comparancia* de nuestros conocimientos científicos!" (Let us not speak of those ignorant individuals!

I feel pity for their lack of culture and the level of brutology in which they find themselves in comparison to our scientific knowledge! [136]). Ancieto's redundant phrasing, along with his inability to use his complex vocabulary correctly, immediately raise the question of the catedráticos' own level of ignorance or, as he puts it, "brutología" (brutology)—their own protests to the contrary clearly notwithstanding.

Deeply concerned with the social advancement of his lineage, Ancieto reluctantly agrees to have his daughter, Dorotea, marry Crispín's son. Being of the same class and racial categorization as Dorotea, Ricardo offers no opportunity for social improvement: "El partido no es muy ventajoso," Ancieto notes, "pero al fin, no es ningún guatíbero" (The match is not very advantageous, but in the end, he is no *guatíbero* [137]). Ancieto is soon shocked to learn that in the meantime she has been propositioned by none other than an "ignorante individuo" (ignorant individual): the negro bozal, José, who enters "en mangas de camisa con un sombrero de paja viejo, sin zapatos, muy sucio" (in long sleeves with an old straw hat, without shoes, very dirty [143]). The ensuing argument between father and bozal suitor explicitly engages Cuba's prevailing social stratification based on race, class, lineage, and legal status. Ancieto roundly opposes José's bid to marry his daughter because, he says, "ninguno de mi prosapia formará alianza ofensiva ni defensiva con ningún negro heterogéneo sino con los de su *claise* y condición" (no one of my lineage will form any alliance, defensive or offensive, with any heterogeneous black, but only with those of their class and condition [145, italics in original]).[10] Ancieto surmises from José's appearance and manner of speaking that he is a black bozal (thus "more black" than his criolla daughter), lacking the appropriate class attributes (education, clothes) to match Dorotea. José proudly counters that, to the contrary, he meets all the requirements of a good husband: "Yo so congo, trabajaore la muella . . . yo no toma guariente . . . yo so libre . . . yo gana do peso toitico lu día" (I am a congo, a dock worker, I don't drink liquor, I am free, I earn two pesos every day [144]). But Ancieto only cares about socially recognized markers of race and class status, and he refuses the match.

The bozal José counters with the argument that their shared status as blacks should not only make them equals, but should serve as grounds for solidarity. He is suspicious of the catedrático's commitment to the prevailing (white) social order, implying that in itself it calls into question whether the old man is "truly" black. Challenging Ancieto's arrogant claim to be "má mijó que congo" (better than a congo), he asks whether Ancieto does not share the status of all African ethnicities in Cuba: "¿Tú no so negro? . . . ¿no?

. . . ¡Criollo, lucumí, carabalí, gangá, arará, congo, *toitico, toitico* so negro! ¡Negro *toitico*!" (Aren't you black? . . . no? . . . Criollo, lucumí, carabalí, gangá, arará, congo *all of them, all of them* are black! *All* black! [145]). José thus accuses Ancieto of disavowing his own race and lineage. In the process, José's list of African cultural groups in Cuba—which could rival any "real" demographic breakdown of the black population—questions the credibility of this social-climbing criollo as a "real" black social type. He thus puts into play the metatheatrical question of whether the catedrático itself is or is not a "real" black character.

In the catedrático worldview, only class advancement outweighs the potential racial "set-back" (or, as it was then called, a "*saltatrás*," or jump backward) of a criollo marrying a bozal. On learning that José has saved his two daily pesos and is now extraordinarily wealthy, Ancieto approves the "offensive" alliance promptly. As Dorotea quips in verse, "¡Todo cambia el dinero! / Si ayer pobre, era un borrico, / hoy, que sabemos que es rico, / es el congo un caballero" (Money changes everything! If yesterday he was poor, and a drunk, / today, that we know he's rich, / the congo is a gentleman [149]). Both Ancieto and Dorotea believe they can reform the rich bozal: "Ese negro congo dentro de un año ha de ser un diccionario de la lengua clásica" (Within a year that black congo will be a dictionary of classical speech [158]). But once her son Hercules is born, Dorotea acknowledges that money will not quite counterbalance her son's "African" appearance: "No tiene más defecto que el de la nariz por la parte meridional un poco chata" (He has no defect other than his nose being a little flat in the meridional region [178]). Thus when, in the final act of the trilogy, Hercules is able to marry Tomasa, a mulata, the patriarch is greatly relieved; it is "un adelanto muy marcado" (a marked advance) for the family, because their offspring will finally yield that desired "quebrado blanco" or white fraction (207–8).

The bald insinuation of the catedrático into an otherwise plausible taxonomy of social or racial types in Cuba illustrates the use and abuse of blackface on Cuba's popular stage. Ostensibly, the catedrático indeed does bear a relation to an existing free black social class in Cuba. There was, as Deschamps Chapeaux and Martínez Alier acknowledge, a free colored "petty bourgeoisie" in Havana and other major towns throughout the nineteenth century, especially prior to the violent repression of the free black communities during the conspiracy of La Escalera in 1844 (see Deschamps Chapeaux 1971; Martinez-Alier 1989, 98–99). In the early part of the century, members of the colored militias were at the top of this social hierarchy, which was comprised primarily of working artisans, such as tailors or musicians, and their families. José del Castillo provided this remembrance from the 1840s, which seemed to draw the very portrait of the 1868 catedráticos:

Yo me acuerdo de muchos negros y mulatos, algunos de ellos con abundantes bienes de fortuna, que en su modo de vivir, en su traje, en su porte y en su manera de expresarse, imitaban a los caballeros blancos que todavía quedaban en Cuba, y entre ellos no faltaba gente aficionada a leer libros serios y hasta hacer versos. . . . (Franco 1937, 19)

(I remember many blacks and mulatos, some of them possessing a considerable fortune, who in their way of life, their dress, their behavior and their manner of speaking, imitated those white [Spanish] gentlemen who were still left in Cuba, and among them there was no lack of people fond of reading serious books and even of writing verses. . . .)

Lest we too quickly accept this as proof that the catedráticos were modeled on "real" blacks, note the persistence of the theatrical formulation in Castillo's description: a well-dressed black man was not a wealthy black man, but rather an *imitation* of a white *caballero.* So we might well argue the reverse: this description is an early instance of *catedracismo* itself, a racial discourse in which blacks who behaved outside the normative expectations of a racist society were structurally defined as pretenders, ludicrous interlopers in a white world. In this instance of *catedracismo,* certain behavior (dressing well, being educated, reading serious books, "even" writing verse) was structurally coded as white, forcing the conclusion that any black engaging in such behavior was *acting,* pretending to be white—in short, acting in whiteface.

Catedracismo's hold has been surprisingly tenacious: by 1930 the ethnographer Fernando Ortiz assumed that the black catedráticos constituted a "fenómeno social muy advertido en el siglo pasado" (notable social phenomenon in the past century), although he offered no evidence to support this claim. Defining catedráticos as blacks who spoke "con afectación orativa" (with oratory affectation), Ortiz claimed that there existed "nutridas masas de africanos a quienes se quería hacer pasar de un solo salto de la incultura selvática de los bozales a la literaria, sobradamente literaria, cultura de los blancos dominadores" (abundant masses of Africans who were expected to jump in a single leap from the rustic lack of culture of the bozales to the literary, excessively literary, culture of the dominant whites). Ortiz went so far as to claim that the catedrático formed part of a circum-Atlantic, pan-African cultural phenomenon:

El mismo fenómeno, en mayor o menor grado, se ha notado en los pueblos costeros de África y en las poblaciones africanoides de las demás Antillas, del Brasil, de los

> Estados Unidos de América, donde se han dado los mismos contactos entre las dos razas. (Ortiz 1930, 119)
>
> (In greater or lesser degrees, the same phenomenon has been found in coastal towns of Africa, in the Africanoide populations of the other Antilles, of Brazil, of the United States of America, where similar contact between the races has taken place.)

Ortiz's portrait of "abundant masses" of Africans speaking overly-formal speech offered a strange—very strange—rendition of the black Atlantic.

To understand why Ortiz would venture such a notion, we can examine his own explanation of the catedrático phenomenon. Again, the narrative hinged on a crucial relation between the cultural behavior of "African races" and theatricality:

> el fenómeno de transición parece tener como causas específicas ciertos caracteres psicológicos muy comunes entre las razas negras, cuales son las facultades y tendencias sobresalientes para la imitación del prójimo, para la oratoria pomposa y hueca, para la burla y la sátira y para destacar los perfiles grotescos de los seres y de las costumbres. Unid todos esos impulsos del alma africana a la leguleyería, a la vanidad ostentosa y a la palabrería fanfarrona, en un ambiente tan dado a la cultura literaria como fue el de la sociedad colonial de Cuba, y os explicaréis el lenguaje de los catedráticos por presuntuoso y prematura acercamiento al de los blancos literatos. . . . (Ortiz 1930, 119–20)
>
> (this transitional phenomenon appears to have specific roots in certain psychological characteristics common among the black races, which are the exceptional faculties and tendencies for imitation of his fellow man, for pompous and hollow oratory, for jokes and satire, and for highlighting the grotesque outlines of beings and customs. Unite all of these impulses of the African soul to the chicanery, the ostentatious vanity, and the showy chatter, in an atmosphere so given to literary culture as was Cuban colonial society, and you will explain the language of the catedráticos as a presumptuous and premature approximation of that of the white literati.)

As with the Castillo description almost a century earlier, black behavior outside white norms was immediately equated with showiness and ostentation. The weight of Ortiz's ethnological expertise, marked here by such scientific language as "transitional phenomenon," and "Africanoide populations," not only lent authority to his claim, but also helped to naturalize his perceptions. Showiness, pomposity, and ostentation were rendered the inherent "psychological characteristics" of all "African races." Ortiz diagnosed these as the root "cause" of catedracismo, when in reality the reverse was operative: black ostentation was an *effect* produced by the ethnological analysis. *Catedracismo*, it appears, did not refer to African behavior, but to a white mode of perceiving it. Because Ortiz's worldview did not allow for an African to enjoy literary culture in "normal" circumstances, the fact that "abundant masses" nonetheless might have attempted such enjoyment could only be understood as a symptom of all Africans' inherent desire to imitate their fellow (white) humans.

Ortiz thus offered the catedráticos as proof that imitation (and particularly cross-racial imitation) came naturally to all African races as one phase of their cultural development. However, his claim was based on phantom evidence: there is, of course, no record of "abundant masses" of African catedráticos on any part of the Atlantic rim. Perhaps Ortiz's generalization was based on some recollection from his childhood, as was José del Castillo's. Far more likely, however, is that his claim was based on a memory of black behavior not on the street, but instead in blackface on the teatro bufo stage, which Ortiz no doubt encountered (perhaps in "abundance") as a young man in the 1880s and 1890s. Indeed, the blackface performances of the bufos provide the only "evidence" anywhere of the catedráticos as a social phenomenon.

So it is not entirely surprising that the occasion for Ortiz's comments was a 1930 reprint of a bufo play, *Los novios catedráticos* (The catedrático newlyweds), by Ignacio Benítez del Cristo, which was itself a direct takeoff on Fernández's 1868 *Los negros catedráticos.* The play was first published and performed after the first war of independence in Matanzas in 1877, and published in a second edition in 1888. Ortiz elected to reprint the play in the journal of the *Archivos del folklore cubano* (Archives of Cuban folklore) not as a record of bufo performance (which could, perhaps, be recuperated as Cuban folklore), but rather as an evidentiary document of "real" catedrático speech and behavior itself: "el sainete tiene un valor filológico documental que conviene conservar" (the sainete has a philological documentary value that is worth preserving). He conceded that the play errs on the side of "exceso corrección en el lenguage puesto impropiamente en bocas incultas" (excessive correction of the speech improperly placed in uncultured mouths); the real catedráticos actually "hablaban peor" (spoke worse). But the play retains its documentary value since it reflects "tipos y costumbres de popular comicidad" (popular comic types and customs), and especially because of "la imitación del lenguage de los negros congos bozalones al romper a hablar español" (the imitation of the broken speech of black *congo bozalones* when speaking Spanish [Ortiz 1930, 120]).

We see here the complex interplay among notions of race, ethnographic truth, and performance that surrounded the blackface catedrático, both in its own day and in critical appraisals thereafter. The "original" or "real" catedráticos on which the bufo performances were presumably based were little more than performative aftereffects of the performances themselves and the (proto)ethnographic discourse around them, each serving as evidence for the other in a tautological embrace that extended from the 1860s to the emergence of Cuban ethnography in the work of Fernando Ortiz and beyond. The bufo performances circulated a protoethnographic (costumbrista) idea of a black persona prone to the (poor, comic) imitation of wealthy white culture. Yet that idea was enacted by white men and women performing in blackface—that is, by white people who were themselves prone to the enthusiastic (comic, poor) imitation and parody of black people. Later critics, including Fernando Ortiz and a number of Cuban theatre historians, took the bufos' pseudo-ethnographic claims at face value: the performances became evidence, however distant or imperfect, of "real" catedráticos who "must have" existed, since they were, after all, portrayed on the costumbrista stage along with other credible social types and customary cultural behaviors. This assumption perfectly elided any analysis of the evident *white* enthusiasm for cross-racial performance—and, indeed analysis of why such enthusiasm was re-dressed as an inherent feature of black peoples instead. So even as we acknowledge that there was race and class stratification within Cuba's black community, it does not finally matter whether there actually were some number of individuals who dressed or spoke like catedráticos; what matters is why and how such figures were reinvented on stage and in the popular protoethnographic imagination as a Cuban social "type."

If Creto's blackface bozal had earlier allowed white audiences to flirt with the idea of being "Africanized" while still carefully containing such a process, the expression enabled by the blackface catedrático was substantially less ambivalent. The catedrático allowed white audiences unabashedly to project the fear of being African onto the African himself: being and becoming African were strategically elided, such that the already black/African Ancieto himself fears "becoming" African. Ancieto is able to voice—in sesquipedalian fashion—compelling social reasons that a fear of *being* "African" in racist Cuba would be reasonable. However, the white social order directly responsible for slavery, racial segregation, and discrimination is conveniently absent from this stage world. Ancieto's terror of things "African" cannot therefore be recuperated as a critique of the difficulties and injustices of black life in Cuba. The catedrático is a ventriloquist for white racist fears of becoming "African," displaced fully onto the black(face) man himself.

Make no mistake: this dimension of catedracismo at times allowed for the unadulterated expression of race hatred—a sentiment made all the more ugly by placing it in the mouths of "black" characters. In *El negro cheche*, for example, Ancieto momentarily regrets his decision to accept the bozal José as a son-in law:

> si sus bémbicos labios no hubieran conquistado el virgíneo corazón del fruto de mis amores conyugales, no sufriría yo estos bochornos en medio de las frequentadas calles de esta populosa capital. [. . .] Usted es la llave que ha dado cuerda a esa máquina horrísona e infernal. Usted no tiene más que sebo y manteca dentro de su voluminoso cuerpo. Usted es un indígeno ingrato y desagradecido, que no ha sabido apreciar en lo que vale el honorífico honor que se le concediera, ligando sus acuáticos sentimientos con los glóbulos homeopaticos de las bóvedas incógnitas y sensibles de mi desgraciada hija. (Fernández and Pequeño 1868, 188–89)
>
> (if your large lips had not conquered the virginal heart of the fruit of my conjugal love, I wouldn't suffer these embarrassments in the middle of the highly frequented streets of this populous capital. [. . .] You are the key that has started this horrifying, infernal machine. You have nothing more than grease and butter in your voluminous body. You are the ungrateful and wretched native who did not know to appreciate the value of the honorific honor bestowed on you, joining your aquatic sentiments with the homeopathic corpuscles of the unknown and sensible cranium of my unfortunate daughter.)

Through the character of Ancieto, the play blames the African—perhaps all Africans—for the public "embarrassment" of his very presence in the capital, casting him as the key to the "horrifying, infernal machine" of race conflict. Here we find a racist allegory about Cuba itself, in which the displaced African is ungrateful for the "honor" of living free in Cuba, and is blamed for ruining the "virginal" purity of Cuba's population.

This trenchant discourse about race and nation harbored within it a more ambivalent anticolonial discourse. Primarily through its gleeful recourse to tropes of linguistic play, the blackface persona became the vehicle for the expression of social alternatives to the status quo, enabling the emergence of a "Cuban" humor, style, and rhythm. Like the bozal, the catedrático mimicked educated speech, but subjected it to a round abuse of grandiloquence, circumlocution, and catachresis. The special appeal of the catedrático, like that of the bozal, lay in its intense distortions of Spanish, and it is no coincidence that the term "catedrático"—like the term "bozal"—denotes a style or manner of verbal expression as much if not more than it denotes a "black" persona. The contrast between the lexical distortions of the catedrático and the bozal are instructive and crucial to the operation through which blackface was appropriated by its protonationalist Cuban audiences as a form of anticolonial ventriloquism.

Witness, for one example, the comic interplay in *Los negros catedráticos* between Ancieto and José, as José struggles to become "more" catedrático. Ancieto offers lessons on fatherhood:

Ancieto: Escucha ahora que estamos en las tinieblas de la soledad el deber que como padre te impone la vida social para con el hijo de tu elocuencia. Primero: el desarrollo común didáctico y epitalámico de las ciencias médicas y naturales. Segundo: el mantenimiento necesario a su robustez abdominal. Tercero: el conocimiento de los binomios, polinomios, letras, coeficientes, signos y esponentes de las cantidades algebráicas. Cuarto: la colocación de ese vastago en las posiciones comerciales, periodísticas y mercantiles, y por último, el señalarlo con la tinta del matrimonio sin perturbar sus adoraciones amorosas.

José: Bueno; usté criba esa cosa aritméticamente pa que yo luego con linfáticamento lo jace uno estudiamento escolapio. (172)

(*Ancieto*: Hear, now that we are in the darkness of solitude, the obligation that as a father social life imposes on you toward the son of your eloquence. First: the communal development, didactic and epithalamial, of the sciences, medical and natural. Second: the necessary maintenance of his abdominal robustness. Third: knowledge of binomials, polynomials, letters, coefficients, signs, and exponents of algebraic quantities. Fourth: the placement of said offspring in positions commercial, periodical, and mercantile, and lastly, to mark him with the ink of matrimony without perturbing his love adorations.

José: Well; you write that thing arithmetically so that later I can with lymphaticment do it a scholarly study.)

If the bozal delights in the melodic vowel-laden slur of Castilian, the catedrático delights in the exaggerated, rhyming, staccato crispness of its Latinate base. Both are parodies of spoken Spanish, and both are mapped onto the "black" bodies of José and Ancieto. Part of the humor is that neither José nor Ancieto can speak Spanish "properly." Yet when Ancieto rattles off his overeducated jargon, part of the comic critique, it seems, is directed at the pretenses of highbrow Castilian itself, and not just the funny "African" trying to speak it. Note that the publicity for bufo performances often used catedrático language; for example, a June 1868 press advertisement promised melíflua y sinagógica sinfonía por la orquesta. El metafísico jugete en un acto, original del Conguito [Luis Cruz] . . . *La gallinita ciega.* La numismática y funébrica canción *La muerta viva.* La hipodrómica pieza *Los negros catedráticos.* La cuadrilátera guaracha, *El negro bueno,* y el onomatopéyico cuadro de costumbres etiópicas *Un minué.* (Leal 1975b, 29).

(mellifluous and synagogical symphony by the orchestra; the metaphysical farce in one act, original by "El Conguito" [little congo] . . . *The blind chicken.* The numismatic and funereal song *The living dead.* The hippodromical piece *Los negros catedráticos.* The quadrilateral guaracha, *The good negro,* and the onomatopoeic portrait of Ethiopian customs *A minuet.*)

Here we find a parody of the kind of language that might otherwise describe highbrow opera performance. Through the catedrático, white audiences delighted not only in making fun of socially pretentious black people, but also of the pretentiousness of aristocratic culture.

A small circular entitled *La Sopimpa* illustrated the full potential for both this humor and critique. The name *La Sopimpa* refers to a particular dance of purported African origin; the paper's subtitle was "periódico bailable a todo orquesta" (newspaper danceable to full orchestra). Like other publications of the day, and like Creto Gangá before them, this one's text favored the theatricality of printed speech. The first issue presented this (untranslatable) poem, entitled "Aleluya," a satire of both Latin and black cultures. Presenting a variation on catedrático speech, the poem uses the frame of a Latin prayer or ode to celebrate the dance "la sopimpa" throughout the city. The vernacular term "sopimpa" is "translated" into Latin as "Sopimpam," such that "laudate sopimpam" means "praise the sopimpa." It begins,

Yam ñañigui non reñibunt,
Quia bailabunt Sopimpam.

Laudate Sopimpam de Manglare,
Laudate Sopimpam in Sitiis.

Laudate Sopimpam negriti
Laudate Sopimpam mulati e chini.

Laudate Sopimpam in fututo,
Yn tamboribus et güiris.

Laudate Sopimpam in guitaris,
In sambombis bene templatis.

Laudate Sopimpam á Roncali
Usque ad Resintum muralle.

Laudate Sopimpam las de peli solti,
Omnes ninfe fregatrices.

Highly idiomatic references to black life and musical culture in Cuba have been translated to fake Latin: "ñáñigos" becomes "ñañigui"; the predominantly black neighborhood of "Manglar" becomes "Manglare"; "negros," mulatas, and "chinas" become "negriti," "mulati," and "chini"; the "recintos de muralla" (the outskirts of the city walls) become "Resintum muralle"; and the women dancing with their hair down (a pelo suelto) become "les de peli suelti," apparently "washerwomen nymphs" or "ninfe fregatrices." What's funny about this joke? The sacrilegious idea of monks droning in Latin about sopimpa-dancing washerwomen, the idea that the sopimpa could merit a Latin ode, the idea that Cuban slang could be translated into the high-culture language of Latin, the idea that Latin, in turn, could be tainted with such vernacular terms. It is a simple joke, finally, but one that encapsulated in full the central logic of the catedrático: in a popular culture saturated with the notion that the future of the colony would be either Spanish or African, both African and Spanish had to be displaced to enable the emergence of the Cuban as an alternative. The catedrático served as a convenient—and necessary—site for such simultaneous displacement.

Catedrático language came to be associated with parody of high colonial culture, especially its crowning achievement: the opera at the Tacón. Beyond offering burlesque versions of specific operas playing at the Tacón, the bufos were associated with the satire of the culture for which that theatre stood. This is the pretext of one 1868 catedrático play, *El ensayo de Don Juan Tenorio* (The rehearsal of Don Juan Tenorio), a "descarillamiento cómico" (shameless comedy) in which a number of catedráticos attempt to stage Zorrilla's play of that title.[11] The protagonist, Domingo, has decided to "afiliar[se] en el batallón de los actores líricos-trágicos" (align himself in the battalion of lyric-tragic actors), his obvious lack of acting talent notwithstanding. Domingo has chosen *Don Juan* over his first choice, *La africana*, because, for one, "en el patio no debía caber el embarcación marítima" (the maritime embarkation wouldn't fit in the patio). Besides, "¿quién consigue tanto traje?" (who can find that many costumes?). He continues, "es verdad que yo con mis relaciones íntimas, podia adquirirlos en el teatro Tacón, pero . . ." (it's true that I could, with my intimate connections, surely acquire them from the Tacón theatre, but . . .). His cohort, Eleuterio, interrupts, "Mal hecho, amigo. Los periodistas dicen que la ropa del Teatro de Tacón es anacronísima" (Bad idea, friend. The newspapers say that the clothes at the Tacón theatre are most anachronistic), and so on, over the course of the rehearsal. In this play, catedrático language, which all of the characters spout both on and off their rehearsal stage, served to ridicule the pretensions of Spanish colonial theatre as much as the attempts of blacks in Cuba to join that high society.

The teatro bufo of 1868 forced its association between aristocracy and black culture in another strain of catedrático humor: the catedrático as black aristocrat, best illustrated in the "disparate catedrático" (catedrático joke) *Un minué* (A minuet), debuted by the Bufos Habaneros at the Teatro de Variedades on 22 August 1868. This fascinating one-act comedy casts its catedrático protagonists, Don Serapio and Doña Petrona Tragabuches (their last name meaning something like "swallowbellies"), as members of a fictional black aristocracy in Havana. "Toda la aristocracia de los círculos aplomáticos de la Habana" (All of the aristocracy of aplomb-atic circles of Havana [8]) is invited to their home for a minuet in honor of their daughter Juliana's social debut. Much of the play revolves around the ritual introduction into the dance hall of each guest and his or her entourage, all in full formal regalia. *Un minué* presents a fanciful African social world, populated by the likes of the Marqués Tintorera (Marquis of Clothing-dyes), the Marquesa de la Zamaritana (Marchioness of Zamaritana), Srta. Jacinta the Vizcondesa de Liby (Miss Jacinta, the Vice-countess of Liby), and the African bozal-speaking Sr. Macario, "Presidente del areópago carabalí" (Mr. Macario, president of the carabalí tribunal), whose linguistic repertoire does not exceed his much-repeated introduction "Macario, carabalí pá seví á osté y á tatá Dió" (Macario, carabali to serve you and father God [10]). For his part, the Marqués Tintorera finds being an aristocrat "un túnel de desgracias" (a tunnel of misfortune [9]); like Ancieto from *Los negros catedráticos*, he has recently suffered the indignity of having a "negro hidrofóbico mal nacido" (poorly born hydrophobic negro) ask for his daughter's hand in marriage. Serapio also laments the loss of respect for nobility, saying that this is no doubt "el fruto de las doctrinas democráticas" (the fruit of democratic doctrines [9]). He immediately undermines the claim, however, by noting that "ya no se respetan las posiciones adquiridas con los billetes de la Real Lotería," (now not even positions acquired with Royal Lottery bills are respected [9]), implying that they form part of a *nouveau riche* class, rather than an old aristocracy.[12]

Several other teatro bufo plays were conscious of and interested in the social hierarchies in the African cabildos in the city. Cabildos were mutual aid societies organized according to African ethnic group or "nation." Sanctioned by the colonial authorities, they were generally self-governing and often replicated or reinvented social hierarchies from their communities of origin. In the play *De hombre a hombre* (From man to man), for example, the surprise ending reveals that the heroine's father is actually an African king, whose authority and status thus exceeds that of her skeptical future father-in-law, the head of a local African cabildo. No such insight graces *Un minué*, although it almost certainly harbors a satirical agenda against the black aristocracy that had been installed in nearby Haiti.

The ambiguous referent for this aristocracy allows the play to satirize both the very idea of blacks forming (or joining) an aristocracy, and Havana's existing, *white* aristocratic set, largely composed of colonial, Spanish nobility. The controversial fact that black characters here refer to each other with the appellations *don* and *doña* would not be lost on Cuban audiences. As a practice open to white people only, it would cue audiences to read these black aristocrats as parodies of white dons and doñas as much as parodies of Africans per se. Here "blackness" and "aristocracy" each serve as the means to satirize the other. At the end of the play Don Serapio beseeches a policeman to not confuse "las diversiones tersicoreñas de los etiópicos, con las de la categoria clásica de los de la capital de la perla de las Antillas" (the terpsichorean diversions of Ethiopians with those of the classical category of the capital of the pearl of the Antilles [Cuba] [14]). His request aside, the play invites precisely such a confusion: the "classical" Spanish aristocracy is presented as no more valuable than a group of self-involved dancing Ethiopians, and likewise, those social-climbing "Ethiopians" offer nothing better than the worst ostentation of Cuba's colonial excess.

The anticolonial undertone of *Un minué*'s satire is redoubled in its relation to music and dance. By choosing a minuet, the black aristocrats make recourse to a decidedly imported, European form of entertainment. The play makes their disdain for contemporary Cuban musical forms a constant source of humor. Juliana, for example, has to assure the "Stephanoni" sisters that they are hosting "una *soiré* sistemática y no un tango fúlgido (a systematic *soirée*, and not a glowing tango [6]). Emetrio, the (white) gallego house-servant suggests that, while awaiting the arrival of the "músicos con sus *clarinetotes*" (musicians with their clarinets), they should give in to the "dulzuras de una danza tropical" (sweetness of a tropical danza [11]). The aristocrats are firmly opposed: "donde se baila al MINUÉ que es el baile clásico, anfibológico de las personas cúbicamente decentes, bailar danza es como hechar sardina de nantes en un tabernáculo de néctar soda" (dancing a *danza* where one would dance a minuet, the classical dance of all cubically decent people, is like throwing sardines in a tabernacle of sparkling nectar [12]). The joke is metatheatrical: it is not just that these European-identified aristocrats fail to appreciate the attractions of the newly popular Cuban danza, but that their aesthetic tastes run directly counter to the audience in attendance, who may well have enjoyed a "tropical" danza at the close of the evening's entertainments. This play demonstrates the degree to which the aristocratic tastes and behaviors of the catedráticos (whether coded as African, Spanish, or otherwise) were explicitly marked as different from those of the audience. These plays are not, for the most part, self-parodies, but rather exercises in self-definition by negative inference. As the teatro bufo gave shape to a new "Cuban" reality, it defined the parameters of that new reality against that of its perceived "others." The comic black aristocrat dancing a European minuet simultaneously embodied Cuba's internal other (blacks or mixed race peoples) and its external other (Spain as a European, colonizing power).

Sounding *Candela*: Revolution, Race, Rhythm

The *contradanzas* popularized by the teatro bufo and rejected by the catedrático Tragabuches were themselves a racially charged genre. French in origin and enjoyed in Cuba by Spanish colonials, the contradanza was gradually altered in its Cuban practice, until its newly energized form traveled back to Europe as the *habanera.* As early as 1837, Félix Tanco y Bosmeniel was able to point to the contradanza as a prime site for the "Africanization" of dance; in a letter to Domingo del Monte, he wrote,

> "¿Quien no ve en los movimientos de nuestros mozos y muchachas cuando bailan contradanzas y valses, una imitacion de la mímica de los negros en sus *cabildos*? ¿Quien no sabe que los *bajos de los dansistas del país* son el eco del tambor de los *Tangos*? Todo es africano, y los inocentes y pobres negros, sin pretenderlo [. . .] se vengan de nuestro tratamiento. (*Centón epistolario* 7, 87–88)

> (Who does not see in the movement of our young men and women when they dance contrandanzas and waltzes an imitation of the mimicry [also, gesticulation] of the blacks in their *cabildos*? Who does not know that the *bass* [rhythm] *of the dancers of the country* is the echo of the drums of the *Tango*? Everything is African, and the innocent and poor blacks, without intending to, [. . .] avenge our treatment of them.)

The contradanza was, apparently, the site of dizzying impersonation, as white dancers "imitated" the "mimicry" of the Africans through the "African" performance of otherwise European choreography. Alejo Carpentier notes that by the mid-nineteenth century, it was popularly believed that *contradanzas* were "better" when played by colored or black orchestras; the black musicians reportedly inflected the traditional European dance music with slight variations in rhythm and style that gradually redefined the genre (Carpentier 1946, 320). As the contradanza was thus gradually "Cubanized," it also more frequently embraced subject matter related to its black and African musicians. Carpentier cites the example of Santiago in 1856, when at a formal celebration honoring the visit of the Captain General Concha, the aristocratic guests indulged for much of the evening in the "tropical" danza *Tu madre es conga* (Your mother is a conga), whose musical phrasing introduced the rhythm that would later come to be known as the *conga*. Carpentier and the music historian Zoila Lapique Becali cite a number of other contradanzas whose titles indicate "black" themes, either from their content or by the (untranslatable) supposed African origin or sound of the name: these include "La chupadera" (from *chupar*, or "suck"), "La caringa," "La sopimpa," "La fambuá," "En subiendo la lomita" (Going up the hill), "Maní Totán," "Aronga," "Cambujá," "Ma-Anica la vieja" (Ma-Anica the old woman), "Los ñáñigos," "Mandinga no va, o los tres golpes" (The mandinga doesn't go, or the three blows), "El mulato de Guanabacoa" (The mulato from Guanabacoa), "El mulato en el cabildo" (The mulato in the cabildo), "Lo de atrás palante" (Those in back come up front), "La negrita" (The little black girl), and "Sandunga" (Spark/excitement) (Lapique Becali 1979, 40–42; Carpentier 1946, 316–20).

Thus, although black Cubans were strictly relegated to representation by blackface proxy on stage, they played a significant role in the orchestra pit. Several music historians have already noted with interest that blacks outnumbered whites as professional musicians throughout the nineteenth century, performing both concert music and more popular genres.[13] Lapique Becali attributes this racial imbalance to the early association among Spanish colonists between music and manual labor. Although educated white young men and women might learn a musical instrument as amateurs, it was considered socially inappropriate to pursue music as a professional career; young, middle-class white men instead pursued more stable and lucrative professions in medicine, law, and the clergy. Robin Moore suggests that "musical labor straddled a cognitive boundary between white-collar and blue-collar (Moore 1997, 17; Lapique Becali 1979, 25; Agüero y Barreras 1946, 119). By the late eighteenth century, free people of color filled the ranks of musicians in local orchestras and small musical groups; for the first decades of the nineteenth century, numerous blacks found access to steady employment and social notoriety as composers and performers in a wide range of musical genres, prompting some white intellectuals to protest. José Antonio Saco lamented in 1831,

> Las artes están en manos de la gente de color. Entre los enormes males que esta raza infeliz ha traído a nuestro suelo, uno de ellos es el haber alejado de las artes a nuestra población blanca. (Carpentier 1946, 315)

> The arts are in the hands of people of color. Among the huge misfortunes that this unhappy race has brought to our land, one of them is having distanced the arts from our white population.

Saco did not examine the whites' own self-imposed alienation from artistic labor or from the blacks who otherwise performed it. This state of affairs was interrupted by the alleged slave conspiracy of La Escalera, which resulted in the violent repression of the free black population, including the imprisonment of many well-known black musicians. It was not until 1852 that then Captain-General José Gutiérrez de la Concha pardoned musicians still in jail—among them the popular black composer Claudio Brindis de Salas Sr., who named his newly formed orchestra in the Captain-General's honor, La Concha de Oro (Lapique Becali 1979, 25). Thereafter blacks again dominated the professional musical scene, populating orchestras or ensembles for the theatre, masked balls, and especially salon dance venues.

The fact that blacks were regularly employed as musicians in the theatre and other popular performance venues provided an important context for the so-called "Africanization" of Spanish dance and music forms. The regular contact between the races in the performing arts was what allowed music historians such as Odilio Urfé to cite music as one of the primary venues for the mestizaje that defines Cuban culture (Urfé 1984, 181, 188). But Carpentier is quick to point out that although the black musicians did bring inventive new inflections to salon dance music in the latter half of the nineteenth century, the so-called "African" elements of the contradanza were not yet fully integrated into the composition, as they would be later during the so-called *afrocubanismo* movement of the 1930s. In the nineteenth century, he writes, the contradanza borrowed only superficial features of African music and dance, including the obsessive repetition of a single phrase; a marching rhythm reminiscent of the African comparsas (street processions performed by the African cabildos, primarily on their Three King's Day celebration); and a brief, clearly demarcated musical motif that returns repeatedly throughout the composition, "to the point of saturation" (Carpentier 1946, 399).

Interestingly, Carpentier characterizes these African borrowings as "epidérmico" or "skin-deep"—a kind of musical blackface (Carpentier 1946, 398). If the catedráticos of the play *Un minué* are "black" characters dancing in whiteface, then the white audiences indulging in "tropical" danzas are, similarly, dancing in blackface. Like the teatro bufo's characterization of black peoples, the contradanzas, danzas, and guarachas of the teatro bufo selectively borrowed from ostensibly African sources in order to conjure a sense of a fresh "tropical" reality. As with the use of blackface, here the white audiences' cross-racial desire for and enjoyment of "African" music emerged only when accompanied by a sharply delineated fantasy of its opposite: the fantasy of *black* cross-racial envy.

The combination of these two elements, the blackface catedrático and "African" dance and music, illuminates the racial contradiction at the heart of this emergent Cuban anticolonial nationalist sentiment. The ostensible "Cubanness" of the dance music was predicated on the unique mix of precisely those elements that were also combined in the catedrático: the African and the colonial Spanish. But whereas the catedrático was the subject of vicious parody, the music was openly celebrated—often in the press in downright giddy rhetoric. The crucial difference in treatment lay in the popular attitude toward the racial investment of each figure. On the one hand, the catedrático was clearly *raced*; that is, she or he was marked as a racialized figure most powerfully through the practice of blacking up. The cross-racial investment of the contradanzas or guarachas was, on the other hand, naturalized into a racially nonspecific "Cuban" practice, contrasted on an ostensibly cultural—not racial—level with Spanish culture. The visual economy of blackface and the aural economy of Afrocuban music may well have attenuated each other: although the satirical catedrático may have allowed for the safe celebration of "black" music, the music may have lent an aura of "Cubanness" to the catedrático. This mutual mediation was rather literal: free blacks performed in the orchestras along with white musicians, but never performed in this period as actors on stage, much less in the role of the negrito in his bozal or catedrático incarnations. Audiences *heard* African-influenced music, but *saw* the comic blackface catedráticos. Thus, the two racializing economies were kept rigidly separate, but each informed the reception of the other.

The one festivity in which these two economies—visual and aural—

were allowed to converge in public for the black community was the Three Kings' Day Festival held annually on 6 January, in which African cabildos staged a vibrant processional. The event was met with panic or disdain by most white audiences. In early 1869, one commentator in the *Diario de la Marina* worried aloud,

> No deseamos sino que todas las personas que nos quieren bien se vuelvan sordas desde las ocho de la mañana hasta el anocher [sic], y que todas las que nos quieren mal se vean asediadas por todos los *diablitos*, ya solos ya acompañados con sus músicas infernales, y que no los abandonen hasta que les dejen los bolsillos como la ropa al ser entregada por la lavandera. (5 January 1869)

> (We only wish that that all those who love us well will go deaf from eight in the morning to nightfall, and all who wish us ill find themselves beleaguered by all the little devils [*diablitos*], alone or accompanied by their infernal music, and that they don't abandon them until they leave their pockets like the clothes turned in by the washerwoman.)

The boisterous processional through the center of Havana by African cabildos became a hallmark of Havana's limited public culture throughout the century, much remarked upon by commentators and foreign visitors to the city—particularly the drumming and dancing associated with the closed all-male black brotherhood of "Abakwa" (also "abakua," known to outsiders more often as "ñáñigos"), whose masked spirit dancers (the *ireme*) were known to white Cubans as "diablitos" or "little devils." The commentator went on to worry about the effect such a spectacle might have on a foreign visitor: "Deseamos tambien que no lleguen ese día á nuestras playas extranjeros que no tengan que seguir viaje á las pocas horas para que no formen de nosotros un juicio á lo Duvergier d'Hauranne" (We also hope that no foreigners disembark on our shores that day who have to continue their journey in a few hours, lest they form a judgment of us like that of Duvergier d'Hauranne), referring to the French writer, Ernest Duvergier de Hauranne, known for his judgmental accounts of life in the United States during the Civil War (see de Hauranne 1974). The Cuban imagined the European visitor encountering a scene in which Havana's racial hierarchies had seemingly been reversed, and through which the European could mistake African dance, music, or culture for Cuban. Yet these very forms were celebrated as "Cuban" in white popular theatre—but only when divorced from black embodiment, performance, or agency.

The productive, if uneasy, dissonance among the representational economies of blackface, "black" music, and white nationalist sentiment is well illustrated by the popular guaracha frequently performed in repertory with *Los negros catedráticos,* "El negro bueno." The lyrics of "El negro bueno" draw a portrait of a street-savvy black man "de rompe y raja":

Aqui ha llegado *Candela,*
Negrito de rompe y raja
Que con el cuchillo vuela,
Y corta con la navaja.

Estribillo:
¡Ay! ¡Ay¡ ¡Ay! ¡Ay!
Vamos a ver
¡Ay! Chinitica
¿Qué vamos a hacer?
Si al negro bueno
Lo quieren prender;
Al negro bueno
Quieren desgraciar;
Pero ninguno
Se quiere atracar
Porque si tira
Se puede clavar

Del Manglar al Monserrate,
Y de la Punta a Belén,
Todas doblan el petate
Si toco yo a somatén.

Donde se planta *Candela*
No hay negra que se resista;
Y si algún rival la cela,
Al momento vende lista.

Candela no se rebaja
A ningún negro valiente;
En sacando la navaja,
No hay nadie que se presente.[14]

(Here comes *Candela*
Defiant/streetwise negrito
Who flies with the knife,
And cuts with the jackknife.

Chorus:
¡Ay! ¡Ay¡ ¡Ay! ¡Ay!

We will see
Ay! Chinitica
What will we do?
If they want to capture
The good negro;
They want to ruin
The good negro;
But no one
Wants to get in a fight
Because if he draws
One could get nailed

From Manglar to Monserrate,
And from the Punta to Belén [Havana neighborhoods],
All the women fold the bed mats
If I sound the alarm [or call to war].

Wherever *Candela* stands
There's no black girl/woman who can resist;
And if some rival traps her,
In a moment he sells out [takes a bribe].

Candela does not lower himself
To any valiant black man;
In taking out the jackknife,
No one will come forward. [italics in the original])

The song introduces the important figure of "Candela," who—along with the catedrático—became an important feature on the racialized landscape of Cuban representation on the eve of war. The word "candela," which literally means "candle," carried a far wider set of meanings in Cuba in the nineteenth century (as it still does) and to an extent became a euphemism for a particularly compelling form or style of Cubanness itself. Used as an adjective to describe a dance, for example, "candela" can be imagined as the nineteenth-century equivalent of calling the dance "hot," "hip," or "happening," resonant with the way these terms have historically described African diasporic music and dance forms generally. Although it need not literally describe black music or culture (one can simply say, for example, that a party was "candela"), the term carries an archaeological trace of its racialized past: the measure of being candela is always, at some level, in proximity to the kind of fully present "coolness" evoked by African diasporic music and dance. In the guaracha "El negro bueno," the connection between race and the idea of being "candela" is made explicit. "Candela" names a streetwise, sexually potent black man—a striking portrait for the day, given that the lyrics do not try to control or contain the figure's violent or sexual energy, as was the norm with other contemporary portraits of black men in print and performance. Consider, for example, the very different chorus to the guaracha "El negro Rafael": "Mentira que no tiene nada / Este negro Rafael; / Con tantos hijos que tiene, / Pero ninguno es de él" (It's not true he has nothing / This black man Rafael; / With all the sons he has / But no one of them is his [*Guarachas cubanas* 1982, 66]). By comparison, Candela is strong, sexy, angry, and dangerous.

How did such a potentially controversial song enjoy such wide popularity in Cuba's race-stratified society? Candela was the opposite, it seems, of the teatro bufo's favored negrito, the pedantic catedrático: Candela was the "negrito de rompe y raja" (streetwise/defiant negrito) who had no truck with social piety or any law beyond the street. Yet Candela was able to emerge only because he was most often performed on the bufo stage, right next to that insipid pedant. Next to the catedrático, the Candela of "El negro bueno" appears instead like another costumbrista portrait—a fascinating, "exotic" black curiosity from the colored neighborhood of Manglar, just beyond the official city limits. Candela's world, like that of the catedrático, was populated only by other blacks: the black women who couldn't resist him, and the "negros valientes" (brave black men) who dared not confront him. As long as Candela was not armed against white authority, he might be contained within the costumbrista frame. Defusing its implicit racial challenge, the frame of the teatro bufo left the song available instead for appropriation on broader cultural terms.

This might explain how this racially provocative song came to enjoy such popularity as a specifically "Cuban" anticolonial anthem in 1868. In his footnotes to the reprinted lyrics in 1963, Anton Arrufat noted that "El negro bueno" was one of the most popular guarachas of all time, originating in the teatro bufo of 1868, but also sung that same year by the revolutionaries (the *mambises*) on the battlefront [*Guarachas Cubanas* 1982, 66]. Emilio Bacardí confirms the anticolonial associations of the song, noting that in October 1868—the same month that war broke out in the Eastern provinces—the Bufos Habaneros toured to Santiago. Their visit was a great success, "siendo aplaudida con furor la canción 'El negro bueno,' que se tuvo como una especie de canto o proclama revolucionaria" (the song "El negro bueno" was applauded with fury, and was taken as a kind of revolutionary proclamation or chant [Bacardí y Moreau 1973, 50–51]). In this context, the defiant Candela was a racialized—one might even say blackface—image of the Cuban insurgent: armed, defiant, and ready to play the "somatén"—to sound the call, perhaps for war. To sing in the name and voice of "Candela," then, allowed for the expression of a particular way of being Cuban at this historical juncture. In January 1869, for example, the allegorical drama, *La vida privada* (Private life), published in the liberal newspaper *El Alacrán Libre* (The free scorpion), used the song as its stirring conclusion. The play is a rather stilted melodramatic portrait of a mother (representing the Spanish crown) who favors one son (Spain) over another (Cuba); the ensuing rebellion of the latter leads to the family singing "El negro bueno" in a semiconciliatory ending. Somehow, for this playwright, the confrontational blackface song seemed the appropriate ending with the power to resolve problems within the "private life" of this political family.

El Negro Bueno was also the title adopted by one of Havana's newspapers during that short period known as the "libertad de imprenta," or "freedom of the press," appearing on 7 January with the subtitle "con intenciones políticas" (with political intentions). The newspaper appeared days after the Spanish general Domingo Dulce, a former Captain-General of the island, was sent to replace General Lersundi to provide leadership against the insurrection. In a move seen by some as a preemptive, pacifying strategy, the General immediately closed the commission on censorship, and allowed greater freedom of the press and of assembly. Although the freedoms did not last long, cut short by the conflict at the Villanueva Theatre on 22 January 1869, the first weeks of January saw an efflorescence of expressive culture, in print and in performance, with more than seventy-five new newspapers appearing in Havana alone. The Bufos Habaneros, for their part, reprised "El negro bueno" in the honor of the general, who attended a bufo performance within a week of his arrival. Presumably in gratitude for the new freedoms, the Bufos revised the lyrics, which were published the next day in the newspaper *La Voz*:

Aquí ha llegado Candela
negrito de sociedad
gritando que se las pela
que ¡viva la libertad!
¡Ay, chinitica,
ya no hay reunión
porque quitaron
la Comisión!
¡Ay, chinitica,
qué vamos a hacer
si el hombre libre
ya tiene el poder;

y el pueblo entero
ya pué respirar
y con franqueza
contento gritar.
Que ya ha triunfado
el partío liberal.
Todo el pueblo reunido
repite con ansiedad
el grito dulce y querido
de ¡Viva la libertad!
No hay goce más lisonjero
ni de más intensidad
que ese placer verdadero
que brinda la libertad. (Leal 1982, 54–55)

(Here comes Candela
high society negrito
shouting that we're dying for it
long live liberty!
Ay, chinitica,
there's no meeting now
because they took away
the Commission [of censors]!
Ay, chinitica
what are we going to do
if the free man
now has power;
and the whole country
now can breathe
and with frankness
happily yell [*gritar*, or cry]
Now the liberal party
has triumphed.
The entire country gathered
repeats with anxiety
the cry, sweet and loved
of: Long live liberty!
There is no joy more gratifying
nor of greater intensity
than the true pleasure
offered by liberty.)

Candela, that "negrito de rompe y raja," streetwise and defiant, had been drafted to support liberal, reformist policies, and was thus redressed as a society-black, a "negrito de sociedad." The verse that claims that the people repeat the "grito dulce y querido de ¡Viva la libertad!" (cry, sweet and loved, of Long live liberty!) pays homage to Dulce's reformist policies, underscoring the people's loyalty with the pointed reference to Dulce himself in the phrase "dulce y querido" (dulce means "sweet"). Yet the same verse just as easily celebrates the more famous "grito" for liberty, the Grito de Yara, which had launched the insurrection only a few months prior. It was one of these *¡vivas!* from the bufo stage that sparked the Sucesos de la Villanueva just two weeks later.

Sucesos de la Villanueva

The day before those Sucesos, the Habaneros' producer, Luis Nins y Pons, launched his own newspaper entitled *Los Negros Catedráticos*, which listed the Villanueva Theatre as its publishing house and the now "liberal" Bufos Habaneros as correspondents. Like other quick-run periodicals of the day, the paper was a single, large sheet, folded to offer four pages of text. It appeared only one time, and its contents suggest in part why Spanish soldiers were out in force to police the theatre the following day. The paper's subtitle, "periódico físico, matemático y recreativo, con sus ribetes de político acusativo" (physical, mathematic, and recreational newspaper, with touches of political accusation) evoked catedrático language, which riddled the subsequent articles. The promised "touches of political accusation," however, gave ideological dimension to what otherwise might have seemed nonsense speech. The mission statement celebrated the new liberties, and deliberately exploited the political ambiguities housed in celebrations of freedom: "La libertad (de imprenta ó la que sea ó como cada cual la quiera tomar) ha sido la llave dorada con que se han abierto las puertas del año actual" (Freedom [of the press or of whatever or how each may understand it] has been the golden key with which the doors of the current year have been opened). The "golden key" may have been turned by Governor General Dulce in extending freedom of the press, or perhaps by the Spanish generals who deposed the existing monarchy, or by the insurgents fighting for "Cuba libre" in the east. The editors declined to specify: "Nosotros no nos metemos á averiguar secretos de nadie, y dejamos cada cual con su opinion" (We don't get involved in uncovering anyone's secrets, and leave each to his or her own opinion). Their own opinions, however, were mapped through winking double entendre and catedrático evasion:

Se ha dado el *grito conmovedor, consolador, inspirador* y todo lo acabado en *or*, y el fuego ha comenzado por disparar periódicos. No hay uno solo, periódico se entiende, que no huela á pólvora desde léjos, y el nuestro con mas motivo tiene que trascender á chamusquina por haber tendido muy cerca la *candelada.* [. . .] Liberales fuimos antes y despues de *catedratear.* Así, no hay que estrañar que hoy sin la mordaza que nos cortaba el *uso de la palabra verbal*, acompañemos á Quintero diciendo con toda la *fuerza motriz* de nuestros pulmones:

"Un viva por los que han muerto!"

¡Hurra por la libertad!

Políticos nosotros, hasta perdernos en los mas *recóndito* de los *círculos metafísicos*, [. . .] y libres como *el aire de los espacios circunflexos*, emitimos nuestra opinion sobre los que se nos antoje, aunque *frailes sopimperos* empleen toda su elocuencia por hacernos torcer la inclinación.

Quede, pues, sentado, que este periódico tambien es libre. Y existe hoy alguno que no lo sea? [. . .] En fin, ya nada nos queda que agregar. Nada prometemos. *Nuestros hechos nos justificarán.* [. . .] Ahora, lector, paga los diez centavos convenidos: *elévate al cubo del cuadrado* y sigue leyendo.

(The *grito* [cry] has been sounded, *moving, consoling, inspiring,* and everything ending in *ing*, and the firing begun by shooting out newspapers. There is not one, newspaper that is, that does not smell of [gun] powder from a distance, and ours has more reason to emerge with scorching, having been so close to the *candelada* [candle/candela; a reference to the "heat" of the insurrection in the eastern provinces, from which the Bufos Habaneros had just returned]. [. . .] We were liberal before and after being catedráticos. Thus, it should be no surprise that today, without the gag that cut short our *use of the verbal word*, we join Quintero[15] in saying with all the *motoring power* of our lungs:

"Long live those who have died!"

Hurray for liberty!

We are political, to the point of losing ourselves in the very *depths* of *metaphysical circles*, [. . .] and free like the air of *circumflexive space*, we emit our opinion on all those we please, even though *weak sopimperos* employ all their eloquence to make us turn our inclinations. Let it be a given, then, that this paper too is free. Is there one today that isn't? [. . .] Well, we have nothing left to add. We promise nothing. *Our deeds will justify us.* [. . .] Now, reader, pay the agreed ten cents: *square yourself to the nth cube*, and keep reading. [italics in the original])

The text drew on catedrático nonsense, combining and misusing the Latinate jargon of mathematics, philosophy, or philology ("espacios circunflexos," "cubo del cuadrado") for comic effect, along with the mock-braggart tone ("emitimos nuestra opinion sobre los que se nos antoje") so typical of these small political circulars, especially in their staged competitions with each other, as when the editors of this paper hold no fear of the rival "sopimperos," referring to the writers at the "republican" newspaper *El Sopimpero* (whose title, in turn, refers to a dancer of the "sopimpa"). This marked verbal ostentation housed, and perhaps was meant to obscure, language more explicit in its anticolonial sentiments than most. Although the celebrated "grito" was not named (was it the Grito de Yara, the grito that brought constitutional rule to Spain?), it was aligned with the well-known yearnings for Cuban independence of José Agustín Quintero, a poet associated with the generation of del Monte, exiled for a second time in 1868. The text insisted that the bufos had been "liberal," "political," and "free" all along; removing the "gag" of censorship allowed the sputtering catedráticos finally to say what they meant. Proof of their ongoing "liberal" edge was their proximity to the "candelada," a euphemism for the style that—like the protagonist Candela of "El negro bueno," and like the notion of being "candela" itself—was "hip," was "hot," and set the rhythm and pulse of its community. If the catedrático is mask, the "candelada" is soul.

The blackface characters of the teatro bufo, including "el negro bueno," each offered a contribution to the newspaper, translating their stage performances into the discursive blackface of print. El negro bueno offered an article complaining of his ill treatment at the hands of commercial theatre producers, who refused to give him credit or royalties for his music, particularly the now ubiquitous guaracha, "El negro bueno." El negro cheche, in turn, offered a song satirizing the sudden antiroyalist enthusiasm:

Cuando todo el mundo era
Hijo de la Monarquía,
Yo infeliz hijo del pueblo
Odiaba la tiranía. [. . .]

Me place que todo el mundo
Goze y grite sin desden;
Pues así los mas tiranos
Son liberales tambien.

(When everyone was
Son of the Monarchy
I, unhappy son of the people,
Hated tyranny. [. . .]

I'm pleased that everyone now
Enjoys and shouts without disdain
Because then the most tyrannical
Are liberal as well.)

Relaxed censorship still did not tolerate mention of slavery or the "race question" on the island. While the black(face) cheche did not state that his early hatred of tyranny was tied to racial inequality, we can assume as much: Nins y Pons was not the first to use the figure of the slave to illustrate the multiple oppressions of colonial rule, nor the first (as we saw earlier in the paper *La Mentira*) to pose the "race question" against calls for universal constitutional rights.

Either way, the black catedráticos of the newspaper assumed that they had earned such rights, and printed the proceedings of the first meeting of the "club catedrático etiópico" (Ethiopian catedrático club), presumably protected by the new right of freedom of assembly. The aged Crispín, one of the patriarchs from the play *Los negros catedráticos*, explained "freedom" to his comrades:

> *Indivíduos científicos y eméticos, catárticos, botánicos, dramáticos* de ambos *hemisferios* [. . .], la *libertad* de la *idea* del *pensamiento libre,* no es otra cosa que la *alegría universal, elevada al cuadrado en razón directa de sus masas y el cuadrado de las distancias,* segun las leyes de Newton y Kepler, sábios *anatómicos* de la *antigüedad de los tiempos pasados. Basandonos* en esta *base incombustible,* cada *ser existente,* que vive á manera de un *epitafio,* puede arreglar la *bóbeda celeste y terrestre* como mejor le parezca.
>
> (*Scientific and emetic individuals, cathartic, botanical, dramatic* from both hemispheres [. . .], the *freedom* of the *idea* of *free thinking,* is nothing other than *universal joy, squared in direct proportion (reason) to its masses, and squared by distance,* according to the laws of Newton and Kepler, wise *anatomists* of *antiquity of times past.* Based on this *incombustible base,* every *existing being,* who lives in the manner of an *epitaph,* can arrange *celestial and terrestrial silliness* as they please. [italics in the original])

Crispín was our first introduction to the catedrático figure of the "ciudadanito" or "little citizen," a figure important on the later bufo stage in the 1890s. The *ciudadanito* satirized black political discourse and the notion of black citizenship. For Crispín, "liberty" was the right to arrange "celestial and terrestrial" nonsense according to whim—a right he exercised to comic effect in this very speech. Like the ciudadanito of later plays, Crispín enacted his own lack of skill at republican citizenship even as he purported to embrace that citizenship.

Although continually marred by linguistic absurdities, Crispín nonetheless offered a pointed critique of police activity in the city. He called for a new company of "azulejos" (literally meaning "tiles," but evoking "blue ones"), who would be prohibited from lounging or loitering in the corner bodegas all day; they would instead walk a beat every two blocks from each other, and have a system for collaborating in keeping public order. Their bosses, Crispín said, would need to get up before noon. The "secretary" recording the speech interjected parenthetically, "Aquí dieron mil vivas á la libertad y se cantó el Himno de Regio" (Here they called a thousand ¡vivas! and sang [the Spanish Republican] Hymn of Regio). When Crispín suggested that the police should be assisted by elected auxiliaries, the crowd "lanzó *los sombreros cubridores de la cabeza* al aire, y cantó la Marsellesa" (threw their *hats for covering their heads* in the air, and sang the "Marseillaise"). Again the catedrático sliced its humor in two directions simultaneously: at the "Ethiopians" who had not mastered the script of Republican behavior, and at the colonial authorities, ill equipped to respond to the needs of the people, before and after granting them the right to express them.

When the "negro congo" José joined this fray, it was to express his bewilderment at the social upheaval of the times: "Po señó: la gente ta borotao; to la mundo ta cribí y hata la compañero mio, ese negro parejero que se lo ñama catierática, se lo ha mitío tambié in la jormiguero ese" (Well sirs: people are breaking out; the whole world is writing and even my companion, that black partner people call catedrático, has gotten into that same ants' nest). Under pressure from his father-in-law, Ancieto, José decided he too should make his voice heard. Thus José told a story of two friends, who were slaves, listening to a sermon on "lamo malo" or bad masters:

> —Vosotro lo que lo tiené criao, disia la pare cura, no se lo purá pa que trabaja ma de lo que su fuesa lo permite, poque eso so uno pecao. [. . .]
> —Cucha, compañero, disi uno de lo carabela, cucha que cosa ma güeno lo ta jabrando lo pare.
> —¡Uh, uh! contetá la notro: no laba hata que no caba.
>
> (—Those of you who have slaves, said the Father priest, don't pressure them to work beyond what their strength permits, as that is a sin. [. . .]
> —Listen, companion, said one of the fellows, listen to what good things the Father is saying.
> —Uh, uh! replied the other: don't talk until it's over.)

The narrative continued with the priest insisting that masters should provide for slaves, buy them clothes and shoes, reward loyalty, and allow them to attend their cabildos on Sundays. For each admonishment, the first slave expressed joy, and the second repeated his refrain: "no laba hata que no caba" (don't talk until it's over). Finally, the priest noted that if a slave was a "remolón" (a slacker), the master should beat it out of him. The second slave was thus vindicated: "ahí tá. ¡Qué se lo disia yo! No son bobo, carabela, acuédase oté de la sermon simpri y no laba hata que no caba" (There it is! What did I say! Don't be stupid, friend, remember the sermon always and don't talk until it's over!). The wiser slave knew to be suspicious of the moralizing sermon, waiting for the revealing moment of hypocrisy: the priest advocated ethical treatment of slaves, but never so far as to question the immorality of slavery itself. Given that critiques of slavery were still rigorously censured, this story was surely provocative. José immediately recuperated: "Caballero letor, di 'la Catieráticu', no vaya oté disí argo: ese no quié disí na: no son na ma que uno cuento pa que te lo ditraya uno rato" (Gentleman reader of "the Catedrático," don't go saying anything: this is not trying to say anything: it's nothing more than a story to distract you for a while). Because the paper's editor and authors fled into exile within days of the paper's publication, we cannot know whether this publication, with provocative tales like this one, would itself have earned censure.

The newspaper concluded with an announcement of the evening's performances. Most notable was the advertised new play entitled *Lo que vá de ayer á hoy, ó el destronamieno de una reina de cabildo* (From yesterday to today, or the dethroning of a queen of a cabildo). Surely no representation of the dethroning of a queen could fail to resonate with the recent deposing of Isabel II in Spain, making the connection between black and peninsular monarchies explicit. The play included a new guaracha entitled "¡¡¡YA CAYO!!!" (It/she/he finally fell!), which the newspaper explained was to be set to the music of "El negro bueno":

Ayer se dió mucho tono
Porque eterna se creyó:
Hoy mira en tierra su trono
Porque el *reinado tronó.*

¡Ay! ¡ya cayó! ¡ay! ¡ya cayó!

(Yesterday she gave herself airs
Because she thought herself eternal:
Today she sees her throne on the ground
Because the reign imploded [thundered].

Ay! she finally fell! ay! she finally fell!)

As with most of the references in popular theatre, this one was multiply voiced, literally referring to the fictional queen of the cabildo, obliquely referring to the Spanish monarch, and generally celebrating the fall of any authority, including perhaps, colonial rule. In the most immediate context, the exact phrase "¡Ya cayó!" had been circulating as a headline in the press for much of the prior week, in reference to the fall of the city of Bayamo to Spanish troops on 12 January. Bayamo had been the home of the revolutionary leader Manuel de Céspedes, and residents had burned the town to the ground rather than surrender to the Spanish. Most newspapers celebrating the fall of Bayamo were supportive of the loyalist cause; the bufo song recuperated the phrase for liberal or even insurrectionist ends, especially by setting the lyrics to the tune of "El negro bueno," already understood or viscerally experienced as a kind of Cuban political anthem.

On the twenty-second of January, then, bufo performance at the Villanueva became the site at which competing notions of liberty came to a violent confrontation. A few days before, the radical newspaper *La Chamarretta* had appeared with the provocative subtitle "Periódico que huele a machete y sabe a horquetilla" (newspaper that smells of machete and tastes of pitchfork) with this frankly anti-Spanish critique on its front page:

> Libertad: hé aquí la palabra pronunciada por todos y para todos, desde el Palacio hasta las mesas del Diario de la Marina y la Prensa. Sin embargo pocos han comprendido la estensión de esa palabra, en todas partes se oye el grito de "Viva Dulce" "Viva la libertad" ¿Que hemos ganado con eso? —Nada. [. . .] No queremos promesas, queremos hechos, queremos garantías. [. . .] ¿Qué quieren esos hombres que hace tres meses luchan en el departamento Oriental? Qué piden? libertad! No la palabra sino su significado; piden una cosa justa, una cosa puramente humanitaria, y si no se les concede diré yo con todos los defensores de ella nada con España, ni por España.
>
> (Liberty: here is the word spoken by all and for all, from the Palace to the desks at [the newspapers] *Diario de la Marina* and *La Prensa*. However, few have understood the extent of that word, everywhere we hear "long live Dulce" "long live liberty." What have we gained by this? —Nothing. [. . .] We don't want promises, we want deeds, we want guarantees. [. . .] What do those men want who have been fighting for three months in the east? What do they demand? liberty! Not the word, but its meaning; they ask for something just, something purely humanitarian, and if it is not granted, I will say with all of its defenders nothing with Spain, nor for Spain.)

La Chamarretta finally said the obvious: at stake in the mounting cries for "liberty" were not minor changes in censorship policy, but a redefinition of basic sovereignty and rights for the people of the island. On the second page of this inflammatory paper, was a "theatre note" that linked the Bufos Habaneros to this demand for liberty:

Se nos dice que el viernes se trata de dar una función en Villanueva, por los Bufos Habaneros, cuyo fondo se destinan para un fin muy laudable, esperemos que todas nuestras simpáticas amigas y nuestros leales compañeros contribuyan con su asistencia. No se permitirá entrar á quien no lleve un garabato ó una horquetilla.

(They tell us that on Friday they are planning a performance at the Villanueva, by the Bufos Habaneros, whose funds are destined for laudable ends. We hope all our sympathetic (girl) friends and our loyal companions will contribute with their attendance. Entrance will de denied to anyone not wearing a *garabato* [an S-hook] or an *horquetilla* [a hairpin; also means pitchfork].)

The *garabato* and *horquetilla* are references to gendered and politicized fashion: horquetilla, for example, likely referred to the particular hairpins used by women following the then new fashion of wearing their hair down, held only by a hairpin, as opposed to up in a bun. Because the hairstyle was associated with new "liberty" for women, it was at times associated with "revolutionary" behavior. *La Chamarretta* referred to it as wearing "pelo á la Céspedes" (hair in the style of Céspedes).[16] In any case, this newspaper linked the Bufos Habaneros and the Villanueva with financial support of the insurgents: over the weekend the Villanueva accordingly filled with supportive men and women (with their hair "a lo Céspedes"), along with increased numbers of suspicious, armed Spanish *voluntarios*. On Friday the Bufos Habaneros performed as promised; on Saturday, in the same theatre, the Bufos Caricatos took the stage. *La Chamarretta* recorded what happened: "Anoche se dió una función en el Villanueva, cuyos fondos se destinaban para un fin que todos saben, y no dejó de haber la concurencia numerosa que se esperaba" (Last night there was a performance at the Villanueva, whose funds were destined toward an end everyone knows, and the expected audience did not fail to attend [Leal 1982, 59]).

That Saturday night, the actor playing the character Matías in the play *Perro huevero* delivered the line "No tiene vergüenza ni buena ni regular ni mala, el que no diga conmigo [gritando] ¡Viva la tierra que produce la caña!" (He has no shame, not good, regular or bad, who does not say with me [shouting] Long live the land that produces the sugar cane!) Some sources reported that the actor delivered a different line, and instead said, "viva la *gente* que produce la caña!" (long live the *people* who produce the sugar cane!), thereby shifting the emphasis from Cuba as a place, to Cuba as a people. The *people who produce the sugar cane* might refer not only to the Cuban landowners, but also to all their workers—including slaves. Accounts differed wildly on what happened next, but all agreed that the voluntarios opened fire on the audience. Some, like the editorial in *El polizonte*, argued passionately that there was no expression of support for independence, or for Céspedes from the stage. Others, including the *El Noticiero de la Habana*, recounted an elaborate plan:

a mitad de función y a una señal dada desde las tablas por un cómico, se levantaron la mayor parte de los concurrentes, y entre ellos algunas señoras, que vestidas de blanco y azul, y adordandas de estrellas, se hallaban en los palcos, lanzando vivas a Cuba y a la independencia, seguido luego de algunos mueras a España e inmediatamente después, de varios disparos de revólveres. (Leal 1982, 64; *El Noticiero de la Habana*, 30 January 1869)

(halfway through the production, at a signal given from the stage by a comic, the better part of the audience stood up, among them some women who, dressed in blue and white and adorned with stars, were in the theatre boxes, launching "vivas" to Cuba and to independence, followed by "die" to Spain, and immediately afterward, by various revolver shots.)

Whatever did transpire after the "¡Viva!" from the stage, the shots fired into the audience brought the violence of the war to the capital, and ended the bufo theatre season of 1868.

In the immediate aftermath of the Sucesos de la Villanueva, as blackface figures vanished from the stage, blackface voices in the press comprised one of the few protests of the killings. One paper provocatively titled *Los Cimarrones* (The maroons), appeared for the first time on the 7th of February, ostensibly edited by two runaways, Quindembo and his sidekick, Pata de Jamón (literally, ham shank).[17] Their mission statement claimed to support "Libertad para todos, igualdad para todos, union y fraternidad con todos los seres de la especie humana" (Liberty for everyone, equality for everyone, union and fraternity with all beings of the human race). Quindembo complained, perhaps in response to the new circular on censorship, "Que mal estamos así, Sr. Pata de jamón, pues sabe V. camará que se conoce que estamos en *Cuba*, pues ni podemos menea ni la *pluma*" (How bad we are like this, Mr. Ham Shank, since you know, comrade, we know we are in Cuba, since we can't even shake [move/dance] our *pens*." This one phrase nicely captured the repression that followed the violence at the Villanueva: both performance and print were forced to stop "dancing." In one of the only humorous comments on the Villanueva killings, *Los Cimarrones* published this joke under the title "Escenas de Villanueva" (scenes at the Villanueva):

—No me mate voluntario yo gritaré lo que vuete quiere.
—Quien vive?
—España.
—Que gente?
—Sr. nosotros no somos gentes sino unos pobres islenillos que andamos paseando.

(—Don't kill me soldier I'll shout what you want.
—Who lives?
—Spain.
—What people?
—Sir we aren't people rather just some poor little islanders that were passing by.)

We do not know what happened to the editors of *Los cimarrones*, but no further issue appears to be extant. As the short window on freedom of the press closed, another paper tried to pay homage to the Villanueva deaths, and petitioned to use "Enero 22" (22 January) as its title; when the request was denied by colonial authorities, the paper appeared with the title *Titulo Borrado* (Title erased). It is perhaps fitting that it was the paper named *El Negro Bueno* that condemned the murders outright, in a lengthy editorial on the 4th of February: "*El negro bueno* considera," it began, "que no hay razón que autorice, ni disculpe siquiera el asesinato, ni el derramamiento de sangre humana" (*El negro bueno* believes that there is no reason that authorizes or excuses murder, nor the spilling of human blood). It seems that *El Negro Bueno*, Candela, the blackface hero, got a final parting word, as the bufos went into exile.

Chapter 3
Black(face) Public Spheres, 1880–1895

In 1893, Cuba's leading activist for racial equality and Cuban independence, Juan Gualberto Gómez, wrote in the black activist newspaper *La Igualdad*, "We want equality in all that is related to public and social relationships. We respect the prejudices that our [white] neighbors might encourage in their homes, which we will never enter. But in the common sphere we want the end of differences based solely on skin color" (Helg 1995, 39). In a later speech, he reiterated, "¿qué pide la raza negra de Cuba? Pues sencillamente la igualdad de derechos, y, con ella, la igualdad de trato en todas las esferas públicas," (What does the black race in Cuba demand? Simply, equal rights, and, with them, equal treatment in all public spheres [*La Igualdad* 10 May 1894]). Here as elsewhere, Gómez articulated one of the primary tenets of antiracist activism in the postslavery era: activism for equal rights focused not on ending white racism as such, but on gaining the legal and cultural sanction for blacks to participate in the public sphere of Cuban society at large. Gómez invoked an important social geography of race relations, separating a private, domestic realm that, he said, blacks would not enter (either because they were not welcome or because they had no interest in fraternizing with white racists), from the public sphere of "social relationships" to which blacks demanded full and equal access. If we worry, with hindsight, about Gomez's concession to white racism in the so called "private" sphere, it is not only because private racism refused, again and again, to be contained in the ostensibly benign space of white homes, but because the discourse around race was one of the foundational terms through which notions of public *and* private were determined in the first place. As became evident in the white backlash against the civil rights legislation passed in late 1893, the dominant conception of the public sphere was already developing as a sphere of white fraternal intercourse defined in part through the "common" experience of racial and sexual privilege.

The term "public sphere" appeared with frequency and passion in black activist oratory and press in the interwar years; that is, in the years between the end of the first unsuccessful war of independence in 1878 and the beginning of the second in 1895. Gómez's insistence on separating the public and private spheres is striking, not least because the notion of a "public" sphere was only just gaining currency for all Cubans in this period. The negotiated peace at Zanjón, which ended the Ten Years' War, in 1878, established key terms that shaped a new period of public expression and performance in Cuba. Concessions offered by Spain included the relaxation of censorship of the press, of the theatre, and to some extent of restraints on free assembly, along with new constitutional rights, including limited electoral representation in the Spanish Cortes. As a result, Cuba witnessed the development of a significant public sphere for the first time in its colonial history. Crucial to this new public sphere was the end of slavery, which occurred through a gradual process of "patronage" in 1880, and was officially over in 1886.

It is useful to engage the development of the public sphere in the sense lent to the term by Jürgen Habermas in his 1962 *Structural Transformation of the Public Sphere* (1991) and by his subsequent interlocutors Oskar Negt and Alexander Kluge (1988), along with Michael Warner (1993), Nancy Fraser (1993), and others. Although Habermas focuses on the emergence of a public sphere through bourgeois, liberal interaction in modern Europe, his notion is generative in the study of anticolonial culture, since it designates a site of discursive deliberation, negotiation, and imagination among "citizens" (or other social subjects) that is by definition distinct from the "official" discourse of the state or colonial apparatus, and distinct from the private realm alongside which it emerges.[1] Partha Chatterjee calls on us to account for the constitutive role of colonial and anticolonial contexts in the development of postcolonial nationalisms,and in this chapter, we will explore how notions of the public sphere are differently constituted under pressures of colonial dominion (Chatterjee 1993). In Cuba, this public sphere (or spheres, as was the case) was the site in which Cuban subjects gradually organized themselves *as* a public and publicly as "Cubans" for the first time. Those publics emerged in constant relation to and against official colonial discourse on the one hand, and internal codes of exclusion, which positioned women, people of color, and Chinese immigrants as nonsubjects, on the other.

This chapter will argue that Cuba's public sphere was not fundamentally *literary* in its logic. Instead, the technology of performance—of theatre, dance, and music and of impersonation, embodiment, and spectatorship—was central to the new Cuban "publicity" of the interwar years. The implications of such a contention are illustrated by analysis of two major forms of performance that emerged during the interwar years: the forceful return of blackface performance in the teatro bufo, beginning in 1879 and continuing unabated through 1895, and the sharply contrasting emergence of black social performances, known as *veladas*, sponsored by black mutual aid societies, which took shape by 1888 and also continued with increasing frequency through the beginning of the war in 1895. Both sites relied on performance as the central mode through which to conjure performatively a new "Cuban" public sphere.

Print and Performance

At first glance, nineteenth century Cuba seems to have followed the general model of most emerging communities in modernity—from the liberal bourgeois public sphere described by Habermas to the emergent "imagined community" described by Benedict Anderson (1991)—in so far as the period witnessed the sustained proliferation for the first time in Cuba's history of a print culture, primarily through a wealth of newspapers. Habermas describes eighteenth century Europe's "literary" public sphere as an "apolitical precursor to the political public sphere." Through this "literary" public sphere, "culture became a commodity and thus finally evolved into 'culture' in the specific sense (as something that pretended to exist merely for its own sake)." Thus "it was claimed as the ready topic of a discussion through which an audience-oriented [. . .] subjectivity communicated with itself" (1991, 29). In Cuba, literature provided a space for public reflection focused on the uniqueness of the island's own emerging national community. Costumbrismo was the *lingua franca* of this "literary" public sphere throughout the century, from the work generated by del Monte's literary salon in the 1830s through the renewed costumbrismo of the 1880s. Yet we cannot speak of the emergence of an actually existing public sphere until the 1880s; strict censorship and social control disabled anything but the formation of a clandestine and irregular Cuban community prior to the Ten Years' War.

The aftermath of the Ten Years' War saw a dramatic proliferation of newspapers, magazines, and other small publications. New political parties quickly adopted major newspapers as their "official" representation, and a host of smaller newspapers and revistas emerged devoted to literature, science, and customs, often combining an interest in these three. The press at times delineated a range of social positions and newly public identities: some were professional, with *boletines* devoted to associations of doctors, professors, or particular labor guilds, such as firefighters or *commerciantes*. Others addressed the interests and experiences of particular immigrant populations, including *El Ixuxu, Periódico dedicado a la Romería Asturiana* (El Ixuxu, Newspaper devoted to the Asturian Pilgrimage [romería]); *La Gaita Gallega* (The [Galician] bagpipe); *Eco de Canarias, Defensor de los Intereses Canarios* (Echo of the Canaries, Defender of Canarian Interests); and *L'Almogavar, Periódico Bilingue consagrado a los Intereses Generales de Cataluña* (L'Almogavar, Bilingual Newspaper dedicated to the General Interests of Catalonia). The emergence of the black press functioned in comparable manner: constituting a newly articulate social and political community through the interpolation of its literary address. Other serial publications were directed specifically at women, and to theatre, to sports, and to other specialized interests. As a whole, the papers textualized a complex social reality, allowing the emergence of an objectified self-representation and self-reflection impossible in any other form. "The public that read and debated this sort of thing," as Habermas says of the *Tatler*, but could equally say of new publications as varied as *El Fígaro*, *El Ixuxu*, or *La Fraternidad*, "read and debated about itself" (43).

The literal weight of the archival record might lead us to assume that Havana became an eminently literary society between the wars, but this is in part an archival illusion, one that neither captures the precise nature of Cuban print culture nor understands the relation print held to the other major "technology" of Cuba's new public sphere: performance. This period witnessed in particular the proliferation of new spaces for public gathering—cafés, social dances, baseball clubs, skating rinks, and, not least, theatres—in which performance was the favored mode of public interaction. In each arena, the social codes of access according to status, class, or race reiterated the presiding racial norms.

Dance comprised the backbone of Havana's social scene, for all classes and races. Cafés and theatres sponsored some dances, which charged admission and were almost always segregated. The venues that were not segregated were known then euphemistically as "arroz con frijoles" (white rice and black beans). The most famous were late-night *rumbas* held in the patios of private homes or at a local *solar*. Only the elaborate masquerade balls held during carnival, for which there were frequently all-white and all-black venues, rivaled these dances.

Baseball, brought to Cuba in part by exiles who returned from the U.S. at the end of the Ten Years' War, quickly became a favored activity. More than two hundred teams—either white or black, but segregated—were formed across the island, as were "exile" Cuban ball clubs in New York,

Philadelphia, Tampa, and New Orleans. Avid identification with local clubs promoted a sense of regional pride and enabled open pursuit of quasipolitical rivalries between teams; at the same time, the sport's popularity across lines of class and race seemed to offer, as Louis Pérez Jr. has argued, "the possibility of national integration" (Pérez 1994, 506).[2] Black ball clubs were the site of a discourse of racial pride and achievement within the larger national frame.

Theatre too, as we shall see, grew in thematic scope and aesthetic complexity, and the number of theatres operating in Havana grew substantially. The Villanueva was never restored, but the Albisu had joined the old Tacón and opened during the war, catering to distinctly Spanish colonial sensibilities.[3] The rival 2,500-seat Gran Teatro Payret (also called "La Paz" or "Peace" in honor of the pact at Zanjón) opened in 1877. The Ariosa, originally built as an art theatre by the Robreño brothers in 1869, was renamed Cervantes in 1874 when it switched to popular entertainments, becoming infamous for its showgirls. The Circo Teatro Jané was inaugurated in 1881, and the 1,640-seat Irijoa (later the famous Teatro Martí) opened in 1884. Meanwhile the smaller theatres Salon Trocha, Teatro Torrecillas, and Teatro Habana opened in 1877, 1887, and 1888, respectively. The Teatro de Verano and the Circo Metropolitano offered seasonal circus, equestrian shows, and other family entertainment. Finally, several Chinese theatres, catering to the Chinese laborers in Havana's boisterous *barrio chino*, were in operation during this period (Leal 1982, 77–80, 90–92,100–103, 106–7; Bonich 1933, 325–35).

Far from representing clearly distinct genres for social or aesthetic performance, these many activities more often developed in relation to one another: for a long time, an evening of social dance was the *de rigueur* ending for baseball games; cafés and theatres regularly hosted masquerade dances; skating rinks, newly popular with young women, were sites of social performance otherwise associated with more formal dances; and theatre spaces themselves were used by fledgling political parties, labor unions, and mutual aid societies from both the black and white communities as public meeting spaces. It is worth remembering too that the ostensibly "literary" press indulged in constant performative behaviors. Witness the penchant for pseudonyms, pen names, racial aliases, and role playing in the popular press; the use of dialogues and song lyrics as vehicles for editorial commentary; the use of countless created personas, and the invention of fictionalized and publicly celebrated rivalries between such personas writing for competing newspapers. The editorial press also had a penchant for writing in theatricalized voices (writing "black," writing "guajiro") much as Crespo y Borbón had done, capturing the nuances and idiosyncrasies of pronunciation or pace through phonetic spellings and italicized or otherwise highly marked text.

All of these genres of social or aesthetic performance showed persistent fascination with embodied "national" behaviors, and especially with practices of impersonation. This is perhaps owed to the fact that crossings between the press and theatre were frequent. Often bufo playwrights, who could rarely make a living on the limited royalties generated by one-act plays, also ran or worked for newspapers. The prolific playwright Ignacio Saragacha, for one, edited a newspaper devoted to the newly popular game of baseball, *El Sportman Habanero*, in 1882. Pedro N. Pequeño, founder in 1887 of *El Moscón, Periódico Político, Zumbón, Jocoseria y Agridulce con Caricaturas* (The Botfly, Political Newspaper, Buzzing, Comico-serious, Bittersweet with Caricatures), was the co-author of the third play in the *Negros catedráticos* trilogy in 1868, and the author of the 1882 blackface bufo play, *La africana.*

La africana illustrated the new social role that blackface performance would play in interwar years. Written in the full midst of Cuba's economic stagnation in the aftermath of the war, the play features two actor-brothers, Dima and Suárez, who complain that their traditional, lyrical guarachas (one of which opens the play) are simply not earning them enough money. Dima's reflections on their hunger and poverty offer performance as one antidote to anticolonial anger. Claiming that music helps him cope with his envy of the aristocratic life he sees in Havana, he says, "no envidio el infecundo / aristocrático manto" (I don't envy the infertile / aristocratic mantle [Pequeño 1885, 4]). Yet their new guaracha, "La muerte," which reminds aristocrats that death is the great equalizer, expresses their desire for revenge: "Tú tienes mucho dinero / dinero conque tirar: / yo metido en mi abujero / también me sabré vengar" (You have a lot of money / money to shoot with: / me, stuck in my hole, / I'll also know how to take revenge [5]). Unable to earn a living through their traditional music, and seeing the success of the new bufo actors Salas and Mellado (whom he later calls the "new aristocrats" of the theatre world), Dima decides that their only viable solution will be to form a bufo company, which, he believes, "que haga temblar á la tierra" (will make the world quake [6]). The ensuing discussion between Suárez and Dima places blackness and blackface at the center of their imagined success:

Suárez: Pero chico, si de bufos está la Habana que apesta.
Dima: Si lo está: de bufos blancos, que nada nuevo presentan.
Suárez: ¿Y somos negros nosotros?
Dima: Teniendo la cara negra

con el tinze que usarémos
no habrá quien se atreva
á registrarnos el cuerpo
para adquirir la certeza
si somos negros pintados
ó somos negros de veras.
Nos marchamos de la Habana
á poblaciones pequeñas
y regresamos gorditos
y con la bolsa repleta. (6–7)

(*S*: But man, Havana is so full of bufos it stinks.
D: Yes it is: full of white bufos, who present nothing new.
S: But are we black?
D: With our faces black
from ink we'll use,
no one will dare
check our bodies
to be certain whether
we are painted blacks
or blacks for real.
We'll leave Havana
for small towns,
and come back good and fat
with our wallet full.)

Dima decides to capitalize on the profitable formula already proven by Salas: Havana crowds will pay for blackface performance. But his "innovation" takes the formula one step further: rather than simply perform in blackface, they will make their own racial status intentionally ambiguous, tantalizing audiences with the intriguing possibility that they are a real black bufo company. No one—especially less experienced audiences in the provinces, they speculate—will be sure whether they are real or fake blacks, and so they'll bring home the cash. They enlist their friends to fill stock roles of a bufo company: the heroine/mulata, the drunk (played by an ostensibly "real" drunk whom they pull from a bar), and even the Galician policeman (el sereno), who will be played by their own "real" Galician servant, Domingo, who auditions by singing an "authentic" Galician song. Their friend Franco wins the role of the hero (the *galán*) by declaiming Spanish poetry, according to the stage directions, "en carácter negro y con gestos duros" (in black character and with rough gestures [13]). Dima notes that, in addition, he himself offers special skills in magic, to round out the company's talents and make their act more authentic; he studied magic under the tutelage of a real black *brujo* or witch. They conclude that all that remains is to find a suitable name. After rejecting such names as "Sociedad anónima" (Anonymous society) and "La risa" (The laugh), they decide on "La Africana" as the most compelling. Although their act will indeed reduce blackness to no more than a joke and an anonymous mask, they prefer to underscore their pretend Africanness. They propose to celebrate "Africa" in the song that closes the play:

No me asustan los cantantes
de todo el mundo bufón:
si hay moneda en el cajon . . .
¡Africa! fuego y palante.

Salga el sol por Rusia ó Nante
suene ó no suene el cañon:
si hay moneda en el cajon . . .
¡Africa! fuego y palante. (17)

(I am not afraid of all the singers
in the whole bufo world
if there's cash in the box . . .
Africa! fire and onward.

If the sun comes up in Russia or Nantes
if the cannon sounds or not
if there's cash in the box . . .
Africa! fire and onward.)

The song does not so much celebrate Africa as it does reiterate the certain connection between Africanness and hard cash in colonial Cuba. So long—but only so long—as there's cash filling the register, they will happily play at being African, regardless of other social or aesthetic trends.

The lesson offered by *La africana* is not that representations of Africa or Africans, credible or otherwise, will meet with popular and profitable success on the bufo stage, regardless of how much the play playfully indulges this idea. The actual lesson of *La africana* is that *impersonation* itself, especially racial impersonation, is what pays off: the actual performance of the play *La africana*, of course, involves no black actors or even Galicians, but is an ironic treatment of the notion of authentic performance itself, rendered through a dizzying array of doubled and redoubled racial impersonations. Here a white actor portraying a "real" drunk pretends he will become a white actor playing a black drunk; here a non-Galician white actor portrays a "real" Galician who imagines himself as a black actor playing a Galician in white-face. The fact that blackface performance pays off does nothing to change or challenge the racism that otherwise permeates the cultural environment. In fact, one of their concerns in picking an appropriate name for the company is that if they do not, the press will accuse them of conducting themselves like "real" blacks: "á fin de que no nos digan los periódicos diarios que hacemos las cosas como negros, es de prescindible necesidad bautizarla con un nombre característico" (just so the newspapers won't say that we do things like blacks, it's imperative that we baptize the company with a characteristic name [15–16]). The performance of Africanness in *La africana* does not present an allegory of racial integration and exchange in a new Cuba; performing blackness is simply the means through which Cubans like Dima and Suárez take their financial revenge on Spanish aristocrats.

The image of Franco mangling Spanish poetry through blackface performance, or comedic concerns about how theatrical "Africanness" will be represented in the press suggest another dimension of how performance organized the new public sphere in Cuba. Although the new publicity was organized around performance, its practices did not strictly exclude the "literary" as much as provide a means through which to engage (or take revenge) on notions of the literary and of literacy itself. Benedict Anderson has elsewhere been faulted for insisting on the primacy of literacy in the development of Latin American national identities, foreclosing as it does serious consideration of the important contributions of Latin America's many oral- and performance-based cultures to national self-imagination (Rowe and Schelling 1991, 25). The practices of the teatro bufo illustrate how white criollos used (fictions of) Afrocuban performance to organize their own national imagination, and thereby articulate a new, more useful relationship between performance and print.

Performing Politics

The political parties that emerged after Zanjón engaged this sphere through familiar forms, coalescing into separate conservative, liberal, and radical organizations. The conservative party, known as the Unión Constitucional, advocated a strong relation to Spain, governed through constitutional reform;

Cuba should be nothing less than a province of Spain, with the same rights and governance as the provinces on the peninsula. The liberal party, known also as the Partido Autonomista, supported autonomous, but not fully independent, governance for the island, so that Cubans would be primarily responsible for policy. These two parties were the primary competitors for the limited electoral representation granted to Cubans in the Spanish Cortes. Finally, radical calls for Cuba's independence were organized largely by veterans or patriots, such as José Martí in exile in New York or Madrid, Antonio Maceo, (who had resisted laying down arms at Zanjón, and was responsible for the Guerra Chiquita), and Juan Gualberto Gómez, the leading black civil rights activist of the day and future leader of the Cuban insurgents in 1895; these eventually formed the Partido Revolucionario, or Revolutionary Party. Each political party had at least one newspaper as its official mouthpiece.

Each of these ideological and political orientations was premised on a different understanding of the relation of race to nationalism, and as such, on different understandings of the social meaning of mestizaje. In the broadest strokes, conservatives tended to reinforce the division between the races, and understood their claims to Spanish political subjectivity to be based in large measure on their shared racial heritage and privilege with their Spanish brethren. For the Unionistas, then, mestizaje was an unwanted and often alarming dilution of the racial difference on which their personal and national identity was based. Liberal arguments for autonomy, on the other hand, engaged a social poetics of national self-definition that centrally evoked mestizaje—glossed as the unique offspring of Spanish and African culture—as the defining "structure of feeling," to borrow Raymond William's formulation (Williams 1977, 133), for an emergent sense of Cuban identity. As such, liberal Cuba frequently showed keen interest in black and mulato life and culture in Cuba, even as it was equivocal about, if not overtly hostile to, black civil rights or black political participation. Radical nationalism embraced an explicitly antiracist agenda, and understood "Cubanness" as the key to a post-racial social future.

Cuban nationalism emerged from the contest and interplay of both radical and liberal nationalism. If radical nationalism emerged in reference to the experience of interracial, male bonding on the revolutionary warfront, then liberal nationalism emerged in reference to the palpable realities of urban racial contact and conflict, particularly those surrounding interracial sex, in civilian life. If radical Cuba proposed a notion of nationalism based in the transcendence of race, liberal Cuba harbored a nationalism based in the experience of race itself. If radical Cuba proposed nationalism as the corrective answer to racism and race-based behaviors, liberal Cuba proposed race-based behaviors as the necessary precursor to the emergence of nationalism. Finally, if the former created a homosocial public sphere based on notions of fraternity, the latter cast women themselves—mulatas in particular—as the site for the very articulation of Cubanness; in either case, women themselves were definitionally excluded as participating subjects.

As such, the Cuban public sphere departs in principle from that outlined by Habermas. First, in Cuba the concern was at no time with "privateness" in the service of bourgeois individualism as it was in Europe or the United States. Emerging under—and in response to—the pressures of colonial exploitation, Cuban nationalism was not constituted by private individuals gathering "freely" as a public; rather, from the outset that public was constituted in part by its shared experience of exclusion from the political and social freedoms granted to peninsular subjects. In this sense, the Cuban public sphere is more akin to what Negt and Kluge have called "proletarian counter-publicity" (1988, 61) or what Nancy Fraser names "subaltern counterpublics." These counterpublics are "parallel discursive arenas where members of subordinated social groups invent and circulate counterdiscourses, so as to formulate oppositional interpretations of their identities, interests, and needs" (Fraser 1993, 14). To be sure, the protagonists of Cuba's public sphere were neither proletarian nor subaltern, bearing considerable privilege and power as predominantly white criollo males; it was the emerging black political activism, represented by such associations as Gualberto Gómez's Directorio or the black women's journal *Minerva: Revista Quinceanal de Mujeres de Color*, that created a specifically subaltern counterpublic, which both overlapped and contested the unspoken racial limits of the emerging "Cuban" public norm. However, the systematic exclusion of all Cuban-born subjects, across class and color lines, from direct power over their own affairs endowed the Cuban public sphere with its deeply oppositional character.

Bufos de Salas

"¡Ha llegado Salas con su compañía! . . . ¡Se salvó el País!" (Salas is here! . . . The country is saved!), or so claimed a local Cuban press commentator at the return of the teatro bufo actor-director Miguel Salas, whose Bufo company—called simply los Bufos de Salas—restored bufo performance to prominence after the war (Leal 1982, 210). A young member of the Bufos Habaneros during the explosive season of 1868, Salas had fled into uncertain exile—along with virtually all of the other bufo performers from that era—following the political violence of the Villanueva in January 1869. Relocated to Mexico, the Bufos Habaneros attempted a revival of their blackface fare in Mexico City in June 1869, with their signature play *Negros catedráticos.* Not surprisingly, they met with disastrous reception: this racially charged repertoire, so carefully calibrated to the sensibilities of Cuba's criollo class on the eve of anticolonial war, found no corresponding audience in Mexico of the late 1860s. Moving to the United States, Puerto Rico, or the Dominican Republic, the expatriate actors—including Francisco Fernández, author of *Negros catedráticos*; Jacinto Valdés, the revolutionary *guarachero* whose performance sparked the Sucesos de la Villanueva; Saturnino Valverde; and Miguel Salas—struggled against poverty in exile throughout the long Ten Years' War.[4]

The peace at Zanjón in 1878 allowed for amnesty of insurgents and their supporters, enabling the return of the bufos from exile. This new, uneasy peace—which lasted until 1895, interrupted briefly by Cuba's so called Guerra Chiquita in 1879–80—ended the decade-long suppression of bufo entertainments on the island. Throughout the war, the term "bufo" itself went into exile; after the explosion of "bufomania" in 1868, the sudden absence of the term in the press for the subsequent decade is striking.[5] Although *Cuban* blackface disappeared, there are periodic mentions of U.S. blackface minstrels on tour: for example, a "parodia minstrélica" (minstrel parody) entitled *La esencia de Virginia* (The essence of Virginia) in 1870; the Ainsleys performing *Los negritos del norte* (The negritos from the north); and Adams and Lee featuring *Los negritos musicales de Mississippi* (The musical negritos from Mississippi) in 1877. By mid-decade, the new teatro Cervantes partly filled the vacuum of irreverent humor left open by the bufo's departure: it was the Cervantes that offered comic opera bufa, most often Spanish in origin, and Spanish zarzuelas, with titles such as *¡¡Casa de locos!!* (Madhouse!), *El proceso del can-can* (The trial of can-can, discussed later), and *El último mono* (The last monkey). Only José Dolores Candiani, veteran actor of the Bufos Caricatos, continued to perform the bufo repertoire with some regularity during the war. Usually performing in small or amateur theatres outside of Havana, on the periphery of the watchful view of colonial authorities, Candiani reprised his cross-dress role as the comic, crass guajira of Juan José Guerrero's plays. The fact that his performance crossed lines of gender rather than race likely made his reappearance more palatable in a moment of tense civil disagreement, in which the question of race and slavery was paramount.

The return of the bufos under Salas certainly did "save" Cuban vernacular theatre, although not, perhaps, the country, from its desultory state. Beginning in 1879, the Bufos de Salas and their several rival bufo companies thoroughly revitalized the Cuban popular stage, and firmly established the teatro bufo as the predominant popular genre of the interwar years. Although one critic complained that all bufo plays were "reducido[s] á cuatro tipos y cuatro argumentos" (reduced to four types and four plots [*Don Circunstancias,* 17 July 1881]), the teatro bufo did indeed develop a far more complex and substantive repertoire of plays and dance music than it had in its first season in 1868. This period saw the emergence of at least three major playwrights: Ignacio Saragacha, who dominated the bufo stage from 1880 to the end of the century beginning with *Un baile por fuera* (A dance on the outside, 1880) and ending with his pro-Cuban critique of U.S. intervention in Cuba's final anticolonial war, *¡Arriba con el himno!* (Up with the hymn!) in 1900; the satirist Raimundo Cabrera y Bosch, who introduced frank political content into the teatro bufo, especially in his acclaimed *Del parque a la luna* (From the park to the moon [1888, 1975]); and José Maria de Quintana, whose immense theatrical production was specially notable for its delineation of the theatrical mulata.[6] These dramatists were joined by numerous actor-playwrights, including Miguel Salas himself and his frequent partner, Manuel Mellado y Montaña, whose play *Perico Mascavidrio, o la víspera de San Juan* (Perico Mascavidrio, or the eve of San Juan) was the hit of the 1881 season and became a Cuban standard.

For this new wealth of teatro bufo plays there emerged a number of important Cuban actors, remembered now as among the first to lend serious professional talents to an increasingly complex range of Cuban characters. Starring in Mellado's play, Miguel Salas popularized the figure of the drunkard, or "mascavidrios" (literally "glass-chewer," in the vernacular of the day). Salas also specialized in negrito roles; one viewer remembers him, in verse, as a "feliz imitador del negro congo / ante quien muda se postró la Habana / salvador de los bufos" (happy imitator of the negro congo / before whom Havana fell mute / savior of the bufos [*Don Circunstancias,* 21 August 1881]). Salas's popularity was such that at his benefit performance at the Albisu Theatre in 1881, one witness recounted,

> El teatro estaba que reventaba de *lleno.* Espectador ví sentado sobre una de los apartados del gas, por no haber dado con más cómodo asiento. Los corredores estaban cuajados de gente, y hubo *papá* que se vió obligado á tener sobre sus hombros á dos niños, que lo ménos pesarían, uno con otro arroba y medio. (*Don Circunstancias,* 18 September 1881)

(The theatre was so full it was ready to explode. I saw a spectator sitting on one of the gas boxes, not having found a more comfortable seat. The aisles were filled with people, and there were fathers obliged to seat two children on their shoulders, weighing between them an *arroba* and half.)

Manuel Mellado too was a popular actor; one contemporary remembers him as a "caudal de exactas observaciones de nuestro peculiar ambiente criollo" (cauldron of exact observations of our peculiar/particular criollo environment [Villoch 1946, 22]). Elvira Mireilles, the so-called "mulata rosa" (mulata rose) from the guaracha of that name, which she popularized, was the leading bufo actress, and regularly played sentimental mulatas, in brownface. She was often joined by Maria Valverde, whose performances were admired for their "candor y gracia" (candor and humor [*Don Circunstancias*, 21 August 1881]).

As with the bufos of 1868, the new bufos alternated blackface humor with a widening array of African-inspired dance and music. An initial run by the Caricatos Habaneros in late 1879 featured, over the space of several weeks, a reprise of *Los negros catedráticos*, *La suegra futura* (The future mother-in-law), *Un guateque en la taberna* (A celebration in the tavern), *De la tribuna al tango* (From the tribune to the tango), and even the formerly controversial *El perro huevero . . .* (Egg-hunting dog . . .); the guarachas "El negro bueno" (The good negro) and "Que te vaya bien, chinita!" (Hope it goes well for you, Chinita); along with new plays like *Una noche en un ingenio* (A night on the sugar plantation) and *Curros y lucumies* (both terms for "types" of black people);[7] and new musical pieces, with such titles as "Los negros rumberos" (the black rumba players), "La guabina," "La mulata rosa," "Los calseros" (the black carriage drivers), and "Los mangos."[8] By 1882, the Bufos de Salas performed a repertoire whose titles included *El negro*, the new catedrático plays *La duquesa de Haiti* (The duchess of Haiti) and its sequel, *La condesa del camaron* (The countess of shrimp, perhaps also a play on "Cameroon"), and *Los políticos de guinea* (The politicians from Guinea) with its guaracha "El negro candela," along with new guarachas "La mulata bailadora" (The dancing mulata), "La prieta santa" (The saintly black woman), and "La mulata María" (The mulata Maria). This latter was performed "in character," as guarachas about mulatas often were, by the young Miss Valle, the youngest in the company.[9]

The guaracha was soon joined by the danzón—a genre as electrifying to the population as it was controversial. A satirical dialogue in the press, ostensibly between a supporter and detractor of the teatro bufo, commented that guarachas and danzones were an "inprescindible necesidad" (indispensable necessity) for the teatro bufo: "Que el asunto pierde interés, guaracha salvadora; que el público empieza á bostezar, danzón al canto" (If the matter loses interest, savior guaracha; if the public starts to yawn, danzón to the rescue). The dialogue continued,

—Tambien á mí me deleitan esas preciosas producciones musicales, llenas de gracia, de dulzura y de un *no se que* que retrata esta apacible *dolce far niente,* característico del país. Pero no puedo ménos de censurar el excesivo abuso que de ellas se viene haciendo, que parece demostrar escasez de fantasía, falta de inventiva en los autores que emplean.
—Advierta usted, sin embargo, que como ellos llevan al teatro las costumbres de la tierra, y aquí se baila tanto, tanto. . . .
—Cierto; pero aquí no está bailando siempre, mientras que en esas piezas bufas baila hasta el mismísimo traspunte. (*Don Circunstancias,* 17 July 1881)

(—I too am delighted by those precious musical productions, full of good humor, of sweetness, and an I-don't-know-what that illustrates the mild *dolce far niente,* so characteristic of the country. But I cannot but condemn the excessive abuse of dance, which seems to demonstrate a lack of fantasy, a lack of imagination on the part of the authors that use them.
—Bear in mind, nevertheless, that they bring all the customs of the country to the theatre, and here we dance so, so much. . . .
—True, but here we are not always dancing, whereas in the bufo pieces even the prompter is dancing.)

Judging from reports of full theatres and high box office receipts, theatregoers did not share the critic's reservations. With its compelling combination of music, humor, and social delineation, the teatro bufo of this period became the foundation for virtually all popular Cuban theatre, dance, and music from that time forward.

The avid celebration of a humor, music, and dance distinct to the Cuban experience tended to align the teatro bufo with the emerging liberal view in politics, and its political party, the Autonomistas. Yet, as a genre, the teatro bufo was generally anathema to formal political affiliation. Its cultivation of *choteo* as a sense of humor and an irreverent attitude toward imposed order did not lend itself to representing any party line. As Loren Kruger's work on national theatres suggests, we should not assume a particular ideological relation between the generic structures of theatrical practice and structures of political formation, whether oppressive or revolutionary. Kruger, for one, believes that what is ultimately at stake for certain national theatres is cultural legitimacy; she analyzes national theatres in relation to parallel structures of political representation that helped legitimate the nation-state (Kruger 1992). In Cuba's anticolonial context, the teatro bufo differed from other "national" theatres, reveling instead in its "illegitimate" status. One late bufo play, *Los hijos de Thalía, o bufos de fin de siglo* (The sons of Thalia, or end of the century bufos [1896]) gleefully announced itself as a "desconcierto anti-literario, cómico-bufo-lírico-burlesco y mamarrachero, en verso y prosa" (an antiliterary dis-concertment, comic-bufo-lyric-burlesque and nonsensical, in verse and prose), and serves as one among hundreds of similarly impertinent and genre-bending examples. In this sense, the teatro bufo seemed closer to the "political party" outlined by the new costumbrista newspaper, *Don Circunstancias* (Mister/Sir Circumstance) in 1879, edited by satirist Juan Villergas and the famous caricaturist and lithographer Víctor Patricio Landaluze. Unimpressed by the formation of new political parties and the noise of their respective newspapers, the editorial figure Don Circunstancias proposed his very own party. "¿Cuál es, pues, este último partido, cuya denominación nadie conocè?" (Which is, then, this latest party, whose name no one knows?):

> Si lo dijéramos, guardaríamos floja consecuencia con lo prometido de este semanario. Si lo dijéramos, faltaríamos á la costumbre de las reservas de efecto, que se va introduciendo en el palenque de la publicidad. Si lo dijéramos, en fin, todo el mundo sabria tanto como nosotros, en el particular de que se trata, y á nosotros, ya que en otras materias sabemos muy poco, nos gusta saber en dicho particular más que todo el mundo.
>
> (If we were to tell, we'd hold the promises of this weekly in weak stead. If we were to tell, we'd lack the custom of keeping newsworthy items on reserve, to be dispensed in the arena of publicity. If we were to tell, in short, every one would know as much as we do about the detail in question, and since we know so little in other areas, we like to know more in this matter than every one else.)

The paper proceeded to argue that its nameless political party in fact won a majority in the recent elections, demonstrating through a chain of puns and jokes that the party believed in all forms of union, healthy constitution, and especially "conservaduria" or "conservatism," particularly when related to the conservation of eggs. In short, the satirical discourse favored nothing, and staked its social and political ground through irreverent humor.

Although *Don Circunstancias* abandoned its fictional party ultimately to align itself with conservative politics, in its way the teatro bufo carried on this party with no name. It treasured its brazen illegitimacy precisely because it contrasted so sharply with the ostensibly "legitimate" art of European drama, colonial opera, and concert performance, and called into question that theatre's corresponding aristocratic ideology. This is, for example, the central joke of Ignacio Saragacha's *Esta noche sí* from 1881, in which an aristocratic, opera-going husband and wife hide from each other their secret love affair with the teatro bufo. Manuela uses the occasion of her husband's visit to his brother to entertain Carmen del Valle, her favorite bufa performer, in secret. Her husband Miguel, in turn, has no intention of meeting his brother, and plans instead to attend secretly a performance by Valle herself. Trying to hide their mutual deception, the two exchange views on the teatro bufo:

Miguel: ¿A los Bufos? ¡Jamás! Yo contribuir con mi óbolo a esa profanación del arte puro, del arte . . . sano, ¡jamás!

Manuela: Tienes razón, amigo mío, no seré yo quien te aconseje semejante cosa; ese espectáculo tan a la moda hoy demuestra el grado de incoherencia en el cual esta modesta Babilonia, renegando sus dioses de otros tiempos, se entrega al desprecio de todas las convenciones que son la base inquebrante de las sociedades. (Aparte) Uf! (Sarachaga 1881, n.p.)

(*Miguel*: To see the Bufos? Never! Me, contribute my wealth to that profanation of pure art, of healthy art, never!

Manuela: You're right, my friend, far be it from me to suggest such a thing; the performances in fashion now demonstrate the degree of incoherence in which this modest Babylon, renouncing its gods of old, gives itself over to total disregard for all conventions that form the unshakable foundation of society. [Apart] Ugh!)

Their protests notwithstanding, both Miguel and Manuela cannot help but indulge their attraction to the new performance form. The implication of this bufo play is that even those who patronized the opera out of cultural arrogance or class obligation were nonetheless vulnerable to seduction by the passion and energy of the "profane" teatro bufo.

In its "exact" portraiture of Cuban customs and types, the vernacular theatre formed part of a wider discourse that mapped social life in Cuba through increasingly elaborate classificatory systems. Both a newly invigorated costumbrismo and the emerging practice of anthropology in Cuba were premised on the development of such social typologies, whether the more formal categories of race proposed by anthropologists, or the more anecdotal portraits of Cuban "types" offered by costumbrista authors or painters. It was not simply that, in an era of reduced censorship, Cuba's arts and sciences were able to draw increasingly articulate portraits of its cities and peoples; rather, the very idea of seeing and understanding social development, behavior, and identity through the revelation of orderly systems of social classification itself enjoyed new relevance and popularity in both popular and scholarly contexts. Thus, this period saw the much-anticipated publication of a new *Tipos y costumbres de la isla de Cuba* (Types and customs of the island of Cuba), illustrated by Victor Patrício Landaluze in 1881, and the publication of the full version of Cirilio Villaverde's celebrated costumbrista novel on the life and death of a mulata, *Cecilia Valdés, o la loma del angel* (Cecilia Valdés, or the angel's knoll) in 1882.

The new Anthropological Society, formed in 1877, understood Cuba as a rich microcosm of racial "types": the island of Cuba, noted one of the members, "es el país que en menos territorio contiene mayor número de razas así como de mestizos resultado de la mezcla de estas mismas (is the country that in the least territory contains the greatest number of races, as well as of mestizos, resulting from the mix of these [*Boletín de la Sociedad Antropológica*, 1879, 53]). In his inaugural address to the society, Dr. Luis Montané cast Cuba's racial "others" as the first priority for anthropological study and representation: "Dos razas con las cuales vivís íntimamente deberán en primer lugar ser objeto de vuestras perseverantes investigaciones: la raza negra africana y sus descendientes criollos, entre los cuales distingue el antropólogo notables diferencias y la llamada raza mongólica" (Two races with which you live intimately should in the first place be the object of your persevering investigation: the black African race, and the so called Mongol race). These races, he continued, presented "las múltiples variedades que caracterizan al género humano. Variedades anatómicas, psicológicas, patológicas, intelectuales, lingüisticas" (the multiple varieties that characterize the human species. Anatomical varieties, psychological, pathological, intellectual, linguistic [*Boletín de la Sociedad Antropológica*, 1879, 13]). The Anthropological Society aimed to understand these many "varieties" of racial formation, and did so with a decided local—and national—orientation: understanding racial difference and racial mixing in Cuba would be the Cuban anthropologists' own contribution to the otherwise European and metropolitan field of anthropology.

It is in relation to such discourses that we should understand the teatro bufo's growing "ajiaco" of "national" characters throughout this period. Salas and his company populated the stage with a widening gallery of blackface characters, including the by now familiar negrito, in both the bozal and catedrático incarnations. As the official end of slavery approached, the teatro bufo created a range of black male "criminal" figures, all of which would later find protagonizing roles in Fernando Ortiz's 1906 study, *La hampa afrocubana*, including *negros cheches*, *brujos*, *negros de manglar*, *negros curros*, and so forth.[10] In the theatre, as in the new fields of criminology to which Ortiz's early work belongs, each of these different black male "types" was associated with varying degrees of vagrancy, street crime, or other unsavory practice. New to the stage in this period was the mulata, a highly eroticized figure whose proliferation in the theatre—as in lithography, painting, narrative, and scientific discourse of the same period—made her the literal and figurative embodiment of Cuban mestizaje, replete with the complex anticolonial investment, racist panic, and nationalist desire that this implied. She was, as we shall later see, at once a pathologized figure of dangerous racial encroachment ("Africanization"), a miscegenating temptress, and a symbol of the innocent, tropical Cuba to be rescued from the lascivious Spanish imperialist. The negrito and mulata were gradually joined by the curious, comic figure of the *gallego* (Galician), almost always a heavily accented, white houseservant, and later the policeman, pining for the attentions of the demure mulata. In his 1887 play, *Perico*, the actor Manuel Mellado wrote into the script the commentary of a *bufo-guarachero*, who notes that in all plays written for the bufos, "se ha hecho una necesidad presentar un borracho, una mulata, el catalán de la bodega, ó el sereno gallego, por que son tipos que hasta hoy, han conquistado mas simpatías. (It has become a necessity to present a drunk, a mulata, the Catalan of the bodega, or the Galician policeman, because until now these types have conquered the greatest sympathies). Without these key ingredients, he says, "la medicina no da resultado (the medicine gives no results). The guarachero nonetheless insists that through these stock types, the teatro bufo was presenting "la verdadera comédia del país" (the true comedy/theatre of the country [Mellado 1887, n.p.]). Audiences agreed: by the early twentieth century, this cast had been refined to the triad of mulata, negrito, and gallego, which became *the* defining characters of the Cuban vernacular stage for decades thereafter. For Rine Leal the comic interplay among these three earned them the title of "tropical *commedia dell'arte* characters": a black Harlequin, mulata Columbine, and white immigrant Pierrot (Leal 1975a, 17). This competition between two men—one black, one white; one African, one Spanish—over the sexual favors of a biracial island-born woman clearly carries out an ongoing and heightening discourse of colonial contest and nationalist longing.

Engaging the representational range of both anthropology and costumbrista letters, the teatro bufo of the 1880s offered a popular ethnographic elaboration of the aesthetics of everyday life: the rich cacophony of sounds of a Havana *solar*, a typical urban, poor tenement built around a communal patio; the languid sense of time on an afternoon street corner; the pace of a mulata strolling; the intensity and heat of fiesta on a rural bohío (palm hut, typical slave housing on sugar plantations); and even the peculiar shape, flavor, and pronunciation of the tropical *quimbombó* or *aguacate* (okra or avocado). More than replicate scenes of daily life, the teatro bufo's costumbrismo reframed these elements within a national optic, allowing one to see each element as part of a related and systemic fabric of national culture. In José Tamayo's parody, *Traviata, o la morena de las clavelinas* (Traviata, or the mulata of the carnations, no date, probably late 1880s), a brownface parody of the *La traviata*, itself a retelling of the Lady of the Camelias, for example, the *quimbombó* that overwhelms the mulata protagonist is not just tasty or tropical but explicitly "Cuban"; it is as (ostensibly) "Cuban" as the mulata herself, who is revived by the rhythm of an equally Cuban danzón. The fanciful, and sometimes ironic, tone of these national self-representations adds, rather than detracts, from their power as sites for nationalist discourse: tongue-in-cheek irony itself, in the form of what Cubans were then just beginning to call choteo, was itself a celebrated feature of the newly emergent cubanía.[11] It is no exaggeration to say the teatro bufo did more for the development of a pleasurable, palpable—lived, embodied—sense of cubanía than any other single activity in the years leading up to the final war of independence in 1895.

Salas thus "saved the country," in addition to the theatre, by saving and elaborating a "structure of feeling" of a Cuban national community before the social and political conditions for such nationhood had emerged. This is what essayist and playwright Federico Villoch, a young man in the days of the Bufos de Salas, illustrated in his remembrance of the popular theatre, written in 1946. The era of the Bufos de Salas, he wrote, was one in which "el alma criollo se expansionaba [. . .] hasta lo indecible oyendo sus guarachas y sus canciones, y riéndose hasta perder el aliento con sus dicharachos y chistes de sus tipos populares" (the criollo soul expanded beyond description hearing its own guarachas and its songs, and laughing until out of breath with its own word-plays and jokes from its popular characters). For the first time in memory, he noted, Havana was home to "un teatro lleno todas las noches de bote en bote meses y meses" (a theatre chalk full every night, month after month). For Villoch, the teatro bufo evoked deep affection precisely because it enabled a feeling of national community: the teatro bufo "ha quedado viva y latente en el recuerdo de los antiguos habaneros" (has remained alive and latent in the memory of older Havana residents). In a remarkable formulation, he said that "Se la recuerda con más fijeza y cariño siendo como *un adelanto a cuenta de Cuba Libre, . . .*" (We remember it with more clarity and affection *as an advance credit on Free Cuba*, italics mine). This theatrical, virtual, and borrowed "Cuba Libre" was manifested, he recalled, in

> la honda emoción que estremecía al público apenas se hacía en escena la más ligera alusión al ideal de independencia; los estruendosos aplausos que se le tributaba apenas aparecía un tribuno popular en el teatro; el regocijo que se experimentaba viendo en escena un bohío, una carreta cargada de caña. (Villoch 1946, 23)
>
> (the deep emotion that shook the public at the slightest allusion on stage to the ideal of independence; the thundering applause [provoked by] the mere appearance of a popular public figure in the theatre; the joy one experienced seeing a bohío on stage, an oxcart filled with sugarcane.)[12]

The teatro bufo's imaginative recombination of topical jokes, fictional sugar plantations, and real political figures, along with intoxicating music and dance created a palpable experience of national community—but one that was nonetheless decidedly virtual, a "credit" against the Free Cuba yet to come. In Villoch's testimony, then, theatre was the site of enormous nationalist "cariño" or affection—an emotion that Timothy Brennan elsewhere calls "national longing" and Benedict Anderson has called "political love" (Brennan 1990, 44–70; Anderson 1991, 143). If Villoch experienced the teatro bufo as "advance credit" on a Free Cuba yet to come, then bufo plays (such as Pequeño's *La africana*) make clear that blackness and black Cubans are the real currency that underwrites that loan.

Performing *Fraternidad*

"En la noche, en la memorable noche del 12 de Julio, hemos arrojado el guante á la faz de aquellos que con tanto *cinismo* y desenmascarada *maldad* afirman [. . .] que todavía no hemos ni siquiera tocado a las puertas del progreso" (On that night, that memorable night of the 12th of July, we threw down the gauntlet against those who with *cynicism* and unabashed *ill-will* insist [. . .] that we have not so much as knocked on the doors of progress [italics in the original]). So wrote the black Cuban exile Pedro D'Aguirre from Panama to the activist newspaper *La Fraternidad* (Fraternity) in the fall of 1888. The night in question—12 July 1888—marked the first so-called velada or "soirée" for the black community held in Havana, which featured an extensive evening of performance, including oratory, poetry, and a three-act drama, along with original classical music, and hours of social dance. Called the Velada Gómez-Fraternidad, the performance was a benefit to support the black patriot and civil rights leader Juan Gualberto Gómez in exile in Spain, and a demonstration of black unity, combining the efforts of the black press and several leading black mutual aid societies. Held only two years after the official end of slavery, this night of elegant performance revealed for D'Aguirre and others that, despite continued white resistance to supporting black education and black integration in the larger public sphere, black Cuba nonetheless excelled at white Cuba's most valued measures of "culture" and "progress"—the performing arts. Like Villoch before him, D'Aguirre sees in the theatre a portal to a better future. "Orgullosos debeis estar" (You should be proud), wrote D'Aguirre, "por haber colocado la primera piedra angular del magnifentísimo monumento de nuestra dignificación" (for having placed the cornerstone of that magnificent monument to our dignity [*La Fraternidad*, 20 October 1888]).

The letter itself lends insight into the central dynamics of the Cuban black public sphere that emerged between abolition in 1886 and the beginning of the final war for independence in 1895. First, D'Aguirre's letter makes clear that the black public sphere exceeded the boundaries of the island; newspapers like *La Fraternidad* and its counterpart, *La Igualdad* (Equality), maintained an extensive community of predominantly black Cubans, which encompassed a local audience as well as a network of Cuban exiles throughout the Caribbean and Central America, and in New York, Tampa, Miami, and Madrid. A strong commitment to an international, particularly hemispheric, black community informed much reporting; features explored the state of black Americans in the United States, Haiti, Jamaica, or elsewhere in the Caribbean and Central American region, often comparing quality of life, political successes, or continued racial oppression with conditions in Cuba. At the same time, nationalist and anticolonial sentiment saturated the editorial pages of this black press: throughout the period, black patriot-intellectuals used performance and the press to advocate for a racially integrated Cuban national future (see Ferrer 1999, chapter 5; Deschamps

Chapeaux 1963). The fact that the veladas were marshaled in support of both these aims—Cuban nationalism and black solidarity—made them a site for authentic "fraternidad," as a newspaper editorial argued:

Esta es la verdadera solidaridad de intereses que debe existir y nunca olvidarse entre los hombres de color cubanos; sin olvidar tan poco que esa solidaridad de nuestros intereses no excluye, antes al contrario, impone de manera imprescindible, otra solidaridad: la de los intereses de la patria que son communes á todos sus hijos. (*Fraternidad*, 9 July 1888)

(This is the true solidarity of interests that should exist and never be forgotten among Cuban men of color; without forgetting either that this solidarity of our interests does not exclude—to the contrary, it imposes in an indispensable way—another solidarity: that of the interests of the nation, which is shared will all her sons.)

Thus, the public that was both constituted and represented by these performances and the press evinced both a black transnational solidarity, as well as a transracial national solidarity.

The veladas became a regular and vital feature of the black public sphere in Cuba from 1888 through the beginning of the war in 1895. Almost always hosted by a mutual aid society to benefit its social work or to fund a particular initiative—the building of a school, for example—these performances were directly tied to the progressive development of the community. The veladas were ambitious, involving hours of oratory, music, and theatre, followed by social dance well into the night. The full—and very lengthy—program for the Velada Gómez-Fraternidad is revealing:

Primera Parte (First Part)

1. Abertura á gran orquesta, dirigido por el Sr. Raimundo Valenzuela (Opening, with full orchestra, directed by Mr. Raimundo Valenzuela)
2. Discurso por el Sr. D. Enrique José Varona (Oratory by Don Enrique José Varona)
3. Poesía por el Sr. Gerardo Betancourt (Poetry by Mr. Gerardo Betancourt)
4. Poesía por el Sr. D. Ancieto Valdivia (Poetry by Don Ancieto Valdivia)
5. Poesía por el Sr. D. Felipe López de Briñas (Poetry by Don Felipe López de Briñas)
6. Discurso por el Sr. D. Miguel Figueroa (Oratory by Don Miguel Figueroa)

Segunda Parte (Second Part)

1. Primer Acto del drama en tres actos, originales del modesto poeta y educador de la juventud de color, Sr. D. Antonio Medina y Céspedes, titulado: (First act of the drama in three acts, an original play by the modest poet and educator of the youth of color, Don Antonio Medina y Céspedes, entitled:)

   Jacobo Girondi, con el siguiente reparto: (Jacobo Girondi, with the following cast:)

Isabel, hija de . . . (daughter of)	Sta. (Miss) Medina, C.
Pietro, pintor (painter)	Sr. (Mr.) Valdés, N.
Jacobo	Sr. (Mr.) Medina, M
Rodolfo, conde (count)	Sr. (Mr.) Medina, A.
Lorenzo, criado (servant)	Sr. (Mr.) Flores, J. V.
Enriqueta, criada (servant)	Sra. (Mrs.) Corujo, A.
Gerónimo, bandido (bandit)	N. N. (no name)
Salvador, ídem (the same)	N. N. (no name)

   Título de los actos: 1. Los Rivales, 2. El rapto, 3. El padre y el hijo (Title of the acts: 1. The rivals, 2. The kidnapping, 3. The father and the son)
2. Rondo Caprichoso para piano, ejecutado por la Señorita Momoytio—Mendelssohn (*Rondo Caprichioso* for piano, played by Miss Momoytio —by Mendelssohn)
3. Fantasía para clarinete, por el Sr. José de Jesús Ponte (Fantasia for clarinet, by Mr. José de Jesús Ponte)
4. Nocturno num. 2, op. 9, por violín y piano, por los Sres. Cuevas y Falcón —Chopin (Nocturne, num. 2, op. 9, for violin and piano by Misters Cuevas and Falcón—by Chopin)

Tercera Parte (Third Part)

1. Segundo acto del drama (Second act of the drama)
2. Concierto, op. 16, para violín y piano, por los Señores Arango y Falcón —Berliot (Concert, op. 16, for violin and piano, by Misters Arango and Falcón—by Berliot)

3. Romanza para violín con acompañamiento de cuarteto, por los Sres. Pacheco, Valenzuela, Valdés, Isla, Jimenez (hijo)—White (Romance for violin, with accompaniment by quartet, with Misters Pacheco, Valenzuela, Valdés, Isla, Jimenez (junior)—by White)
4. Fantasía sobre motivos de la ópera *Sonambula*, para clarinete y piano, por los Sres. Valdés y Falcón—Caballini (Fantasia on the opera *Sonambula*, for clarinet and piano, by Misters Valdés and Falcón—by Caballini)
5. Capricho para violín, por el Sr. Arrondo—Prune (Caprichio for violin, by Mr. Arrondo—by Prune)

Cuarta Parte (Fourth Part)

1. Acto tercero de la drama (Third act of the drama)
2. Sinfonía en Sol á dos violines y piano por los Sres. Arango, Vazquez, y Falcón (Symphony "en Sol" for two violins and piano by Misters Arango, Vazquez, and Falcón)
3. La chistosa comedia en un acto, original de Sr. D. Mariano Pina, titulada: (The funny comedy in one act, an original play by Don Mariano Pina, entitled:)

   La novia del general, con el siguiente reparto (*The General's Girlfriend*, with the following cast:)

Eladia	Sra. (Mrs.) Teresa Montes de Rodriguez
Martina	Sra. (Mrs.) Dominga Pajés
Alfredo	Sr. (Mr.) Pascual Hernández
Gregorio	Sr. (Mr.) Ambrosio Labastida
4. BAILE (Dance)

Much can be said about this extensive program, involving more than twenty-five different performers over what must have been hours of performance. Although the genres of performance are varied, they are drawn from a repertoire normally associated with European "high art": not just music, but classical German and Italian composition; not just any instruments (and definitely not instruments associated with African Cuba), but violin, piano, and clarinet; not just theatre, but a three-act serious drama; and so forth. Reviews in the black press of later veladas show considerable attention to the quality of performance, particularly to the arts of speech: pronunciation, diction, intonation, and so on.[13] Having so long suffered ridicule for "improper" black speech, the veladas were also an occasion to model "proper" speech and demonstrate beyond reproach black skills in oratory.

Overall the veladas offered an opportunity to showcase the talents of black actors and musicians. At this first velada in 1888, the orators, poets, and playwrights, however, were almost all white, as indicated by use of the term "Don" before their names. The legacy of slavery had, it seems, still left its racial imprint on the practice of "literate" culture; the veladas of 1893 and 1894, by contrast, showed a wider range of writers and orators, and began regularly to include women of color as well as men. The white orators of the first velada were important advocates of the black cause in Cuba. Enrique Varona was one of Cuba's foremost intellectuals, an early champion of positivist philosophy and education in Cuba, supporter of early anthropological research (as we shall see in a later chapter), and ultimately a key member of the independence movement—he would subsequently serve as vice president of the republic from 1913 to 1917. Miguel Figueroa was a well-known lawyer and diplomat, deputy to the Spanish parliament, and an outspoken advocate first for abolition and later for Cuban autonomy. The presence of these respected white leaders conferred prestige and legitimacy on the event, marking an important solidarity between black and white political interests on the island. On his return from exile, José Gualberto Gómez was by far the favored orator at these events, but the overall formula did not vary: the veladas always began with explicitly political or activist speeches, thus framing the rest of the performances of classical music or poetry, integrating them as part of that larger cause.

At this velada, Enrique Varona placed the event in the context of historic black struggle: "¿Quién hubiera podido soñar hace cuarenta años que habíamos de estar celebrando esta fiesta?" (Who would have dreamed forty years ago that we would be holding this celebration?). The account of his speech printed in *La Fraternidad* noted repeated "aplausos prolongados" (prolonged applause) as Varona lauded the struggle against slavery, linking it to the martyrdom of black soldiers in the war of independence. Despite the "ruinous" chains of slavery, said Varona, "a pesar de todo esto, de allí, [. . .] se levantó la obra ¡la obra santa! de aquella generación de mártires; de allí se levantó,"—he said in crescendo—"de allí surgió la redención de vuestra raza, vuestra libertad, ¡Oh negros cubanos!" (despite all this, from there [. . .] arose the work, the holy labor! of that generation of martyrs; from there arose, from there emerged the redemption of your race, your liberty, Oh black Cubans!). The rousing speech confirmed the bond between antiracist and anticolonial projects, and celebrated the assembled audience not only as black, but also as Cuban. At a historical juncture when progressive Cubans were, as Varona put it, "profundamente disgustados por el espectáculo de nuestra vida social" (profoundly upset by the spectacle of our social life), the veladas provided a space not only of well-earned repose, but also "casi de esperanza" (almost of hope). As a demonstration of black talent and development, the network of performances assembled at the veladas continued to function as sites of hope against the odds, seeding hope for the future of the race and the country.

Aline Helg and Ada Ferrer seem to contradict the notion that performance was central to the development of this black Cuban public sphere by illuminating the importance of the press and a literary sphere for black anticolonial and nationalist practice in this very period. Yet both note that literacy was very low for both blacks and whites across the island: only 35 percent of whites and 12 percent of blacks could read or write in 1887. In Havana those numbers climb to 70 percent of whites and 28 percent of people of color (Ferrer 1999, 116). With reference to the black community, Ferrer argues that the press nonetheless had a wider influence than the numbers suggest: the *pregones* (the street calls) of newspaper vendors shared the contents of the papers with nonliterate passersby; literate members often read the papers publicly to audiences at their mutual aid societies; many of the articles were transcriptions of speeches, spoken poems, and other forms of public oratory (often first delivered at the veladas); and tobacco workers had books, articles, and poems read aloud to them as they worked by so-called *lectores*. All of this evidence, while compelling, affirms that the encounter with "literature" (whether the press, autobiographies, or serial novels) was often mediated through performance, rather than conforming to our contemporary notions of reading.

Through both "literary" performances and a "performative" press, Gómez and his colleagues sought to define a Cuban public imaginary that was grounded first in an ethic of fraternity, as he explained in an editorial in *La Fraternidad* about the importance of the paper's title. "Fraternity" referred both to fraternal solidarity among people of color, and to fraternity between whites and blacks on the island. Gómez himself was largely responsible for advancing a collective notion of a "raza de color" (literally, race of color) that could unite blacks in Cuba in a common cause against racism and the legacies of slavery. The long history of slavery, he argued, itself produced palpable and crucial differences between whites and blacks:

No ya sólo diferentes por el color de la piel, sino diferentes por la procedencia, por la cultura, y por los medios de vida, por el órden político y jurídico a que respectivamente estaban sometidos, ¿quién puede extrañarse de que la separación entre ambos grupos étnicos haya sido tan real en lo pasado como resulta en el presente? (*La Igualdad,* 15 September 1890)

(Now not only different in the color of skin, but different by provenance, by culture, and by the means of life, by the political and juridical order to which each was respectively submitted, who can be surprised that the separation between both ethnic groups was as real in the past as it is in the present?)

As another activist wrote, "los hombres de color deben más que nunca hermanarse, fraternizar [porque . . .] todos los negros en Cuba participamos de las mismas desgracias" (now more than ever, men of color must become brothers, must fraternize, [because . . .] all blacks in Cuba participate in the same ill fortune" [*Igualdad,* 2 December 1893]). Gómez had founded the Directorio Central de las Sociedades de Color (Central Directory of Societies of Color) to consolidate the resources and political power of Cubans of color.

At the same time, Gómez hoped that relations of equality and fraternity between all Cuban men, white and black, would eliminate race and create a radically new form of social fraternity. "From the instant that differences in the public and social spheres do not exist between whites and blacks," an editorial from the Directorio wrote, "there will not exist the organization of a race." Toward that end, the leadership of the Directorio advocated for and eventually won crucial concessions from the Spanish colonial government in December 1893 that ended official racial segregation in public life in Cuba by granting blacks equal access to all areas of theatres, cafés, and public parks; by integrating public schools; ending the practice of separate official birth rolls for people of color; and granting blacks equal access to the courtesy titles "Don" and "Doña," which had previously been reserved for whites only. Acting in the name of "la raza de color," Gómez understood activism *based* on race as a key step toward the *eradication* of race as we know it: "the man of color will consent to live in order to give birth to a man without adjective. In this supreme hour," the editorial stated with optimism, "the gravest Cuban problem will be satisfactorily resolved" (Howard 1998, 198–99).

The theatre proved especially difficult to wrest from the white supremacist ideology that had until then organized its use. Days after the passage of the new civil rights legislation, *La Fraternidad* and *La Igualdad* began to record instances of white resistance to the law. At the Teatro Tacón, wrote *La Igualdad* on 2 January, several black women bought tickets with seats in the "tertulia," or the balcony seating; the usher refused to seat them, directing them instead to the "cazuela" or the highest balcony, formerly reserved for black patrons. The women demanded return of their money and left. In Cienfuegos, the president of a well-known mutual aid society, pointedly referred to as *Don* Nicolás Valverde, went to the elegant Teatro Terry with several others, also people of color. "Apenas ocupó su luneta" (He had barely taken his orchestra-level seat), wrote a witness to *La Igualdad* on 6 January, when "empezaron a circular por la sala rumores de hostilidad, rumores que fueron creciendo haste que se condensaron y desataron en gritos desaforados de ¡fuera los negros! ¡fuera Valverde!, promoviendose con tal motivo un gran escándalo" (there began to circulate throughout the hall rumors of hostility, rumors that kept growing until they condensed and exploded in unabashed screams of "out with the blacks! out with Valverde!," thereby causing a great scandal). Valverde wished to hold his ground, but the (white) police finally intervened, insisting that he leave "for his own safety." In Matanzas, meanwhile, black patrons were boycotting the Teatro Estéban, since a group of threatening "*preocupados*" (preoccupied ones), as resistant racists were euphemistically called, had prevented black people from taking preferential seats. When a freemason lodge named "Los Puritanos" (The Puritans) planned a benefit performance at the Teatro Estéban, their members announced that people of color would be welcome in all seats of the theatre; however, a newspaper also announced that people of color themselves "procediendo con una sensatez y buen juicio [. . .] han decidido ocupar las localidades altas para que nadie pueda decir que ellos han contribuído á ahuyentar del teatro á los escrupulosos y timoratos," (proceeding with a sense and good judgment [. . .] have decided to occupy the high balcony seats so that no one can say they have contributed to the departure from the theatre of the scrupulous and timid [*La Igualdad*, 17 April 1894]). The report was, as many black Matanzas residents would attest, entirely false, but designed to persuade people of color not to jeopardize the proceeds. As the white press swelled with complaints and protests from white "preocupados," the black press similarly swelled with evidence of continued racism and lack of compliance with the law.

Only a few months after Gómez's landmark civil rights legislation, the teatro bufo answered with the play *Con don, sin don, ayer y hoy* (With Don and without Don, yesterday and today [1894]), written by Laureano del Monte (a preocupado of great proportion), which was a deeply racist blackface satire of Gómez, the directorio, their legislation, and their celebrated veladas. As the title suggests, the play proposed a review of recent Cuban history, analyzing the social place of blacks with and without access to the courtesy title "Don" and "Doña." The first two scenes, "yesterday," are set on a plantation in 1850, and those of "today" are of contemporary black social life. Each scene is a scenario in which black protagonists have the opportunity to prove their social or moral standing; this scathing play, more reactionary than any in the teatro bufo repertoire, presents a catalogue of their failures, in which the black characters, almost all men, only prove their unworthiness—yesterday, today, and presumably tomorrow—to share in the social or moral standing that the term "Don" designates for whites. It does so by holding blacks—rather than whites—morally accountable for slavery, abuse, and social arrogance.

If radical black leaders presented citizenship as a new social discourse that would transform and transcend Cuba's racism, the anxious white response in the teatro bufo turned this notion against itself: race consciousness and citizenship were presented as mutually exclusive, but only to recuperate citizenship as the provenance of unmarked whiteness. Laureano del Monte's *Con don, sin don, ayer y hoy* maps conditions of near impossibility for black citizenship. Its bald racism offers insight into the normative expectations of whiteness associated with the homosocial bonds of fraternity, equality, and liberty as understood by a larger white Cuban public sphere (perhaps better, a "preoccupied" public sphere).

The first two scenes, entitled "El rapto de Candelaria" (The abduction of Candelaria) and "El asesinato de Candelaria" (The murder of Candelaria), enact the abduction, attempted rape, and murder of Candelaria, a young black female slave whose steadfast resistance to the lewd sexual advances of the white overseer, aided by his black assistant Francisco, is punished with her death. The play is subtitled a "caricatura trágico-bufa, lírico bailable" (tragic-bufo caricature, with dance and music), and Candelaria's story—atypically violent for any teatro bufo play—provides the "tragic" content. Her death serves as pretext to judge the depth of the male slaves' loyalty to her and their courage. The slaves, almost all "negros congos" speaking in thickly rendered bozal, are horrified at the news of her murder, and resolve to murder the overseer. The male slaves take up their machetes in a chorus of rising cries, "¡Muera ese perro asesino! [. . .] ¡Muera la mayorá! ¡muera!" (The murderous dog should die! [. . .] Death to the overseer! death!). For his part, the overseer is undaunted and challenges the men to kill him. Not only do the enraged slaves then fail to attack Candelaria's murderer, they are immediately terrified of him and drop their machetes on command. When the overseer threatens lashings, the slave Tranquilino quickly betrays his comrades and names the instigators of the plot, who are sent away for beatings. In a final coup over the men, the overseer grants them permission to dance and sing until dinnertime; the cries for his death are thus replaced with equally energetic cries of "Viva el Mayoral!" (Long live the overseer!), as they begin dancing the zapateo and the *congo*. Under his breath, the overseer borrows Candelaria's word to call them all "sinverguensas," noting that the only way to treat these "dogs" is with a whip in one hand and bread in the other. "¡Que malos son!" (How bad they are!), he notes, "ya no se acuerdan de la pobre Candelaria. [. . .] Ella misma tuvo la culpa, se resistió y la maté. Poco se ha perdío. Ea, muchachos, á divertirse" (they have already forgotten about poor Candelaria. [. . .] She herself is to blame, she resisted and I killed her. Not a great loss. Hey, boys, go have fun, [Monte 1894, 12]).

The racism drawn here is breathtaking, and entirely strategic in its mapping of the relation between gender, race, and cultural capital. The scene traces an interracial contest between men to prove their respective moral resolve and physical strength—in short, their manhood. That the contest revolves around a sexual crime betrays the gendered dynamic inherent in notions of "brotherhood" and "fraternity" that the play evokes. If blacks and whites are to be "equals" or even "brothers" in bearing the title "Don," then that equality will be measured by their respective abilities as "real" men. Not coincidentally, this particular test immediately reinstantiates racial difference by testing whether black men will protect "their" women against the sexual offenses of white men. The unspoken irony, of course, is that the only white man in these scenes is a rapist, murderer, and abusive slave driver, and surely the least deserving of the title "Don" in this system of honor, but the play leaves this matter aside. Indeed, the play implies that the slaves' cowardice and failure to avenge Candelaria's death is equally if not more shameful than the overseer's attempted rape and murder. The overseer's assistant Francisco, in particular, embodies this nefarious lack of ethics: he abducts the innocent Candelaria, leads her to her death, betrays his fellow black men, and ultimately leads the chorus of "Vivas" that celebrates the white murderer. The racist double standard of the story asks, how indeed could whites ever trust black men to be "brothers" when they so clearly lack loyalty even to one another? If this were not enough, the play (written eight years after abolition) suggests that black men themselves are largely responsible for the "sins" of slavery. The failure of the slaves to attack the overseer, when they have an opportunity and clear advantage, only proves that they themselves are partly to blame for their continued abjection. On a simple command, they drop their machetes to dance the *congo*. No wonder, *Con don* implies, slavery so long persisted in Cuba.

This reactionary telling of the history of slavery is the backdrop for the equally reactionary re-dressing of the present, in a scene titled "El Meeting," which focuses on a black political gathering—almost certainly a parody of Gómez's Directorio. The African slaves of the first half of the play have now been transposed into postabolition "citizens" carrying out civic duties. In the process, the characters make the by now familiar switch from bozales to catedráticos, as each presiding functionary expresses himself in an overcomplicated parody of what we would call "legalese." The black leaders have been assembled, we are told, in order to assess the "patriótico y sívico prosedimiento" (patriotic and civic progress) of the "lucha constante y perseverante del renasimiento de nuestros legítimos y morrocotudos derechos" (persevering and constant battle of the renaissance of our legitimate and hugely important rights [13]). Of course in "catedrático" language, every third word is intentionally mispronounced or grammatically misplaced, creating the effect of a speaker unable to master language he speaks. The earlier catedrático helped shape the common derogatory understanding of blacks as negritos; the new catedrático reframed the negrito as ciudadanito, or little citizen: a parody of citizenship itself.[14]

The leading ciudadanito in this racist discourse is Juan Gualberto Gómez himself, who is satirized in this play through the character of Don Juan Gualberto, leader of the assembly. The play presents black men's desire to use the title "don" as a strictly racial presumption: they seek not to be the equals of whites, but to become white themselves. This is illustrated in the central joke of the scene: when J. Gualberto begins his speech with "Hoy que nuestra rasa de color . . ." (Now that our race of color . . .), he is met with angry grumbling from the crowd. He quickly corrects himself, apologizing for the "laso lingüitico de la lengua" (linguistic lapse of the tongue). "He dicho de color, sin acordarme de que ya todos somos blancos" (I said of color, forgetting that now we are all white [13]). His fellow ciudadanito, Juan María de la O, elaborates: before gaining the title "don," they were "una planta parásita, inorante y silvestre" (a parasite plant, ignorant and wild), but with "don" they are "la leche, la nieve, el armiño, el alabastro" (the milk, the snow, the ermine, the alabaster [14]) and so on. To be a "don" in this stage world is to imagine oneself to be white.

In the play, J. Gualberto argues that having achieved the title of "don" will inspire the newly whitened black men to participate in the new discourse of citizenship in Cuba:

debemos todos unirnos, 3 cabesas de ajos, en apretada ristra y dispensar nuestras huestes, para que, con sus profundos conosimientos en materia de democrasia, igualdá, hermandá y liberalismo, vayamos como nuestro apostol Abraham, por el monte de Sinaí pregonando nuestra doctrina, como si fueran huevos frescos. (14)

(We must all come together, like heads of garlic, in a tight braid of garlic, and dispense our follower-cloves, so that, with their profound knowledge in matters of democracy, equality, brotherhood and liberalism, we can go like our apostle Abraham on mount Sinai, peddling our doctrines, as though they were fresh eggs.)

In catedrático fashion, here garlic and activism, fresh eggs and religious inspiration are arbitrarily combined for comic effect, thereby calling into question J. Gualberto's professed understanding of democracy, equality, and fraternity. His rousing speech inspires one "Don Solloso" (meaning Mr. Sob) to offer explosive sobs as testament to the joy experienced by black men in their new relation with whiteness: "ya somos blancos! Ya somos todos iguales!" (now we are white! Now we are all equals! [15]). Thus, the play resignifies key words in the black civil rights movement, separating liberty and equality from the project of antiracism, and instead mapped as the domain of white Cubans in a newly developing polity.

The critique of radical nationalism is particularly intense here, surely in response to heightened concerns in the mid-1890s over anticolonial insurgency and the role of blacks therein. In the same period that this play was performed at the then new teatro Alhambra in 1894, José Martí and Juan Gualberto Gómez had agreed that the latter would serve as the Cuban-based leader of the planned (and still clandestine) insurgency in Cuba. Although this fact was not public knowledge, the alliance between insurgent exiles and black activists in Cuba was evident: the black press regularly drew parallels between the colonial condition of Cuba and the condition of blacks in contemporary Cuba and it published essays by known independence supporters, such as Rafael Serra, from exile in New York.

The remaining scenes of the play compound the racial double bind into which these black(face) men have been cast. Scene four illustrates the daily negotiation of power and social prestige between one of the new black (or is it white?) citizens, Don Francisco, and his white gallego servant, also called Francisco. Now that blacks have the title of "don," the immigrant servant believes that he too should be addressed with that title; if the former slave Francisco can be a Don, why not today's servant Francisco? Separated by race and class distinctions, the two Franciscos ostensibly illuminate the hypocrisy and, indeed, racism of the new black power elite. The arrogance of white supremacy is thus displaced onto the black community, and the problematic of racism is strategically elided into the field of class struggle. Don Francisco, the play implies, wants to be "don" not because he actually believes in racial equality (if he did, would he not address his servant as "don" as well?), but because he wants access to the racial and class privileges formerly reserved for whites. Again the presumption of white racial privilege is not in question, only blacks' desire to access it; when they do, it becomes a mark of black racism, leaving white racism entirely out of the frame.

The final scene, "El Soirée," levels its scathing satire onto the new black veladas, drawing on familiar terrain from *Un minué* (A minuet) of 1868. In addition to the requisite stiff performance of a minuet, this soirée features a (blackface) Italian opera scene, whose wildly exaggerated highbrow performance—replete with several monumentally overtragic deaths—sends the guests into paroxysms of admiration. Later two guests confess that they are not certain what the term "classical music" actually means. The joke is the same—blacks humorously fail to enact proper aristocratic behaviors—but its politics have shifted. Rather than implicitly critique Spanish aristocratic society through this double-voiced image, this blackface soirée is aimed solely at contemporary black cultural practice. If people like Pedro D'Aguirre felt that successful black performance of classical music, drama, and oratory would provide proof positive of black progress and integration into civil society, in this play black performance is understood instead as poor racial mimicry. When black bodies sing opera or dance a minuet, they sing and dance in whiteface. Following the implications of the previous two scenes, the "real" aspirations of black citizens are thus exposed: blacks care nothing about equality and liberty, and seek only to hoard (white) wealth, power, and prestige.

In a *coup de grâce,* Don Francisco reluctantly agrees to allow the performance of a danzón; the guests perform the dance in "la manera más aristocrática posible" (the most aristocratic manner possible [25]). Here blacks are so thoroughly inadequate in their social performance that they cannot even dance the eminently Cuban dance that "they" as "Africans" are credited with inspiring. The contradiction encapsulates the political double bind for black men that the play relentlessly traces: black men can never be proper "Cubans" or "citizens" or even real men ("dons"), because they are incapable of even being "true" to their own race. The more loyal they are to their "own" kind, the more deserving of white respect they will be; if Don Francisco were less "false" in his class and race aspirations, he would no longer require such strident parody. But, of course, if the black men were to pursue race-based identification, they would only provide evidence of the fundamental racial difference on which white supremacy and racial segregation are based. And that, of course, is the point: blacks are here encouraged to follow their "true" civic duty to stay out of the (white) public sphere. The play thus carefully stages, and argues for, the impossibility of black entry into the discourse of Cuban citizenship.

Despite such rabid critique, the veladas continued to provide a key context for a black public sphere, and even began to act as structures for a utopian political imagination—a space for imaginative social rehearsal as important, if entirely different, from that offered by the teatro bufo to white criollos. A velada held in 1889 was described by a commentator in *La Fraternidad* as an "essentially democratic festivity," in which one could witness "mixing in agreeable intercourse white men and black men, the noted man of letters with the humble man of industry or arts. In that balcony an aristocratic white Lady, in another a virtuous black woman worker." He continued, in a remarkable commentary,

> Contemplamos aquel cuadro grandioso por el eternal espíritu que lo animaba, y no pudimos menos que exclamar: "Si siempre fuera así, si el espectáculo que esta noche se da, transcendiera afuera, e informara todos los actos de la vida política y social de este país, otro fuera el destino de Cuba!"
>
> (We viewed that grandiose picture, and could not help but exclaim: "If only it were always so, if the performance of that night could transcend [these walls], to inform all acts of social and political life in this country, another would be the destiny of Cuba!")

Although still mapped along vectors of class, race, and gender, this site of interracial performance—focused on the audience more than stage—engendered a political hope that otherwise had no form of representation.

The commentator's pessimistic assessment of the power of the veladas raises an important question: why *didn't* these veladas succeed in transcending the limits of the theatre and reshaping the destiny of Cuba? The answer is easily found, in redux, in that mean blackface play, *Con don, sin don, ayer y hoy*. Its lesson is stark: blackness and genuine political identification are mutually exclusive; by definition, the political sphere is a domain of whiteness. No matter what Gómez or his compatriots said in this arena, they would be heard not as black men, but as black men in whiteface. The fact that white actors portrayed them in blackface behaving as though in whiteface only compounded the inability of a credible black political identity to emerge. The velada could not quite extend its social power beyond the theatre because it could not command discursive or material control over the intertwined meanings of blackness, desire, and impersonation—simulated blackness as a particular structure of Cuban feeling—that were, by 1893, already central to the making and maintenance of normative white Cuban *fraternidad.*

Theatrical Bodies: Incorporation, Impersonation

The implications of considering Cuban public spheres as shaped by performance, rather than print, are many. First, print culture has been understood as foundational to the formation of not only the public sphere as understood by Habermas, but also of the nation, as articulated by its pioneer theorist, Benedict Anderson. Where Habermas bases the development of the bourgeois public sphere on the rise of print culture, Anderson bases the rise of nationalism on what he calls print-capitalism. Although the two notions—public sphere and nation—have frequently and for good reason been opposed by critical theorists, momentarily viewing them together yields important insights into their related investments in the idea of print, and into their assumptions about the necessary relations among culture, nationalism, and literacy. For both theorists, a community of readers is the stuff by which the public sphere or national community is made. Both are constituted through a foundational moment of social projection in the activity of reading: as I read the newspaper—the privileged print genre for both public sphere and nation—I imagine that others read as I do, and share in this particular way of arranging and mapping the social world, and so "we" must share a greater communal bond. Michael Warner describes this experience as "social subjectivity," one in which "we adopt the attitude of the public subject," marking our identity with others; in so doing, we momentarily disavow our own particularities of class or gender or race, thus also "marking to ourselves our nonidentity with ourselves" (Warner 1993, 234). Through the ongoing production of this social subjectivity the nation is "imagined" (per Anderson), and the public is "incorporated" (per Habermas). For both nation and public, the culture and technology of print provides the mediating ground between the private imagination and social incorporation; that is, print culture enables the production of the social body.

But what kind of body is this textually produced social body? Warner explores the formative contradiction of this social body, arguing that the process of social incorporation demands a corresponding process of "disincorporation" from each of its subjects. The bourgeois public sphere, he writes, "claimed to have no relation to the body image at all"; in theory, citizen-subjects of any race, gender, sexuality, or class could partake of the process of becoming "public" subjects, since the public sphere was, by definition, structured through a process of disembodied self-abstraction. The technology of print thus carried the utopian promise that no body would be required to create the new social body, hence its appeal to liberal, democratizing discourse—a theory not unlike or unrelated to that informing certain enthusiasm for new virtual technologies today. In practice, however, the public sphere (like Anderson's nation) continued to rely on features of some bodies: "Access to the public came in the whiteness and maleness that were then denied as forms of positivity, since the white male *qua* public person was only abstract rather than white or male. The contradiction is that, even while particular bodies and dispositions enabled the liberating abstraction of public discourse, those bodies also summarized the constraints of positivity" (Warner 1993, 239). Both nation and public sphere thus safeguard for certain bodies a privilege that is disguised and elaborated—rather than averted—by the technology of print culture. Thus, as Saidiya Hartman argues at length about the post-Emancipation United States, "the stipulation of abstract equality" between subjects does not simply fail to enact fully the "fragile 'as if equal' of liberal discourse," but itself *produces* "white entitlement and black subjection in its promulgation of formal equality" (Hartman 1997, 116). This bourgeois, liberal print culture, then, maintains a relation of bad faith with the bodies of its subjects: even as it promotes a disembodied, virtual equality, its process of selective disincorporation exiles some groups—women, people of color, gays and lesbians—by forcing them to acknowledge their own positivity as the mark of their difference from the "public" norm (Warner 1993, 241). Consigned to bodies, rather than the public subjectivity of reading and abstract personhood, they are denied complete entry into the public sphere.

What kind of social body, then, does a *theatrical* imagination make possible? What different economy of public representation emerges if national community is organized not through the culture of print, but instead through the technology and culture of performance? This question does not presuppose the use of performance as a means to recuperate the liberal-individualist notion of an ideal public sphere, or to establish an inherent good-faith relation between self and body through performance. It is not meant to suggest that the representation of bodies through performance is any less mediated or complicated than it is through print or other media. Not only would such claims be suspect, but absolutely nothing in the Cuban historical context would support them: Cuban blackface performance, for one, was very much a process of "disincorporating" blackness in order to "incorporate" a white racial norm. The question merely serves to enhance understanding of the insistent presence of performance as a major form of publicity in Cuba's anticolonial setting, particularly racial impersonation. Why did anticolonial Cuba need such performance to form its national community, and what is the nature of the social body that is thereby constituted? In other words, what is the difference between *impersonation* and *incorporation* in the constitution of public spheres in relation to race?

We can find one potential answer in analysis of the criticism leveled against Anderson by Partha Chatterjee. He contests Anderson's characterization of the nation as having a "modular" structure, applicable to any number of social terrains and insists that the specificities of the colonial situation defy transposition of European patterns of development.[15] To stage his objection, he offers the stubborn popularity of Bengali drama as an example of how the literary aesthetic corresponding to the "modular" European nation state was flatly rejected by the nationalist, educated, bilingual Bengali elite of the nineteenth century, an elite that might otherwise have taken its cues from modern Europe. Chatterjee contends that the "conventions that would enable a play to succeed on the Calcutta stage were very different from the conventions of [. . .] European drama," and he reduces this difference to an insistent—and for him, inexplicable—commitment on the part of Bengalis to "their" drama, "a literary genre that is the least commended on aesthetic grounds by critics of Bengali literature" (Chatterjee 1993). In short, Chatterjee notes (and wonders why) the Bengali elite indulged a taste for its own "bad" drama. He does not, however, consider that this attachment might be explained as a loyalty to *performance* over and against the literary conceits of both European colonists and subsequent "literary" critics, Bengali or otherwise. By his own brief description alone, this theatre defies easy reduction to a "literary" genre, and is oddly described as "drama." Something about this mode of performance—rash, urban, modern, but relentlessly *not* "literary"—*worked* for the Bengali elite in their national self-imaginings

So it is not just that European literary models may sometimes "fail" to take hold in the colonial setting, as Chatterjee claims. In Cuba, performance offered a useful, perhaps necessary, alternative technology for mobilizing, organizing, and otherwise constituting anticolonial public subjectivity. Consider briefly the play that launched playwright Ignacio Saragacha to fame, *Un baile por fuera* (1880, 1990), which the Bufos de Salas performed regularly to great acclaim. *El Fígaro*'s leading theatre critic Rafael Pérez Cabello (who wrote under the alias "Zerep"), remembered this play ten years later as by far the best play of the genre ever written (Pérez Cabello 1898, 9). What makes the play interesting is certainly not its storyline, which is a variant of a standard plot found in dozens and dozens of other teatro bufo plays: the young heroine, Rosa, wants to marry her young (Cuban) beaux, Chicho, against the wishes of her father, José, who has already promised her hand to the older, wealthier (Spanish) Ramón. The plot charts Chicho's efforts to dissuade the father from his course, with the help of his clownish friends; he finally succeeds, and the play closes with the announcement of the new wedding date.

We, like Chatterjee, can wonder why a play of such minor merit would provoke such enthusiasm. Its merits lie instead in the play's costumbrista aesthetic and especially in the performance style through which it is rendered. The real protagonist of the play is neither Chicho nor Rosa, but Cantúa, the local shoemaker and drunkard ("mascavidrios")—performed, no doubt, by Miguel Salas, in whose honor the play was written. Although the character plays no real part in the plot, he acts as bemused witness, offering salty metacommentary throughout. His steady stream of language is frank and streetwise, thickly rendered in "aural" costumbrismo. Costumbrista detail guides the setting as well, the front of a local bodega (named after that particularly Cuban fruit, "El Mamey Triste," or The Sad Mamey), and replete with true-to-life details: "ventana y puertas grandes, como las del país" (window and large doors, typical of the country), "una banqueta de zapatero; encima de ésta un letrero que diga 'Sapatos pa'guajiro de vaqueta' (a shoemaker's bench, with a [misspelled] sign on top that reads "cowhide shoes for peasants," [Saragacha 1990, 35]). The plot develops during a dance party hosted by the father; although the dance serves no purpose to the plot, it provides a pretext for several lively guarachas and danzones, and allows a steady stream of local characters—musicians, dancers, a magician, a firefighter, a police officer, and so forth—to sail across the stage. This play, so top-heavy with extra details, characters, and songs unrelated to its plot, was an instant success in Havana no doubt precisely because it provided a compelling vehicle for the organization and display of such details. Indeed, Zerep praised the play's "evidente exactitud" (evident precision) in portraying "Cuban customs" (Pérez Cabello 1898, 9, 167). What *Un baile por fuera* did, then, was evoke a social style, a manner of being public, and a feeling of the city and its inhabitants that audiences felt was overfull with truth.

However, even as bufo performance evoked a sense of embodied cubanía, the complex racial dynamic of anticolonial Cuba pressured performance into other service as well. Performance not only offered white criollos a medium through which to organize themselves against the literary conceits of colonial Spain; it was also the required medium through which to engage, negotiate, and incorporate—in Habermas's sense—the active influence of African and Afrocuban cultures on the island as well. The myth of Cuban mestizaje would have us believe that performance—dance and music particularly—"naturally" emerged as Cuba's national genres through the inevitable encounter of African and Spanish cultures, citing the importance of performance to traditional African cultures. This myth has, for some contemporary ethnohistorians, been codified into a pseudoscientific theory of cultural development, frequently buttressed by Fernando Ortiz's otherwise compelling theory of transculturation. Certainly, performance is important to black cultures in Cuba. However, it is the degree to which performance formed the basis of social bonds and social memory for most African ethnocultural groups in Cuba that is most significant. Black activism through performance has, time and again, been crucial to black survival and resistance on the island (see Howard 1998). Indeed, when traditional political initiatives failed, as they did so violently in the massacre of black politicians and intellectuals during the so-called "race war" of 1912 (see Helg 1995), it was black ingenuity in performance in the 1920s that in part made possible black incorporation into the Cuban national imagination during the afrocubanismo movement (see Moore 1997).

In addition, although it is certainly true that centuries of racial contact have yielded genuinely new forms of culture, especially performance, in Cuba, the myth of the benign origins of Cuban mestizaje and the role assigned to performance therein, and the myth of a disinterested, undirected process of racial "mixing" could not be further from the reality of white racial panic in colonial Cuba and the barrage of social, legal, and cultural controls intended to manage and discourage racial contact. Proponents of these views of Cuba's history further propose music and dance as the "natural" domain of "African" cultures in Cuba, while rarely acknowledging the fact that it was illegal for slaves to be literate, and that, through the so-called "blood code" in effect until 1878, free blacks could not attain education beyond the primary level. These myths of Cuban mestizaje were manufactured in the nineteenth century by and for white Cubans, and they coalesce to form one of the reasons black participation in the national community was so often *limited to*—rather than represented by—modes of performance.

To state the matter differently, if the European liberal bourgeois public sphere imagined that it had no body, Cuba's most certainly did, and it was in blackface. The anticolonial public sphere "had a body" because, by simple virtue of violating the unspoken norms of positivity defined by the peninsular Spanish citizen, the white criollo subject could not quite occupy the sphere of unmarked public subjectivity. By the fact of his birth, he—and it is *he*—could not fully "disincorporate" (from) himself to join the dominant public sphere, whose normative range was defined by peninsular-born subjects who enjoyed greater political freedom and social rank than those born in Cuba. The public sphere constituted through print was both materially and discursively tied to peninsular constellations of power, educated literacy, and social subjectivity. As Angel Rama's seminal study of the Latin American, *Lettered City*, suggests, the "documentary umbilical cord" that brought Spanish letters—in all senses of the word—to the Americas provided "the linguistic models for [Latin American] *letrados*" or the elite class of American-born, literate bureaucrats, the compradors, that brokered power for the metropole. The "rigid semantic system of the city of letters," writes Rama, which discursively interlinked legal and literary practice, "required the most univocal language possible" (Rama 1996, 33, 59). Competency in such language was required for participation in the public sphere defined by the lettered city, and formed the basis of elite criollo power; yet, in this colonial context, full competency was premised on birthright, excluding even elite criollos from the highest echelons of social and political power.

Emerging through this discursive grid of literate power, we can imagine the populist criollo subject retreating into the otherwise undervalued domain of embodied subjectivity as a tactical maneuver, providing an alternate site from which to critique the dominant ideological structure and mount his own bid for power. This Cuban public sphere indulged embodied performance practices as viable alternatives to the print models proposed (but then prohibited) by Spanish colonial rule. At the same time, however, white criollos performed an identical repressive operation on blacks in Cuba, prohibiting their participation in the field of letters and literacy during slavery and impeding it thereafter, thereby consigning them too to the domain of the body and of performance. The black patriot intellectuals who organized the elegant veladas of the late 1880s and early 1890s made counterclaims not only in the realm of performance, but also in direct relation to "literate" culture: theirs was, to borrow an insight from Houston Baker, a "stolen literacy"—by which is meant a "radically secular and critical structure of feeling gained from reading and writing" (Baker 2001, 7). Oratory, recitations of poetry, and drama were the markedly literate performance media through which black publicity made its bid to enter the white city of letters.

The field of performance, then, represented not a site for unproblematic, reciprocal racial mixing and exchange, as some would have it, but the contrary: a site of profound social contestation and negotiation. It is no accident that the myth of racial diversity entered the public scene through the teatro bufo, a white criollo genre whose organizing trope was not racial contact or collaboration, but the contrary: racial impersonation. The penchant for racial impersonation throughout this period should signal the degree to which white interest in black performance derived as much, if not more, from a nervous desire to know and control the only public expressive medium available to African Cuba as from an interest in how African performance might please or serve white anticolonial needs.

We could think of the teatro bufo in this period as a keen example of what Arjun Appadurai calls (echoing Anderson) the *imagination as social practice*, with emphasis on the multiple nuances of the word "practice" (Appadurai 1993, 269–96). As a primary site for the formation of national community and Cuban public, the teatro bufo engaged the dialectical relation between practice as rehearsal and practice as realization. Between the rehearsal and the realization, we find the infinitely complex process whereby the social was imagined and became real. It is the process by which, as Michael Taussig puts it, the real is "really made up" (1987, 366–70; 1993, xiii–xix). This intersection between rehearsal and realization—or between imagination and incorporation—is also the crucial and difficult conjuncture between performance and performativity itself: between the really made up and the made up real. Illuminating just a fraction of this process, in the teatro bufo was an imagination of Cuba that was, as it were, making its bid for the real. Along the way, the history of the teatro bufo may illuminate how notions of race and racism organize not simply the shape of national communities, but also one's embodied sense of the real itself.

Two corollaries to Anderson's notion of the nation as imagined community may apply to Cuba's performance culture. First: the national imagination is not mimetic. What it imagines is not a "true" reflection of what is or will be; the imagination shapes the real through socioaesthetic strategies other than realism. This is worth restating in the Cuban case, since costumbrismo's most insistent (and insidious) promise was to represent reality exactly, to provide a voyeur's glimpse into real daily life on the island. How many times, to this day, have lengthy passages of the novel *Cecilia Valdés* been reproduced and cited as reliable sources of information on nineteenth century Cuba? How often, to this day, have Victor Patrício Landaluze's lithographs and illustrations been reproduced as transparent windows into Cuban life, allowing us to peer directly into nineteenth century Havana homes and streets?[16] We must beware of costumbrismo's claims to represent colonial reality accurately. The fact that costumbrismo so consistently favored images of African and black Cuba reflects less what was actually happening on Havana streets or homes than *who* was looking and what concerns organized their view. That is, white men don't appear at the center of these images because they are already imagined as the primary point of view, from the other side of the frame. These often-reproduced lithographs enact this logic: white men occupy a position of disembodied subjectivity, and women and people of color are the bodies against which and through which their sense of social self is articulated. Although in the teatro bufo the repeated fantasy of mestizaje did indeed bring notions of racial diversity forcefully into a newly constituted Cuban public sphere, it did not therefore reflect or create the racial diversity it described. Mestizaje was instead a strategy for using, containing, and controlling race in that public sphere.

This leads to the second corollary, summarized well by Chatterjee's rejoinder to Anderson when he asks, "*Whose* imagined community?" If the nation is an imagined community, we do well to remember that only certain segments of a given community are the ones imagining, and they do so from a particular and partial social orientation. The others, those without power underwriting their imaginations, end up *living* in imagined landscapes not of their own making. From one view then we can say that Cuban criollos live in a surreal landscape produced by the imagination of colonial Spain. From another view we can say that black Cubans, Asian migrants, and women live a contradictory imagined landscape produced in part by colonial Spain and in part by white male criollos (those "preocupados") whose imaginations are shaping a newly emerging public sphere. For those whose imaginations don't matter (that is, materialize), this protonational "imagined community" is a surreal and deeply compromised place to live indeed: the social contradictions and arbitrary allocations of power and resources that make up the imagined landscape are, from this orientation, raw, unfinished, illogical, disjointed—in short, not fully naturalized. The teatro bufo and its costumbrista cousins are—far from tropical reflections of European naturalism—instead part of that ongoing socioaesthetic produced by colonial violence sometimes named "magical realism": an aesthetic in which the social "magic" of the real is always half complete, half visible, haunting and continually distorting the lives of the living.

Chapter 4

National Rhythm, Racial Adulteration, and the Danzón, *1881–1882*

When the mulato composer, Miguel Faílde, created the "danzón" in 1879, this new dance engaged a complex discursive terrain of racial, sexual, and national identity in the full midst of Cuba's anticolonial era. Film critic Ana M. López has noted that Latin America as a whole has produced not only foundational fictions, as argued in the important work of Doris Sommer, but foundational *rhythms* as well. Because so-called "Latin" dances and music palpably evoke the rich cross-fertilization of cultural influences—most frequently African and Spanish—in the Americas, they have functioned as near "perfect markers of the instability of borders" at the same time that they have provided "indices of the imaginary demarcations that constitute the process whereby Self/Nation defines itself (and is defined) in relationship to Others" (López 1997, 310). This is especially and provocatively so of the Cuban danzón, a music-dance form that emerged forcefully on the Cuban scene in the early 1880s, disseminated in part through the entertainments of the teatro bufo. In the energetic debates of the early 1880s on the morality, sexual meaning, and racial origins of the dance, we find that the discourse surrounding and including the danzón encapsulates a generative contradiction between what López calls "national rhythm"—consolidating, framing a pleasing tempo of national life, inviting uniform participation—and what Barbara Browning has called "infectious rhythm"—overwhelming, chaotic, forcefully seducing dancers into bodily pleasures and a loss of self-control (López 1997, 323; Browning 1998). Operating in dialectical counterpoint in Cuba's newly developing public sphere, these competing interpretations of the danzón presented a new and contradictory Cuban social body, invested in dance with competing gender and racial coordinates: that social body was, at one and the same time, a public (usually male) "Cuban" body dancing to its own feminized, sensual, non-European (mulata) tropical rhythm, and a new and innocent (now female) Cuban body in grave danger of being overwhelmed by (now male) African, sexualized rhythms. In both cases, gender and race were mutually formative and foundational features of this national imagination, and—as we shall see—dance functioned as a form of national embodiment inextricably linked to racial performance and impersonation.

Early variations of danzón choreography reportedly took shape in black dance halls of the 1870s. Osvaldo Castillo Faílde notes that the term "danzón" had been used earlier to describe the choreography of certain dances performed by African comparsas on plantations or during the *Día de Reyes* (Three Kings' Day) festivals in Havana, well before the term danzón referred to a specific compositional form. However, the dance as we have come to know it did not enter wide circulation until Miguel Faílde adapted the musical structure and choreography of the then-popular Cuban danza, incorporating choreographic elements of what had otherwise been known as "danzón," to create that first danzón, entitled "Las Alturas de Simpson." Unlike the danza, the new danzón moved to a much slower, subtle tempo, incorporating a walking sequence to give the dancers a chance to rest (or socialize) between dance sections—a welcome pause, as many commentators then and now have noted, in the tropical heat of Cuba. Unlike the contradanza, the danzón jettisoned most line, circle, and square formations in favor of closely partnered choreography. Set to 2/4 time, the music began with the undanced *paseo* (walk) or introduction, followed by the first "*trio*" featuring lyrical clarinets or flutes, followed by the second trio, where violins set a slower but more virtuosic pace, and ending with the energetic third trio, dominated by trumpets, whose upbeat tempo was said to have the quality of "street" music, much like that of local—and usually black or African—rumbas. Similar in structure to the *habanera*, the danzón distinguished itself by the double repetition of the paseo between each trio (Castillo Faílde 1964, 29–30, 83–95; Rodríguez 1994, 81–84; Daniel 1995, 38–39).

The combination of variable tempo and close partnering created a remarkably sensual dance, whose tendency to excite sexual tensions earned it as many converts as critics. The dance's popularity across the island was immediate, and so sweeping that by 1882 one press commentator complained that:

> Habana es un escandalo. Se baila en nuestras sociedades de recreo, que son numerorisísimas los domingos y los días festivos; y en las academias conocidas vulgarmente como escuelitas. En cada esquina de culta población se estaciona de la noche a la mañana un organillo, que con sus chillonas notas molesta a los vecinos pacíficos y saca de sus casas a las inexpertas muchachas. (*La Aurora del Yumurí*, 3 September 1882; Castillo Faílde 1964, 158–59)

> (Havana is a scandal. People dance [the danzón] in our recreation societies, which are very numerous on Sundays and holidays; and in [dance] academies known vulgarly

mutual aid groups or more public?

as "little schools." On every street corner in respectable neighborhoods they set up a little organ from night until dawn, whose loud music bothers peaceful neighbors and lures inexperienced girls from their homes.)

During the height of its popularity, the danzón was a standard feature of Cuban public entertainments, shared at masquerade dances during carnival season, at dance festivities following baseball games in both the black and white communities, and at major social dances for all classes and races. Regular work at social dances supported new composers, such as Faílde and his friendly rival Raimundo Valenzuela; dancers and composers alike mutually challenged each other into new forms, more complex rhythms, and a wider repertoire of danzones.

The danzón became a regular feature of the teatro bufo entertainments as well. Bufo plays were a regular context for the debut of new danzónes by Faílde or Valenzuela, and the danzón joined and at times replaced guarachas as the musical component of teatro bufo plays from 1880 through the end of the century. The intense popularity—and equally intense condemnation—of the dance also provided the theme for numerous bufo plays. *Los efectos del danzón* (1881) celebrates the revitalizing effects of the new dance on the island's population, while *Los rumberos* (1882) offers instead a cautionary tale of the grave dangers posed by drink, dance, and especially dancing (mulata) women. The latter, however, was the exception: the teatro bufo almost always championed the dance, in frequent and often explicit response to moralist attacks from the press, as in José Tamayo's *La Traviata o la morena de las clavelinas* (La Traviata, or the mulata of the carnations [1879]), a parody of Lady of the Camelias, Ignacio Saragacha's *Un baile for fuera* (A dance on the outside [1880]), *Un baile por dentro* (A dance on the inside, [1880]), *En la cocina* (In the kitchen [1881]), and Mellado's *Perico Mascavidrio o la víspera de San Juan* (Drunk Perico, or the eve of San Juan [1880]). Yet none defended the danzón as comprehensively as Ramón Moralez Álvarez's 1882 play, *El proceso del oso* (the trial of *el oso*), which focuses on the newest version of the danzón called "el oso" or "the bear," and which will merit our pause in the pages to follow.

In the foregoing pages, I return to the formulation posed by Raymond Williams in his important, brief essay "Structures of Feeling" and invite us to think about choreography and the kinesthetic experience of the dancing body as a site for the production of important "structures of feeling." We can consider the emergence of the danzón as a new structure of feeling that organized a series of lived relationships to notions of sensuality, gender, race, and national belonging in Cuba of the early 1880s. The tremendous power exerted by this dance lay in its ability to recalibrate the bodily experience of national desire, race, and gender in ways that surprised, seduced, or scandalized the public that participated in or witnessed it. The dance enabled the experience of an important "change in presence," as Williams would say, whose vital connection with competing ideological and political concerns of the day is visible to the historian only in the seismic waves of written condemnations and defenses that followed the dance itself. As we, in turn, try to understand the complex role of the danzón in this social terrain, we should ask how the danzón restructured the experience—the feeling, the "practical consciousness"—of race, or gender, or national identity. How was race, sexuality, or gender embodied, lived, in the act of dancing? What relations did that embodied experience have to the prevailing debates over race, sexuality, and national identity? What pressure did the dance exert on those discourses? Williams notes that even as we "acknowledge (and welcome) the specificity of these elements—specific feelings, specific rhythms," we must still find ways of "recognizing their specific kinds of sociality" (Williams 1985, 133). To do so, we return to the question of performativity: in order to understand what the dance "meant," we must ask, what did it *do*? What social experience did it shape and make possible? The rhythm of the danzón, I argue, structured feelings of race and gender, and provided an emergent structure for the feeling of "Cubanness" itself.

This analysis rejoins a question posed in the previous chapter: how does the lived sociality proposed by emerging performance forms differ from and possibly reorganize the sociality proposed by the structures of literature and cultures of print? What possibilities does dance, and more specifically rhythm, offer to complicate or intervene in the regime of print culture? The immediate and extensive written response to the dance, as we shall see below, itself dramatizes the competition between performance and print in public culture. Those written responses—rebukes, celebrations, condemnations—work tirelessly to reestablish narrative and interpretative frames of reference over the dance and its possible social significations. As we analyze the discourse surrounding the dance, I do not assume full access to the "true" social content of the dance beyond print, because our understanding of the historical dance has been so fully mediated by textual representation. However, I invite us to imagine rigorously how its social content may have been experienced in its historical moment, because it is precisely the claim to embodied truth—however inaccessible to us now and however phantasmatic in its "original" moment—that gave the dance its appeal. That embodied, performative sociality is the ineluctable structure of feeling that prompted the pleasures, passions, and controversy that the dance occasioned.

Immediately on arrival, before its popularity had spread beyond the city of Matanzas, the danzón provoked debate on how the dance displayed—or publicized—the national body. The first attack, launched in *El Diario de Matanzas* on 7 November 1878, posed the question, "¿progresamos?" (is this progress?) in disbelief. Whereas refined women ("madres dignísimas," most dignified mothers) in years past might have enjoyed *watching* a dance similar to the danzón performed by their slaves during carnival, "como aceptamos en el teatro el espectáculo de una cuadrilla de Offembach [sic]" (like we accept the performance of a square dance in the theatre in an opera by Offenbach), they certainly never *danced* such a "voluptuousa melodía, pausada, ardiente, incitante, concebida en cerebros africanos al calor de este suelo tropical" (voluptuous melody, slow, ardent, inciting, conceived in African brains to the heat of this tropical ground). The "doloroso sorpresa" or painful surprise for the commentator is that the very daughters of these most dignified women—far from eschewing the slave dance altogether—now dance the dance themselves. Is *this* the direction of progress? (*El Diario de Matanzas,* 7 November 1878, in Castillo Faílde 1964, 122–23).[1] In the dance the commentator sees Cuba's most dignified women—mothers and virgins, no less—becoming "more" African, and by racist inference, "less" culturally progressive. The distinction he makes between watching and performing is crucial: viewing a pleasing performance and actually taking pleasure from embodying it organize totally different registers of social conduct. While the former is tolerable and does not challenge the social differences between the refined woman and her slave, the latter contaminates the social body itself, making her vulnerable to the seductions of the "voluptuous" African melody and all it represents.

Those defending the dance did so by calling into question the critic's understanding of the ontology of rhythm. It is not the rhythm or even the choreography that determines the meaning of the dance, wrote a dissenting commentator the following day, but instead the dancers themselves. "El Danzón," he writes, "puede llevarse a la exageración y disgustar a las personas celosas de la moral pública" (can be exaggerated and displease those zealous about public morals), but the danzón will not cross such lines "mientras lo bailen personas que sepan respetar la sociedad" (so long as it is danced by people who know to respect society). In response to the question of progress, this defender insists that "efectivamente progresamos, porque [. . .] de un baile ridículo y despreciable, hemos hecho un baile tan decente como la misma danza tan aceptada" (indeed this is progress, because [. . .] from a ridiculous and despicable dance we have made a dance as decent as the *danza* itself, so widely accepted [*El Diario de Matanzas*, 8 November 1878]). In response to the ongoing debate another Matanzas critic reiterated the same point to his female readers:

> sabed que este humilde gacetillero os considera tan puras y tan virtuosas cuando bailaís el danzón como cuando no la bailaís. Determinados bailes no hacen decentes a las personas, sino las personas decentes hacen decentes todos los bailes. (*El Diario de Matanzas*, 9 October 1879)

> (know that this humble essayist considers you as pure and virtuous when you dance the danzón as when you do not. Certain dances do not make people decent, instead decent people make decent all dances.)

In other words, rehearsing a racist trope not new to Cuba, apparently whiteness is more contagious than blackness: if a white woman dances an African dance, she whitens it.

Another critic, in December of 1878, rehearses this same point—"hasta el *tango* puede bailarse con decencia, [. . .] todo depende del actor" (even the *tango* can be danced with decency . . . it all depends on the actor)—in order to lament that this most "Cuban" of dances has been so harshly criticized: "nos duele ver que los mismos hijos de Cuba que deberían defenderla son los primeros en atacarla" (it hurts to see that the very sons of Cuba who should defend the dance are the first to attack her). Besides, he asks pragmatically, "¿Habrá alguno que pueda decir que su esposa, su madre, su hermana, su hija, no la bailó?" (Is there one who can claim that his wife, his mother, his sister, his daughter has not danced it?) And, he continues, even if there were any truth to the charges of Africanization, "La ropa sucia se lava en casa" (dirty laundry is washed at home [*El Diario de Matanzas*, 22 December 1878]). Here the danzón is a site for the production of (female, white) Cubanness, whose very constitution requires a repressed African source. What matters for this critic is finally not the dance, but the dancer—more specifically, the race of the dancer. The danzón publicized a new social body, but here its racial litmus was exposed: no matter how many Africans may have developed and danced the dance, the danzón is true, decent, and Cuban only when danced by a white public. Any extent to which that is not true, implies the admonishing critic, is better kept from public view.

One recurring concern, from both sides of the debate, was how the dance represented Cuba as a nation, both to the newly developing citizenry and to a larger community of nations. As López notes of various "Latin" dances in twentieth century film, explicitly national rhythms are ostensibly the "rhythms of the 'people' (rather than of individual characters) and simultaneously serve to unify the nation by providing an identity and to market the nation abroad" (López 1997, 323). While both of these functions of the danzón—one national, one international—involved the fabrication of a singular, frequently homogenized, national identity, the question of race immediately illuminated the tension between them. The dance's defenders extended their essentialist logic on race to the matter of national identity as well. Dance, said one, is "almost natural": "todos los pueblos desde los más salvajes hasta los más civilizados tienen sus bailes propios que nadie se los ha enseñado, pues entre ellos mismos han nacido" (all peoples from the most savage to the most civilized have their own dances which no one has taught them, since it was born among them alone). Cuba's danzón is no exception: he compares the unique passion of its rhythm to the "grave and taciturn" rhythm of the Russians or the "majestic" *contradanse* of the French, on the one hand, and the "ardent" "madness" of the congo or the "disagreeable" and "frenetic" enthusiasm of the Comanche Indians, on the other (*El Diario de Matanzas*, 6 November 1879). But his treatise walks a careful line: the dance that is otherwise accused of being, precisely, "savage" and "African," is here recuperated as "naturally" Cuban, having no history and no relation to either its European or African ancestry. But the critics were firm in the contrary: "*El chingüingüí* y *El paso de la malanga* son los nombres de . . . ? los obras de arte de Africa? –No: de dos obras de arte *cubano*, de dos danzones [. . .] Algún trabajillo costará á la señorita que tenga que hablar de ellos, pronunciar nombres tan groseros. (*El chingüingüí* and *The pit of the malanga* are names of . . . . works of art from Africa? No: of *Cuban* works of art . . . some little effort it will cost the young woman who must speak of them, to pronounce names so gross [*El almendares*, 3 July 1882]). Another danzón celebrant countered by eliminating the question of "savagery" altogether: "En todas partes del mundo civilizado, [. . .] el detalle principal es el baile" (In every part of the civilized world, [. . .] the principal detail is dance). Dance itself, whatever the rhythm, is what qualifies a nation for entry into the "civilized" world. And Cuba, "patria por excelencia del baile" (nation par excellence of dance), has a special place in that civilized gallery of nations (*La Aurora del Yumurí*, 2 November 1879).

In the early 1880s, some liberal nationalists became concerned that Cuba's passion for the dance was perhaps excessive, giving bad publicity to Cuba at the very time when the island was otherwise enjoying new social and political freedoms. One commentator asked, "¿Niega [Usted] que existe en Cuba una exagerada pasión por bailar?" (Can you deny that there exists in Cuba an exaggerated passion for dance? [*El Diario de Matanzas*, 20 March 1881]). An offended patriot insists that dancing does not serve the real work of nation building:

> Si es verdad que tenemos *voz y voto* no es porque se lo debemos a los bailadores de danzones, a los que se peinan conchitas, a esas cajas ambulantes de perfumería. Esos patriotas (?) no dan más que descredito. [. . .] No nos oponemos a que aquí se baile, criticamos sólo la licencia, la pasión desenfrenada por las piruetas, y creemos que se respeta más al país valendo por su buen nombre y progreso, que alentando a esa desgraciada juventud que emplea su tiempo bailando "La guabina" y "La mulata rosa." (*La Aurora del Yumurí*, 30 June 1881)
>
> (If it is true that we have *voice and vote* [after the 1879 peace pact at Zanjón] we don't owe it to the dancers of *danzones*, to those combing their hair in buns, to those walking boxes of perfume. Those patriots (?) do no more than discredit us. We don't oppose dance, we simply criticize the license, the unbridled passion for pirouettes, and believe that one respects the country more by valuing its good name and progress, than by giving breath to that unfortunate youth that spends its time dancing "La guabina" and "The mulata rose.")

Through a sleight of words, dancing is here represented as a predominantly female activity—for those with fashionable hair and perfume—while their required male partners are ignored entirely. It is mindless women who, given to unbridled passions, distract men from the more meaningful (although similarly embodied) work of using voice and vote, and who tarnish Cuba's "good name."

From this ideological view, the danzón challenges the "good name" of both white women and Cuba, in ways that either collapse them into one, or rigorously exile them from each other. On the one hand, white women are asked to stand for the body of Cuba; by dancing they put themselves and Cuba's "good name" in danger, threatening their own and Cuba's sexual and racial purity. On the other hand—given that not only daughters but dignified mothers insist on dancing regardless—some critics, like the one quoted above, find no recourse but to exile women altogether from the nation itself, temporarily safeguarding it from the dangerous public performance of reckless women. The frustration caused by the image of "their" women dancing to "African" rhythm was, for some Cuban men, extraordinarily acute. Witness one exasperated Cuban in 1881:

> la regeneración intelectual y por consecuencia el progreso será imposible entre nosotros mientras haya padres de familia que [. . .] lleven a sus hijas, vírgenes de la patria, al desenfreno del baile de hoy día [que] no es más que una degeneración del tango africano. (Castillo Faílde 1964, 144–45)
>
> (intellectual regeneration and therefore progress will be impossible among us so long as there are fathers who take their daughters, the virgins of the nation, to the madness of today's dance, which is nothing other than a degeneration of the African tango.)

The discourse of control and progress in the making of a new nation was, it seems, roundly disturbed by women who refused to play their part as virgin patriots, or fathers who failed to appreciate the full value to the nation of safeguarding their daughters' racial and sexual purity. For the women, who kept dancing anyway, perhaps the danzón provided an instance of what José Piedra has evocatively called "hip poetics," a form of "feminist posturing of African origin" that has historically allowed women (usually of color) to negotiate a public arena whose sexism and racism might otherwise render them invisible and speechless: dance provides an alternate, if frequently politically compromised, "signifying bodily attitude" (Piedra 1997, 96).

The attempt to safeguard and police white women's virtue remained fully embedded in a discourse about the nature and control of the public sphere. Because white women were the imagined embodiment of social virtue, their own mobility, visibility, and experience within the public sphere in theory illuminated the "path" of public virtue. A common trope for male writers in the press was to cast themselves in the subject position of female viewers, imagining the girls' scandal at the city's decayed morals. This complaint, from *El almendares*, sets the scene: "A los mil atractivos que reune nuestro Parque Central, como son: chinos ciegos, billeteros, carteristas, vendedores de flores, etc., hay que agregar los petardistas. En breve, ni al Parque podrán ir nuestras bellas" (To the thousand attractions assembled in our Central Park, like blind Chinese men, lottery vendors, pickpockets, flower sellers, we must add the swindlers. In short, our beauties cannot even go to the park [21 August 1881]). The paper, whose readership is imagined to be largely female, presumably registers its complaints on behalf of women. Ideally, the park would be a "natural" site of leisure graced by beautiful women. In practice, however, those "beauties" compete with the poor: vagrants, vendors, and menacing youth. The laments typically add raced subjects to their list of "obstacles" to white female enjoyment on the city's public streets:

Las calles de esta populosa ciudad están llenas de pordioseros blancos, negros, chinos, mulatos, billeteros de ámbos sexos, floristas, vagos, carteristas, ñáñigos, hombres sin piernas, chiquillos desnudos, gente de mala facha, etc etc ¡Y la llaman culta! Parece una ciudad donde no hay asilos y que el presidio anda suelto.

(The streets of this populous city are full of white, black, Chinese, and mulato beggars, lottery vendors of both sexes, flower sellers, vagrants, pickpockets, ñáñigos, men without legs, naked children, people with bad looks, etc. etc. And they call it cultured! It looks like a city where there are no asylums and the jailed run free.)

Cuba's racial "others"—unbecoming whites, blacks, Chinese, mulatos, ñáñigos—are criminalized and pathologized along with vagrants and the ill. A cultured city, apparently, would lock up people of color and leave the streets free for white beauty. When men indulge questionable behavior, their behavior is similarly racialized, as in the strident complaint on a hot summer day, when men were seen swimming naked in the ocean, leaving (white) women consigned to their homes "por no ver el más repugnante de los cuadros: un enjambre de hombres, hijos de un pueblo civilazado, que se baña como una tríbu de salvajes en el interior de África (to avoid seeing the most repugnant of pictures: a swarm of men, sons of a civilized society, bathing like a tribe of savages in the interior of Africa). Debates about the public morality of the danzón, then, condensed these broader discourses, and made explicit their discourse of race, sexuality, and contagion. If women could be "contaminated" in proximity to Chinese, blacks, or "black" behavior as a witness on the city street, imagine the scandal of Havana's beauties dancing a perceived "African" dance. For conservative critics, those girls were not so far from the barbarous men bathing in the nude, revealing in the very heart of Cuba the savage interior of Africa.

The most heated controversy about the dance reemerged in the summer of 1881 and lasted for a year. Despite the initial controversy, the dance had in two short years become *the* dominant form of entertainment in Cuba, crossing lines of race, gender, and class. Several conservative newspapers, lead by the Matanzas-based *La Aurora del Yumurí,* and later joined by Havana papers like *El almendares,* launched an all-out attack on the morality of the danzón. The attacks reprised and refined the two central objections to the dance: its "Africanizing" effects and its sexual impropriety. Both charges assumed and elaborated a more fundamental premise: the rhythm of danzón operated as a palpable contagion on real and figurative social bodies. The fact that this criticism emanated primarily from conservative (procolonial) quarters allows us to understand these critiques as an attempt to recode the otherwise "Cuban" meanings with which the dance had by now been invested. That is, if many (although not all) liberals celebrated the dance as a "national rhythm," a sign of Cuba's unique and independent cultural identity, then the critics attempted to recast that rhythm as a nefariously "infectious" one.

One conservative, insisting on his adoration of Cuba, illustrates the procedure well. His editorial in *El aprendiz*, in the town of Regla, firmly casts the danzón as African, and proposes the (Spanish, peasant) zapateo as the better Cuban beat. "Para desgracia nuestra," he says, "la raza negra ha logrado introducir en familia cierta perturbación" (the black race has managed to introduce a certain perturbation in the family); the black race has interrupted the unified "family" of Spanish-born and Cuban-born whites on the island. Repeating the claim that danzónes are nothing other than "degenerations of African tangos," he contests any contrary claim that it is Cuban:

> ¿Queréis [. . .] probarnos que la danza y el danzón son buenos y morales? ¿Queréis probarnos también que son cubanos? [. . .] para nosotros la danza y el danzón son bailes extraños, porque para nosotros el baile que nació en el país, y aún vive en el, se nombra ZAPATEO.
>
> (Can you prove that the danza and the danzón are good and moral? Can you further prove that they are Cuban? For us the danza and danzón are foreign dances, because for us the dance that was born in this country, and still lives here, is called ZAPATEO.)

The writer, of course, has strategically rewritten the genealogy of all three dances: whereas the choreography of danza and danzón did, of course, initially develop only in Cuba, the zapateo originated in Spain, and was brought to Cuba by Andalucian immigrants who settled primarily in Cuba's countryside. While Cubans did elaborate their own variation of zapateo (sometimes called simply, zapateo cubano), the dance was certainly no more and arguably less "native" to Cuba than the African-influenced danza or danzón.

In her analysis of metaphors of contagion in the reception of African diasporic cultural forms in the Americas, Barbara Browning notes that all infectious rhythms "spread quickly, transnationally, accompanied by equally 'contagious' dances, often characterized as dangerous, usually overly sexually explicit, by white critics" (Browning 1998, 6). And so it was in Cuba, where virtually no discussion of the dance during the moralist attack was free of metaphors of contagion. In one paroxysm of condemnation, the performances at the Cervantes Theatre (known, indeed, for risqué performance genres like the can-can) was accused of hosting "letal veneno de una desenfrenada corrupción, donde mujeres deshonestas se ofrecen en asquerosa caricatura, entre pirápicas danzas y lésbicos abrazos" (lethal poison of an unstoppable corruption, where dishonest women offer themselves in disgusting caricature, between burning dances and lesbian embraces [Leal 1982, 182]).[2] Drawing a picture of poisoned women indulging in heated dances and otherwise "perverse" pleasures of racial impersonation and female desire, popular performance is imagined as a venom infiltrating the body politic. The vector for this contagion was, apparently, the pleasure of performance itself, which is as addictive as it is dangerous. One editorial from *La Aurora del Yumurí* explained:

> Y tanto la danza y el danzón como los bailes africanos tan sólo hablan a la materia, y en ellos todos, a medida que se baila más, más y más se despiertan los sentidos y más y más se desea la continuación, hasta que el cuerpo, jadeante y sudoroso, cae, rendido por la fatiga que proporciona un placer desconocido. (*La Aurora del Yumurí*, 30 July 1881)

> (The danza and danzón alike, like African dances, only speak to the embodied, and in all three, the more you dance, the more and more your senses awake, and the more and more you desire to continue, until the body, panting and sweating, falls defeated by the exhaustion produced by an unknown pleasure.)

This orgasmic description was meant to scandalize the public, although here as in countless other critiques, we find a remarkable if inadvertent paean to the reputedly fantastic pleasures offered by the new dance.

Conservative commentators capitalized on liberal men's fear of "their" women losing control in the face of the dance's magical powers of seduction, presenting this as further evidence that Cubans could not control their women, much less their own political affairs. Female chastity and political independence were, apparently, firmly interconnected: "Sin pudor," announced one moralist, "no hay madre posible, no hay sociedad buena, ni pueblo digno, ni espiritú digno, ni espiritú noble, ni países libres" (Without modesty, there is no mother possible, nor good society, nor dignified people, nor dignified spirit, nor noble spirit, nor free country [D. Luis Arias, *La Aurora del Yumurí*, 28 August 1881]). Or, consider this taunting axiom, written by a rabidly anti-Cuban essayist: "Bailando los hombres se afeminan y las mujeres se prostituyen; los pueblos pierden su energía y su amor a la independencia" (By dancing men are feminized and women prostituted; nations lose their energy and love of independence [W. A. Insúa, "Variedades" in *La Aurora del Yumurí*, 9 August 1882]). The most frequent and no doubt effective image broadcast in the conservative press was of Cuba's white virgins willingly giving in to the seductions of a powerful African rhythm—a rhythm that another writer characterized as "ese grito africano que lleva a sus sonidos la exclamación viril del salvaje" (that African scream whose sound carries the virile exclamation of the savage [*La Aurora del Yumurí*, 20 July 1881, parodying a defense of the dance as a "Cuban dance" in the *El eco de las Villas* [Castillo Faílde 1964, 140–41]). The picture intentionally exacerbated the already unreasonable but prevalent fear of black rape of white women. Witness this near pornographic portrait of one of Cuba's virgins in the fullness of the dance:

> La mujer en brazos del hombre; dejando oprimir fuertemente su flexible talle, confundiéndose sus alientos, envolviéndose en una misma magnética mirada, meciéndose, columpiándose, rozándose, aniquilándose en el deleite del pensamiento, y en el deleite del deseo, embriagándose con las notas saturadas de armonía y de sensualidad del danzón, perdiendo toda idea de pudor y de castidad, sintiéndose agitado el corazón por extrañas sensaciones y la mente enardecida por mas extrañas ideas, he ahí el cuadro. (W. A. Insúa, *La Aurora del Yumurí*, 9 August 1882)

> (The woman in arms of the man, allowing him to firmly press her flexible figure, their breaths mixing, becoming enveloped in one magnetic gaze, rocking each other, swinging together, brushing against each other, losing herself in the pleasure of the thought, the pleasure of desire, intoxicated by notes saturated with the harmony and sensuality of the danzón, losing all notion of modesty or chastity, feeling her heart agitated by strange sensations and the mind heated by the strangest ideas, there is the picture.)

Here white women are the discursive currency—the object to be rescued, exchanged, or lost—between rival white male ideological positions on the fate of Cuba; "she" is the metaphor for the public body over whose control white men compete. Following a common strategy from earlier in the century, the more conservative position used explicit threats of "her" "Africanization" to paralyze liberal action.

These threats took on new meaning in the early 1880s, when the implementation of abolition was already in progress and its final passage imminent. The Moret Law of 1870 technically freed elderly and infant slaves; new legislation in 1880 replaced the slave system with the *patronato*, which legally renamed slave-holders *patronos* (patrons, a term far more benign in rhetoric than in practice) and which marked the eventual release of the slaves, now renamed *patrocinados* (the patronized). For the commentator quoted above, Cuba's passion for illicit, "African" dance threatened to turn "her" not only African, but into a slave: "Bailad, que con vuestros pies, forjaréis la cadena que, como escalvos, os sujete siempre a la inmoralidad. [. . .] Cuba será una pobre esclava constantemente martirizada no por gentes ajenas sino sus mismos hijos. ¡Cuba despierta!" (Dance, so that with your feet you'll forge the chains that, like slaves, will link you always to immorality. Cuba will be a poor slave, constantly martyred not by foreigners but by her very sons. Cuba, awake! [W. A. Insúa, *La Aurora del Yumurí*, 9 August 1882]). Through dance, Cuba—now double cast as both mother and virgin daughter—would be undone by her very own sons: by indulging this "African" dance, the "stain" of slavery would remain with her despite the progress of abolition. The end of slavery would, in other words, signal no moral progress if white Cuba allowed the culture of former slaves to "infect" or "Africanize" white civil society.

Conservative critics were in fact partly correct in associating the dance with an increasingly public black social community. While the dance's exact "African" origins are debatable, the dance was nonetheless important to a coalescing black public sphere in the 1880s. The popularity of the dance with white culture catapulted mulato composers like Miguel Faílde and Raimundo Valenzuela to fame and considerable fortune, which they in turn frequently lent to the black community. For example, the black mutual aid society La Unión, in Matanzas, held a benefit in May 1879 at the Teatro Estéban (the primary home of the danzón and the teatro bufo in Matanzas) to raise funds to build a school for black children. Attended by both whites and blacks at a time when seating in theatres was still segregated, the evening's entertainments were notable for featuring black comics and orators on stage before this mixed-race audience, a rarity in Cuban theatre. Alfredo Torroella, longtime guaracha and later danzón composer for the teatro bufo, headlined the event. In another example, all of the major danzón orchestras gathered in December of 1881 at the café El Louvre in Havana for what may have been an all-black affair to honor the black activist-politician Juan Gualberto Gómez. Miguel Faílde and Raimundo Valenzuela joined three other orchestras in a long evening that culminated with all five playing the celebrated danzón "El Siglo XX" or "The twentieth century" (Castillo Faílde 1964, 97, 122–23). For many black Cubans, urban black entertainments (whether "African" in origin or not) were thus clearly an important part of black Cuban social and political relations, enabling the expression a vision of Cuba's future more consonant with their antiracist and nationalist views. Honoring the island's foremost civil rights activist with a display of danzones by leading composers, the event proposes a future Cuba of "El Siglo XX" that counts on creative black collaboration, participation, and intervention.

Years later, on return from a long exile, Juan Gualberto Gómez was called upon to reflect on the meaning of the dance for the black community in the aftermath of abolition, answering charges that Cubans in general, and black Cubans in particular, simply dance too much. One editorial expressed a view that appeared with some frequency in the black newspaper *La Fraternidad*: "para desgracia nuestra, muchas [sociedades] olvidan su alta misión é indebidamente se intitulan de "Instrucción" cuando sólo se dedican al recreo, siendo el principal de ellos el baile, del que se abusan demasiado" (to our ill fortune, many [mutual aid societies] forget their high mission, and improperly name themselves [sites] of "Instruction" when they only dedicate themselves to recreation, principal among them dance, which they abuse excessively [*La Fraternidad*, 21 August 1888]). Another put the matter more succinctly: "Bailemos menos; acordémos que somos hombres" (Let us dance less; let us remember that we are men), suggesting that the "real" work of the black community would be performed by men with no recourse to the apparently feminizing distractions of dance (*La Fraternidad*, 20 December 1888). Both critics, and many similar concerned voices in *La Fraternidad* and *La Igualdad* over the years, worried aloud that the constant association of black people with dance, either in the minds of whites or in the practices of blacks themselves, itself was injurious to the project of black development and enfranchisement.

Gómez, who only rarely departed from overtly political commentary in his oratory, took a moment to defend the dance and its role in the formation and, in his term, the "progress" of the black community in the years since the patronato:

> ¿No es verdad que los bailes de las sociedades de la clase de color han servido mucho para el progreso, la cultura, y la moralidad de nuestra raza? Los hombres que han llegado á la hora segunda, ó á la tercera, no saben cómo encontramos á la raza de color, sobre todo en la Habana, los que desde la primera hora empezamos a trabajar por su rejeneración. Nuestra juventud, en buena parte, se dedicaba á los juegos de ñáñigos, á los tangos, á los bailes inmorales de la *cuna* de Guanabacoa, y de los *altos* de Albisu. No teníamos otra cosa que ofrecer á esa juventud y entonces se crearon las sociedades y sus bailes vinieron á representar un positivo progreso sobre el *tango* y sobre las contorciones del ñáñiguismo. En ese sentido, debemos gratitud al baile. (*La Igualdad*, 14 March 1893)
>
> (Is it not true that the dances of the [mutual aid] Societies of the people of color have greatly served the progress, the culture, and the morality of our race? The men who have arrived at the second hour, or at the third, do not know how we found the race of color, particularly in Havana, when those of us at the first hour began to work. Our youth, in large measure, dedicated itself to ñáñigo games, to *tangos*, to the immoral dances of the *cuna* in Guanabacoa, or the upper floors [*altos*] of the Albisu. We had nothing else to offer that youth, and then we created the Societies and their

dances came to represent a positive progress over the tango and the contortions of *ñáñiguismo.* In this sense, we owe gratitude to the dance.)

The stakes for such dances were high, Gómez notes, enabling not simply moral "uplift" but survival, in a threatening social context where, he recalls, everyday brought news of the injury or death of four or five black people as a result of the "prácticas bárbaras" (barbarous practices) found in rough urban neighborhoods.

If white commentators accuse the dance of attracting white youth toward a dangerous "Africanizing" practice that distracts them from their Spanish present, or a Cuban future, Gómez poses the reverse for black youth. The great black social dances, and later the celebrated veladas, of the 1880s mark a path of progress away from those practices most associated with an African past, like ñáñiguismo, and toward a Cuban future. The contrast between white conservative discourse and that of Gómez is striking. When the newspaper *El Almendares* joined what it called the "crusade" against dance, it too described a scene of degradation and "ñáñiguismo" at the salons of the Albisu and other sites, where

> hay *escuelitas*, es decir, centros de depravacion. Allí acuden jóvenes de todas clases, que bailando y tomando por pretexto el baile, se hacen de amistades peligrosas, se aficionan á toda clase de vicios y se van infiltrando poco á poco de ideas y gustos de la peor especie. No es extraño que de aquí salgan los *ñáñigos distinguidos* de quienes se valen algunos para hacer befa del país. (*El Almendares*, 3 August 1881)

> (there are little schools [*escuelitas*], that is, centers of depravity. Young people of all classes, dancing and taking dance as a pretext, make dangerous friendships, they become interested in all class of vice and they are infiltrated little by little by ideas and tastes of the worst kind. It is no surprise that from there emerge those *distinguished ñáñigos* who serve as cause for some to ridicule the country.

Several weeks later, *El Almendares* raised the alarm again, now decrying the "indecent" dances at the Café El Louvre: "Los títulos de los danzones y de las personas á quienes son dedicadas . . . dan asco" (The titles of the dances and the persons to whom they are dedicated . . . are disgusting [*El Almendares*, 25 August 1881]). White and black moralists, apparently, agree on this much: the *escuelitas* teach morally questionable behavior in addition to, or perhaps through, dance. For *El Almendares*, the *escuelitas* are the sure road to dangerous dance, emblematized by the danzón as the prime site of immoral "infiltration." In September, it drew this scandalized genealogy of Cuban dance: "Empezamos con la danza, vino el danzón, ahora el *oso*, enseguida vendrá la *rumba*, y como es natural, acabaremos bailando *ñáñigo* (We began with the danza, then came danzón, and now *el oso*; soon will come the *rumba*, and as is natural, we'll end up dancing *ñáñigo*.) The danzón marks a movement "downward" on a quasi-evolutionary scale from Europe to Africa. The commentator then imagines this portrait of eventual Cuban dance:

La orquesta de Valenzuela suprimiría sus instrumentos de viento y en su lugar tocarían tambores. Entraría una familia en un baile: papá por delante con el *palo mecongo* ó *mecombe;* la mamá con las marugas; el hijo mayor vestido de *ñáñigo* y el mas chico con el ramo de escoba amarga; las muchachas con coronas de maní y farolitos de colores entonando un punto de clave. [. . .] Si esto ha de succeder, [. . .] preferimos morrirnos ántes de presenciarlo.

(Valenzuela's orchestra would eliminate their string instruments, and in their place play drums. A family would enter a dance: father in front with the *palo mecongo* or *mecombe* [percussion instruments]; the mother with *las marugas* [shakers]; the eldest son dressed like a *ñáñigo*, and the youngest with a branch of *escoba amarga* [plant used in Afrocuban religious practice], the girls with crowns of peanuts and colored lanterns singing a *punto de clave*. If this must come to pass, we'd rather die than witness it.)

The commentator suggests that enjoying the danzón is already a process of "putting on" "Africanness," whose logical outcome can best be illustrated by outfitting the normative patriarchal white family with the clothes, instruments, and accoutrements of a "degenerate" musical scene, all moving to the beat of Valenzuela's drums. The costume and rhythm are imagined as having a precise racializing effect: the portrait draws a "respectable" family in scandalous blackface. Yet even as the author wishes death before such a future, his own seeming fluency with the genre of "African" performance (down to the specification between the "palo mecongo" *or* "mecombe") suggests that he has already grasped and unwittingly accepted an essential grammar of these supposed "African" (but actually Afrocuban or black Cuban) musical forms. However scandalous he may find African diasporic performance, he does not find the music or its context undecipherable: he is able to reconstruct, to a point, the key elements that might produce the distinctive rhythm he otherwise abhors. He is, it appears, already more "infected" by the music than he himself admits.

For Gómez, in turn, the social dances hosted by the black community—often headlined by Valenzuela, and attended by black men and women and their children, almost always dancing danzones—are instead the sure road *away* from the dangers of the *escuelitas* and their "Africanizing" influence.

Gomez is no more friend to ñáñiguismo than his white counterpart; but for Gómez the danzón sits on a different, almost inverse, scale of progress, moving away from drums and toward strings, away from the dangers of street life and toward "wholesome" family and social gathering. In his same *Fraternidad* editorial from 21 August 1888, Gómez contests the related assumptions that the danzón is inherently "African," that it is inherently "immoral," and that black Cubans would therefore have a special affection for it. First, he notes that "El danzón lo bailan aqui elementos de todas las razas y de todas procedencias" (The danzón is danced here [in Cuba] by elements of all races and from all backgrounds). As for immorality, he argues, far greater scandal can found in the dances he saw in exile in "cultured" Paris; next to the can-can (which also made its way to Cuba in the early 1880s), the danzón is a "una pulcritud bendita" (a saintly pulchritude). Against the widely broadcast notion that "la clase de color no [hace] mas que bailar y que [esta] corrumpida por el danzón" (the class of color does no more than dance and is corrupted by the danzón), Gómez insists: "No! La clase de color trabaja, estudia. Y progresa mas de lo que baila" (No! the class of color works, studies. And it progresses more than it dances).

Underwriting these discourses—liberal, conservative, black, white—is a complex set of assumptions about performance, social identities, and ideas of movement. These communities, defined by race, gender, age, or nation, apparently move "up" or "down" a ladder of civilized behaviors by virtue of practices like dance; and they move "backward" to or "forward" from "primitive" beginnings, foreign pasts, or national futures. Temporal and spatial coordinates are mapped in the terms of the other: Africa can be made present in Cuba through dance or other practices, but is temporally marked as "before," or "behind" an ideal present. To keep Cuba in a present covalent with Europe and other "civilized" nations, and not fall "back" to Africa, Cubans must keep dancing—the right dance. Dance stands as one key site for the imagining of such social movement: located in the body, but learned and shared collectively, dance expresses both essential identity and social development. It is both without history, emanating from the body in a repeated present, and the site of all history, whose rhythm apparently reveals the atavistic codes, like so much DNA, of its constituent racial and national pasts.

The fact that dance was evidently important to blacks in Cuba, served as one ground for the conservative attack on liberals in the debates of 1881 and 1882. They argued that the cross-racial popularity of the dance would not only "Africanize" whites, but would break down racial barriers altogether. The moralists of the *Aurora del Yumurí* crusade were particularly concerned by rumors the Teatro Estéban allowed certain persons of color—usually light-skinned mulatas—into its Sunday dances. On the question of racial segregation they were adamant: "o deben ser exclusivamente para personas blancas o exclusivamente para personas de color, pues esa amalgama de razas [. . .] entraña el orígen de un mal grave para el porvenir de la sociedad" (they should be exclusively for whites or exclusively for people of color, since that mixing of races harbors the beginning of a grave ill for the future of society). The critic then conjures another cautionary image of racial chaos to chasten readers:

> Pero ya que esto no es así, no deben existir las preferencias; que bailen todos, negros, pardos y blancos, que bailen todos; que ante los repugnantes goces que proporcionan esos interminables danzones que se tocan en 'Esteban' desaparecen todas las diferencias y todas las razas.
>
> (But seeing that this [racial segregation] is not the case, then there should be no preferences: let everyone dance, blacks, mulattos and whites, let them all dance; in the face of those repugnant pleasures meted out by those interminable danzones played at the Esteban, let all differences and races disappear.)

The writer assumes, perhaps correctly, that his white readers will be scandalized by the image: under the shadow of impending abolition, all social structures that separate the races and regulate racial behaviors could crumble, to be replaced by the chaotic miscegenation of a wild danzón. Yet this same image—no preferences, no differences, no racial distinctions—may well have been precisely the image of racial equality that Faílde and Valenzuela may have traced in their danzón vision of "El Siglo XX" (the twentieth century) and it is most certainly the rule of law imagined and advocated by Gómez for Cuba's public sphere. Here the danzón offered a different structure of feeling for white and black participants: race and sociality are dialectically re-formed and differently semanticized in the practices of the dance.

Why then did liberal Cubans embrace this dance, given that it left them open, like black Cubans, to charges of racial adulteration, lack of civilization, and sexual depravity? What did this dance *do* that others had not or could not? What mode of presence, what form of sociality did this dance structure? What made people *feel* Cuban when dancing this dance? Ramón Morales Álvarez's teatro bufo play *El proceso del oso*, performed by the Bufos de Salas at the Teatro Torrecillas in January 1882, points to some answers. In the play, we are told that the conservative attack on the danzón has reached such a pitch that it has alarmed the very muse of dance, Terpsichore, who decides she must investigate the controversy herself. Tired of the complaints, she convenes "todos los bailes residentes en la isla de Cuba" (all resident dances of the island of Cuba) to witness a trial of the latest and most "voluptuous" version of the danzón to date, "el Oso" or the "the bear" (10).[3] After a thorough review, which includes a lengthy performance of the dance itself, the suspect danzón is ultimately acquitted of all charges.[4] Here, as we will see, it was precisely the image of Cuban racial harmony through dance that liberal Cubans strategically recycled and resignified to counter the conservative assault; significantly, they did so not in print, but through performance.

The primary conceit of *El proceso del oso* is that each dance is anthropomorphized and made to embody the national, racial, or ethnic characteristics of the region the dance ostensibly represents. The entry of each dance onto the stage is an occasion not only to display the choreography of each dance, but to underscore a range of prescribed social markings associated with each dance's region of origin. By the time all of the dances have arrived on stage—including the ultrarefined European Minué (Minuet); the foot-stomping throaty Spanish Zapateo; the drum-beating African, a comic bozal "Congo Luango"; the sentimental mulata Danza; the flighty female Francophone Can-can who enters to a scandalous version of "Les enfants de la patrie"; and the doltish English Lancer; along with the full range of danzón-based dances of the day including the *cocoyé*, *papolote*, *caringa* and the *fambuá* (danced by blackface negros curros, costumed in the flamboyant Andalucian-style dress for which they were famous)—the procession has mapped not only a folkloric genealogy of Cuban dance, but the social, sexual, and racial profile of Cuban culture itself. Assembling all to stand in judgment of the new danzón named Oso, Terpsichore commands the dignified, European Minué to act as prosecutor, and the well-spoken mulata, Danza, to serve as the danzón's defense. This fanciful scenario itself advances a counter-offensive to the conservative critics: the danzón will be judged from the point of view of dance itself, thereby eclipsing any arbitrary moral stance against the social-sexual expressive culture of the body in the first place.

The innovation of the play lies not in its basic scenario, which Morales Álvarez borrowed wholesale from an earlier Spanish one-act play, *El proceso del can-can*, performed in Cuba in 1876 by a touring Spanish company during the war. In the earlier play, the protagonist on trial was the Can-can, portrayed as a French womanizer, accused by a range of Spanish and European dance figures (the English Lancer, the German Polka) for his scandalous seductions and betrayals of two Spanish dances, allegorized as young women. The subsequent trial of Can-can stages the competitive contrast between

Spanish and French dance, and by extension Spanish and French culture, morality, and taste, and ultimately indicts and exiles the Can-can from serious theatres in Spain.[5] *El proceso del oso*, in turn, brings greater complexity to the notion of "national" dance: rather than stage a community of dances in which each form "represents" its corresponding nation, the Cuban play explores how and when different dance forms have made claims to be "Cuban" at all, thereby gradually establishing the grounds on which the danzón can claim legitimacy as a national dance.

The first of these grounds draws on the then prevalent rhetoric of Darwinian evolution to draw a genealogy of dance's development in Cuba through time, in addition to marking its complexity in the present. On entry, each dance positions him or herself in the progressive development of dance in Cuba. Minué, for example, is nostalgic for "aquellos días patriarcales" (those patriarchal days) when he "formaba las delicias de los bailadores" (formed the delights of dancers [18]), but realizes that his dominance, like all other things, "está sujeto a las leyes del transformismo, según los que nos hacen descender del mono y del orangután" (is subject to the laws of transformation, according to those who would have us descend from the monkey and orangutan [19]). His successor, Danza, recalls her evolutionary rise and fall as the darling of Havana's social scene in a striking monologue, remarkable first as a valuable if anecdotal thumbnail history of the dance, and also as a prime example of costumbrista prose. Her rhythmic recitation of the evocative, vernacular names of danza variations, in addition to being virtually untranslatable, offers an important conceptual frame for the performance of the dance itself. She explains that she began as a dance of choreographic floor patterns (*un baile de figuras*), but that her choreography was simplified over the years under the pressure of the changing experience of time itself:

> Se empezaba por la cadena . . . venía luego la media cadena . . . en seguida el sostenido y por último el cedazo . . . pero vino el progreso, rugió la locomotora . . . nació el relajo y se armó la bulla, time is money, según la máxima americana; mis partidarios comprendieron que bailar de esa manera era perder el tiempo miserablemente y que reducida solamente al cedazo, que vino a tomar distintos nombres según la manera de ejecutarlo y se llamó sube y baja . . . de vaya y venga, de me duermo bailando, a lo guanajay. Y apareció el cangrejito, la sopimpa . . . la cachumba, la caidita, el ladrillito, el chiquito abajo, el infanzón, la palanca y el cedazo de malanga. ¡Y sabe Dios todo lo que hubiera salido! [. . .] Todavía me acuerdo del zungambelo, del canelo, del mandinga ciguato, de Ábreme la puerta, cielo, Aronga, mamita; Sereno toca el pito, Quindembo, Suelta el peso que es del rancho, y apaga la vela. Pero ya voy de capa caída . . . Me han desterrado del Louvre. (25)

(It began with the *la cadena* [the chain] . . . later came *la media cadena* [the half chain] . . . soon followed by *el sostenido* [the supported/sustained] and finally the *cedazo* [sifter, similar to the waltz] . . . but along came progress, the locomotor roared . . . the *relajo* [joke] was born and raised a ruckus, *time is money* or so says the American maxim; my partisans understood that dancing that way meant a miserable waste of time, and so I was reduced to the *cedazo* only, which came to be known by various names, depending on the style of execution; so I was called *sube y baja* [rise and fall]. . . *vaya y venga* [come and go], *me duermo bailando* [I sleep while dancing], *a lo guanajay* [like a fool]. And then appeared the *cangrejito* [little crayfish], the *sopimpa* . . . the *cachumba*, the *caidita* ['little fall'], the *ladrillito* [little brick], the *chiquito abajo* [little one below], the *infanzón* [big baby], the *palanca* [the lever] and the *cedazo de malanga* [malanga waltz]. Who knows how it would have turned out! [. . .] I still remember the *zungambelo*, the *canelo*, the *mandinga ciguato* [jaundiced African/mandinga], *Ábreme la puerta, cielo* [Open the door for me, honey], *Aronga, mamita*; *Sereno toca el pito* [Watchman blow your whistle], *Quindembo*, *Suelta el peso que es del rancho*, and *apaga la vela* [blow out the candle]. But now I am in rough shape . . . They've banished me from the Louvre café.)

The evolutionary rhetoric proposes the notion that for each successive social era there is (and should be) a corresponding dance. The combination of Danza's celebratory costumbrismo along with a presentation of the dance itself (the cedazo, danced by Danza with the male Danzón) indulges the audience's—and certainly the critics'—nostalgia for bygone days, well before the arrival of the danzón and the confusing or threatening social-sexual-racial complexities of the 1880s. For many, the danza was associated with the days of Spanish hegemony, slavery, strict racial segregation, and rigid colonial social order. For just this reason, the danzón can be recuperated in the play as the necessary expression of Cuba's postwar age, now characterized by greater autonomy and social freedoms for whites and black alike. The evolutionary rhetoric positions the danzón as the only and rightful successor to the nostalgic Danza, and positions attacks of the danzón as an attack on the very "locomotor" of social progress.

When Danzón enters the scene as "la última palabra del arte coreográfico" (the latest/last word in choreographic art), the representation of the dance re-signifies the contemporary critiques in several important ways. When Danzón claims that "Las niñas me piden a gritos [. . .] y hasta las viejas se embullan al son del . . . ¡entra, guabina!" (the girls ask for me with screams, and even the old women get moving to the sound of "entra, guabina!" [lyrics to a popular danzón, 26]), we find the dance still associated with extraordinary powers of seduction over women, young and old alike. However, unlike conservative discourse, the play does not allow these women to stand in for the "innocent" or "pure" body of Cuba, but rather, substitutes them with the dance itself: now Cuba is a virile young man, whose power and potency are amply measured by his undisputed ability to seduce Cuba's coveted women. The powers of seduction that made the dance suspect in the eyes of conservative critics are now harnessed in service of the new nation. The play presents the dance's virility as the necessary correlative to a newly invigorated Cuban society, one that anticipates Cuba's revolutionary independence in the years to come. Indeed, Danzón (with tongue firmly in cheek, of course) insists that whereas the French revolutionaries went to the gallows singing the "Marseillaise," the Cubans will surely meet their destiny singing "la mulatica revoltona" (the sashaying mulata), a popular danzón of the day (26). Now it is no longer Cuba's white virgins who are threatened by the danzón (to the contrary, it is implied that they are well satisfied by the dance), but rather conservatives who must beware the seductive political powers of the dance.

However, even as the play reverses the gender terms of conservative discourse to cast the Cuban public body as inherently male, it cannot fully elide questions of the danzón's supposed African heritage. Instead the play—like so much Cuban vernacular culture of the day—pursues a course of strategic ambiguity where issues of race are concerned. *El proceso del oso* acknowledges this potential disturbance in its evolutionary rhetoric by elaborating a joke about the Danzón's questionable parentage. Danzón introduces himself as the "hijo natural de la danza . . . y de padre . . . no conocido; pero bautizado en la casa cuna" (natural son of the danza, and of a father . . . unknown, but baptized in the city orphanage [also slang for dance venues]). His baptism in a casa cuna is significant, as it tells us that he—like many mixed-race children of unmarried mothers in nineteenth century Cuba—was placed in an orphanage at birth so that he would be granted a proper surname (usually Valdés) despite the lack of father. Clearly, as the "natural son" of the mulata Danza, the play makes no pretense to cast Danzón as white, but the unknown father leaves open the possibility that he may be less or more white than she. Nothing in the text of the play or in extant commentaries indicates how the Danzón was represented on stage, whether he was played in blackface, brownface, or without makeup. Several things are certain: the play does not use language to mark the character as being in any way "African," the typical marker of comic blackface in teatro bufo plays. Instead, that linguistic humor is lent primarily to the bozal figure of the African Congo. Danzón speaks a fairly straightforward, locally inflected Spanish idiom throughout. Thus, while the play keeps open the possibility that Danzón may have a black father, the story of his baptism seems rather to prompt the opposite assumption: white, not black, fathers were more likely to disavow a child of their union with a mulata; mixed-race children of white, not black, fathers were most frequently placed in Havana's casa cuna. This story allows the author, Moralez Álvarez, to evoke a common anticolonial allegory found in other teatro bufo plays and in popular fiction, in which Spain is cast as the tyrannical father unable or unwilling to let his own son come of age and control his own affairs. In *El proceso*, we glimpse Spain as a colonial hypocrite who has slept with a Cuban criolla, and is now unwilling to acknowledge the "natural" result of their union. Again it is colonial Spain—not Cuba's women—that shows a lack of sexual control and proper moral conduct.

While Cuba is presented as an almost-white virile male, the general body politic whose loyalty he commands is represented as the embodiment of racial and gender mixing itself—a body marked by new modes of inhabiting race and gender in Cuba's newly "democratic" age, a body difficult to define with prevailing categories. Witness Danzón's testimonial of the social scene he caused the previous night:

La concurrencia se componía de lo principalito de la culta capital de la perla de las Antillas. Allí estaba la crema, la flor y nata de la juventud masculina, femenina, neutra, común de dos epicena y ambigua; campeando la democracia, pues no había distinción de clases, colores, ni condiciones.

Bailaban allí el yambú
de una manera asombrosa
las negras Coleta y Rosa
y Juanita Chambicú.
Ya estaba como un merengue
la heterogénea hembrería,
y sin embargo decía
que toquen el Tengerengue.

Entre las señoras se hallaban las bellas de Benitón, Perico Mascavidrio y Palanqueta, las respetables de Congo, las distinguidas de Mandinga, y las nunca bien ponderadas como se debe, duquesa de Haití y condesa del Camarón. (27)

(Those attending were composed of the principal [group] of the cultured capital of the pearl of the Antilles [Cuba]. There was the cream of the crop of today's youth—masculine, feminine, neutral, both, epicene and ambiguous; championing democracy, as there was no distinction of class, color, or social status.

Dancing the *yambú* [an Afrocuban dance]
in a surprising manner

were the black women Coleta and Rosa
and Juanita Chambicú.
The heterogeneous womanhood
was already going like a *merengue*
but still they asked
that they play the Tengerengue

Among the ladies were the beauties of Benitón, Perico Mascavidrio, and Palanqueta, the respectable [ladies] of Congo, the distinguished [ladies] of Mandinga, and the never as well thought of as they deserve, the Duchess of Haiti and the Countess of Camarón/Shrimp.)

This is a striking image of the Cuban body politic: gender bending (although largely female), racially "heterogeneous," sexually charged, egalitarian, and of course, avidly dancing. The play draws upon existing discourse of Cuban nationalism as founded on a notion of racial mestizaje: the play itself is subtitled an "ajiaco bufo-lírico-bailable" (a bufo-lyric-danceable ajiaco), and, like Creto Gangá's own ajiaco, parodically celebrates racial diversity as central to Cuban national sentiment. The slight *catedracismo* of Danzón's speech ("epicena," "heterogénea hembrería") indicates that, like Creto Gangá before him, we cannot take his claims at face value; yet he strategically uses racial and gender difference as the decisive marker of the scene's Cubanness ("lo principalito de la culta capital. . ."). The image is the parodic—but not unserious—double of that evoked by Faílde's "Siglo XX" in honor of Gómez. Speaking to the female Terpsícore, Danzón breaks into a seemingly "authentic" song (and dance?) in the middle of his otherwise wry narrative ("allí bailaban el yambú") perhaps to embody the rhythm itself, inviting—seducing—her to partake in the same heated merengue that had the negras calling out for more. The evocative image of those black women dancing is immediately followed by one of a mock black aristocracy: the ladies of Benitón, Congo, and Camarón are stolen from the teatro bufo's latest catedrático hits, perhaps performed in repertory with this very play. In *El proceso,* the blackface aristocracy no longer acts out a whiteface charade of the European minuet, but instead follows the latest social fashion, dancing the democratic danzón. The danzón is then comically but explicitly linked to new social reforms in the capital. When Terpsícore asks whether Lady Moñonga had not joined the aristocratic seraglio, Danzón explains that she was busy investigating the latest public works, studying the latest reforms to the sewer system, fire alarms, and municipal taxes (27). The presence of these mock aristocrats in Danzón's narrative is as much a tongue-in-cheek testament to the dance's democratizing effects (embracing white and black[face] aristocrats alike), as it is a covert critique of Spanish aristocrats who might enjoy the dance as well, despite their public protests to the contrary.

Casting Cuba as a virile male allows the play to protect his/Cuba's body from difficult questions of social reproduction: Cuba can be celebrated as sexually potent, without being subject to the same concerns of sexual or racial purity otherwise expected of Cuba's "patriot virgins." In the play, all sexual-social reproductive concerns are displaced onto the subplot, which focuses on the mulata Danza, who is—as in so many teatro bufo plays—torn between two suitors, one black and one white. In this case, it is her love for the black Congo (a variation of the negrito), and her obligation to love the English Lancer (who here stands in for the thick-witted gallego). Her love story carries the burden of Cuba's national allegory, choosing between an African and European future. From the outset Terpsícore chooses for her, noting that Lancer is the only reasonable choice: "hoy por hoy los matrimonios deben obedecer a la conveniencia. Para eso estamos en el siglo de las luces" (in today's world marriages should obey convenience. That's why we're in the age of Enlightenment [31]). Just as, says Terpsícore, East will encounter West and the Atlantic will embrace the Pacific through the engineered miracle of the Panama canal, so will the tropical Danza finally join the northern Lancer. When Danzón reminds Terpsícore that Danza has, after all, been having relations with the African Congo, Terpsícore makes it clear that Danza's future will not include that part of the globe: "los casaremos aunque sea por lo militar" (we'll marry them, even if by military means). As it turns out, Danza's own indecision costs her Congo's love; she acquiesces to Terpsícore's wish that she marry the Englishman.

The ensuing, rather cryptic, exchange between Danzón and Terpsícore on how Danza's marriage should be made official returns the play to the controversy between essence and form, actor and rhythm. Terpsícore insists that one should look always for the essence of all behavior and disregard the specific form; Danzón suggestively replies, perhaps in reference to the danzón itself, that he knows of "forms that speak volumes" (32). Danzón implies the principle on which the rest of the play is premised, and the principle by which the danzón el Oso will be acquitted: the truth of the danzón, like Cubanness itself, is only manifest to those who can *dance* it. Here nationalism presents itself as a kind of bodily, kinesthetic knowledge, an epistemology which must be performed, and performed well, to be known at all. The foolish Lancero's inability to dance illuminates the point. He is greatly attracted to the danzón—so much, he says in broken Spanish, that "mi gusta más que al rosbif," he likes it even more than his decidedly English roast beef. However, he fears he'll never be able to capture the rhythm: "Mí ponga bien los pies y la cabeza; pero no puede menea la cuerpo" (I can put my feet and head right, but I can't move my body [33]). The Englishman has the same problem performing "Cuban" speech as well. Trying to convince Lancer to approach Danza, Minué resorts to what he believes are ice-breaking Cuban euphemisms, asking Lancer how he feels about Cuban women, especially mulatas, through a string of increasingly idiomatic vernacular sayings. When Lancer protests that Minué's meanings don't match those in his Spanish dictionary, Minué's attempts to explain himself only plunge them deeper into comic miscommunication. Exasperated, Lancer demands to know if there is more than one type of Castilian, to which Minué must confess the affirmative (34–37). As with the danzón, it is the specific performance of the choreography or of the words that carries their actual social meaning, not a disembodied essence otherwise imputed to them.

The trial of el Oso elaborates this assertion. The legal context is incapable of appreciating the importance and relative "innocence" of the dance until all the bodies in attendance are able to dance it. Neither the prosecution as articulated by Minué or the defense as spoken by Danza can address the appeal and value of the dance; their respective haughty dissertations can do no more than parody the inadequate discourse already available in the press. Taking the stand, Minué becomes an outright parody of conservative critics, caught in full paroxysm of moral offense: "Yo me horrorizo, me estremezco . . . me hago una tortilla de camarones cuando veo esa juventud . . . el Oso es [. . .] el camino mas recoto para el vivac . . . el aldabón asqueroso conque se toca a las puertas del hospital. Yo me espeluzno . . ." (I am horrified, I tremble . . . I become a shrimp omelet when I see that youth . . . el Oso [. . .] is the fastest road to the police station . . . the repulsive door knocker on which one knocks at the doors of the hospital. My hair stands on end . . . [52–53]). Danza, in turn, cannot manage to defend Oso in the courtroom context, except by making recourse to unbridled catedracismo, presenting and parodying the pseudo-anthropological idea that choreography is determined by environmental factors such as the tropical climate:

> La preponderancia estética, metafísica, y si quiere antropológica, que de una manera tan vertiginosa [. . .] van adquiriendo las piezas sueltas, es la prueba más tangible [. . .] fehaciente, palpitante y axiomática de la protección priotécnica que se dispensa en los círculos paralelógramos de nuestra patria a todos los artículos importados del extranjero. [. . .] Esos bailes, como la nieve, deslumbrantes y fríos presentan todos los caracteres químicos y geológicos [. . .] [que se] recomiendan única y exclusivamente para los glaciales y aristocráticos salones de las hiperbóreas de los polos. (53–54)

(The aesthetic, metaphysical and, if you will, anthropological superiority that, in a manner so vertiginous, single dances acquire, is the most tangible, reliable, palpable, and axiomatic proof of the pyrotechnic protection dispensed in the circular parallelograms of our country against all articles imported from abroad. [. . .] Those dances, like the snow, dazzling and cold, present all the chemical and geological characteristics [. . .] recommended only and exclusively for the glacial and aristocratic salons of the hyper-borealis of the poles.)

Danza's impenetrable and hyperbolic defense suggests that foreign dances from the northern hemisphere, like the minuet and lancer, can have no meaning in tropical climates, and that fortunately Cuba has developed strong natural defenses against such foreign imports. Her catedracismo, however, suggests again that the dance will not be adequately defended through description alone. Even Danza is unconvinced by her own pedantic speech; in mid-defense, she breaks out of her catedracismo, to offer an aside in "Cuban": "pero a mí esto me huele a chicharrones de pellejo . . ." (this smells to me like cooked pork rind . . . [54]). Danzón, acting as witness, concurs, and translates her entire speech into plain "Cuban": "en los países intertropicales todo debe ser candela" (in inter-tropical countries everything should be candela, [54] which, among other things, means hip, hot, cool, all the rage, and in the groove). It is precisely this ineluctable candela quality which the danzón el Oso captures for Havana in 1881–82, and which saves the dance from legal censure in the play. For his own part, el Oso is all rhythm: he presents no defense (we are told he is mute) other than the rhythm itself, to which all the attending parties are compelled to move at his very appearance. Against such powers of communal seduction, who could resist? The tribunal is impressed, and drops all charges against him.

This appeal to the "tropical" nature of the rhythm hides the same racial ambivalence we find elsewhere in the teatro bufo, and in much 19th century Cuban cultural production. The very term "tropical" functions here as a charged code word which can mean both "Cuban" and "African": one on hand, "tropical" appears in much literature and theatre as a nationalist euphemism for the term "Cuban"; on the other, "tropical" is used as frequently in the same discourse to evoke a sense of Cuba's "Africanness" without actually calling it by name. The slippage between the two belies the racial debt Cubanness has to Africanness, and the degree to which that debt was so fully disavowed. To be "tropical" in this discourse was to be non-European, in the far peripheries of the West, where life is slower, hotter, wilder, in short: where life is candela. Hence the slower version of the waltz developed in Cuba (it was said, to accommodate the summer heat) was named the "vals tropical." The poet Fernando Romero Fajardo objected to the term in an 1889 editorial, insisting that the appropriate term was "Cuban" rather than "tropical": "protesto en contra del adjetivo tropical que por moda o por capricho, [. . .] se viene aplicando al cadencioso y pausado vals que comúnmente se baila en este país. Ese vals es cubano por el orígen. Ese vals ese cubano por el uso" (I protest the use of the adjective tropical that through fashion or whim [. . .] is being applied to the cadenced and slow waltz that is commonly danced in this country. That waltz is Cuban in origin. That waltz is Cuban in practice). After a detailed explanation of the latter, he affirms: "la propiedad en el lenguaje [. . .] exige que se denomine CUBANO y no tropical . . ." (correct use of language [. . .] demands that it be called CUBAN and not tropical [Castillo Faílde, 83–84]). But in fact Romero Fajardo is wrong: correct language does not call for the word Cuban, even though this is frequently the central meaning evoked by the term. The "tropical" was valued (then and sometimes now)[6] precisely for its ambiguity: it enabled a strategic slippage and doubling on matters of race and national identity.

Like the term "tropical," the danzón itself offered to liberal Cuba a way of literally inhabiting one's national and racial identity that was both alluring and abounding in a sense of shared and perhaps transgressive secrecy. For many white Cubans, the danzón was itself a form of erotic choreographic blackface that allowed them to live, to embody, their sense of public self in a tantalizing new way that felt African, sexy, transgressive, non-Spanish, anticolonial, and as such, Cuban. I reiterate that the dance's actual African or Afrocuban heritage, which is complex, quickly became immaterial to white criollos; the dance and the discourse surrounding it became a new structure of feeling that produced and organized its own new expressions of racial identity (which frequently precluded the actual experience of Cuba's black population), new expressions of public sexuality, new combinations and relations between the two ("epicene and ambiguous"), and thus a newly invented sense of public or national self. Clearly, these many evocative secrets—of nation, race, and sex—kept by or projected onto the dance were central to its appeal.

Ramón Moralez Álvarez's play *El proceso del oso*, takes as its starting point the conservative critics' accusations that the danzón is a gravely "infectious" rhythm, whose contagion will jeopardize the racial and sexual purity of Cuban women and the moral health of the nation. By recontextualizing the dance in the world of performance, and by repeatedly embodying the choreography itself, the play gradually re-signifies these conservative sexual-racial-national associations so that the dance's rhythm, while still racially and sexually charged, is finally heard—felt, danced—as a "national" rhythm: a rhythm that can be experienced only by those for whom it is intended, and can be valued only by those capable of embodying its communal potential. The danzón was, eventually, embraced as Cuba's "national dance. "El danzón habria de ser, hasta cerca de 1920, el baile nacional de Cuba" (The danzón was to be the national dance of Cuba until about 1920), writes Alejo Carpentier. "No hubo acontecimiento, durante cuarenta años, que no fuese glosado o festejado por medio de un danzón" (there was no event, for forty years, that was not glossed or celebrated by way of a danzón [Carpentier 1946, 239]).

To be sure, many were not convinced: when Saturnino Valverde staged the play in 1882, after its more successful performance by the Bufos de Salas in 1881, a critic again decried the play, the dance, and the entire genre in which both were presented, complaining that "Tal parece que el África ha invadido y ocupado el campo del arte, que la inmoralidad es nuestro ambiente, y por último, que la pérdida más absoluta y completa del sentido moral y del gusto estético son nuestra manera de ser" (it appears that Africa has invaded and occupied the terrain of art, that immorality is our environment, and last, that the absolute and total loss of morality and aesthetic taste is our way of being). The critic lambastes Valverde for allowing his daughter, a performer in the company, to dance *el oso* in public, to tell jokes of a questionable sexual nature, and to use "como si fuera su propio idioma, toda esa *jerga* de los *ñáñigos*" (as though it were her own language, all that *jargon* of the *ñáñigos* [*El almendares*, 20 June 1882]). Like the many fathers accused of endangering their "patriot" daughters by escorting them to social dances, so too Valverde endangers his own daughter, and through her, the purity of Cuban artistic expression and public morality. The competing interpretations of the play and the dance, then, represent competing ideological positions on the future of Cuba between colonial dependence and autonomy, competing political parties and positions between the so-called conservatives and liberals, and more broadly, competing ideological investments in the "proper" role of the body—especially women's bodies and black bodies—in the public sphere.

In keeping with its "inexplicable" but decidedly "Cuban" appeal, the Afrocuban rhythms on which the danzón is based have been imagined as the repository for anticolonial and specially Cuban secrets. Alejo Carpentier, arguing against those who refuse to recognize black influence in Cuban music, points to the insistent presence of the complex five-beat rhythmic structure of the *cinquillo* associated with African musical forms. The cinquillo, he says, "salido de las manos de los negros franceses de Santiago, había hecho su camino, lentamente, a través de la isla, sesgándose para pasar al lado de l tradanza habanera sin marcarla, antes de afirmarse, de pronto, con d propio de cubanidad, en el baile nuevo" (having left the hands of French blacks of Santiago, had slowly blazed its path across the island, obliquely passing by the contradanza without leaving a mark before affirming itself, suddenly, with its own right to cubanidad, in the new dance [Carpentier 1946, 239]). Thus the cinquillo comes from the heart of black liberation—from the slaves brought to Santiago, the large city in the eastern part of Cuba, by French planters fleeing the slave insurrection in what is now called Haiti; from Santiago, the cinquillo traveled westward, "conquering" the island of Cuba for black sound. In an often-rehearsed legend, the great danzón composer Raimundo Valenzuela is said to have refused to answer questions on the structure and performance of cinquillo. In Fernando Ortíz's version of the story, Valenzuela "decía que nunca la explicaría porque el cinquillo era 'un secreto' y si los músicos extranjeros lo llegaban a descifrar le quitarían su 'vivío' a los artistas cubanos. Su música es su secreto" (said that he would never explain it, because the cinquillo was "a secret" and if foreign musicians managed to decipher it they would take away the 'life' [verve/élan] of Cuban artists. Their music is their secret [Ortiz (1965) 1993a, 94]).[7] It is not just the structure of the rhythm itself, but the particular—"indecipherable"—way in which it was performed by Cuban artists that allows it to organize, in Valenzuela's view, the very vitality, the uniqueness, of Cuban artistic expression. But this very structure, the cinquillo, is also considered by ethnomusicologists such as Ortiz and Gaspar Agüero (whom Ortiz cites) and perhaps Raimundo Valenzuela, to be the "célula rítmica de segura africanidad del danzón" (the rhythmic cell-structure of certain African [origin] of the danzón [Ortiz (1965) 1993a, 204–5]). So the cinquillo may harbor a Cuban secret from foreigners, but at the same time may keep an African (perhaps Afrocuban) secret from whites—perhaps explaining why Valenzuela refused to explain his music to the white Cuban ethnomusicologists interrogating him.

Who then keeps the national secret? And from whom? Is Afrocuban rhythm the national secret white Cuba holds against colonial Spain? Could Afrocuban artists thus take the national secret hostage, to be used toward their own ends? The Valenzuela legend, while perhaps itself a fiction, illustrates the central racial ambiguity of Cuba's national rhythm: in the early 1880s, white and black Cuba did not dance in an easy transculturated embrace, but rather through the danzón used rhythmic secrets to maintain a tense, eroticized distance from each other.

Chapter 5
Racial Ethnography and Literate Sex, 1888

Incendio que devora
llama que abrasa
fiebre que consume,
volcán que estalla
es el amor, señores,
de la mulata. (Sánchez Maldonado, *La Herencia de Canuto*, 1896, n.p.)

(Fire that devours / flame that sears / fever that consumes / volcano that explodes / is the love, sirs, / of the mulata)

So begins one of many theatrical guarachas on the mulata. Conjuring the hyperbolic terms of contagion and sexual abandon reminiscent of those attributed to the danzón, paeans to the figure of the mulata appeared with increasing frequency in guarachas, danzones, and plays of the teatro bufo in the years immediately before and well after the end of slavery in 1886. Indeed, the widespread erotic fascination with the mulata prompted detractors, such as the medical doctor Benjamín de Céspedes, to condemn the many writers who "han falseado por empeños literarios ó efectistas, el tipo verdadero de la mulata, describiendola con los calidos tonos de la cortesana mas refinada del placer sensual" (have falsified the true type of the mulata through literary or theatrical conceit, describing her with the heated tones of the most refined courtesan of sensual pleasure). Céspedes insisted: "No existe tal cortesania, ni cultura, ni belleza ni halagos en ese tipo semisalvaje de la mulata ordinaria que solo posee el arte de voltear las caderas acrobáticamente" (There exists no such courtesanry, nor culture, nor beauty nor flattery in that semi-savage type, the ordinary mulata, who only possesses the art of turning her hips acrobatically [Céspedes 1888, 174–75]). Playwright and doctor here marked opposed ends of the discursive range of white representation of biracial women. The vehemence that each lent to his admiration or repudiation assures us that the mulata functioned in the 1880s and early 1890s as a central figure through which emergent notions of social, sexual, racial, and ultimately national purity were negotiated in an emergent Cuban public sphere.

Like the danzón, the mulata embodied the intersection, both tantalizing and terrifying to white Cuba, where sex and race were ineluctably and irreversibly mixed. As the guaracha indicates, "she" was invested with unparalleled powers of seduction and contagion: her love afflicted the (male) body and body politic like a powerful disease for which there was no cure. More than the danzón, the female figure of the mulata explicitly foregrounded questions of Cuba's social reproduction. Assumed to be the offspring of a white Spanish man and an enslaved African woman, "she" powerfully embodied an origin tale of Cuba's colonial history, often standing in for the very idea of criollo identity. Her mestizaje offered an ambivalent vision of Cuba, standing at the threshold of at least two possible futures: on the one hand she promised a progressive "whitening" of Cuba; her unsurpassed beauty and sexual appeal were coded as a sign of Cuba's increasingly refined national identity. On the other, the mulata stood at the abyss of Cuba's social disintegration, heralding continued "Africanization" of the island and the unabated confusion of moral and sexual values represented by "her" own birth.

Although these two approaches to mestizaje seem opposed, they draw on the same narrow discourse of essential racial difference: adored or despised, the mulata was imagined first and foremost as an ethnological phenomenon whose value and meaning—cultural, theatrical, or scientific—was assessed as a function of her particular racial composition. Standing in the ground between races and their competing claims to national belonging, the mestizo in general and the mulata in particular became the primary ground for staking claims—scientific and national—about race, nation, and the complex relation imagined between them. In anthropology as in literature and popular performance, the mulata confounded the very project of stable racial knowledge, bringing such projects into a crisis that was both epistemological and national. Thus when the teatro bufo lauded the figure of the mulata, or when early medical ethnography repudiated and pathologized her, such claims were planted as new stakes in a revised social context with a changing set of social, moral, legal, and intellectual moorings. An object of curiosity, display, ethnographic description, costumbrista narrative, or scientific analysis, the mulata was at the epicenter of Cuba's late colonial discourse because her function was finally hermeneutic: "she" helped define the contours of the cultural landscape around her and its normative terms—whiteness, masculinity, heterosexuality, and not least, Cubanness. Across this network of discourses, it is important to remember that the

mulata does not comfortably refer to actual women of color (hence, why "she" has been kept firmly in scare quotes until now), even if her ubiquitous representation had significant repercussions—and continues to have repercussions—for women of color in Cuba. As we shall see, the range of claims about the mulata's meaning and significance proceeded from meticulous renderings of "her" body—textual, visual, theatrical—and illustrated how the mulata was discursively produced through mutually reinforcing forms of representation common to the new social sciences and theatrical arts. Women and men of color, in turn, found increasing opportunity to contest such debilitating discourses. As we shall see, none did so more dramatically than the magazine *Minerva: Revista Quinceanal Dedicada a la Mujer de Color* (Minerva: Biweekly Magazine Dedicated to Women of Color) first published in 1888. *Minerva* authors traced an alternative, if heavily assaulted, social role for mulatas, and themselves modeled alternative relations between literacy, gender, performance, and national belonging, different from any imagined either by the mulata's "admirers" or her detractors.

This chapter illustrates how and why the mulata gained prominence at precisely this historical juncture: why her popularity coincided with the beginning of the formal practice of anthropology on the island, and how the figure of the mulata came to function not simply as a metaphor for the nation, but also as a metonymic site on and through which the changing processes of racialization, sexuality, and nation formation converged with particular force.

Anthropology and Racialization

The vast infrastructure of slavery had offered white supremacist Cuba the legal, material, and social means through which to understand and administer the social separation of the races. As slavery was disarticulated as a social system—a process that began in 1880 with a "patronage" system and officially concluded with abolition in 1886—the discourse of race made a decisive shift. In these same years, Cuba began to embrace the new science of anthropology and its new modes of reifying and systematizing racial difference. The Cuban Anthropological Society was founded in 1877, in the final year of Cuba's first and unsuccessful anticolonial war.[1] Subsequent years witnessed new research and analysis on race and ethnicity in Cuba, much of which is documented in the *Boletín de la Sociedad Antropológica de la Isla de Cuba*, the official publication of the Anthropological Society.

The contradictions and continuities between slavery and anthropology as racializing systems are captured, in part, in the text that the Cuban Anthropological Society quickly reclaimed as Cuba's "first" anthropological study. Henri Dumont's *Antropología y patología comparadas de los negros esclavos* (Comparative anthropology and pathology of black slaves, [(1876) 1922]) was a comparative analysis of African "ethnicities" and their ailments as represented in Cuba's slave population. The French Dumont, who had come to the Americas to study yellow fever and ended working as a doctor on Cuba's western plantations, turned his medical practice into an opportunity for field research, studying and recording anatomical data of his slave patients in order to define characteristics of six African "nations," the Mandingas, Gangás, Lucumís, Minas, Carabalís, and Congos. Dumont's analysis rehearsed three assumptions common to European anthropology of the day: first, that racial essence is consistent across bodies, such that analysis of a small demographic sample might be generalized for the entire ethnic group; second, that such essence has continuity over time and space, such that the middle passage or the context of slavery did not fundamentally alter the social and cultural identity of African subjects; and third, that the task of comparative anthropology is to determine relative degrees of development, progress, and "civilization" among the "races of man." Thus, Dumont studied each "nation" through a combination of generalizing remarks on that group's relative "progress," and a detailed anatomical analysis of one representative subject. The Mandingas, for example, were characterized as comparatively "advanced" in their "natural intelligence" and "progressive spirit" and were illustrated by anatomical documentation of a twenty-two-year-old woman who had been abducted into the slave trade three years prior.

Throughout, Dumont's analysis sought to draw out ethnic essence from particular bodies, literally reading their surface—cranial size, physiognomy, as well as the tattoos and complex scarification that covered so many of the African bodies he studied—for signs of ethnic coherence. Bodies obviously broken or built by brutal slave labor were read for essential racial characteristics: "Los lucumís se distinguen de los demás negros por la altura de su cráneo," he wrote, as well as "la complexión vigorosa de su espalda, por la disposición de sus músculos, cuyo desarollo los capacita para las más rudas labores" (The lucumis distinguish themselves from the rest of the blacks by the height of their cranium [as well as] the vigorous complexion of their backs, by the disposition of their muscles, whose development capacitates them for the most brute labor [21]). Even signs of radical slave resistance or despair were recast as practices "typical" of the group. For example, Dumont explained the "epidemic" of suicide among the Lucumís in relation to the group's religious belief:

La frecuencia del suicidio entre los lucumís, su fácil abandono de la vida, se debe a las creencias religiosas de los mismos; siempre se les encuentra vestidos con su mejor ropa, al pie de un árbol, donde colocan una buena ración de provisiones de boca: todos estos preparativos indican su creencia de hacer, en cuerpo y alma, un largo viaje por su tierra natal. En los primeros tiempos de esclavitud el deseo de emprender el viaje eterno se extendió como una epidemia y el suicidio hizo verdaderos estragos en muchas dotaciones. (26)

(The frequency of suicide among the lucumís, their easy abandon of life, is owed to their religious beliefs; they are always found wearing their best clothes at the foot of a tree, where they have placed a substantial ration of food provisions; all these preparations indicate their belief in taking a long journey, in body and spirit, toward the land of their birth. In the early days of slavery the desire to undertake the eternal journey spread like an epidemic, and suicide made genuine ravages of many holdings.)

However "typical" such death rites may or may not have been in Africa, the idea that the horrors of chattel slavery might have accounted for their frequency in Cuba did not interest the anthropologist.

Dumont's ethnological conceit was undermined by the context of slavery. To interpret his subjects, Dumont more often relied on the slaves' "owners" than the Africans themselves, as so many of the latter had limited command of Spanish. His accounts of life in Africa were drawn in large part from acquaintances in the slave trade, and his own professional charge was at odds with his research agenda. Far from amplify their distinct ethnic practices or identities, his task was to do no more than provide sufficient medical attention to maintain his patients' productivity as slaves. Although Dumont parroted a language of relative cultural and physical "development" common to European and American ethnology, in practice he measured the relative "progress" of each ethnicity most often in terms of their adaptation to conditions of slavery. He wrote, for example, that "Los negros *gangás*, antropológicamente, son inferiores a los *mandingas*" (the black *gangás*, anthropologically, are inferior to the *mandingas* [17]), yet the criteria for such "anthropological" superiority were left unclear. A moment later, Dumont turned to his white colleagues on the plantation for their "expert" comparative assessment: "Según nuestros informes y los suminstrados por los administradores de los ingenios, que confirman nuestro concepto, son preferibles los macúas a los gangás" (According to our information and those working for the plantation administrators, who confirm our understanding, the macuás are preferable to the gangás [20]). Preferable to whom? Was the commodity value of the slave determined in part by perceptions of the African's relative "progress" on the scale of races? Or, more likely, did the anthropological evaluation, wittingly or no, favor those with higher value on the slave market? A few pages later he affirmed that "Sin excepción alguna, [los lucumís] son los mejores y más buscados por los hacendados, a pesar de sus tendencias al suicidio" (Without exception, the lucumís are the best and most sought-after by plantation owners, despite their tendency to suicide [24]). This "first" anthropologist of Cuba thus revealed the complicity between slavery and anthropology as ways of knowing and taxonomizing Africans, and Africanness, in Cuba. The forcible abduction and confinement of Africans provided an "opportunity" for firsthand research; the research revealed "evidence" of the ways that Africans were "naturally" suited for such conditions in the first place.

The Anthropological Society continued Dumont's project insofar as the members too understood the presence of a sizable African demographic in Cuba as a singular opportunity to study "real" Africans. The presence of a large population of foreign-born Chinese laborers (whose conditions of life and labor had often been identical to those of plantation slaves) further amplified Cuba's opportunity for comparative anthropology. The society's president, Fernando Poey, opened the first session by underscoring just this fact: "Nuestra posición social y política nos permite estudiar cumplidamente, bajo el aspecto físico, moral é intelectual, dos razas humanas, la africana y la mongólica" (Our social and political position permits us to study fully two human races from a physical, moral and intellectual aspect, the African and the Mongol [*Boletín de la Sociedad Antropológica*, 1879]). Like Dumont, and like most of their counterparts in Europe and the United States, the members of the Society never seriously considered that conditions of slavery or indentured labor might affect the physical data they could gather about Africans or Chinese in Cuba, much less that the legacy of slavery might operate as a limiting frame on their own perception and evaluation.

Unlike Dumont, however, the society did not limit its interests to African- or Chinese-born subjects or their direct descendants as "pure" representatives of their ethnic group. Rather, the society quickly staked Cuba's unique contribution to the new sciences in the island's special relation to mestizaje. Poey went on to insist that members study " los numerosos mestizos que provienen de los cruzamientos de ambas con la raza blanca" (the numerous mestizos that come from the crossings of both [the African and the "Mongol"] with the white race). Mestizaje offered a compelling and under-studied subject for ethnological research—one that gave the Society's members a clear research advantage over their colleagues in Spain. The inaugural lecturer Dr. Luis Montané, who followed Poey to the podium at the first meeting of the Society, articulated the ethnographic project before them as a distinctly national one. In addition to studying Africans and "Mongols," both of which he defined as inherently "exogenous" to Cuba, he challenged his colleagues to rise to their singular scientific occasion:

> tendreis que abordar uno de los problemas más delicados de la antropología fisiológica; queremos hablar de los cruzamientos étnicos y de su influencia bajo el punto de vista de los productos. Aquí, mejor quizás que en ninguna parte, nos encontramos en disposición de levantar una punta del velo que oculta tan difícil problema.
>
> (You will have to engage one of the most delicate problems in physical anthropology; I mean crossings between ethnicities and their influence from the point of view of offspring. Here, better perhaps than in any other place, we find ourselves disposed to lift a corner of the veil that occludes so difficult a problem.)

Poey admonished his fellow anthropologists therefore to avoid universalizing generalizations and to stay focused on the rich opportunity for research that Cuba's multiracial landscape provided: in a word, he concluded, "sea cubana nuestra Antropología, antes que general" (let our Anthropology be Cuban before being general [*Boletín de la Sociedad Antropológica*, 1879]). From its earliest iteration, then, "Cuban" anthropology—like Cuban theatre before and alongside it—would stake its originality, indeed its claim to authenticity and legitimacy, on its particular access to and representation of mestizaje.[2]

If British or French anthropology accompanied these colonial powers to the heights of their imperial projects in Africa and Asia, allowing the new imperial powers discursively to map hierarchies of race and ethnicity as they literally remapped the globe, in Cuba anthropology took on this distinctly local, national, and even anticolonial relevance—an anticolonial dimension that would, a generation later, manifest itself in the postcolonial ethnography of Fernando Ortiz, where the desire to understand Cuba's racial and cultural crossings would return with critical force in his theory of "transculturation." In science as in literature, music, and theatre, mestizaje provided Cuba with a distinctive profile whose value could be mobilized in international, and particularly anti-imperial, arenas to claim the autonomous development and character of Cuba as a nation. The long discourse of mestizaje was now translated into a scientific project that Cubans were best positioned to practice.

But, just as in the arts, the scientific interest in mestizaje carried a foundational racial ambivalence: the Cuban anthropologists would assert their Cuban distinction to the world, and particularly their Spanish counterparts in Madrid, by studying mestizaje; yet the study of mestizaje was limited at every turn by the need to recuperate their own position—again, as Cubans—as solidly grounded in whiteness. Within months of the society's founding, the members began to acknowledge this ambivalence, concerned that they lacked an appropriate definition of *race* itself. If the "African" and "Mongol" were defined from the outset as "exogenous" races because of their foreign provenance, who then could claim to be endogamous to Cuba, and on what grounds? At first the assembly affirmed without contest that the term "Cubano" referred exclusively to white men born in Cuba. But by the next meeting a month later, a number of members were less certain. One asked: could not the new white immigrants from Galicia or the Canary Islands be considered Cuban? Another noted—although his views were not, apparently, endorsed—that there were no scientific grounds on which to exclude mestizos from the category "Cuban," as they too were born in Cuba. Thus, the attempt to lend scientific rigor to the opportune study of race became instead a renewed effort to define the relation among ethnic, racial, and national identity, or, put differently, to understand whether national identity itself implied a coherent and "pure" racial or ethnic profile.

Scientific Costumbrismo

In 1888, the young medical doctor Benjamín de Céspedes published his highly controversial and still remarkable study, *La prostitución en la ciudad de la Habana* (Prostitution in the city of Havana). Ostensibly a scientific analysis of recent data on the practice of prostitution, the text used prostitution as the occasion to "diagnose" larger social and moral diseases that afflicted Cuba as an emergent nation. From a medical view, Céspedes presented prostitution as the menacing vehicle through which venereal disease would ultimately decimate the population; from an ethnological view, he analyzed prostitution as the social practice that best illustrated and reinforced a weakness of social, moral, and national constitution in the Cuban people themselves. An ardent nationalist and supporter of the failed independence war, Céspedes faulted the island's colonial history for its degradation, most evident—he argued—in its racial "confusion":

> Y el pueblo cubano persiste siendo la abigarrada confusión de razas, intereses, procedencias, y aspiraciones, que riñen discordes desde los primitivos días de la conquista, sin otros fines que la explotación brutal y acelerada de la tierra de la cual procuran ahuyentarse sin amor y sin recuerdos, los más, cuando han realizado su

codicioso objeto; dejando cada cual por única reliquia de su paso sus deyecciones y sus vicios, como el peregrino que sacude la sandalia polvorienta al abandonar la ciudad apestada. (91)

(And the Cuban nation persists as a motley confusion of races, interests, origins, and aspirations, that have been at discordant odds since the early days of the conquest, with no other ends than the brutal and accelerated exploitation of the land that they are sure to abandon without love or memories, especially on realizing their greedy ambitions; leaving their dejection and their vices as the only relics of their having passed, like the pilgrim who sheds his dusty sandals on leaving the pestilent city.)

In Céspedes's narrative, Cuba "herself" was the ill-used lover: feminized, raped, and robbed of her natural wealth and resources by a history of reckless Spanish colonization. Cuba's early conquerors were remembered as "el detritus de un pueblo esquilmado por todos los rigores de las guerras y por todas las opresiones del poder político y religioso" (the detritus of a people sucked dry by the rigors of war and by all the oppressions of political and religious power). He even cited early modern Spain's drama of romance and sexual intrigue, *La Celestina*, as evidence of the debased sexual behaviors such men imported to Cuba, spreading venereal disease in the process. Their present-day counterparts, the Spanish army, were no more than a standing troop of syphilitic johns, or "una muchedumbre de célibes amargos" (a crowd of bitter celibates). The church was implicated in this historic debauchery, as Céspedes recalled incidents of sexual scandal plaguing the priesthood from the earliest days of the conquest. The centerpiece of Cuba's degradation was the history and legacy of slavery that had, he said, "viciado la sangre de todas estas gentes, y lo mismo el español que el criollo" (vitiated the blood of all these people, Spanish and criollo alike [68]). Colonial history witnessed the resulting "cuartones infectos" (infected quadroons) of black women circulating in the dense urban confluence of military barracks and churches, home to a "clientela segura, reclutada entre las gentes del mar, la soldadesca y la cleresía" (secure clientele, recruited from the people by the sea, the military and the clergy [70]).

Through all of these practices, argued Céspedes, Spain had made Cuba a dumping ground for social and racial impurity:

El pueblo cubano, apesar de su gloriosa Revolución politica y social; apesar de la energía, honradez é ilustración de sus principales jefes; es hoy como ayer y como siempre: la cloaca máxima de España donde vienen á desembarcar como arribazón y criadero de peces toxíferos, toda clase de gentes disolutas. Es como ayer, un depósito de Nigricia que nos deshonra, reproduciendo las mismas costumbres salvajes de esos países, en esta factoria ruinosa que flota en los confines del Atlántico, como una nave averiada que encalla y se abisma mas y más, abrumada por el peso de sus históricas iniquidades. Pueblo de dominados y dominadores, de infelices y de poderosos, de fatuos engreidos y de sencillos entusiastas; todos viven disgregados como si le hubiera acometido al organismo social, la descomposición cadavérica. (91–92)

(The Cuban nation, despite its glorious political and social Revolution; despite the energy, honor, and illustriousness of its principal leaders; is today as yesterday and always: the great sewer of Spain, where all classes of dissolute peoples disembark, like a dumping and breeding ground for toxic fish. Cuba remains, as before, a depository of blackness that dishonors us, reproducing the same savage customs of those countries in this ruinous factory that floats in the confines of the Atlantic, like a broken down ship that runs aground and sinks further and further, weighed down by its historic iniquities. A country of dominators and the dominated, of the unhappy and the powerful, of conceited fools and simple enthusiasts; all live splintered, as if the social organism had been attacked by a cadaverous decomposition.)

Again the health of the nation was threatened not only by the "toxins" of colonialism, but also by the impurities of race; indeed, Céspedes suggested that the Cuban patriots who attempted to "save" Cuba during the failed revolution were those who were most "sana en costumbres, menos enervada por los vicios, mas viril y sin mezclas, por el contacto de otras razas" (healthy in customs, least enervated by vice, most virile and without mixtures, from contact with other races [81]). (We should note, for perspective, that this text appeared in the same month that the memorable "Velada Gómez-Fraternidad" was held in honor of the black patriot and civil rights leader, and to celebrate the social advancement of black peoples in Cuba.) Like the members of the Anthropological Society, Céspedes assumed that the Cuban patriot would be male, white, and born in Cuba; the pathologies—sexual, racial, and political—that surrounded him were also peculiar to Cuba, but imagined as by definition endogamous, foreign impositions on an unwilling land.

If Cuba's colonial past had thus left her no more than a decomposing cadaver, Céspedes proposed a careful autopsy of that body, in particular relation to the practice of prostitution. Having conjured Cuba's degradation through his spectacular array of metaphor (Cuba as sewer, as ruinous factory, as pestilent breeding ground), he offered the factual realities of prostitution and venereal disease as scientific proof positive of Cuba's condition. Here the texture of his language and discourse altered, moving away from thick painterly metaphor and instead becoming, in his term, "severamente científico" (severely scientific [1]): offering comparative annual statistics on the numbers of men and women hospitalized for venereal disease, and tabulating data on the race and national origin of prostitutes with venereal disease; and itemizing symptoms of different sexually contracted ailments. Against the wealth of metaphor in the text, he posed an equally overwhelming wall of scientific language, as in his list of the venereal diseases whose instances and symptoms he tabulated: "Blenorragia, Orquitis blenorrágica, Artritis blenorrágica, Chancros blandos, Bubones supurados, Chancro infectante, Sifílides, Irítis sifilítica, Laringitis sifilítica, Sifiloma laríngeo, Placas mucosas, Rupia sifilítica, Sarcocele sifilítico, Goma sifilítico, Ulceraciones sifilíticas, Artritis sifilítica, Ataxia locomotriz sífilítica, Sífilis constitucional, Sífilis visceral, Sífilis cerebral" (84). The contrast between—and, ultimately, the continuity of—language as a repository of evocative metaphor (in which words amplify and double understanding) and scientific naming (in which words concretize and specify understanding) proved crucial to the narrative logic of the text, and the logic through which the doctor advanced his medicoanthropological claims about the relation of race, gender, and sex that placed women of color in general and mulatas in particular at the center of Cuba's social pathology.

Carried out over many pages of data, description, and diagnosis, Céspedes's dread analysis was organized systematically, contrasting "determinant" and "efficient" causes of prostitution, and providing ample expository evidence to illustrate the variants of each category. The chapters devoted to "determinant" causes are why the text was considered by many, including avid readers, to be pornographic: the chapters explored such topics as "provocations to lechery," "seduction and abandon," and "greed and luxury." The "efficient" causes of prostitution—"misery," "concubinage," "domestic service," "the dance," and "immigration"—were each presented as dire social contexts whose only outcome for young women would be sexual labor and accompanying moral doom.

As Céspedes progressively mapped the social factors that lead to prostitution, the text traced a moral geography of Havana's urban landscape, in which the relations he imagined among gender, labor, and public space in the city were gradually illuminated. As the narrative progresses, we find that each "cause" of prostitution finally involved an "unnatural" crossing between the established lines of public and private spheres and the gendered roles Céspedes imagined pertained to each, leading to the ultimate abomination of both public and private domains: public sex. Thus, in his logic, domestic labor lead to prostitution because the young woman hired into a home "interrupted" the order of the private home and the sanctity of the bond between husband and wife, providing too great a sexual temptation for the husband. Dance too was dangerous as a precursor to public sex, he contended, in an argument that rehearsed critiques of the danzón: "Esos mismos padres, tan celosos de la sencilla ignorancia de sus hijas, las conducen á los bailes para que se zarandeen de lo lindo en brazos de todos los mocitos que bailan *sabroso* y saben *picar* y *voltear con bulla* y otros excesos, al son de la música ñáñiga" (Those same fathers who jealously guard the simple ignorance of their daughters, lead them to the dances so that they can shake about prettily in the arms of the good-for-nothings who dance deliciously and know how to *bite* and *turn with excessive movement* [colloquial terms for choreographic moves perceived to be sexual in nature] and other excesses, to the strains of that ñáñiga music [98]). Taken from their "proper" place at home, the ignorant girls encountered sexual advances they were ill equipped to understand or defend against. In his strongest and most controversial critique, Céspedes cited the continued flow of male immigration, both Spanish (Canary Islander) and Chinese, as a major contributor to prostitution—not because this army of single men provided potential clients for prostitution (far from it), but because these men usurped the specific forms of labor appropriate to women (primarily sewing, laundering, and hair-dressing) that would otherwise be viable alternatives to prostitution. Although the private or semiprivate setting of such labor offered poor women a context for dignified labor on the margins of the male public arena, such labor apparently had devastating moral effects on men. That labor, Céspedes strongly implied, feminized the men and lead them to "unnatural" sexual proclivities, making their workplaces hotbeds of "pederasty"—the then prevailing term, both medical and popular, for homosexual sex.

Céspedes levels extraordinary contempt at homosexuality, but he cast the mulata as the source—the disease vector—of Cuba's social crisis. The discourse of medical ethnography allowed Céspedes to make explicit, literal, and "scientific" assertions that the "African" operated as an "infection" on the white social body: "En el organismo linfático de la sociedad cubana, el abceso supurante de la prostitución, radica en las costumbres de la raza de color" (In the lymphatic organism of Cuban society, the suppurative abscess of prostitution stems from the customs of the race of color [171]). Here medical terms—lymphatic organism, suppurative abscess—were transformed into metaphors in a racializing discourse that, in turn, lent a scientific gloss to the metaphor of essential African contagion. Despite his own statistical evidence that venereal disease was also spread by white women, and of course, also by men, Céspedes cast women of color—all women of color, it seems—

as the source of the disease: "su contacto íntimo infecciona todo cuanto toca" (her intimate contact infects everything that it touches). It is precisely the level of intimacy with white men that posed such extraordinary threat. He asked, "¿Qué mayor venganza pudo jamas cumplirse en los destinos históricos de nuestro pueblo, en favor de la raza agraviada, que la lenta pero segura infusión corrosiva de todos sus vicios y abyecciones en lo más interno del organismo social?" (What greater vengeance could ever have been exacted on the historic destiny of our people, in favor of the offended race, than the slow but sure corrosive infusion of all its vices and abjection in the very interior of the social organism?). Prime evidence of this "corrosive infusion" was racial mixture itself: "los uniones carnales más peligrosas para la salúd y la moral pública, son las que se establecen entre individuos de diferentes razas y condiciones" (the most dangerous carnal unions to public health and morality are those established between individuals of different races and conditions [170–72]).

In an elision common to the discourse of mestizaje, the doctor made no mention of mixed-race men, but expended all his vitriol on the mulata. What most defined the mulata was, apparently, her skill at deception: she was the most susceptible to venereal disease, yet the most capable of hiding its symptoms; the most unhygienic in her ablutions, but most able to appear otherwise; the most prone to "clandestine" prostitution (which is to say, unregistered on the municipal rolls, and therefore inaccessible to Céspedes), but somehow more prolific in her "máquina infernal de fornicación" (infernal fornication machine). This skill at deception, claimed Céspedes, enabled her to gain occasional employment in domestic work where she "profaned" "honorable" homes. In a remarkable, if frankly maniacal, characterization, he imagined her skin color leaking from her body like so much infectious discharge: "Ella es la verdadera imágen del negro Minotauro, que va destiñendo su piel y manchando todo cuanto toca con la viscosa materia de sus lubricidades" (She is the true image of the black minotaur, whose skin color runs, and stains all it touches with the viscous material of its lubrications [177]). Arguing that the mulata was the genetic combination of the "deformes físicos y morales de la raza africana y los más vulgares de la blanca" (physical and moral deformities of the African race and the most vulgar of the white [172]), this racial "minotaur" was a monstrous body. But her monstrosity was all the more salient in its concealment: in this paranoid imagination, she was able to make her own skin fade, becoming more white and thus more difficult to identify as black the more she darkened the white world around her. She not only crossed boundaries of public and private, black and white, but she also emblematized the dissolution of meaningful boundaries themselves.

The middle section of Céspedes's analysis overlaid his moral geography of public and private spheres with a racial ethnography, in which he offered a study of different races, each in terms of the practice of prostitution. Like Dumont before him, Céspedes created a "tipografía," or "typography" of prostitution organized as a hierarchy of racial and sexual "decline," placing at the bottom prostitution between people of color (meaning blacks), between minors, between men, and finally between the Chinese. The latter were awarded the lowest nomination, it appears, because the prostitution Céspedes claimed to have witnessed took place between Chinese men, adding sexual "abomination" to innate racial "inferiority." Also like Dumont, Céspedes had experience as a medical doctor, and this experience formed the basis of his field research: he owed his familiarity with prostitution—indeed, his quite intimate knowledge of the bodies of prostitutes—to his position as a municipal doctor charged with the task of regularly visiting all houses of prostitution to ascertain whether the women were free of venereal disease. Prostitution was not illegal; to the contrary, brothels and prostitutes were required to be registered with the city for purposes of taxation. Women were inscribed in a municipal registry, known as "el libro negro" or the "black book." In an effort to curb the rising incidence of venereal disease, the city mandated biweekly medical checkups for the women, who were organized in various "agrupaciones" or "groupings" that roughly corresponded to neighborhood, and hence, also to race.[3] Again, like Dumont, Céspedes's research (to understand the causes of prostitution) was in tension with the objective of his medical practice (to keep prostitutes healthy on the job). A violence simmered through these early medical ethnographies: the patients were required to make their bodies available for intimate analysis by doctors whose "expert" testimony would pathologize their condition and most likely consign them to the very social misery that caused their physical ailments in the first place.

Although reminiscent of Dumont's work, the discursive rendering of these "types" places Céspedes's text in genealogical relation to costumbrismo as much or more than to European ethnography. Indeed, this text might best be read as a form of "scientific costumbrismo," in which the narrative conventions of costumbrista aesthetics were enlisted as the primary means through which to make persuasive ostensibly "scientific" claims about race, gender, and culture. Consider, for comparison, Cuba's most famous literary portrait of the mulata, Villaverde's *Cecilia Valdés.* The protagonist is introduced over several long paragraphs that render her body in thick detail:

> Sus cejas describían un arco y daban mayor sombra a los ojos negros y rasgados, los cuales eran todo movilidad y fuego. La boca tenía chica y labios llenos, indicando más voluptuosidad que firmeza de carácter. Las mejillas llenas y redondas y un hoyuelo en medio de la barba, formaban un conjunto bello, que para ser perfecto sólo faltaba que la expresión fuese menos maliciosa, si no maligna. (Villaverde [1839/1882] 1981, 15)

> (Her eyelashes delineated an arc, and gave greater shade to the eyes, brown and almond-shaped, which were all mobility and fire. The mouth was small and lips full, indicating more voluptuousness than strength of character. Her cheeks, full and round and a dimple in her chin, formed a beautiful ensemble, which to be perfect only needed her expression to be less malicious, if not malignant.)

This fragment illustrates the procedure: each feature of her body is itemized, detailed, and then read as a potential index of her moral character. The fullness of her lips, the amount of curl in her hair, the precise line of her nose, or the relative darkness of her lashes provide "empirical" evidence of her racial and thus moral status. For Villaverde, the detailed review of her anatomy culminated in his central question, "¿A qué raza pertenecía esta muchacha?" (To what race did this girl belong? [16]), a question that hangs rhetorically and ominously over the girl's fate for the next several hundred pages of her tragic life. The central contradiction here, of course, is that even as her body is presented as a corpus of evidence on the truth of her racial identity, it does so only to define her as the racially *dissembling* body *par excellence*—the body that is black but can pass for white, and is thus tinged with malignancy.

Céspedes followed a comparable strategy when making claims about the various racial types he itemized. For example, he offered a lengthy account of a poor young white woman driven to prostitution in order to care for her sister, then dying of tuberculosis. Her story was shared as a narrative biography; this episode was structured as a testimony of her decline into poverty, desperation, and prostitution. But Dr. Céspedes claimed to have the met the girl long before her decline, when he was called to attend to her dying father. Even though the story is meant to illustrate the effects of poverty on (white) women, it turns out that Céspedes was able to "read" her moral degeneracy in that first encounter with her body:

Bien plantada, erguida, dibujando atrevidamente el arco adorable del talle, descubría en su pecho alto y ancho, la florecencia exuberante de dos senos rebeldes por su turgencia y dureza á mantenerse firmes en las escotaduras del corsé. [. . .] Era su tez de color trigueño y sano propio de los temperamentos ardientes y resueltos. Un vello finísimo afelpaba, como un polvillo afrodisíaco, unos brazos robustos, torneados y sanguíneos que parecian destinados á ceñir y desainar hombres con sus lascivios abrazos. (108–9)

(Handsome, upright, daringly tracing the adorable arc of her figure, her tall, broad chest revealed the exuberant florescence of two breasts that, firm and overfull, rebelled against being held in the low cut of her corset. [. . .] Her complexion was olive-skinned and healthy, proper to ardent and determined temperaments. A fine velvety down, like an aphrodisiac powder, covered robust arms, shapely and ruddy that appeared destined to cling and tighten about men with their lascivious embrace.)

These departures into near pornographic renderings of his subjects earned the text its controversy—and no doubt its popularity. But even as Céspedes indulged in descriptive titillation for his own or his readers' benefit, he advanced his claims by a firm logic: the composition of the woman's anatomy already carried her moral destiny, and it was the task of the author—doctor or poet—to isolate, itemize, and interpret her physical signs.

When it came to mulatas, the anatomical catalog told a drastically different tale—indeed one meant to counter the seductive portraits offered by costumbrista poets and novelists such as Villaverde. Céspedes's summary description of the mulata "type" began thus:

La complexión huesosa de la mestiza, se caracteriza por el predominio de ángulos que se aguzan bruscamente en las epifisis, rompiendo con la trabazón armónica de las junturas. Las extremidades de su cuerpo son deformes, viscosas, semejan mucho á la coloración del vientre de los animales anfíbios que reptan en las orillas pantanosas. En cambio heredan del blanco, la flojedad y la atrofía muscular que agravan con sus hábitos indolentes, hasta el punto de aparecer enjutas y descarnadas, unas veces, y otras infiltradas enormemente por el tejido grasiento que las envuelve en una gordura desigual; pues, mientras persisten encanijados los muslos y las pantorillas; el vientre, los pechos y los brazos, se desbordan con la blandura malsana de las carnes sueltas y fofas. (173)

(The bony complexion of the mestiza, is characterized by the predominance of angles that sharpen abruptly in the epiphyses, interrupting the harmonic linking of the joints. The extremities of her body are deformed, viscous, greatly resembling in coloring the abdomen of amphibious animals that slither on the shores of swamps. On the other hand, from the white [race] they inherit the muscular slackness and atrophy that they exacerbate with indolent habits, to the point of appearing at times gaunt and emaciated, and at other times enormously infiltrated by a greasy layer that unevenly envelops them in fat; since, as long as the muscles and calves remain shrunken, the belly, breasts and arms overgrow with the unhealthy tenderness of loose flesh and flab.)

The line between poetic license and medical diagnosis is very thin. Medical description borrowed from costumbrista portraiture and claimed itself as science; in the cases of both Céspedes and Dumont, the doctor's "authority" rested on his status as witness, and his ability to draw meaning from each detail—the angle of a jawbone, hair on her arms—relied on its inherent scientific and social meaning.

Céspedes followed costumbrista aesthetics even further in structuring portions of his text as a series of vistas into the literal and figurative geography of the city—rehearsing a long trope in Cuban letters and lithography that had been a regular feature of Cuba's lithographic printing presses since the 1840s. Céspedes's view fastened exclusively on the moral and sexual scandals allegedly on regular display in Havana. He asked his viewers to imagine themselves as visitors to the city, disembarking in Havana's port, shocked by the evidence of prostitution marking every turn, every major corner, and the public throughways near cafés, near theatres, and even near churches and honorable homes (132). Céspedes's accounts were painterly, with clear vistas and points of view; included in the frame were the half-open doors, windows, window bars, and shadows by which sex labor was both revealed and hidden. Looking up from a major public avenue, one might have spied through the open windows the bed of a prostitute, on which the woman posed. A panoramic street view of the carriages leading to and from the theatre on any given night revealed the contrast between honorable women guarding their modesty in closed carriages, and the wealthier prostitutes who brazenly passed in negligee in open carriages. Another view—which clearly echoed Víctor Patrício Landaluze's famous portrait of the mulata from 1881—framed mulatas on the street with moving hips visible under tight gowns, one hand clutching a handkerchief, the other coyly hiding and revealing her face behind a slow-moving fan. Another series of narrative vistas fastened on naked black bodies: the bodies of naked children curiously darting about doorways; the arms and backs of women working and laundering in the summer heat; the bodies of destitute men, barely covered by tattered rags (132–34). What costumbrismo and ethnographic discourse shared in this instance was the ability to hide the position of the witness-researcher. He did not reflect on his own position or mobility as a white man circulating the city, entering houses of prostitution at will, moving in and out of public and private spaces, crossing urban boundaries of racialized neighborhoods. He acted on the privilege of his race and gender to gaze at and condemn destitute bodies on the street, to return fully the gaze of the prostitute in her window even as he condemned her lack of modesty for looking out at all.

The text was endorsed in a prologue by the then young Enrique Varona, a respected member of the Cuban Anthropological Society, supporter of Cuban independence, and frequent supporter of black civil rights. Varona celebrated Céspedes's text as a model of the social utility of anthropology:

> La ciencia estudia al hombre, aislado y en sociedad, lo analiza y descompone, y le enseña á conocerse y á regirse. Le da la voz de alerta para que se precava, le muestra la sanción ineludible que las leyes naturales saben imponer á sus transgresores, y al mismo tiempo le enseña como puede fortificarse contra las causas de destrucción, llámense enfermedad, vicio, ó injusticia. (ix)

> (Science studies man, isolated and in society, it analyzes and deconstructs him, and it teaches him to know and govern himself. It gives warning so that he may be on guard, it illustrates the inescapable sanction that natural law imposes on its transgressors, and at the same time it shows him how he can fortify himself against the causes of destruction, whether these be illness, vice, or injustice.)

Varona's characterization of the work of science was not so far, in retrospect, from the claims made on behalf of costumbrismo almost a century prior, when it was praised for its ability "to correct vices, by painting them in their own colors so that when seen, with horror, they will be detested."[4] Céspedes had, in many ways, accomplished the early mission of the society, lending the methods and tools of scientific analysis to the study of those racial and interracial formations proper to Cuba, and cast as its protagonist the figure who was already at the center of Cuba's aesthetic self-reflection, the mulata.

Sex, Dance, Brownface

When the figure of the mulata began to make regular appearances on the teatro bufo stage, its representation immediately departed from the racial logic advanced by scientific discourse and most costumbrista representation. If ethnography and costumbrista narrative could carefully study the mulata's body for "evidence" of its intrinsic racial meaning, the teatro bufo by definition could not: the theatrical mulata had no "essential" body, as she was played by white actresses in brownface—or at the very least, by women who could pass for white and wore brownface. Wittingly or not, these performances contested essentialist understandings of race, and presented race itself—as we shall now see—as the domain of performative enactment. Like the danzón, with which the mulata was often paired on the bufo stage, the mulata was a discursive site for the exploration of whether and how race might be materialized through particular kinds of movement, choreography, and behaviors. Yet here as in Céspedes's study of prostitution, the representation of race doubled as a spatial practice, mapping the contours of public and private arenas and the gendered and racial logic of their separation.

The mulata and the danzón were, in the 1880s, explicitly linked in the costumbrista figure of the *mulata de rumbo* (sometimes *mulata de rumba*), a popular character in the teatro bufo, the visual arts (most famously in Víctor Patrício Landaluze's 1881 portrait of the mulata published in *Tipos y costumbres*), and—as we have seen—in literature, like Villaverde's *Cecilia Valdés.* The *mulata de rumbo* was precisely the "typical" representation of mulatas that Dr. Céspedes abhorred, and against whom he marshaled his ethnographic evidence. Unlike his pathologized women, this mulata was typically a stunning beauty who confidently heated up local *rumbas* (and the white men who have come to watch) with her special talent and appetite for dance; she did not labor, and was not yet a wife or mother, but was instead a single woman who spent her days waiting and preparing for her *rumba* nights. This figure captured the many connotative meanings of the term *de rumbo*: *of the rumba*, in reference either to the *rumba* as a social dance event usually held in black urban *solares*, or to the rumba as a dance itself; *of the street*, connoting prostitution and loose morals; and *of direction* or *of destiny*, connoting confidence and (sexual) brazenness. The mulata de rumbo was doubled in popular discourse by the *mulata de rango*, or the "mulata of rank," which referred to a similarly beautiful, seductive, and talented mulata, but one who had managed to achieve substantial wealth or social standing, usually through the "patronage" of a wealthy white benefactor and lover. In some representations, such as the protagonist of *Cecilia Valdés*, the mulata de rumbo and mulata de rango are one and the same person, at different stages in their lives; in others, the two figures are invested with contrasting class or ethical values. Either figure could be sentimentally depicted as a moral (white) woman betrayed by her (black) racial status, or as the embodiment of the immorality associated with her racially mixed (read black) heritage.

The play *La mulata de rango* by the leading bufo playwright of the mulata genre, José María Quintana, illuminates the complexity of this brownface representation.[5] Unlike fiction or lithography, where, as Vera Kutzinski has well illustrated, the association of mulatas with tales of moral decline was constant throughout the nineteenth century (1993), the teatro bufo hardly ever subjected its protagonist to a punitive fall from grace. The mulata plays in the teatro bufo are in fact notable for their lack of plot structure: in most "mulata" plays precisely nothing happens and the troubled mulata ends up in exactly the same place she began. No doubt, as Rine Leal speculates, a tragic demise was incompatible with the generic expectations of comedy (Leal 1975a, 37–38),[6] and a conventional happy ending—in the form of new wedding vows—was equally incompatible with the prevailing racial ideology, since in the mulata's case a wedding would almost always be interracial.

Rather than drawing the arc of her life (and death) as so many other representations did, the teatro bufo meditated her present identity as a social problem, with fascinating social satire as a result. *La trichina*, for example, centers on the conflict between the defiant mulata de rumbo and her catedrático uncle, who urges her to capitalize on her whiter skin to make greater advances into white society. Subtitled a "disparate bufo-crítico" (a bufo-critical joke), the joke is not at her expense, but rather at his, satirizing his investment in passing in white society. *La mulata de rango* similarly portrays the mulata in largely sympathetic terms; her resigned anger at being denied full entry into wealthy society provides the excuse for a scathing parody of Spanish aristocratic hypocrisy. In both cases, the moral story is less about her than about the contradictions in the social context that produced her troubled circumstance in the first place. The question organizing teatro bufo plays ceased to be whether the mulata was "really" black or white, since this ostensibly empirical research could not be addressed adequately on stage. The theatre instead asked how her *performance* of either identity—how she dressed her body, "wore" her race, and publicly presented her racialized self—was received and engaged by the respective communities for which it was intended. Would she be accepted by whites? By blacks? Would she find a way to feel that she truly belonged, or would she always feel she was "acting," passing for white or black? The theatre thus shifted the emphasis away from the body as a locus for essential racial identity to the body as a locus for the contextual performance of race.

La mulata de rango dramatizes the notion of race as performance as a central part of its plot. Julia is torn between her two contradictory identities, the mulata de rumbo who thrives while drinking and dancing with friends and who loves the poor guaracha-player Pancho, and the mulata de rango, her wealthier self that enjoys fine dining and refined company thanks to the amorous patronage of several aristocrats. She articulates her dilemma to the unrequited Pancho thus: "Crees acaso que la mujer que se ha acostumbrado á esta vida; que la que no cesa de ver á sus piés hombres que le rinden su nombre y fortuna, lo abandone así de cualquier modo?" (Do you think perhaps that a woman who has become accustomed to this life; in which she never ceases to have men at her feet who surrender to her their name and fortune, would abandon it for any reason? [Quintana 1891, 19]). Julia is not torn between her competing racial identities (at least, not in any simple way), since Pancho, like her other suitors, is white; she is instead sentimentally torn between her incompatible class aspirations: should she enjoy her participation in wealthy society (however limited by her race), or should she renounce access to wealth in order to follow her pleasure at the lifestyle of a dancing, celebrating mulata de rumba? Either way, Julia knows that it is neither her race nor her class that determines her ability to chose these paths, but her gender identity as perceived by all concerned. When her mulata maid, Angela, expresses her admiration for Julia's extraordinary social position, Julia is quick to remind her that it will last only so long as her beauty: "Ahí tienes tú marcado el tiempo de mi grandeza. Durará lo que mi belleza. Apagada ésta, no seré otra cosa que la mulata Julia hija de la negra Juana" (There you have marked the time of my grandeur. It will last only as long as my beauty. Once that is gone, I'll be nothing other than the mulata Julia, daughter of the black Juana [11]). Her ability to cross boundaries of race and class, then, is contingent on the uncertain continuity of her particular gender identity.

In the only real plot development of the play, Julia is persuaded to reconsider her role as the mulata de rango by her white father, Manuelillo, a poor drunk—a typical stage *mascavidrios*, whose own role is, apparently, to articulate the racial conscience of the piece, albeit in his heavily slurred and stumbling performance. Early on, he admonishes her to consider her obligation to the black community:

Manuelillo: Tú que mulata eres, que morena fué tu madre [. . .] favorece á los tuyos; sé la amiga de los negros.
Julia: Y bien á todos los quiero.
Manuelillo: Y cumples con tu conciencia! Ellos tus hermanos son; hasta ayer fueron esclavos y ya que la ley les dá el derecho de hermanos, como tal hay que tratarlos. (61)

(*Manuelillo*: You, as a mulata, as the daughter of a black woman, [. . .] favor your own kind; be a friend to the blacks.

Julia: I love them all well.

Manuelillo: And so you do right by your conscience! They are your brothers; until yesterday they were slaves and now that the law gives them the right to be brothers, so we must treat them.)

This passage is a rather remarkable embrace of racial equality, especially spoken by a white actor before white audiences in 1885, a year before the final vestiges of slavery were dismantled. Yet they harbor a familiar ambivalence: he does not suggest that Julia always should have considered blacks her brothers, only that she do so now that the law mandates it. For Julia, at any rate, his admonishment (which is then echoed by Pancho) forces her to acknowledge her fundamental enjoyment of her local, mixed-race, poor community, in which (and for whom) she can indulge her role as the consummate mulata de rumbo. She thus decides momentarily to abandon her identity as the mulata de rango to become, for one evening only, the mulata de rumbo she so enjoys.

The transformation from one role to the other illuminates the play's interest in the controversial idea of race as performance: the transformation is marked on stage through a radical change in costume, demeanor, and speech pattern. We can imagine that in performance this transformation was greeted with a certain wonder at how thoroughly the beautiful mulata had changed in so little time. In this reverse-Cinderella tale, Julia leaves the stage in her glamorous dress, carefully coifed hair, and well-heeled shoes, with the promise to return as the mulata that Pancho so desires. In her intervening absence, the maid Angela ponders aloud, "Qué le ha entrao á Julita? Pues no lo entiendo. Está poniendose las chancletas y dice: 'Hoy voy á ser feliz! Hoy soy Julia! Hoy soy la mulata criolla!'" (What has gotten into Julia? I don't understand. She's putting on her *chancletas* [hard-soled slippers, like clogs] and says, "Today I'll be happy! Today I am Julia! Today I am the criolla mulata!" [21]). Indeed, when Julia returns in her chancletas, her transformation is complete. Chancletas were the signature feature of the mulata de rumbo, signaling both her moral disrepute and her sexual attraction: their street-worn, unsightly appearance marked her low social class; the open heels and her bare ankles marked her lack of modesty, and brazenly flaunted bare flesh in public. Finding the freedom to wear her chancletas, she leaves behind the compromising social role that being the mulata de rango requires: "Así es como estoy yo a gusto, y no con tanto polizón y tantos perendengues" (This is how I am at ease, not with so much hiding and elaborate costume [*perendengues*] [23]). She announces that tonight her home will be turned over to a grand rumba, in which even her servants will be free to participate.

This temporary suspension of social roles, relaxing the strict obligations of class, race, and gender, presents the rumba as a momentary refuge from the exigencies of social normativity. As such, the *rumba* is positioned outside the normative public sphere, a semiprivate space that nonetheless allows for a different kind of public to assemble, one that imagines a more egalitarian relation between races and classes. But the rumba is only temporary—compensatory relief from the psychological labor of racial and class conformity in everyday life. As Julia comments, she cannot choose to stay in her chancletas all the time, because if she did, "entonces dicen que una es chancletua" (then call her a *chancletua*), a derogatory nomination that Julia's dignity cannot tolerate). "En fin," she says, "no hay más que conformarse con las exigencias de eso que llaman la sociedad y que cuando viene á mi casa, hago con ella lo que me dá la gana" (In short, there's nothing to be done other than to conform with what is called society and when it comes to my home, do with it whatever I please [23]). Mulatas, she claims, have no place or function of their own in the public sphere, and limited opportunities for social advancement or social change.

While she implies that the doors to her home are what separate her public and private lives, this is not quite so: the social obligations of the mulata de rango also require that she entertain the aristocratic set in her home (as she does in Act 2) since, as a mulata, she is not welcome in the public spaces or homes where aristocrats socialize, especially if they are also patronized by their white Spanish wives. Thus, to the contrary, it is not her home as such, but rather the change of racial performance from mulata de rango to mulata de rumbo, from highbrow soirée to local rumba, that makes possible an alternate, if temporary, public arena in which different rules governing gender, race, and class might prevail.

However, even as the play indulges the idea that racial identity is mutable and potentially contingent on performance, it nonetheless returns—ferociously—to a discourse of racial essentialism before it arrives at what would indeed be a radical theory of the performativity of race and racial identity. For Julia, the move from mulata de rango to the mulata de rumbo is a move from the "fake" to the "real" and "authentic" mulata. In her relaxed dress and demeanor, she announces herself, again and again, as the "real" mulata: "He aquí la mulata de verdad!" (23). The following day, when she is consigned to her rango costume and duties, she complains, "Ayer la verdad! Hoy la mentira . . !" (Yesterday the truth! Today the lie . . ! [25]). She insists, in frank terms, that she only acts at being the mulata de rango as a form of opportunistic revenge for the racism she has otherwise endured:

> Hoy mi casa será invadida por los tipos más orgullosos de la sociedad, y sin embargo, vienen á mi casa á rendir tributo á Julia, á la mulata Julia. Y tengo que tratarlos bien? No y mil veces no! Me recibirán en su casa siquiera un momento? Pues que sufran mi desprecio y sean esclavos de la vanidad de que ellos mismos me han alimentado. (25)

> Today my home will be invaded by the most arrogant types in society, and despite this, they come to my home to render tribute to Julia, the mulata Julia. And must I treat them well? No and a thousand times no! Would they receive me in their homes even for a moment? Well then let them suffer my disdain and be slaves to the vanity that they themselves have fed me.

Her home is her limited arena for participation in this public sphere, but here at least she has a modicum of control. She capitalizes on the hypocritical adoration of white men against them, intentionally taking on the role of the object of their desire. The mulata de rango, the play tells us, is all an act, a lie that does nothing more than illuminate the hypocrisy of the men who desire her. Indeed, all of Act 2 displays her shrewd "acting" ability, and satirizes the racist hypocrisy of the Spanish aristocracy.

However, Julia's obsessive assertion that the mulata de rumba is her true identity is repeated again and again—most likely—not because the author or audience firmly believe it, but because they begin to doubt it. The repeated assertion is, in other words, required by the racial insecurity of the play, because nothing in this discourse or social ambiance assures us that her performance of one role is fundamentally different from the other. Julia herself signals the radical slippage between acting and being when she decides to shed her mulata de rango act: "me voy a disfrazar, es decir, voy á volver á mis primeros días y á ser la mulata Julia, la verdadera mulata" (I am going to disguise myself, that is, I'm going to return to my earlier days and be the mulata Julia, the true mulata [21]). For Julia, every role available to her is precisely an act, a way of wearing or presenting her racially marked body; in short, it is a kind of blackface. Everyone plays a racially marked social role that can be framed and analyzed as such. The difference is that Julia is never allowed to stop consciously performing the racial scripts already written for her. More importantly, she is never allowed to understand herself in other terms that might exceed, complicate, or interrupt these gendered, racial scripts. True or false, she is always the mulata.

Julia's father suggests that choosing the path of the mulata de rumbo is what her "conscience" should dictate: that role allows her to "favor" her "own" kind, and be fraternal with blacks as her brethren. He forces her hand at the end of the play by publicly attacking and humiliating her rich male suitors. When the aristocrats revile against the old moralizing drunk, Julia finally rejects them; in the closing moments of the play, she agrees to replace her soirée with yet another rumba. But what "favor" does being a mulata de rumbo lend to her community? What actual change is made possible when she exchanges one set of dancing shoes for another? Despite her many protests to the contrary, becoming the mulata de rumbo does not, in fact, alter her racial or gender behaviors at all: she remains, in both contexts, the beautiful, desired mulata who plays hostess to communal gatherings of men in her home. In both contexts she is surrounded by white men, and those black "brethren" her father invokes never appear. The fact that the minuet is danced in one and rumbas in the other makes no substantial difference to her situation—although it is crucially important, of course, to her white male guests. To the contrary, from her perspective, the rumba—the space in which she is ostensibly "herself"—denies her access to wealth and limits her overall agency, since her father and lover are quick to discipline her "true" identity. Pancho and Manuelillo's enthusiastic concern for "their" mulata, then, illustrates a substratum of class and gender conflict underlying this play and the entire discourse surrounding the mulata that the play represents: these poor white men cannot tolerate "their" mulata succeeding in the social world from which they are exiled, especially by using her coveted sexuality to do so. They insist repeatedly that her "true place" is to serve and please them. The fact that she is black and they are white only exacerbates their own racist and paternalistic presumption to dictate her "true" self.

In the fascinating conclusion, Julia announces the end of the play and perhaps her identity as la mulata de rango as she begins to dance a yambú:

Y con un cubano tango
Bailado en este local
Verá el público el final
De *la mulata de rango.* (45)

(And with this Cuban tango
Danced in this locale
The public will see the end
Of the *mulata de rango.*)

The sudden introduction of the term "cubano" for the first time in the play conjures the nationalist and anticolonial agenda implicitly organizing the play from the outset. The mulata is used in the theatre to illuminate competing worlds of white men—one Spanish and wealthy, one "Cuban" and poor. No black community, where a mulata might indeed find other avenues of social work and behavior, ever appears on the scene. Indeed, even her black mother has been killed off before the story begins. When she dances her yambú, then, she resigns herself to a series of deeply problematic social norms, which only serve the aims of a select group of white Cuban men: as a woman, she will serve "her" men; as a near-white woman, she will not desire or fraternize with black men, but instead seek to further "whiten" herself; and, finally, as a black woman, she will not only tolerate poverty, but embrace it as her only and "true" social place. Adopting such a role, she draws on the African, or perhaps more accurately Afrocuban, culture of rumbas and yambú to which she ostensibly has "authentic" access to reaffirm not blackness, not racial equality, but "Cubanness" itself. Rather than act as kept mistress to the Spanish aristocracy, she will be the cooperative dancing trophy of a rising Cuban nation that understands her "place."

This constellation of race, gender, and nation is further extended by the subplot of the play, which centers on Julia's two servants: the mulata Angela, who acts as Julia's racial double throughout the piece, and the gallego Santiago, a poor Spaniard struggling to fit in and become "more" Cuban. Unlike Julia, Angela cannot afford to languish as either the mulata de rango or de rumbo; she earns her living by serving Julia and seeks opportunities to reach the relatively comfortable status that Julia enjoys. Santiago, in turn, lusts after Angela and is offended by her rebuffs, constantly reminding her that as a servant she should have no presumption to marry anyone of higher class or social status than he. One exchange between them draws the contour of this negotiation between gender, race, and national belonging:

Santiago: Yo te quiero de verdad; pero de verdad pura.
Angelita: Pero D. Santiago, usted sabe lo qué necesita una mulata?
Santiago: Fuerza! mucha fuerza! [. . .]
Angelita: Oigame: lo que una mulata necesita, es dinero, dinero y dinero.
Angelita: Y unas palizas de cuandu en cuandu.
Angelita: De eso sí que no llevo yo.
Santiago: Pues si te enredas conmiju, y no andas derecha . . . tan derecha como una vela, te gorobo de un trancazu que te desconponjo toda.
Angelita: [. . .] Mira como habla todos los dicharachos del país.

Santiago: Y en cuantu me arrejle contijo, ¡criollu completo! purque tú al fin tendrás que quererme. [. . .] Yo quieru una muger para mí. (7–9)

(*S*: I love you in truth, in pure truth.
A: But Don Santiago, don't you know what a mulata requires?
S: Strength! a lot of strength!
A: Hear me: what a mulata needs is money, money and money.
S: And a few beatings from time to time.
A: That I won't take.
S: Well if you mess with me and aren't straight, straight as an arrow, I'll [split] you with one blow, and mess you up completely. [spoken in idiomatic Cuban expressions]
A: Look how you use all the expressions of our country.
S: And when I settle things with you, I'll be a complete criollo! Because at the end you'll have to love me. [. . .] I want a woman of my own.)

Angela is required in this play to counterbalance the relatively positive treatment of Julia: one constant feature of the representation of mulatas, from which the teatro bufo does not stray, is that the mulata is always in large measure responsible for the unfairness she faces in life. Here greed is the mark of both women's lack of moral standing. So even as the sentimental mulata Julia learns to reject her greed and embrace poverty as her "natural" destiny, her comic double succumbs to her equally "natural" greed: all that Angela wants is money—even if a battering husband is the price. Indeed, reprising a scene from the 1868 *Los negros catedráticos*, Angela has a quick change of heart about Santiago when she learns he has become wealthy.

The two mulatas, Julia and Angela, revisit the dialectic between class and race established in the earlier catedrático plays. Angela becomes the new Dorotea, quick to set aside all other concerns over social position, class, race, or ethnicity if her suitor has enough money. Julia, in turn, is cast as a new iteration of the "negro congo" José from *Los negros catedráticos*, the fundamentally good though flawed black character whose attempts to attain a higher social standing only prove that he really was much happier in the place where he "truly belonged," which is to say, in poverty. The two figures advance a racist national ideology in lockstep: Angela proves that mulatas do not have the moral fortitude to ever join high society; Julia proves that even if she were moral, being so would make her loyal to her own kind and keep her from white society. In either case she does not belong near wealth and power. For his part, the comic gallego Santiago completes the nationalist logic of the play. To be Cuban apparently requires two things: first, appropriate linguistic performance—that is, speaking Spanish like a Cuban rather than a Spaniard; second, control over one's very "own" mulata, that paradigmatic criollo object of national desire.

The fiction that the rumba is the site of an active alternate black public sphere is, of course, just that: a fiction. In the theatre, unlike the local solares in the *ciudadela*, the rumba is staged entirely for the benefit of a largely white, and more often male viewing audience. Far from being a compensatory copy of the real thing, the theatrical rumba offers its white male viewers a privileged and specially erotic position from which to witness the event: like Dr. Céspedes, they are voyeurs into the "private" life of an alluring mulata who may sternly refuse, but cannot control, their desiring gaze. Further, if these plays thematize the idea that the mulata is a central vehicle for understanding a public sphere from which she is denied entry, then the actual performance of these plays seals this racist norm. Played by white women (including Elvira Mireilles, who played Julia and other mulata protagonists in brownface), the performances signal the total structural absence of black women from the public sphere, certainly in the theatre. The prevalence of brownface on white women in the teatro bufo also suggests that the sexual appeal of the mulata on stage had less to do with actual mulatas than it did with the erotic titillation of the "scandal" of interracial sex that her birth represented. Whereas the representation of mulatas in fiction or visual arts could only portray the moral consequence of such transgression as it rippled through the mulata's life, the theatre evoked the illicit transgression itself through the fact of blackface. Like Cuba's white virgins dancing the "African" danzón to unknown pleasures, the image of a white woman in brownface playing the erotic and sexually available mulata provided an embodied, overdetermined figure of interracial sexual contact and pleasure. Her whiteness made this desire all the more illicit (unlike mulatas white women were not defined by the dominant cultural discourse as sexually available), at the same time that it made her performance of mestizaje all the more appealing. The white woman in brownface, perhaps more than an actual brown woman, provided a palatable fantasy of liberal Cuba herself: a white, virgin, patriot, and erotic Cuban *rumbera*, all in one—object of "national longing," indeed.

Thus far, Céspedes's writings and Quintana's play may well seem diametrically opposed in their treatment of the mulata, illustrating how wide the range of perception and representation of mixed-race women was in Cuba of the late 1880s. The former mounted relentless textual evidence to disparage the mulata; the latter offered her adulation, however ambivalent its effects. Both men were Cuban nationalists: one situated the mulata as the toxic, foreign element that most threatened the literal and figurative health of the nation; the other looked to the mulata for the style, speech, and rhythm that would serve as anthems to a new national structure of feeling. Both avidly "read" her body, interpreting its racial signs: where the doctor looked for essential racial meaning in her anatomical composition, the playwright illustrated how performance transcends anatomy, allowing her to pass between regimes of race. Yet, however opposed, both ultimately relied on her representation to map social space in postslavery Cuba; both used her to map the relation of white and black worlds, public and private spheres. In early ethnography—or costumbrista science—as in the popular theatre, the mulata was denied entry into the public sphere even as, in her own liminal domain, she herself was defined as an object of public access and pleasure. She had, in short, no rightful place in either the public or private spheres, and was instead the key marker by which such terms were made meaningful, practiced, and policed in discourse.

Literate Women

"¿Y pregunto, seguiremos siempre así? . . . ¿Seguiremos impávidas contemplando el estado de la decadencia moral en que vivimos?" (And I ask, we will continue always like this? Shall we continue impassively contemplating the moral decadence in which we live?) So begins an angry editorial in the magazine *Minerva*, Cuba's first publication by and for women of color. It appeared the same year that Céspedes's tract on prostitution was published and Quintana's play was performed, and it could have been directed at either or both of these men. The writer continued, "Sensible sería que la mujer negra no sirviese en Cuba más que para los deleites de la danza" (It would make sense if black women in Cuba served for nothing more than the pleasures of the dance) because, she argued, no one had organized to offer her any education in the aftermath of slavery. She warned black men, "si los hombres de mi raza siguen en el indiferentismo que viven no podrán constituir [el hogar] porque . . . *le faltarán mujeres*" (if the men of my race continue in the indifference in which they live they won't be able to constitute households because . . . *they will be missing the women* [italics in the original]). A wake-up call to men and women alike, the journal *Minerva*, published between 1888 and 1889, became a focal point for activism on behalf of women of color in Cuba.

It is a curious historic irony that one of the leading writers of Cuba's first publication by and for women of color, *Minerva,* wrote under the single name "Cecilia," allowing us to imagine that a symbolic Cecilia Valdés had claimed her own voice, and jettisoned the generic last name—Valdés—routinely given to Cuban children with no father to claim them. It is possible, of course, that Ursula Coimbra de Valverde chose her *nom de guerre* with Villaverde's protagonist in mind.[7] So too is it possible that her colleague, África Céspedes, invented a name that proudly combined a claim for Africa with the last name of Cuba's most famous patriot—Manuel de Céspedes, responsible for launching Cuba's first war of independence—although there is no hard evidence that hers was a pseudonym. What is certain is that from the moment these women chose to create a sphere of self-representation in writing, every printed word acted as a counterdiscourse to prior representations of women of color in the entire history of Cuban letters. For Cecilia and África Céspedes, along with their collaborators Lucrecia González, América Font, Onantina and others, the pages of *Minerva* were the opportunity, so long withheld, to extend their own person and presence into the wider realm of writing, and to conjure a community of readers that, in the magazine's brief life, extended throughout the island and to Jamaica, Florida, and New York. These are the pages in which, we imagine, Villaverde's Cecilia and the battalion of mulatas de rumbo in the teatro bufo might indeed resist their confinement and set the record straight; or that an alternate combination of gender, race, and nationalism could take shape in a figure proudly called "África Céspedes"—a feminist, antiracist Céspedes to counter that Dr. Céspedes whose arguments about gender and race were so widely disseminated in 1888.

The readers and writers of *Minerva* certainly understood their task as Herculean. A reprinted letter to "Cecilia" from February 1889 addressed her as the "heroina de nuestra raza" (heroine of our race) for her "misión noble y generosa [. . .] de regenerar á las mujeres de nuestra raza" (noble and generous mission [. . .] to regenerate the women of our race): "A tí te ha cabido la grandísima gloria de llamar á nuestras hermanas á empuñar la armas del saber" (To you has fallen the greatest glory of calling our sisters to wield the weapons of knowledge). The authors frequently correlated writing with a form of heroic armed struggle, as did one writer calling on others to take up their pens and write for the press:

> Ayudarnos á luchar, y si por desgracia, no vencéis, tendremos la satisfacción de haber partido con vosotras las fatigas que nos han sorprendido en el camino que hemos

emprendido; tendréis la convicción de haber cumplido con uno de los más santos deberes y de haber contribuído á colocar la primera piedra en el templo de nuestra reorganización: piedra que, no lo dudéis, se transformará en grandioso edificio y que le dirá al caminante: ¡detente y mira la grandeza de los desheredados de la suerte; ellos por sí se han levantado y colocado á la altura de los grandes! (30 December 1888)

(Help us to fight, and if by ill chance you fail, we will have the satisfaction of having shared the hardships that surprised us along the path we have chosen; you will have the conviction of having fulfilled one of the most sacred duties and having contributed to the placing of the first stone in the temple of our reorganization: a stone that, have no doubt, will be transformed into a great edifice that will say to the passerby: halt and behold the greatness of those disinherited by fortune; they raised themselves to the height of the greatest!")

Like their male counterparts in the black press, the women who created *Minerva* were part of the vast effort to restructure civil life for former slaves. Central to those efforts was the struggle to bring literacy and education to black Cubans; black voices in print, whether in Juan Gualberto Gómez's *La Fraternidad* or in *Minerva*, were crucial assertions of black entry and participation in the white "lettered city" (in Angel Rama's phrase) that otherwise guarded access to basic human dignity, subjectivity, citizenship, and other rights of fully acknowledged personhood. In this struggle, the women of *Minerva* shared with their male colleagues a commitment to transnational black solidarity, and hence reached out to a wide audience of women of color beyond Cuba's borders and took interest in the progress of black women in the United States and elsewhere. At the same time, they seem to have shared in a crossracial nationalist project, whereby Cuba's struggle for independence might herald further dismantlement of the social order that had for so long sustained slavery.

The women of *Minerva* further brought a critique about gender to bear on this complex terrain of social struggle. Many articles addressed issues that might be taken for granted as "appropriate" for a women's publication, such as marriage, child rearing, and the home. But in a context in which black women historically were denied access to marriage and respectability as mothers and as keepers of their own—rather than their masters'—homes, these topics took on an explicitly activist dimension. One editorial said, "Si la raza de color desea cordialmente dignificarse y ocupar en las funciones públicas el lugar á que están llamados todos los elementos componentes de la sociedad, empiece por formar familia dentro de los preceptos dictados por la moral, y exigido por las leyes" (If people of color cordially wish to dignify themselves and occupy in public functions the place to which all constituent elements of society are called, begin by forming family within the precepts dictated by morality and required by law [30 December 1888]). In other words, the editorial suggested, black women and men had to begin by firmly redrawing the boundaries of public and private life, and allow marriage to serve as the ritual assertion of that boundary for black Cubans as it had long served for whites. We already know, from Dr. Céspedes's study and from the teatro bufo, how easily white Cuba held blacks themselves—rather than slavery—accountable for the prevalence of concubinage, and how easily white Cuba cast black women as "public" women by social definition, sexually available and destined for immoral sexual conduct. The editorial in *Minerva*, apparently written by a man, faults men of all races for taking advantage of black women outside of marriage. "Todos los hombres nos creemos asistidos en derecho de ir á ese campo abierto, á ese bazaar de carne á proveernos, no de compañeras, sí de parejas para nuestras miserias, para nuestras asquerosas orgías" (We men all believe ourselves entitled to go to that open camp, that bazaar of meat to procure, not a companion, but a pair for our misery, for our gross orgies). The editorial goes on to advise men of color to seek wives with honor and education, and take seriously their roles as husbands and fathers. "No exija todavía que su elejida sea hija de mujer casada; recuerde que esa madre fué esclava" (he should not yet require that his intended be the daughter of a married woman; remember that that mother was a slave [30 December 1888]). Thus, the regular marriage announcements and congratulations that appeared on the pages of *Minerva* may not appear so different from those in *El Fígaro* or other publications dedicated to women, but each announcement proclaimed one more woman's possible—if still compromised—entry into a larger public sphere—one less rumbera, one less woman to garner the contempt of men like Dr. Céspedes.

Yet there is evidence in the pages of *Minerva* that some women, if not men, were wary of accepting white heteronormative patriarchy wholesale as an ideal for either gender relations or black enfranchisement. Almost every issue of *Minerva* included articles on the rights of women and on the importance of making education widely available to girls—all girls, not only those of color. "La mujer debe aspirar," wrote América Font in November 1888, "á salir de la esclavitud de la ignorancia; y para poder ser libre, en este concepto, deber ser instruida; pues donde no hay instrucción, no hay libertad" (A woman must aspire to leave the slavery of ignorance; and to be free, in this sense, she must be instructed; because where there is no instruction, there is no liberty). Black women would not be free, she argued, if they aspired to no more than the ignorance to which many white women were already subject. A woman is not, she said "una máquina, más ó ménos perfeccionada, de hacer calcetas" (a machine, more or less perfect, for knitting). Font eventually qualified that "of course" women should not devote themselves exclusively to their studies—to algebra, classical jurisprudence, or astronomy—at the expense of the domestic duties entrusted to women, she said in a well-fashioned understatement, "por una costumbre que se ha hecho ley" (by a custom that has become law). A later notice in *Minerva* shared the bitter news that "Cecilia" had that month nearly died in childbirth; although the doctors had saved her life, they were not able to save her child. In addition to revealing that "Cecilia" had been pregnant throughout the life span of the magazine that she founded, the news occasioned a short reflection from África Céspedes to Cecilia on the politics of motherhood:

> He sufrido mucho, porque aunque no he sido madre, ni con esperanza de serlo, reflexionaba profundamente sobre nuestra constitución orgánica que hasta para dar al mundo ciudadanos dignos que nos enaltecen ó monstruos que nos depriman, exponemos nuestra existencia á los azares de inminente peligro. (28 February 1889)
>
> (I have suffered greatly, because although I have not been a mother, nor have hope of becoming one, I reflected profoundly on our organic constitution that even to bring to the world dignified citizens that ennoble us or monsters that depress us, we expose our very existence to the vicissitudes of imminent danger.)

We do not know why África Céspedes had no children, and whether this was her choice. We do know that she saw in the "organic constitution" of women a painfully arbitrary fate, whereby her friend Cecilia should have to risk her life for that of another—perhaps a monster that would depress them. The dangers of childbirth, she said, allow for no discrimination on the relative value of women's lives. Like the discourse of scientific costumbrismo, África read a measure of destiny in women's biology. Yet unlike the novelist or the scientist who cast women of color into a sexual drama that inevitably ended in moral and usually physical death, and unlike the bufo playwrights who could not even trace an imagination of women of color that would allow for them to be good mothers or public intellectuals, much less both simultaneously, África's public condolence for her friend's loss acknowledged that such risks were not destined, but weighed and chosen, by women who—through different means—would stake themselves for the future.

Minerva's writers were conscious of the prevailing attitudes that shaped perception, practice, and policy concerning black women. One columnist,

"Elvira," regularly chastised readers for the incommensurate attention paid to dance in the Sociedades, the mutual aid societies: "la misión que en el presente momento se tiene [es] de crear generaciones inteligentes y estudiosas, no *generaciones danzonianas*" (the present mission is to create intelligent and studious generations [of women], not *danzón-dancing generations* [italics in the original, 28 February 1889]). Elvira complained that the frequent veladas in the black community, which she otherwise admired, regularly featured "piezas de cuadro" or square dances by children, who would spend a month in rehearsal rather than devoting their time to school. She noted that parents frequently explained their children's absence from school on the grounds that the children had no appropriate clothes or shoes; yet the same parents would bring their children punctually to rehearsal in the evening fully groomed and clothed for dance. The sociedades, which sponsored both the schools and the dances, she argued, should reverse their priorities. Otherwise, she warned, they would leave the future ("la venidera") bereft of all "patrimony" save dance. Yet dance—if only dance—was precisely the contribution that white Cuba imagined black Cubans could offer to their developing patrimony, as well illustrated by the popularity of the danzón and (brownface) stage rumberas of the day. Arguing time and again for the literacy of black children, Elvira, like Gualberto Gómez, was at pains to renegotiate the presumed relation among race, literacy, and expressive behaviors lest black Cubans be perpetually exiled from a white literate public sphere.

The public sphere and its race and gender contours mapped by the practice of reading and writing, as opposed to the practices associated with dance or theatre attendance, were in fact illustrated by the relation of *Minerva*'s readers to Dr. Céspedes's *Historia de la prostitución en la ciudad de la Habana*, both journal and book having been published in the same year. It is worth reviewing in some detail the remarkable set of exchanges that surrounded the question of whether women in general, and the women of *Minerva* in particular, should, could, or ultimately did read and respond to Céspedes's text—an exchange that lends insight into the related politics of literacy, race, and public sex. Céspedes began his book by asking honest women not to read it, despite its scientific merits: "Solicito, sin embargo, como escritor cubano que no lean estas tristes y vergonzosas revelaciones, nuestras honestas mujeres, ni tampoco aquellos pudorosos y delicados temperamentos, escasamente familiarizados con esta clase de lecturas" (I ask, nonetheless, as a Cuban writer that these sad and shameful revelations not be read by our honest women, nor by those modest and delicate temperaments too scarcely familiar with this class of literature [1]). This would not be so remarkable, given the prevailing values of the day and the subject matter, were it not that only a few chapters later, Céspedes offered a scouring critique of Cuban patriarchy, arguing that the penchant for undereducating women and leaving them wholly dependent on men had made them incapable of negotiating real life challenges when men failed or abandoned them. Ignorance, he complained in a chapter devoted to the topic, was considered "una virtud y una garantía de virginidad moral" (a virtue and a guarantee of moral virginity). Thus honest and resource-rich white women were trained to be ignorant:

> Para reducirla más á la insignificancia y hacer más intangible su influencia en la sociedad; ha logrado tan viciosa educación exitar enfermizamente su temperamento nervioso, ya de suyo exaltado, transfigurando las mujeres, por artificios de amor y de adoracion, en virgenes, ángeles y séres sobrenaturales, colocados tan altos por la pasión de los hombres, que acaban estas por llegar á ser nada más que figuras decorativas, trofeos gloriosos del amor propio del hombre satisfecho de una conquista. [. . .] La consigna tradicional de estos educadores es no despertar en el alma ni en el cerebro de la mujer, la más remota idea de las *realidades mundanas.* (97, italics in the original)

> (To reduce her even more to insignificance and to make more intangible her influence on society, this vicious education has managed sickeningly to excite her nervous temperament, already exalted from his own, transfiguring women from artifacts of love and adoration into virgins, angels and supernatural beings, placed so high by the passion of men, that they end being nothing but decorative figures, glorious trophies of love that belong to man satisfied with his conquest. [. . .] The traditional consignment of these educators is to not awaken either in the soul or the brain of the woman the most remote idea of *mundane realities.*)

In the proletariat classes, he said, and in women of color, "la ignorancia es total y hasta se llega á dudar, si de esos cerebros tan imbuidos por supersticiones de todos géneros, pudieran brotar alguna idea civilizadora" (the ignorance is total and one even comes to doubt whether from those brains so imbued with superstition of every kind there could emerge any civilizing idea [97]). Dr. Céspedes suggested nevertheless that women themselves organize to ensure their better education, creating "escuelas ambulatorias" or ambulatory schools; associations devoted to teaching trades to women; leagues against indecent dance, lottery, and gambling; protective associations for women of color, for children, and for orphans; and societies that could organize campaigns to promote marriage over concubinage (95). The list of "civilizing" projects with which Céspedes would entrust women is impressive (and indeed, as his critics were quick to point out, most of these projects were already under way, under the leadership of women). Still, honest women were not to be trusted with reading his text.

The question for women, then, was to read, or not to read? The distinguished Enrique Varona—a regular contributor to the black newspaper *La Fraternidad*, who was respected by the black community—had commended the text for exemplifying science's ability to make man a "colaborador inteligente" (intelligent collaborator) in the workings of nature; surely scientific study would have the same benefits for women? Or did Céspedes's text belong to some different "class of literature," whose reading could have deleterious effects on women? When the male readership of *La Fraternidad* first made mention of Céspedes's book, in a headline article on August 21, 1888, the author dismissed anthropology itself as a suspicious class of literature: "Dicho libro es uno de tantos que brotan estos tiempos de observación y análysis, con la pretención de mejorar lo existente" (Said book is one of the many sprouting these days of observation and analysis, with the pretension of improving the present). Among the many outraged protests of the book in the black press, we find another on 10 October 1888, entitled "La raza negra cubana ante la ciencia, la experiencia, la justicia y la conciencia" (The black Cuban race before science, experience, justice, and conscience), that questions Céspedes's cynical use of anthropology to reach white supremacist conclusions about blacks. "Si acude el Dr. Céspedes á la Antropología ésta no puede emitir dictamen sin tener en cuenta las condiciones desfavorables en que se halla colocado la raza negra" (If Dr. Céspedes is to make recourse to anthropology, he cannot pass judgment without taking into consideration the unfavorable conditions in which the black race has been placed). The author, signed "H. B. Peña," challenged Céspedes, and by extension Cuban anthropology, to take full account of the effects of slavery, lack of education, and poor diet and medical care on the condition of black Cubans. He reminded Céspedes of the conditions in which slaves were forced to live and the constant sexual exploitation that black women suffered at the hands of their masters: "así el jóven, el hombre maduro y hasta el viejo, amo ó mayoral, estudiante o letrado, arrendatario ó hacendado, dignábanse arrebatar la mujer al negro" (so the young man, the mature adult, and even the old man, master or slave driver, student or learned one, tenant or landowner, saw fit to steal the woman/wife from black men). The critique of anthropology is strong, faulting its failure to account for the effects of long-standing sexual violence and agonizing exploitation. Even so, the critiques tended to position black men as the offended party (which they surely were, along with women), and the debate as a contest between men in defense of "their" women. One letter to the editor, dated 20 October 1888, demanded to know what punitive reprisals would have ensued if the tables were turned, if a black man had published such scathing insults toward white women? But some letters, like one that appeared 31 August 1888, called on black men to admit their complicity in denigrating the mulata; another, in the same issue, suggested that Céspedes's portrait was more accurate than most would admit.

Black men were not the only offended parties protesting Céspedes's book on the front pages of the press in the early fall of 1888. Most rabid were the condemnations published in *El Progreso Comercial* by members of the "Asociación de Dependientes del Comercio de la Habana," the male workers association that Céspedes had signaled as a hotbed of "pederasty." Céspedes offered a curious portrait of queer street life, arguing that "pederasts" circulate freely, often making company with or competition for prostitutes. He identified them by their "actitudes grotescamente afeminadas" (grotesquely effeminate attitudes), bodies arched and on display, walking with a particular dragging gait, "con contoneos de la mujer coqueta" (swinging their hips like a coquette [190]).[8] His "scientific" evidence for "male prostitution" was based on cases of syphilis whose symptoms were particular to homosexual sex. Céspedes transcribed a dialogue between a fellow doctor and an adolescent "dependiente," or clerk, apprenticing in a local shop who, as was typical, lived in shared quarters with his fellow male workers. Suffering from syphilis, the boy confessed that indeed, he had been the regular sexual partner of his older colleagues for some years, usually against his will. Through the boy's testimony, Céspedes suggested that all such immigrant male workers' associations were likely breeding grounds for "pederasty." His larger critique of contemporary Cuban society suggested, however, that such all-male immigrant associations were sexually suspect first because these men usurped positions of labor that would otherwise "naturally" belong to Cuban women. The accusation was explosive, and outraged protests circulated widely in the mainstream press. The Association in question soon published a "Folleto en refutación al libro que bajo el título de La Prostitucion en la ciudad de la Habana del Dr. Benjamin Céspedes" which collected pages and pages of irate refutations of Céspedes's claims.

All this suggests that Céspedes's book was widely known in Havana, and would have come to the attention of the women then preparing the first issues of *Minerva*. From August through November, when *Fraternidad* and other publications debated the book, no mention of Dr. Céspedes appeared on the pages of *Minerva*. The 15 December issue, however, revealed that the editors had turned to their male colleagues at *La Fraternidad* for advice on whether *Minerva* readers should read Dr. Céspedes's infamous text. The editors reprinted a response from one of the men, part of which is worth quoting at some length:

> No incurriré yo en la candidez de anatematizar la citada obra, ni aconsejar á las mujeres de mi raza no lo lean; sé por experiencia que no podría idearse mejor reclamo en su obsequio, por aquello de "lo vedado . . ." etc. etc.
>
> Me limito á no considerar provechosa su lectura: no provechosa ni oportuna.
>
> No es provechosa á mi ver, porque no perteneciendo á la categoría de las obras deleitables, no habrá de proporcionar solaz, y siendo por su índole puramente analítica, mas propia para el estudio grave y reposado por el observador, no acertamos á ver la utilidad que sacarían nuestras mujeres, en general poco profundas—salvo excepciones—de la exposición descarnada y repugnante de los cuadros, no por reales, menos repulsivos.
>
> No veo el provecho de su lectura, querida señora, porque no arriesgaría, á cambio de un poco de sabiduría, el tesoro inapreciable del pudor.
>
> A cambio del conocimiento de las monstruosidades y miserias que oculta en su seno una sociedad disoluta, veríamos destruida la pureza del alma [. . .]
>
> Yo no comparto la opinión de aquellos que sostienen que debe leerse porque nuestras ciudades presentan perennemente á la candorosa mirada de nuestras esposas y nuestras hijas, cuadros al natural mucho más repugnantes que los del libro del Dr. Céspedes. Por la misma razón: pues si toda persona que desea mantener en su hogar y legar á su prole costumbres puras y hábitos virtuosos, tiene harto que luchar para impedir ó anular los efectos de la corrupción pública, no es cosa de introducir en él un pernicioso disolvente de sus sanos consejos y saludables ejemplos. No echemos en olvido la fatal influencia de la tropical imaginación de nuestras mujeres: más que enseñanzas, podrían hallar en las páginas de ese libro, incentivo violento á desconcebidos é impuros deseos, á causa del contacto con tantas obscenidades y desnudeces.
>
> (I will not fall into the naiveté of condemning the cited work, nor will I advise the women of my race not to read it; I know from experience that one could not devise a better enticement on its behalf, than through "the prohibited . . ." etc. etc.
>
> I limit myself to considering its reading not beneficial, neither beneficial nor opportune.
>
> It is not beneficial in my view because it does not belong to the category of works that are pleasurable, it will not provide comfort, and being by nature purely analytical, more appropriate for calm and serious study by the observer, I am not able to see the utility that could be extracted by our women, in general lacking depth—save exceptions—in the stark and repugnant exposition of such scenes, no less revolting for being real.
>
> I find its reading not beneficial, dear Madam, because I would not risk, in exchange for a little wisdom, the invaluable treasure of modesty.

> In exchange for knowledge of the monstrosities and miseries that a dissolute society hides in its bosom, we would see destroyed the purity of soul. [. . .]
>
> I do not share the opinion of those who maintain that the book should be read because our cities perennially present, to the candid gaze of our wives and daughters, scenes that on their own are a great deal more revolting than those in Dr. Céspedes's book. For this very reason: every person who wishes to maintain her home and bestow on its offspring pure customs and virtuous habits already has quite enough with fighting to impede or annul the effects of public corruption, without introducing into it so pernicious a solvent of healthy counsels and models. And we should not overlook the fatal influence of the tropical imagination of our women: more than learning, they would be able to find in the pages of that book violent incentives to unknown and impure desires, as a result of their contact with so much obscenity and exposure.)

Thus, despite his initial assertion that he would not presume to tell women of color whether and what they should read, the board member mounted a strong case that reading the text posed a grave danger to their moral constitution. If this author were like many of his counterparts in the (male) black press, he would have taken great offense at the racist portrayal of black women, and would have questioned the social aims and scientific integrity of Céspedes's study. If he did hold these views, he chose not to share them with the female readers of *Minerva*—who, as black activist women, might have be interested in such perspective. Instead, his letter suggested that, as women, they were ill equipped to encounter the unflinching truths of "science" harbored in the text. Here the author doubled the position advanced by Dr. Céspedes: although women can be and are the object of "analytical" scrutiny by men, they are to withhold voluntarily their participation in the reception and interpretation of that analysis. We cannot know the author's intention: did he wish to protect the women from yet another round of virulent racism? Or keep them from the text's pornographic passages? Or—as he stated—did he believe that the text had "purely analytical" content that the women, with their "fatal tropical imaginations," could not read with "calm" and "studied" reflection? Whatever the case, the end result is that the man interposed his own protective reading between the women and the book, and made clear that choosing to read it would be morally reckless. Thereafter, none of the women openly admitted to having read the text.

Yet surely it is no coincidence that, only weeks later, África Céspedes composed a long, scathing article pointedly titled "Reflexionemos" (Let us reflect), in which she charted a point-by-point critique of the issues raised by Dr. Céspedes's text, without referring to him by name (dated January 1884, it was published in *Minerva* on 15 February 1884). Hers is one of the most remarkable defenses of civil and social rights for people of color and for women written in nineteenth century Cuba, and worth quoting at length.

Enervado nuestro espíritu por el duro tratamiento de ayer y el torpe juicio de hoy, nos preparamos á la defensa en el constante batallar [. . .] ; y tal haremos hasta que se nos considere tal como somos y no tal como á cada *artista pirata* le ha parecido ó convenido á sus medrosos fines.

Nos invitáis a luchar? Pues lucharemos.

Quemaremos el último cartucho en la defensa de nuestros intereses, hondamente lastimados, en su más sólida base, desangrando, como está, el cuerpo social por los parasíticos que á nuestra costa se han sostenido enhiestos.

Reflexionemos, pues, sin hacer separación alguna de razas, sobre el juicio que de la mujer tiene formado la mayoría de los hombres y hasta de algunas *Maritornes* de esta baja esfera, al mismo tiempo que á nosotras, las de la raza negra, se nos considera en las últimas capas de ese infamante juicio.

(Our spirit enervated by the hard treatment of yesterday and the clumsy judgment of today, we prepare ourselves for defense in the constant battle [. . .] ; and so we will do until we are considered as we are, and not as any *pirate artist* has seen fit or convenient for his cowardly ends.

You invite us to fight? Then we will fight.

We will play to our last card in defense of our interests, so deeply injured, at its most solid base, bleeding, as the social body is from the parasites that have maintained themselves upright at our expense.

Let us reflect, then, without drawing a separation between the races, on the judgment that the majority of men and even a few "maritones" from this lower sphere have formed of women, at the same time that we, women of the black race, have been considered at the last stratum of that loathsome judgment.)

África Céspedes established an important frame, illuminating the "intersectionality" of race and gender oppression long before Kimberle Crenshaw lent such insight to the term, and modeling a form of activist critique that by necessity combined both feminist and antiracist perspectives. The title, "Reflexionemos," seems directed as much to the patronizing black male advisor, who so little trusts women to be "analytical," as to Dr. Céspedes's racist views of the incapacity of black women to have "civilizing thoughts."

The long section that follows is structured as a series of statements, rather than arguments, about the condition and treatment of women, particularly in relation to prostitution. The space—the pause—between each statement scans like a long controlled breath of a woman so angry she works to keep herself calm and "reflective."

La sociedad con tenaz empeño siempre a culpado á la mujer de la prostitución, del libertinaje y de cuanto delesnable conduce á los pueblos á su degradación moral.

¡Nada tan injusto, nada tan procaz, nada tan infame!

La mujer, en manera alguna es la responsable de la disolución en que se agita esa parte de los pueblos, que vive sin freno en los lupanares.

La mujer, sólo es la víctima sobre quien llueven los peores dictados, y más si la desgracia la ha conducido á tomar parte en el mundanal festín.

El lodo, la podredumbre, la inmundicia, en que se revuela esa desgraciada parte de la humanidad, tiene su orígen muy apartado del lugar en que todo el mundo lo señala.

En la bacanal del mundo á la mujer se la ha hecho cargar la responsabilidad de todo.

Para la mayor parte de los hombres la mujer es perversa por intuición.

Para el más insignificante número de los feos, la mujer es la personificación de la bondad.

Grácias á esta divergencia, la mujer ocupa los dos polos opuestos en la planeta social, la perdición y la virtud. [. . .]

¡El escalpelo no funciona!

¡La opinión es un sarcasmo!

No hay juicío que juzgue con acierto, imparcialidad y valentía a la que sólo hace el papel de veleta en el *pináculo* de la perdición. [. . .]

La mujer es el punto á donde convergen todas las miradas del resto de la humanidad.

La mujer es el blanco de todas las injusticias. Injusticias en pro é injusticias en contra.

(With tenacious determination, society has always blamed women for prostitution, for licentiousness, and for anything despicable that leads people to moral degradation.

Nothing so unjust, nothing so obscene, nothing so slanderous!

Woman is in no way the one responsible for the dissolution that agitates that part of society, that lives without brakes [out of control] in the brothels.

Woman is only the victim on whom rain the worst dictates, even more if misfortune has led her to partake of the worldly feast.

The mud, the putrefaction, the filth, in which that unfortunate part of society turns, has its origin far from the place where everyone points.

In this bacchanal of a world woman has been made responsible for everything.

For the majority of men, woman is evil by intuition.

For the most insignificant number of the ugly, woman is the personification of kindness.

Thanks to this divergence, woman occupies the two opposite poles of the social planet: perdition and virtue. [. . .]

The scalpel does not work!

Opinion is sarcasm!

There is no judgment that judges with acumen, impartiality, and valor the one who only plays the role of weather vane at the pinnacle of perdition. [. . .]

Woman is the point at which all gazes of the rest of humanity converge.

Woman is the target of all injustice. Injustices for, and injustices against.)

Her reflections, which oscillate among manifesto, poem, and critique, are like so many bricks, laid systematically one upon the other, in the wall of defense she mounted against Céspedes's attack. One directed surely at him and the sciences he represented, reads, "No certain science allows one to distinguish between virtue and appearance" (a rough translation of "no hay quien sepa á ciencia cierta distinguir la virtud de la aparencia"). Indeed, careful, scientific attention to physical "appearance" is precisely the method by which Céspedes claimed to be able to name and understand social practice and its ethical dimension.

This angry litany of "reflections" was followed by a long quotation of Sor Juana Inés de la Cruz's famous "Redondillas," which began "Hombres necios que acusáis / a la mujer sin razón, / sin ver que sois la ocasión / de lo mismo que culpáis" (Foolish men who accuse / woman without reason / not seeing that you are the reason / for the very thing you fault). This famous poem by a sixteenth-century nun, which África Céspedes quoted at length, might well be seen as the model for her own manifesto. "Reflexionemos" made no attempt at rhyme scheme, but like "hombres necios," it often attempted to capture the contradictions of sexism in one verbal gesture: "Se le ha negado instrucción y se lamentan que sea ignorante" (They deny her instruction, and they regret her ignorance), wrote África. The fact that África Céspedes relied on Sor Juana's poetry as a resource for her own defense against contemporary "hombres necios" suggests that the counterpublic sphere mapped by *Minerva* and its community of readers already embraced a long history of struggle by women—as women facing the exigencies of patriarchy—as well as people of color facing the legacy of slavery and continued practices of white supremacy. Sor Juana was enlisted by África—as she often is by feminists today—as an early and important legitimating model in Spanish letters for feminist critique (see Merrim 1991). Born in what is today Mexico as the illegitimate daughter of a poor criolla mother and a Spanish-born father, Sor Juana because of her early circumstances and eventual erudition served as a particularly poignant model for women, especially women of color, in the years following slavery. Her poverty, her American birth, her colonial experience, and her penchant for critique of the circumstances around her positioned her as a specifically American intellectual, whose insights might also be enlisted in an anticolonial and even nationalist projects. Thus, Sor Juana's work was a prelude to África's explicitly political conclusion: "La mujer sólo pide justicia, pero justicia en toda latitud de la palabra" (Woman only demands justice, but justice in the full latitude of the word).

In the next issue of *Minerva* África returned with a new essay, entitled "A Cuba" (To Cuba), and it becomes clear that Cuba—or at least her ideal version of Cuba as a polity—was the greater power to whom women or people of color might make such demands for justice. África looked to the nation as a site for newly established civil order that could then undo the injustices of slavery, colonialism, and—in África's case, if not her male colleague's—patriarchy. The text is more an ode than an expository essay, celebrating Cuba's destined apotheosis from corruption to purity; celebrating women's entry into civil society with "la exigencia lógica del derecho moderno" (the reasoned demands of modern rights); and celebrating that Cuba now, finally, was harbor for "un pueblo de colonos libres" (a people of free colonists). It finally merited the veneration of its poets, she argued. Cuba would be especially blessed, she said, because "aquellos hijos tuyos que gemían en la más cruel servidumbre" (those children of yours who moaned under the most cruel servitude) would soon make books "their constant study" for the good of family, society, and nation (patria).

Dr. Céspedes's ethnography, José María de Quintana's mulata plays, and the writings of África Céspedes share at least this in common: a passion for Cuba. All elaborated the practices that they felt defined—by positive or negative example—what Cuba was and could be; all made recourse to the central role of women of color in general and mulatas in particular to do so. Each in its turn mapped social space of the emerging nation by carefully locating the coordinates of race, gender, and sexuality. In each case a dialectic of embodied and textual practice emerged: for Céspedes, as for the burgeoning anthropological sciences he represented, writing was the practice that catalogued the intrinsic meanings of bodies and performances; for Quintana and for the teatro bufo, writing about the "true" meaning of the mulata to Cuban culture was in tension with the meaning of its brownface performance; for the women of *Minerva,* writing in itself was a practice they pursued aggressively as a means to enter into a civic sphere that could recode the meanings of race. The intertextual tension among the three sites underscores the ways in which both performance *and* writing—embodied and "disembodied" practices—were heavily racialized in this charged historical juncture. It is no accident that women of color were the axle on which these competing discourses and their tensions revolved: what was at stake in the tension among these sites, and between the claims of text and performance as competing epistemological systems, was the place and position of women—always racialized—in this "Cuban" public sphere. We might recall that Dr. Céspedes had asked "*as a Cuban writer*" that honorable women avert their

reading eyes. Somehow, his devotion to Cuba required that he prote
from books. But África Céspedes had a very different vision in mi
would only be "blessed" and fulfill her destiny when all those "ch
slavery, including women like herself, were able to undertake constant literate study so long denied them.

Conclusion
Cubans on the Moon, and Other Imagined Communities

In 1882, the prolific Cuban playwright Ignacio Saragacha wrote a remarkable little play, arguably one of the most significant in the entire bufo genre, entitled *Los bufos en África* (Bufos in Africa).[1] The play is a metatheatrical reflection on the teatro bufo itself, featuring all of the major bufo actors of the day, at that time all forming part of the Bufos de Salas: Miguel Mellado, Saturnino Valverde, Isabel Velazco, Carmen del Valle, Lolita and Ventura Roselló, Joaquín Robreño, and Miguel Salas are all cast as themselves in the piece. The opening finds the company rehearsing another play, *El último mono* (The last monkey) at the Teatro Albisu, one of the primary venues for bufo performance and where, indeed, *Los bufos en África* may have premiered. Miguel Salas arrives late to the rehearsal with the news that Miguel Arderíus, a major theatre impresario in Madrid, has invited the company to come to the Spanish capital. This particular invitation is worth pause, because Arderíus was the producer for the Bufos Madrileños, the Spanish company that performed in Havana in 1866, and proved to be a source of inspiration for the original Bufos Habaneros in 1868. Thus when Saragacha fantasizes that Arderíus would invite the Bufos de Salas back to Madrid, it is in part a colonial fantasy of the colonial "copy" surpassing its peninsular "original." Thus the actors set out to take their blackface act "back" to Spain—the seat of colonial power—where they will have the opportunity to demonstrate their singularity, difference, and perhaps superior talent in relation to the metropole.

However, Saragacha does not allow his Bufos to fulfill this anticolonial fantasy: in Act 2 of this transatlantic misadventure, the actors are instead shipwrecked on the shores of a remote and decidedly savage Africa. The teatro bufo company is thus sent "back" to the ostensible "source" of its own blackface performance, falling captive to the very Africans whom they otherwise impersonate, mock, and abuse. As it turns out, the Bufos are captured in blackface, since they had been performing on deck for the ship crew when the storm came. While Saturnino Valverde's costume—cross-dressed and blacked up as a comic black woman—seduces the Africans into thinking he is a real woman, the actors' use blackface only further provokes the ire of the Africans. Identifying them as Cuban, the head of the tribe (now played by Mellado) sees an opportunity for revenge: his own father was captured and now lives as a slave in Cuba. The Africans thus hold the actors responsible for the mistreatment and abuse of their fellow Africans in Cuba, both in and out of the theatre. As punishment, the avenging Africans throw all the blackface actors in a pot for that evening's dinner.

This play returns us to the questions with which this study began: what is the relationship between the popular theatre and evocations of Africa? What are these Bufos doing in (and with) Africa—not only in this play, but throughout the period of anticolonial struggle with which the bufo genre coincides? During these years, the teatro bufo proposed—and then energetically rehearsed and revised—a complex imagined geography, one which mapped the literal, cultural, and social terrain between Africa, Cuba, and Spain in an ongoing effort to articulate, celebrate, and direct a developing sense of national belonging. *Los bufos en África* illuminates a key trope in the arts of racialization practiced in this theatre: making constant recourse to distinctly unreal imagined realms in a trope I will call *cartographic fantasy.* Traveling to a fantastic Africa to better define an imagined Cuban community, this play and others like it return us to a more precise consideration of the theoretical concern shaping this study: what does this history of Cuban blackface and nationalism tell us about the relation between the theatrical imagination and invocations of the social imagination, such as Benedict Anderson's "imagined communities," or Arjun Appadurai's "imagined worlds," and other notions of the social imaginary? More simply, what is the relation between a phantasmatic Africa on stage to the making and maintenance of a real place, a nation, called Cuba?

Put differently, we recall that it was precisely the Bufos de Salas' 1882 season at the Teatro Albisu that the writer Federico Villoch claimed that he and other Cubans of his generation could never forget, because to do so—he said—"would be tantamount to forgetting ourselves" (Villoch 1946, 22–23). Those same Bufos de Salas, performing racist jokes in blackface in a pot in a fantastic Africa, prompted Villoch to experience—to imagine—nothing less than, in his words, an "advance credit on a free Cuba yet to come." How do we get from the racist joke to that forceful experience of national belonging; or, how does that racist joke interpellate Villoch into the field of the nation-in-formation? Something about the fantastic travel away from Cuba in this and other similar plays allowed Cubans like Villoch to experience pleasure in the otherwise unfamiliar experience of national belonging. They did not so much learn the intellectual contours of a patriotism, or feel an explicitly politicized need for independence; rather, the plays allowed them to recognize a fundamental desire for national belonging itself. As Slavoj Žižek tells us, fantasy's primary accomplishment goes much further than conjuring an image or a hallucinatory fulfillment of desire; "fantasy constitutes our desire, provides its co-ordinates, that is, it literally 'teaches us how to desire'" (Žižek 1997, 7).

Cartographic fantasies map and remap the coordinates of national belonging in deceptively literal ways, constituting the shape and direction of national desire in the process. Central to the teatro bufo's representational economy was its practice of defining Cuba in the terms of its "others"—both its internal other (Africans, slaves, black Cubans) and its external other (Spain as a colonizing power). Fantastic cartography takes this tendency and spatializes it, providing geographic correlatives to the social, racial, and national coordinates of Cuban life. Edward Soja reminds us that "representations of space in social thought cannot be understood as projections of modes of thinking hypothetically independent of socio-material conditions" (Soja 1993, 126). In this case, fantastic cartographies allow for new, unexpected ways of mapping the relation of these "others" to Cuba that speak to the complex struggle for power facing criollos in their social life. The engagement with geography necessitates an engagement with history: to send Cubans "back" to Africa or Spain rewrites the historic circum-Atlantic movement (to borrow a phrase from Joseph Roach) of Spanish and African peoples to Cuba in the first place. Through fantastic cartographies, the criollos to whom these plays are predominantly addressed could studiously imagine—to practice, to rehearse, to realize—fantastic alternatives to their racially segregated and still colonial society.

Fantastic cartography is present as a trope throughout the history of the teatro bufo and its related arts practices. Indeed, the early Creto Gangá provides a paradigmatic example of fantastic cartography at work: the fictional presence of a slave-turned-reporter at high society balls, operas, masquerades, and other aristocratic functions temporarily suspends the existing social geography of class and race and replaces it with a fantastic alternative in which it might be possible for a slave to enter an aristocratic soirée. Fantasy becomes a staging ground for social change, not because it harbors an implicit social critique (as though, suggests Žižek, it carried a secret, serious message); to the contrary, the indulgence in what was otherwise seen to be patently ludicrous begins to open the imagination to other possibilities. The fantasy may originally function as what Žižek calls an "empty gesture": an offer "which is meant to be rejected," a necessary, but false, opportunity to choose the impossible. Creto Gangá is the empty gesture toward the fantasy of race and class mobility in mid-century Cuba: the system allows us to imagine the possibility that a slave could become a reporter, only so that the slave's ludicrous performance can itself more forcefully reinstantiate the ideological rule that slaves not only should not join civil society, but are incapable of doing so. To maintain what Žižek calls "the phantasmic support of the public symbolic order," the ideological system must allow for choices "which must never actually take place, since their occurrence would cause the system to disintegrate, and the function of the unwritten rule is precisely to prevent the actualization of these choices formally allowed by the system" (Žižek 1997, 28).

But this operation is also what makes an ideological system vulnerable. The lesson of the "empty gesture" is that sometimes the subversive course of action is, again in Žižek's terms, not to "disregard the explicit letter of the Law on behalf of the underlying fantasies, but *to stick this letter against the fantasy which sustains it*" (Žižek 1997, 29). Creto Gangá offered the chance to take the fantasy seriously, to find in its ludicrousness something compelling and worth retaining (in this case a sense of cubanía); that is, by indulging the fantasy of Creto Gangá too long and too often, protonational Cuban began to *accept* the symbolic empty gesture and thereby begin to upset, however subtly, the symbolic order that demanded its refusal. Here we began to glimpse what Žižek calls the "radical ambiguity of fantasy within an ideological space." It maintains a false opening that actually limits the range of available social choices, at the same time that the presence of that false choice evokes the alternate social choices that have thereby been repressed.

The domain of cartographic fantasy is, precisely, ideological space. Creto Gangá's revision of racial and class geography was followed in the teatro bufo by the negro catedrático, the black aristocrat, and later, the black citizen, in a direct lineage from 1840 to 1895. What changed in those years was less the characteristics of the theatrical figure than the social geography to which they refer: if the 1868 catedrático was still an empty racial gesture to be refused by white Cuba, in 1895, the gesture was substantially more nervous, offered to urge racist Cuba to rescind or reconsider their ongoing acceptance of black Cubans into the ideological space of citizenship.

Reference to geographic places outside of Cuba entered the teatro bufo after the first war of independence, and was increasingly used as a plot scenario thereafter. Francisco Fernández's 1879 play, *La fundación de un periódico o los negros periodistas* (The founding of a newspaper, or the black reporters), for example, responds to Fernández's own experience of exile during the war. The play is set in New York, a favored destination for Cuban exiles, but in the place of an exiled revolutionary we find a Cuban slave who has won the lottery and decides (like Creto Gangá) to establish a black newspaper in the northern city. By the 1890s, recourse to imagined travel, particularly to Africa or the African Caribbean diaspora, became an obsessive plot device, represented by such plays as Cacia's *Los africanitos* (The little Africans [1895]) which focused on political corruption in the "African" town of "Magarabomba," Alfredo Piloto's *Un matrimonio en Haiti* (A wedding in Haiti [1893]) and *Del infierno a la gloria, viaje fantástico-cómico-lírico* (From hell to glory, a fantastic-comic-lyric voyage [1897]), Vicente Pardo y Suarez's *Los príncipes del Congo* (The princes of the Congo [1897]), as well as his very popular 1896 play *El sultán de Mayarí o el mono tiene rabia*, (The Sultan of Mayarí or the monkey has rabies.) This trope is fascinating not because it refers to "actual" places, but because it devotes so much energy to marking out the ideological space that allows one to imagine or re-imagine "real" places, including Africa and especially Cuba, to begin with. It is perhaps fitting, then, that this trope focused so intently on "real" national boundaries in the mid- to late 1890s, at the start of the final war for independence when the insurgent movement was at its peak, and when Cuba's status as a viable national republic was at stake. Not coincidentally, all these also mark the final hours of the teatro bufo's own coherence as a genre of anticolonial alienation and desire.

The master of fantastic cartography as a trope is without question the political satirist Raimundo Cabrera, who sent his imagined Cubans not to Africa but to the moon in his 1888 play, *Del parque a la luna* (From the park to the moon [1888]). The play, to which I will lend attention here, is one of the finest in the teatro bufo repertoire, and launched Cabrera to well deserved fame as a playwright.[2] *Del parque a la luna* follows the interspatial exploits of a host of disgruntled Cubans whose unhappy life in the Cuban colony prompts them to take advantage of the latest electrical technology and escape to the moon. Through this fanciful premise, Cabrera stages a comprehensive review of the Cuban citizenry, as each new character enters the stage and tells his or her story. In the process, the opening scenes illuminate the dire effects of colonial economic exploitation on the Cuban social body. Among the desperate citizens, we find workers, teachers, and recent immigrants to the city, all driven to hunger, poverty, and the streets by the economic crisis of the late 1880s. We also find Rosa, the tragic mulata at her sentimental wits end with racial conflict in Cuba: "El Sol de mi patria brillante y hermoso / no ofrece a mis ansías la luz ideal" (the Sun of my shining and beautiful nation does not shed ideal light on my anxieties [145]), she sings, as part of the lyrics of "La Cubana," her farewell serenade to the Cuba who betrayed her. We also find a progressive journalist, whose oppositional writings have inflamed colonial authorities; despite the ostensibly free press, he finds himself with fourteen citations for his arrest thanks to the regular abuse of the law by colonial officials. Finally, we meet a Cuban proprietor who has lost his entire fortune to the Spanish tax collector; the diligent collector, in turn, chases him all the way to the moon and back, and charges him extra for the travel and food. As the Cuban astronauts are electrically vaporized and reconstituted moments later on the lunar landscape in a great flourish of theatrical lighting effects, two men—a liberal and a conservative—watch the lunar launch. The conservative asks, "¿En qué ambición se aferra? ¿Qué buscan con loco anhelo?" (In what ambition do they persist? What are they seeking in such crazy longing?) The liberal responds simply: "¡No hay libertad en la tierra! ¡Van a buscarla en el cielo!" (There is no liberty on earth! They are searching for it in the sky! [149]). Not surprisingly, this last exchange was censored by colonial authorities.

In this play, cartographic fantasy allows the new-age explorers a chance to find or create viable alternatives to the colonial oppression they now suffer. Fantasy is a way to open an explicitly alternative imagination of social place—a mode of counterpublicity—at the same time that this gesture strategically reimagines Cuba's own history by, as it were, replotting its history on a new geographic map. Both *Los bufos en África* and *Del parque a la luna* use cartographic fantasy to return to a primal scene of colonial crime: slavery in Africa, and conquest and colonization on the newly discovered moon. Both use these fanciful plots to imagine alternate historical narratives, alternate ends of colonial history. Oskar Negt and Alexander Kluge, in a fascinating argument on the nature of proletarian "experience" in the public sphere, theorize the role of fantasy as a viable medium of social production for proletarian subjects (Negt and Kluge 1988, 60–82). What, if anything, can fantasy offer to subaltern subjects in the production of what they call "counter-publicity"? Negt and Kluge focus on fantasy as a potential mediator of the alienated labor process, but their analysis is useful in considering the effects of what Ngugi wa Thiong'o calls "colonial alienation" on colonial subjects as well (Ngugi wa Thiong'o 1986, 17). Fantasy, they say, is frequently dismissed as nothing more than the "libidinal counterweight" to unbearable alienation. However, because its mode of production is not necessarily required for the production of capital, fantasy is not fully subsumed by that system, it thus offers a "partly autonomous mode" through which subaltern subjects might produce what Negt and Kluge call "authentic experience." The fact that society otherwise represses and discounts the workings of fantasy is what allows it this modicum of freedom; as Negt and Kluge put it, "one can outlaw as unrealistic the spinning of a web around reality, but if one does this it becomes difficult to influence the direction and mode of fantasy" (1988, 76–77). Fantasizing Cubans on the moon, or captive in Africa, might be seen as the struggle to create alternate discursive spaces, in which an alternate way of experiencing reality might be articulated.

But, as we shall see, the uncanny quality of these whimsical plays marks their limitation as much as their potential for creating such alternate realities. "The chaotic quality of fantasy," say Negt and Kluge, "is not an aspect of its true nature but of its manifestation in situations indifferent to its specific mode of production." Because fantasy takes its cue directly from reality, it "reproduces the distorted concreteness of this reality." Fantasy for subaltern subjects is largely cut off from other modes of production—as opposed, for example, to the fantasies that undergird the symbolic maintenance of public order or of the state that Žižek describes. As such, subaltern fantasy is a "*travestied* mode of social production" arising from "damaged life-contexts" (Negt and Kluge 1988, 78). Fantasizing angry Cubans re-colonizing the moon or blackface actors in the clutches of African cannibals certainly resonates with this sense of absurd, distorted, indeed "travestied" imagination. For me, a "travestied social imagination" evokes something akin to what J. L. Austin describes when he speaks of "unhappy" performatives: acts that attempt but *fail* to fully create what they conjure (Austin 1962, 14–15).

Thus travel to the moon ostensibly sends Cubans to a desired (noncolonial) utopian future, where the frustrated citizens may find freedom and a better life. But this expedition to the moon is, on one level, nothing more than a reiteration of Cuba's own historic colonization. To begin, the moon is presented as an idyllic island, and a decidedly tropical one at that: it is described as "un platanal," a banana plantation, a tropical paradise. For their part, the Cubans immediately betray their own divided loyalties and begin fighting for possession of the newly "discovered" moon. Whatever common cause brought the Cubans to the moon is forgotten in the haste to claim ownership of the newly "discovered" land. Carlos announces, "he tomado posesión el primero; es nuestra, amigo " (I have taken possession first; it is ours, friend) to which Mr. Floripan, the space-ship operator, objects loudly:

"Perdone usted, yo le digo que es nuestra, de mi nación" (Pardon me sir, I tell you that it is ours, of my country [153]). Carlos, presumably speaking for colonial Spain (although he later shows himself to be a liberal "autonomist" reformist), insists on the contrary: "Desde este instante la luna / será provincia española" (From this moment the moon will be a Spanish province), while the infuriated Floripan shouts, "¡No señor, no lo tolero / aunque se oponga Dios mismo!" (No sir, I will not tolerate it, even if God himself is opposed!) Carlos rehearses the same rationales used by the Spanish conquistadors centuries before to bolster his claim: "Territorio abandonado / es del primer que llega" (Abandoned territory belongs to the first to arrive [154]), positioning the moon as "abandoned" well before he has had a chance to find out if there is an indigenous population. The ensuing melee is calmed only when the progressive journalist admonishes: "Que no suceda en la luna / lo que en las islas de España" (Don't let happen on the moon, what happened on the islands of Spain [155]).

Underscoring the degree to which this cartographic fantasy is also baldly male, libidinal fantasy, the arrival of the Cubans on the moon also replays the much glossed scene of first contact in which Columbus meets America, so frequently represented in allegory as a languishing, nude female graciously awaiting her male conqueror. Cabrera's moon is populated by none other than an all-female tribe of beautiful moon-nymphs, led by the beautiful and scantily clad Leonora, reclined under a moon-tree (which bears remarkable resemblance to a palm tree). Understandably, after centuries alone, the moon-nymphs are quite delirious at the news that there are finally real men on the moon: "¡Hombres! ¡Hombres en la luna! [. . .] ¡Qué inmensa felicidad! [. . .] Pero, ¡ay Dios!, que nos sorprenden en *negligé* . . . sin peinar" (Men! Men on the moon! [. . .] What immense happiness! [. . .] But, oh God, they've surprised us in our *negligees*, with our hair uncombed [153]). This fantasy reduces natives and native culture to nothing more (but also nothing less) than a harem of beautiful women, voyeuristically caught lounging in lingerie in their open-air boudoir. As soon as the men and moon-nymphs meet, Leonora becomes a new-age Malinche to her conquistador, Carlos, acting as his translator and erotic partner. In a lengthy monologue, she recounts the highlights of moon culture and history, which has transcended war and death by long ago banishing money and men, the two related causes of all social destruction on the moon. Despite the prohibition, she and the other nymphs are thoroughly seduced by the Cuban danzón, and thus cannot resist the men's presence. And, in any case, Floripan concludes that "las damas / en la tierra o en el cielo / no pueden vivir tranquilas / sin compañero" (whether on earth or in space, women cannot live peacefully without male companionship [167]). Immensely pleased with their "discovery," the Cubans decide to settle on the moon at once.

The problem with the story so far, of course, is that this fantasy is all too familiar. We have heard it all before. Or, in Žižek's terms, this fantasy is not productive: it does not teach us any new desire. While the names of the characters have changed, the fundamental structure of the narrative fantasy has not. We know in advance how this story will end: the male colonizer courts or coerces the feminized colony to conform to his needs. No doubt the latent conflict between the reformist and insurgent Cubans will fuel a conflict of possession. So even as the Cubans explicitly resist repeating on the moon the history of their own colonization in Cuba, the key terms of gender and power in this colonial fantasy have not changed at all. Only now the Cubans imagine themselves as the authors rather than subjects of the fantasy, and have cast themselves as the powerful male conqueror, rather than the feminized, violated, colonized subject. While the plot thus proceeds with tongue firmly in cheek, it is in this respect deeply pessimistic. It tells us that what is at stake in this anticolonial drama is not just the failing economy, unfair taxes, or unequal access to political power, but the social imagination *itself*. And, the play suggests, that imagination may already be colonized beyond repair: even on the moon the Cubans cannot imagine themselves outside existing relations of power and abuse to which they themselves have been subjected. As Carlos says to the journalist, "Ni en el cielo será libre / el pensamiento" (Not even in the sky will our thoughts be free [139]).

In a similar operation, the travel "back" to Africa in *Los bufos en África* ostensibly imagines an impossible place in which Africans would have the power to police their own representation in Cuba, to punish those who abuse it, and to take meaningful vengeance against those who have wronged them. But, in order to stage this fantasy, Africa itself must be presented through the very suspect terms for which the teatro bufo (and the racism of Cuban culture at large) might otherwise be faulted and punished: the Africans in this play are figured as, precisely, illiterate, incoherent, angry cannibals, presented by white people in comic blackface. The play thus invokes and seals the same racist tropes it ostensibly calls into question through its fantastic plot; that cartographic fantasy is thus offered up as yet another "empty gesture," which offers the fantasy of representational power to "Africans" even as its own terms make the fulfillment of that fantasy impossible. This, then, is the *travesty* of the teatro bufo's social imagination: fantastic travel to the moon or back to Africa redoubles, rather than opens, the representational economy through which the teatro bufo aims to practice alternate notions of race and colony in its developing imagination of Cuba's future.

However, the very end of the play *Del parque a la luna* offers a different perspective on the work of cartographic fantasy, illuminating the moment at which that travestied imagination may ultimately produce what Negt and Kluge call "authentic experience" for subaltern subjects. It is that small but decisive moment when theatrical imagination makes a break for the real, finds a fissure in colonial discourse and borrows against a desired Cuban future. Or, put another way, it is the moment when the performative aspiration of this theatre becomes, as it were, happy. After seducing Leonora with a danzón, Carlos proposes to introduce her to the "the people of Havana," all of whom, it appears, are poor examples of Havana's finest citizens. They include a greedy Chinese laborer, an anti-Cuban Yankee-educated young man who whiles away his days roller-skating, a debt collector, and in a moment of self-referential irony, a troupe of bufo actors whom Carlos accuses of profiting at the expense of good morals. Leonora's position as a (false) "neutral" observer enables the play to underscore anything that is seemingly "unnatural" or "non-Cuban" in the scene through her surprised reactions. For example, she reviles against the Chinese laborer, insisting that he may not stay on the moon. Similarly, while she adores the music of bufo actors' guaracha, she detests the quasi-bozal lyrics that parallel the "Negro bueno" in recounting the exploits of a rough black street criminal. That is, Leonora's ostensibly innocent view immediately finds and rejects the "foreign" elements in the Cuban scene. The round of introductions suddenly comes to a halt when the Cubans discover—to their horror—that no bananas will grow in the lunar ground. They decide to leave at once: a miserable, colonial Cuba with bananas is apparently better than any lunar paradise without them.

The closing of the play charts travel from the moon back to the park, mirroring the plot structure that originally brought the Cubans from the park to the moon. Leonora decides to join Carlos on earth, giving him the opportunity to resume in greater detail his introduction to life in Cuba. But having returned from the moon, Carlos now presents a very different vision of what Cuba is. This introduction includes none of the images of Cuba's poverty, hunger, or urban strife that had dominated the opening of the play, and includes none of the moralizing editorials about Cuba's poorly behaved citizens. Instead, in the lengthy concluding sequence, he takes her to Havana's Campo de Almendares, filled with storefronts, roving orchestras, and street vendors. Rather than provide a portrait of rough urban life, it illuminates a grand fiesta, a carnival-style display of Cuba's ethnic types through "typical" songs and dances in a festive celebration of Cuba's mestizo identity. The procession includes different Spanish immigrant groups and Chinese laborers, but specially features African ñáñigos and other black or African/Afrocuban groups. Each group enters in full "typical" costume and regalia, crossing the stage singing and dancing. In the closing lines of the play, Carlos yells emotionally, over the rising din of African drumming, to Leonora:

Oye esos cantos, Leonora,
aquí el pueblo se divierte;
no se acuerda de su suerte,
¡aplaude, grita, y no llora! (177)

(Listen to those songs, Leonora,
here the people have fun,
they forget their lot;
they applaud, scream, and do not cry!)

Thus, the same African (and Chinese) elements that were, moments before, presented as "problematic" elements in the Cuban social landscape are now figured (or, better, remapped) as central participants in a gorgeous display of the diversity of Cuban culture. That diversity in music and performance is simultaneously a refuge from the harsh realities of Cuban social life (a place to forget one's lot) and, at the same time, the reflection of what Cuba "truly" is—that place where "the people" can let go and be themselves.

The true fantasy in this play—that is, the fantasy that might produce "authentic experience," the fantasy that teaches us how to desire differently—lies here. Travel to Cuba from the moon is ostensibly a return to the real from the fantastic. But this return is just an illusion, revealing that Cuba itself is the true subject of the cartographic fantasy. This vision of a Cuba that peacefully and animatedly celebrates its racial and ethnic diversity, its comfortable mestizaje, in cross-racial unity, dancing together in the streets—this image, in 1888, is as fantastic as any trip to the moon. Nothing could be farther from the reality of racial segregation and extraordinary racist panic (only recall Benjamín de Céspedes) permeating white Cuban culture in the immediate aftermath of abolition. If Carlos (or rather, Cabrera) invokes this image, it is not because it describes a Cuba he knows (or even one that he wishes actually to see), but because it outlines the contours of an emerging Cuba yet to come; the image provides, as Raymond Williams would say, an embryonic "structure of feeling" for the Cubanness he lives but cannot name

(Williams 1977, 128). Juxtaposing this image next to images of the moon only serves to strategically disguise the true work of cartographic fantasy: mestizaje is the founding myth of an emergent Cuban nationalism, and blackface itself is the primary vehicle for its embodiment. Blackface performance *is* the anticolonial fantasy that teaches its subjects how to desire their own national belonging: it is this blackface lesson that Villoch has in mind when he says that to forget it would be to forget himself.

As an accident of history, we will never learn what happened to those blackface bufos in Africa, stewing in that pot. If precedent serves, perhaps the actors managed to assuage the angry cannibals with the seductions of a new danzón, a lyrical guaracha, or with the heat of a rumba; or perhaps the cross-dressed, blacked up Saturnino Valverde softened them with his performance of Cuban mulata charm. But we will never know: there is no record of the usual Cuban *deus ex machina* that saved them. The final pages of this little play are lost; all that remains is one handwritten copy, which stops short at the moment the head of the African tribe condemns them to the pot.

Yet this is as it should be. The frozen image of those actors struggling to leave the fantastic Africa of their own invention, lost in a cartographic fantasy, using blackface as a refuge, resource, and camouflage, itself provides a vivid allegory of Cuban colonial alienation throughout the period of the anticolonial wars. At the same time it illustrates the complex workings of protonational consciousness, as white actors use and abuse travesties of Africa and Africans in the theatre in order to practice, rehearse, and realize an emergent national imaginary in the anticolonial era.

Notes

Introduction

1. A word on periodization. I use the term "teatro bufo" to refer to a particular instantiation of popular theatre (*teatro vernáculo*) from 1868 to 1895, and argue that it was during those years—which coincide with the anticolonial period—that this theatre form retained a coherence organized around a discourse of race, nation, and colonial power that is absent from other forms of vernacular theatre. I am partly seconded by Cuban theatre historian Rine Leal in this decision, and my rationale is elaborated in later chapters. An older generation of Cubans (like the informants cited in Robin Moore's *Nationalizing Blackness*) might argue with this periodization, insisting—rightly—that the teatro bufo continued well into the twentieth century. A new iteration of the teatro bufo emerged during the Cuban republic, from 1900 at least through the Cuban revolution of 1959, and was performed at a range of theatres in Havana, across Cuba, and in the Cuban diaspora in the United States. Some elide the term teatro bufo with the male-oriented burlesque entertainments of the Teatro Alhambra, which reopened in 1900 and dominated vernacular entertainments through the 1930s, and whose repertoire did indeed draw from and extend aspects of the teatro bufo, especially the proliferation of the stage mulata, *gallego* (Galician), and negrito. However, the Alhambra departed from its past, particularly in its burlesque and sometimes pornographic nature, enlisting these stage figures toward new social ends. The Alhambra represents its own chapter in Cuban performance history that has yet to be fully written, certainly for an English readership. The teatro bufo that I describe in this book had its afterlife less at the Alhambra and more at the smaller, middle-class Teatro Martí, formerly the Teatro Irijoa, where the teatro bufo's combination of humor, racial impersonation, and national style continued to the early 1960s. The story of that theatre, like that of the Alhambra, has yet to be written.

2. The present text is deeply indebted to Vera Kutzinski's *Sugar's Secrets* (1993). I depart from her analysis on the question of performance as both an object and method for study. It is not just that I focus on theatre and performance and she on literature and narrative, or that my research base is more archival and hers more intertextual and literary. Rather, her method understands the discourse of Cuban mestizaje as a series of "iconographies, sets or patterns of images, discursive effects in both literature and popular culture, that . . . seek to articulate Cubanness" (xx). I, in turn, do not understand the discourse of Cuban mestizaje as a series of pre-formed (racial) images that produce (racist and/or nationalist) effects, primarily because such a formulation cannot account for the mutually formative relation between image and its racial "effect." The image and its racial logic are, in my view, mutually constitutive

in the acts of production and consumption, forming part of the performativity of race itself. Thus, by contrast, I understand mestizaje not as a set of iconographies, but as a *racial formation,* in the rich sense first lent to the term by Omi and Winant: racial formation refers to "the process by which social, economic and political forces determine the content and importance of racial categories, and by which they are in turn shaped by racial meanings" (1986, 60–61). Prime among those social forces is the work of cultural production and consumption as primary sites for the production, maintenance, and contestation of racial difference itself.

3. Martí, 1991, 18. Parenthetical page citations refer to this text. The phrase "cuerpo pinto" could also be translated as a "spotted" or "mottled" body; the image of a spotted native/Creole body would resonate well with Martí's frequent invocation in this essay of the hungry tiger as a metaphor for new world nations.

4. I use the English translation by Alan West-Durán titled *Music in Cuba,* edited by Timothy Brennan (Carpentier 2001, 60–61), italics in the original.

Chapter 1

1. While not written in the voice of a blackface persona, the text still shows fascination with race in Cuba. See Kutzinski's analysis of his poem, "La Mulata" (1993, 33–42), as well as Mary Cruz's analysis of the same poem (1974, 74–81).

2. See Jensen 1988 for a detailed discussion of Tacón and his relation to the press throughout his governance. Tacón imposed strict theatre censorship as well: he was equally notorious for his control of its productions. Even theatre posters had to be approved by his censors, and he once commanded that the word "loyalty" be substituted for the word "liberty" in the performance of an Italian opera. See also Paquette 1988, 92; Leal 1982, 293.

3. The film *El otro Francisco,* directed in 1975 by the Cuban director Sergio Giral, restages Anselmo Suárez's narrative of the life of the slave Francisco, and explicitly questions the colonial, patronizing view Anselmo Suárez imposed on the tale, offering alternate representations of black masculine resistance.

4. "Chinito" probably means *chinita,* a diminutive of china, which while literally meaning "Chinese," was used in the nineteenth century to refer to a mulata, specifically the offspring of a black and a mulato/a.

5. Crespo purportedly played one of these roles; see Cruz 1974, 70.

6. Throughout the nineteenth century, the guajiro or guajira usually referred to a white rural laborer; in today's usage, it would apply to rural laborers of either race. For a discussion of the etymology of the term, see Ortíz 1923, 132.

7. See especially Kutzinski's discussion of representations of race, class, and nationalism in the costumbrista lithographs of the period, including those of Landaluze (1993, 60–69). Zoila Lapique Becali offers a related analysis in "La mujer en los habanos" (1996). See also Norman Holland on proto-nationalist expression in *Cecilia Valdés* in his "Fashioning Cuba" (1992, 122–46). Zoila Lapique Becali authored the definitive history of lithography in Cuba: *La memoria en las piedras* (2002). Laplante's illustrations are reproduced in Cantero 1984.

8. The title of the response reads: "Cuntetasione a mi carabela Siriaco Mandinga

po la cosa dielle que me lo poné en *Lan Frao Sindutriá de la Bana*, la viene disinueve diete mimo mese" (Replies to my comrade Siricao Mandingo about the things he wrote me in the Faro Industrial de la Habana, the twenty-ninth of this month).

9. Oddly, Cruz does not consider the possibility that Crespo could have varied his own orthography when writing under a different pseudonym.

10. Edward Mullen has reedited the original Madden publication in *The Life and Poems of a Cuban Slave* (1981). For a discussion of Madden's translation and editing of the *Autobiografía* see Luis 1990, 92–99; also Molloy 1991, 44–46.

Chapter 2

1. Unlike U.S. blackface minstrelsy, where female "wench" characters were played in drag by male actors, the Cuban popular theatre from the outset included both male and female actors. There were some female characters played in drag; the most famous was the crass Canary Island immigrant mother-in-law played by José Candiani, discussed later in this chapter.

2. On 4 October 1868, for example, the *Diario de la Marina* reports that three bufo companies performed in rival theatres: the Bufos Habaneros at the Teatro Tacón, performing *Los negros catedráticos* and other pieces; the Bufos Caricatos, performing the costumbrista play *El perro huevero*. . . . and a guaracha entitled "Los cimarrones" (The maroons) at the Teatro de Ilusiones; and the Bufos Cantantes, a company focused on music, performing *Los medicos de Haiti* (The doctors from Haiti) at the Villanueva.

3. *Diario de la Marina* quoted in Leal 1982, 27; *El País*, 8 November 1868.

4. On the "Succesos de la Villanueva," see Robreño 1961, 24–26; Leal 1982, 53–67; Arrom 1944, 70–71; De Leuchsenring 1937, 44–45.

5. Guerrero 1864; paranthetical citations refer to the reprint edition in *Teatro bufo siglo XIX, tomo 1*, ed. Rine Leal (Editorial Arte y Literatura, 1975), 95–130.

6. *El espectador* notes that in June the Bufos Habaneros crossed from the Villanueva, where they had been performing their satirical operas, to close a benefit performance for a visiting opera star at the Tacón, who performed with them in one of their "cuadros de costumbres" (sketches of customs) and sang the guaracha, "La mulata." While crossing between the theatres does not seem to have been frequent, eventually the Tacón began booking teatro bufo companies themselves.

7. Beginning in 1860, several U.S. blackface minstrel troupes apparently found receptive audiences in Cuba as well. On 23 January 1860, Campbell's Minstrels began a two-month run at the Villanueva before reportedly touring for an additional eight months in Regla, Guanabacoa, and Cárdenas. Christy's Minstrels arrived for a shorter, less successful run in December 1862, as did Webb's Minstrels in January 1865. Blackface performance was, Isabel Aretz asserts, gaining popularity throughout Latin America in this period, in part because of the increased appearance of U.S. blackface minstrel troupes. See Aretz 1984, 189–226. The bufos themselves may have exerted a strong influence in Latin America while in exile during the Ten Years' War, when many brought their blackface acts to Mexico and Puerto Rico.

8. The composer Raimundo Valenzuela later borrowed the title "Los negros catedráticos" for one of his new danzas.

9. Parenthetical references to Francisco Fernández's *Los negros catedráticos,* are from the version published in Rine Leal, ed., *Teatro bufo, siglo XIX, antología, tomo 1,* 131–62, 1975. References to *El bautizo, segunda parte de los negros catedráticos,* are from the version published in *Teatro bufo siglo XIX, tomo 1,* 163–84. References to Fernández's *El negro cheche, o veinte años despues, tercera parte de Los negros catedráticos,* co-authored with Pedro N. Pequeño, are from the version published in *Teatro bufo siglo XIX, tomo 1,* 185–209.

10. In the nineteenth century, "condición" referred to legal classification in terms of race (white, black, pardo, moreno, etc.) and status in terms of labor (free, slave). Note that "*claise*" (class) is italicized in the original, as are all terms in the play that are intentional misspellings of the Spanish.

11. A.T., *El ensayo de Don Juan Tenorio, descarillamiento cómico* (1868); as there are no page numbers, none will be cited. The piece is almost certainly by Toroella, author of another catedrático play written for the Bufos Habaneros, *El minué.*

12. The Marqués's subsequent response confirms this: "cuando yo era paje, antés de ser Marqués, siempre le hablaba al cochero con el sombrero en la diestra, porque siempre he respetado las personas elevadas" (when I was a page, before becoming a Marquis, I always spoke to the coachman with my hat tilted to the right, because I have always respected elevated persons [9]).

13. In 1827, black males were three times as likely to find work as musicians than whites: the 1827 census finds that of the 16,520 white males in Havana, only 44 were musicians; of the 6,754 black males, 49 were musicians. See Carpentier 1946, 315. By 1846, census rolls list 216 blacks as musicians, comprising over half of those in that occupation; this figure is comparable to the number of free blacks working as coach-drivers (221), cooks (294), or mine workers (166); see Paquette 1988, 107.

14. These are the lyrics reprinted in *Guarachas cubanas, curiosa recopilación desde las más antiguas hasta las más modernas,* originally published in Madrid in 1882; republished under the same title in 1963, and under a second edition in 1982, 64–65. It is possible, indeed likely, that the lyrics collected in 1882 differed from those performed in 1868.

15. "Quintero" is likely a reference to José Agustín Quintero, a Cuban-born poet and longtime supporter of Cuban independence, exiled from Cuba along with del Monte and other patriots in 1848. See Quintero's poems included in the new edition of *El laúd del desterrado,* edited by Montes-Huidobro, 1995.

16. *La chamarretta* records this anecdote:

Paseando anoche por la calle de las Damas varios jóvenes que piensan "á la órden del día" vieron en la ventana de una casa una niñas con el pelo á lo Céspedes, y como los jóvenes son el diablo hubieron de decirles insurrectas, y ellas enfadadas gritaron "Viva la Libertad, Viva!" [. . .] las niñas se están portando como se suele decir de *candela.*

(Strolling last night down the "Avenue of the Damas" (Avenue of the Ladies) several young men who think according to the "order of the day" saw in the window of a house some girls with their hair "in the style of Céspedes," and because the men are devilish they felt they had to call them "insurrectionary," and the furious girls yelled "Long live liberty, long live!" [. . .] the girls are behaving, as they often say, *candela.*)

17. Although it lists 7 January as the date of publication of its first volume, it is likely that *Los cimarrones* simply re-names and continues an earlier publication, as happened frequently throughout the month of January. Quindembo and his "pata de jamón" were, in any case, already known figures, either from earlier press representations, or more likely, from a guaracha or contradanza of that name.

Chapter 3

1. Habermas insists categorically that his notion of a bourgeois public sphere cannot be "transferred, idealtypically generalized, to any number of historical situations that represent formally similar constellations" (xvii). While I appreciate Habermas's commitment to rigorous historiography, I join many other critics in questioning—and disregarding—his assumption that the European bourgeois public sphere should therefore provide the singular ("idealtypical") or normative historical experience of social intercourse, public-ness, or publicity.

2. See also González Echevarría 1999 and Brock and Bayne 1998. During this period, the teatro bufo celebrated baseball's new popularity in such plays as Ignacio Saragacha and José María de Quintana's *Habana y Almendares, o los efectos del baseball* (Havana and Almendares, or the effects of baseball) first performed in 1887 and published in 1892. In addition to showcasing American baseball jargon, it affords a pungent satire of the American umpire, "Mr. Jhones," and the Spanish official who suspects the new sport of anti-Spanish activism.

3. The Albisu was briefly renamed Lersundi. In addition to hiring European opera and Spanish zarzuela companies, the Albisu offered international popular entertainments, at times including American minstrels.

4. While the lead actress of the Bufos Habaneros, Florinda Camps (the original Dorotea of the *Negros catedráticos*) was eventually able to make a stage career in Mexico, her compatriots were not. Miguel Salas moved to New Orleans, where he eventually made a living as a street vendor. Jacinto Valdés was desperately poor in New York City, but continued his activism in support of the war in the form of letters to the expatriate press in the United States. The history of theatre related to Cuba's first anticolonial war has yet to be fully explored, although Rine Leal provides an important overview (1982, 137–44).

5. In 1873 we find mention of an amateur concert by "negritos cheverones" performing the guaracha *El cucurrucucú*, without mention of the word "bufo" whose aesthetic so obviously informed it, but references such as these are rare. In 1877, toward the end of the decade, the return of the bufos was already under way: on 4 August 1877, for example, Ignacio Benítez del Cristo's *Los novios catedráticos* (discussed in the previous chapter) premiered in Matanzas at the Teatro Estéban, with Saturnino Valverde in the lead role.

6. To this list we should also add Olallo Diaz González, whose penchant for political allegory brought depth to popular considerations of Cuba's status in the waning days of colonial rule, even as the pedantic tone of his work frequently separated it from the comic aesthetic of the teatro bufo. His *La caña y remolacha, revista*

cómica-fantástica en un acto y tres cuadros (Sugar cane and sugar beet, comic-fantastic revue in one act and three scenes) is representative.

7. "Curros" refers to a black community with origins in the Andalusian region of Spain; "lucumies" an ethnic group originating in West Africa.

8. *Aurora del Yumurí* (Matanzas), 24 October 1879 – 25 November 1879; the Caricatos Habaneros appears to have been a company formed by José Candiani for a run in Matanzas, which included Manuel Mellado.

9. See *Aurora del Yumurí* (Matanzas), 16 April 1882; *Diario de la marina* (Havana) 3 May 1881 – 27 March 1882.

10. For detailed studies of race and ethnography in the early republic, see Bronfman 2004, particularly her chapter "Social Science and the Negro Brujo" (37–66); and Palmié 2002, particularly his chapter "Una Salación Científica: The Work of Witchcraft and Science in Cuban Modernity" (201–59).

11. While Jorge Mañach's curious and quasi-sociological text from 1940, *Indagación del choteo* (1869), is the first formal study to link *choteo* with a specifically Cuban national identity, this association had long been present in Cuban popular culture. Not coincidentally, the related bufo term *guarachear* (literally, "to guaracha") had a similar meaning to *choetar* meaning to joke or "to party" in the late nineteenth century, as per Fernando Ortiz, in his *Catauro de cubanismos* (1923, 177). While Ortiz claims in his 1923 *Catauro* that the term "choteo" derived from the Spanish gypsy term "choto" (see 35–36), by the publication of his *Glosario de afronegrismos* (Glossary of black-Africanisms) the following year, he was persuaded that the term instead had African origins, as José Muñoz notes. Muñoz argues that the term explicitly connotes a form of performative mockery that both evokes and undermines its own claims to creolization. This purported African/Creole origin of Cuba's national sense of self and humor resonates fully with the ironies of the teatro bufo's use of blackface as a vehicle for the delineation of mestizaje as a national ideology (see Muñoz 1999, 119–41).

12. Villoch's memory is not to be trusted entirely: from my understanding, he remembers several seasons of the teatro bufo from the early 1880s as the "one unforgettable season of 1883." That he nonetheless claims that the events are perfectly emblazoned in his memory only redoubles his point: what was compelling was not any one performance (or season) but the full, propitious sense of the future that their combination evoked. Villoch eventually became a playwright for the twentieth century teatro bufo (the vernacular theatre of the Teatro Alhambra), author of the extant plays *Don Centén or el amigo envidioso* (Don Centen or the jealous friend, 1896); *La cruz de San Fernando* (The cross of Saint Fernando, 1897); and *Xuanón enamorado* (Xuanón in love, 1900).

13. See the review of a velada in the 21 December 1893 issue of *Fraternidad*, in which the author chastises the performers for mispronouncing words and for "improper intonation."

14. Ferrer describes an incident when a black revolutionary solider used this term, ciudadanito, to address a fellow white officer, in a calculated reversal of the usual use of the term negrito to address black men (1999, 41).

15. I note that Anderson's model does not, in fact, focus on Europe, but rather takes colonial—even anticolonial—Latin America as its prototype. However, Anderson

does not fully attend to the role of anticolonial sentiment in the process—or, in Anderson's term, the "style"—by which new national communities are imagined under and in response to colonial regimes.

16. Indeed, this is the primary reason that I have chosen not to use Landaluze's lithographs to "illustrate" my own analysis, as is the case with almost every other recent study of nineteenth century Cuba. I do include one early tobacco lithograph, entitled "Un Minuet," on the cover, which departs from Landaluze's more typical realist pretensions in the representation of nonwhite Cubans. While Landaluze's body of work provides an amazing visual archive well worth analysis, it represents a specific mode of social, racial, and aesthetic representation that does not transparently correlate to or illustrate the realities otherwise encountered on the street, the stage, or in other forms of representation.

Chapter 4

1. The majority of the subsequent citations of contemporary press discussions about the danzón from *El Diario de Matanzas* and *La Aurora del Yumurí* are reproduced in Castillo Faílde 1964; I cite the original press accounts unless his was the only record I consulted.

2. While critics often lumped the performances at the Cervantes with those of the teatro bufo, thus far I have found no evidence that suggests that bufo companies actually performed in this theatre; the Cervantes seems to have been reserved for burlesque-style performance, directed almost exclusively to a male audience.

3. Parenthetical references to Morales Álvarez's *El proceso del oso* (1882) are to the version in *Teatro bufo, siglo XIX*, 9–56.

4. Similar "defenses" of dance and theatre appeared in 1881. *El almendares* loudly complained: "¡¡¡SOCORROOOO!!! Este año, es año de procesos; hemos tenido el del Can-can, el del Oso, el del Danzón, el del año 1881, el de los Bufos . . . el *El*, el de *La* . . . pero el único condenado en todos ellos ha sido el sentido común" (Help!!! This year is the year of trials; we've had one for the Can-can, for el Oso, for the Danzón, for the year 1881, for the Bufos, . . . for Him, for Her . . . but the only one condemned was common sense [20 April 1882]).

5. I follow a summary of the play published in *El Espectador*, 8 November 1876.

6. See Aparicio and Chávez-Silverman 1997, whose essays understand "tropicalism" as the etymological correlative to Edward Said's "Orientalism," and which explore the "tropical" in Latin American and especially U.S. Latino/a cultural practice as a contested site of political containment and of political coalition and resistance.

7. Antonio Benítez-Rojo retells this story (1992, 77) as does Castillo Faílde (1964, 30).

Chapter 5

1. The minutes of the first meeting, held on 7 October 1877, list the attendance of about thirty men.

2. Steven Jay Gould notes a comparable history in the development of the doctrine of polygeny in the mid-nineteenth century in the United States, "one of the first theories of largely American origin [. . .] that Europeans referred to [. . .] as the 'American school' of anthropology." Gould notes: "it is obviously not accidental that a nation still practicing slavery and expelling its original inhabitants from their homelands should have provided a base for theories that blacks and Indians are separate species, inferior to whites" (Gould 1993, 93).

3. The municipal regulation, dated from December 1873, includes the following articles:

Art. 10. El cuerpo facultativo higienista se compondrá de cuatro médicos, que se denominarán "Delegados facultativos de Higiene," [. . .]
Art. 30. Harán dos visítas semanales á las casas que de antemano les están señaladas, anotando el resultado de su escrupuloso exámen en el libro de certificados. Uno de los registros debe efectuarse necesariamente con el espéculo.
Art 40. En el momento que encuentren á una mujer atacada de sifilis ó de cualquiera otra enfermedad contagiosa, la enviarán al hospital de San Francisco de Paula. [. . .]

(Art. 1. The medical hygienist corps will be composed of four doctors, that will be called "Medical Delegates of Hygiene," [. . .]
Art. 3. They will make two visits per week to the houses indicated in advance, noting the results of their scrupulous exams in the book of certificates. One of the exams must necessarily be conducted with a speculum.
Art 4. When they find a woman with syphilis or any other contagious illness, they will send her to the hospital of San Francisco de Paula. [. . .])

4. Text earlier cited from the *Papel periódico de la Habana*, 1792, quoted in Bueno 1985, xi-xii.

5. Other extant plays of this genre include: Quintana's *La trichina* (1885), and his *El demonio es la guaracha, o Felipe Ginebrita, disparate bufo-lírico en un acto y en prosa* (1891); José Guillermo Nuza, *Por la mostaza o La mulata Rosa* (1890), and José Barreiro, *Las mulatas* (1890s).

6. When the politics of race do demand a tragic end for black characters, as they did in José Hernandez's 1885 play *El corazón y la cara* (The heart and the face), it is because the playwright has left the bufo genre for melodrama.

7. "Cecilia" published a brief editorial in *La Fraternidad* on 3 March 1888, after which the paper commented that "Cecilia" is the pseudonym of "una distinguida é inteligente señora de nuestra raza" (a distinguished and intelligent [married] woman of our race).

8. The full passage reads:

Durante las noches de retreta circulan libremente confundidos con el público, llamando la atención, no de la policia, sino de los concurrentes indignados, las actitudes grotescamente afeminadas de estos tipos que van señalando cínicamente las posaderas erguidas, arqueados y ceñidos los talles, y que al andar con menudos pasos de arrastre, se balancean con contoneos de la mujer coqueta. Llevan flequillos en la frente, carmín en el rostro y polvos de arroz en el semblante, ignoble y fatigado de los más y agraciado en algunos. El pederasta responde á un nombre de mujer en la jerga del oficio. (190)

(During nights out they circulate liberally, mixed in with the public, the grotesquely effeminate attitude of these types calling the attention, not of the police, but of indignant passersby, by cynically highlighting their high buttocks, with arched and narrow-waisted bodies, balancing themselves by swinging their hips like a coquette as they take small dragging steps. They wear bangs on their foreheads, carmine (red) on their cheeks and (white) rice powder on their faces, ignoble and fatigued on most, and nice on some. The pederast responds to a woman's name in the jargon of the trade.)

Calling this context "queer street life" may well impose an anachronistic understanding of sexual identity on the scenes Céspedes describes. His are among the few descriptions that lend any detail to nonnormative and/or nonheterosexual behavior in Havana during the period, and prompt us to ask what sexual counterpublics may have existed in relation to the emergent public sphere. One particularly evocative complaint published in the newspaper *El Almendares* from 6 June 1882 (six years prior) may lend some clues:

¡QUE VERGUENZA!—Seguida de un cortejo licensioso é insolente una pareja del O.P. conducia ayer de diez y media á once de la mañana, por la calle de Virtudes á un moreno vestido de mujer que la noche anterior había sido preso en los salones del Louvre. El vergonzoso espectáculo que presenciaron muchas familias honradas pudo haberse evitado fácilmente, con solo cuarenta centavos. ¿Por qué no tomó la pareja del O.P. un coche para conducir á la Alcaldía de Barrio al disfrazado adonis de asabache? ¿Erale acaso preferible oirlas miserias indignas con que la turba desvergonzada apostrofaba al metamorfoseado bailarin, tal vez perteneciente á alguna de esas sociedades cínicas que hoy se conocen con los nombres del CAMARON de la YUCA y de la MALANGA y que tienen como centro sensual los altos de *Albisu* y los salones de *El Louvre?* Es una vergüenza, una verdadera vergüenza lo que pasa hoy en la Habana con esos bailes donde la corrupción y el crimen viven en degradante contubernio. ¿No habrá remedio para tanta desgracia?

(Shame!—Between ten thirty and eleven in the morning yesterday, a pair of policemen, followed by a licentious and insolent cortege, led a moreno [mulato/dark man] dressed as a woman that had been caught the night before in the salons of the Louvre. The shameful spectacle, which was witnessed by many honorable families, could have been easily avoided, for only forty cents. Why didn't the pair of police take the disguised Adonis "de asabache" by car to the neighborhood headquarters? Was it by chance preferable to hear the indignant miseries with which the shameless mob apostrophized the metamorphosed (ballet) dancer, perhaps a member of one of those cynical societies that today are known by such names as "Camaron of the Yucca" or "of the Malanga," and who have as their sensual headquarters the upper salons of the Albisu and the salons of the Louvre [Café]? It is a disgrace, a genuine disgrace, what happens today in Havana, with those dances where corruption and crime live in degrading cohabitation. Is there no remedy for such misfortune?)

As of this writing, I've not found further contextualizing information on "cynical societies" patronized by cross-dressing men of color. We can glean, however, that the term "cynical" carries the connotation of nonnormative male sexual behaviors for its critics, and that (despite Céspedes's complaint) such behavior was indeed subject to policing, criminalization, and public harassment.

Conclusion

1. I cite the manuscript copy of *Los bufos en África* housed at the Biblioteca Nacional José Martí; as there are no page numbers, I cite none.

2. Parenthetical citations to *Del parque a la luna* refer to the version published in *Teatro bufo, siglo XIX, antología, tomo* 2, 125–83, ed. Rine Leal (Havana: Editorial Arte y Literatura, 1975).

Bibliography

This bibliography is organized in two parts, which roughly correspond to primary and secondary materials: the former is listed as "manuscripts and archival texts" and the latter as "additional works cited." I do so to allow for annotation of the former, noting when and where plays were originally produced, if known, and whether the works are to my knowledge available beyond the archives in which I consulted them.

A listing of teatro bufo plays in the Colección Cubana at the Biblioteca Nacional José Martí in Havana (from which my sources largely come) and at the Colección Coronado at the University of Las Villas, can be found in the bibliography to Rine Leal's *Teatro bufo, siglo XIX, antología, tomo 2* (Havana: Editorial Arte y Literatura, 1975), 333–46. See also the well-indexed bibliography by Juana Cobián Dorta and Violeta Cárdenas Echevarría, "El teatro cubano en la Colección Coronado: Recopilación bibliográfica," *Islas* 103 (September–December 1992): 192–259.

Abbreviations

ANC	Archivo Nacional de Cuba
BNJM	Biblioteca Nacional José Martí, Havana, Cuba
ILL	Instituto de Literatura y Lingüistica, Havana, Cuba
CHC	Cuban Heritage Collection, Miami, Florida

Manuscripts and Archival Texts

At the Biblioteca Nacional José Martí, Havana, Colección Cubana, unless otherwise noted.

Armas y Sáenz, Ramón de. 1882. *Los rumberos, pieza en un acto en prosa y verso.* Havana: La Propaganda Literaria.

Balmaseda, Francisco Javier. 1874. *El dinero no es todo o Un baile de máscaras, comedia en un acto i [sic] en prosa.* 2nd ed. Cartagena de Colombia.

Barberá, José Domingo. 1878. *La vizcondesa del almidón (2nda parte de Los estanqueros aéreos); desproposito bufo-lírico-bailable en un acto en verso.* Music arranged by the maestro Valle. Havana: Imprenta el Trabajo. [Written for the benefit performance of the dancer Carolina Quintana, 13 May 1878 at the teatro Cervantes.]

———. 1892. *Los arrancados o en la tea brava, disparate cómico-lírico en un acto, en prosa.* Havana: Imprenta del Batallón Mixto de Ingenieros. [Passed the censor 28 June 1884; performed 1884]

———. 1892. *Los guanajos, apropósito cómico-lírico-dramático en un acto, dividido en tres cuadros.* Havana: Imprenta del Batallón, 1892. [Performed 24 December 1889 at the teatro Albisu.]

Barreiro, José R. 1899. *La fiesta de San Lázaro o los amores de un tabaquero, sainete lírico en un acto y tres cuadros.* Music by R. Palau. Manuscript, Havana, March.

Benítez del Cristo, Ignacio. 1877. *Los novios catedráticos, pieza en un acto, prosa y en verso.* Matanzas: La Antorcha Literaria. [First performed 4 March 1877 at the Teatro Estéban, Matanzas, by the Compañía Habanera. Reprinted, with introduction by Fernando Ortiz, in *Archivos del Folklore Cubano* Vol. V, no. 2 (April–June) 1930: 119–146.]

Bobadilla, Emilio. 1881. *Don Severo el literato, bosquejo cómico-sério en un acto y en prosa.* Manuscript.

Cabrera, Raimundo. 1885. *Viaje a la luna, acto bufo en tres cuadros.* Music by M. I. Mauri. Güines: Imprenta el Democrata, 1885. [An early version of the 1888 *Del parque a la luna.*]

———. 1888. *Del parque a la luna, zarzuela revista cómico-lírica sobre asuntos cubanos, en un acto y en verso.* Music by M. I. Mauri. Havana: Imprenta El Retiro, 1888. [First performed in 1888 at the teatro Cervantes. Reprinted in *Teatro bufo, siglo XIX, antología, tomo 2,* 125–83, ed. Rine Leal. Havana: Editorial Arte y Literatura, 1975.]

———. 1888. *¡Vapor Correo! Revista cómico-lírica en un acto y cuatro cuadros.* Havana: Imprenta El Retiro.

———. 1889. *Intrigas de un secretario, zarzuela en dos actos.* Music by Manuel I. Mauri.

Cacia, A. 1893. *La cosa municipal, revista cómica de actualidad, en un acto y en tres cuadros, en prosa y verso.* Havana: Imprenta Canalejo y Xiqués. [Performed 27 January 1893 at the teatro Alhambra.]

———. 1895. *Los africanitos, zarzuela cómico-taurina en un acto y cinco cuadros.* Music by M. Fraga. Havana: Imprenta el Aerolito. [Performed 19 March 1895 at the teatro Alhambra.]

Carreño, Pedro. 1854. *El industrial de nuevo cuño, zarzuela en dos actos.*

Castillo, Enrique. 1892. *Mi conejo, pieza en un acto.* Manuscript, Havana.

Céspedes, Benjamín de. 1888. *La Prostitución en la ciudad de la Habana.* Habana: Establecimiento Tipográfico O'Reilly Número 9.

Clarens, Ángel. 1897. *Notas mundanas, zarzuela en dos actos y diez cuadros.* Music by Jorge Anckermann. Habana: Imprenta el Fígaro.

Costi y Erro, Cándido. 1892. *Vino de papayina, jugete cómico en un acto y en prosa.* Havana: Imprenta La Moderna. [Performed 8 June 1892 at the teatro Alhambra.]

Crespo y Borbón, Bartolomé José. [Creto Gangá]. 1838. *El chasco, o vale por mil gallegos que llega a despuntar, comedia en un acto.* Havana: Imprenta de D. J. M. Palmer.

———. 1839. *El látigo del Anfibio, o sea colección de sus poesías satíricas dedicadas a los estravagantes.* Cuaderno Primero. Habana: Imprenta del Comercio.

———. 1839. *El látigo del anfibio, o sea colección de sus poesías satíricas dedicadas a los estravagantes.* Cuaderno Tercero. Habana: Imprenta del Comericio.

———. 1847. *Un ajiaco, o la Boda de Pancha Jutía y Canuto Raspadura, jugete cómico.* Havana: Imprenta de Oliva, 1847. [First performed 16 March 1848 at the Teatro del Circo. Reprinted in *Teatro bufo, siglo XIX, antología, tomo 1*, 45–93, ed. Rine Leal. Havana: Editorial Arte y Literatura, 1975.]

———. 1849. "Cuntetasione a mi carabela Siriaco Mandinga po la cosa dielle que me lo poné en *Lan Frao Sindutriá de la Bana*, la viene disinueve diete mimo mese." *La Prensa*, 23 January, n.p.

———. 1854. *Grandísima y sobriensaliente baile de gente de colore en la grugrieta de marinabo . . . Fiestas con motivo de la llegada de Exmo Sr. Don José de la Concha por Creto Gangá.* Havana: Imprenta "El Iris."

———. 1864. *Debajo del tamarindo, jugete cómico-lírico en dos cuadros.* Havana: Imprenta Particular de La Honradez.

———. 1965. "¡Que cuntentura pa mi! ¡Y que rabia pa lo sabio!" In *Antología de la poesía cubana, tomo III, Siglo XIX*, 150–153, ed. José Lezama Lima. Havana: Consejo nacional de cultura.

Cruz, Luis. 1868. *La gallina ciega, jugete cómico en un acto y en verso.* Havana: Imprenta del Comercio. [First performed 11 June 1868 at the teatro Villanueva by the Bufos Habaneros.]

Díaz González, Olallo. n.d. *La caña y la remolacha, revista cómico-fantástica en un acto y tres cuadros.* Manuscript. [Reprinted in *Teatro bufo, siglo XIX, antología, tomo 2*, 83–123, ed. Rine Leal. Havana: Editorial Arte y Literatura, 1975.]

———. 1881. [Un desocupado] *Costumbres populares. Escenas copiadas del natural por un desocupado.* Havana: Librería la Principal.

———. 1882. [Un desocupado] *Las planchas del viejo Antón, disparate bufo-lírico-bailable en dos actos divididos en cuatro cuadros, por un Desocupado.* Havana: Imprenta la Idea.

———. 1887. *Desde Cuba al paraíso, revista cómico-bufa en dos actos, divididos en seis cuadros y en verso.* Matanzas: Imprenta Galería Literaria. [First performed 14 May 1887 at the teatro Irijoa.]

———. 1888. *La perla de las Antillas, revista cómica en dos actos, divididos en cuatro actos y en verso.* Matanzas: Imprenta Galería Literaria.

———. 1890. *El buen camino, revista cómica en dos actos, divididos en seis cuadros y en verso.* Matanzas: Imprenta Galería Literaria. [Performed 7 November 1885 at the teatro Albisu.]

———. 1890. *Los detallistas, revista cómico-lírica en un acto dividida en cuatro cuadros y en verso.* Manuscript. [Reprinted in *Teatro bufo, siete obras*, 173-217. Havana: Imprenta nacional, 1961.]

———. 1891. *Los efectos del billete, o a la celaduria, apropósito cómico lírico, bailable en un acto, en prosa y verso.* Manuscript. [Reprinted in *Teatro bufo, siete obras*, 121–50. Havana: Imprenta nacional, 1961.]

———. 1899. *Cubanos y americanos o ¡viva la independencia! Revista política en dos actos y seis cuadros, en verso.* Manuscript.

Dumont, Henri. [1876] 1922. *Antropología y patología comparadas de los negros esclavos.* Trans. I. Castellanos. Colección Cubana de libros y documentos inéditos o raros, directed by Fernando Ortiz. Vol. 2. Havana.

Fernández, Francisco. 1868. *Los negros catedráticos, absurdo cómico en un acto, de costumbres cubanas en prosa y verso.* Havana: Imprenta la Tropical, 1868. [First performed 31 May 1868 by the Bufos Habaneros at the teatro Villanueva. Reprinted in *Teatro bufo, siglo XIX, antología, tomo 1,* 131–62, ed. Rine Leal. Havana: Editorial Arte y Literatura, 1975.

———. 1868. *El bautizo, segunda parte de los negros catedráticos, jugete cómico en un acto.* Havana: Imprenta de la Real e Imperial Fábrica la Honradez, 1868. [First performed 27 June 1868 by the Bufos Habaneros at the teatro Villanueva. Reprinted in *Teatro bufo, siglo XIX, antología, tomo 1,* 163–84, ed. Rine Leal. Havana: Editorial Arte y Literatura, 1975.]

———. 1882. *Retórica y poetica, jugete en un acto, en prosa y en verso, estilo catedrático.* Manuscript. [Reprinted in *Teatro Bufo, Siglo XIX, Antología, Tomo 1,* 211–30, ed. Rine Leal. Havana: Editorial Arte y Literatura, 1975.]

Fernández, Francisco, and Pedro N. Pequeño. 1868. *El negro cheche o veinte años despues, tercera parte de Los negros catedráticos, jugete cómico en un acto en prosa y verso, escrita en colaboración con Pedro N. Pequeño.* Havana: Imprenta Militar, 1868. [First performed 30 July 1868 by the Bufos Habaneros at the teatro Villanueva. Reprinted in *Teatro bufo, siglo XIX, antología, tomo 1,* 185–210, ed. Rine Leal. Havana: Editorial Arte y Literatura, 1975.]

"Folleto en refutación al libro que bajo el título de La Prostitucion en la ciudad de la Habana del Dr. Benjamin Céspedes." 1889. Havana: Asociación de Dependientes del Comercio de la Habana.

Guerra Garcia, José. 1885, 1887. *Puntos Negros: Revista de actualidades en un acto dividido en dos cuadros original y en verso.* Havana. Manuscript, ANC: Fondo: Gobierno General, Legajo 584 number 28871.

Guerrero, Juan José. 1864. *La suegra futura, pieza cómica en un acto.* Havana: Imprenta Villa y Hermano.

———. 1864. *Un guateque en la taberna un martes de carnaval, pieza en un acto.* Havana: Imprenta de Villa y Hermano. [Reprinted in *Teatro bufo, siglo XIX, antología, tomo 1,* 95–130, ed. Rine Leal. Havana: Editorial Arte y Literatura, 1975.]

———. 1864. *Un tarde en Nazareno, y las bóas de Petronilla, piezas cómicas en un acto, segunda edición de Un tarde en Nazareno.* Havana: Imprenta de Villa y Hermano,

Hernández, José. 1891. *Amor sin interés, comedia en un acto y en prosa.* Havana: Imprenta la Moderna.

———. 1891. *El corazón y la cara, ensayo dramático en un acto y en prosa.* Havana: Imprenta del Batallon Mixto de Ingenieros. [First performed 12 November 1885 at the teatro Albisu.]

———. 1891. *¡¡Toda precaución es poca!! comedia en un acto y en verso y prosa.* Music by Felipe Palau. Havana: Imprenta la Moderna. [Performed 5 February 1887 at the teatro Albisu.]

Iracheta y Mascort, Francisco de. 1893. *Las reformas de Laura o el marqués de Chirivía, revista cómico-política en un acto y en verso y prosa.* Music by Felipe Palau. Havana. [Not performed; censored in July 1893.]

León, José Soccoro de. 1863. *Garrotazo o tente tieso, comedia de costumbres cubanas en un acto y en verso.* Havana: Imprenta de la Viuda de Barcina y Comp.

———. 1863. *Un bautizo en Jesús María, locura cómica en un acto y en prosa.* Havana: Imprenta la Tropical.

Los cubanos pintados por si mismos, colección de tipos cubano. 1852. Introduction: Blas San Millán; Illustrations: Víctor Patricio Landaluze; Engravings D. José Robles. Havana: Imprenta y Papelería de Barcina.

Madrid, Francisco de la. 1868. *Cosas de cuidadelas, jugete cómico en un acto.* Cárdenas: Imprenta la Unión. [Written for La Sociedad Tipos de Cuba, presumably an amateur performance troupe; first performed at the Teatro de Cárdenas.]

Medina, Antonio. 1881. *Don Canuto Ceibamocha o el guajiro generoso, zarzuela en dos actos.* Havana: Imprenta del Ejercito.

Meireles, Eduardo. 1891. *Los matrimonios, jugete cómico en un acto y en prosa.* Havana: Imprenta la Moderna. [Performed 15 April 1891 at the teatro Alhambra.]

Mellado y Montaña, Manuel. 1880. *La casa de Taita Andrés, semi-parodia de la casa de campo, jugete cómico de género bufo en un acto.* Manuscript. [First performed by the Bufos de Salas in 1880. Reprinted in *Teatro bufo, siglo XIX, antología, tomo 1,* 263–303, ed. Rine Leal. Havana: Editorial Arte y Literatura, 1975.]

———. 1880. *Perico Mascavidrio o la víspera de San Juan, disparate cómico-bufo-lírico de costumbres del país.* Havana: Imprenta el Correo Militar. [Performed 1880 by the "Bufos Cubanos de Salas."]

———. 1887. *El sueño de Perico. Teatro cubano. Comedia mágico fantástico-lírico-bailable en dos actos y quince cuadros.* Habana, 25 May. Manuscript, ANC. Fondo: Gobierno General, Legajo 584 number 28874.

———. 1891. *¡Misera humana!, comedia en un acto, en prosa.* Havana: Imprenta del Batallón Mixto de Ingenieros. [First performed at the teatro Torrecillas.]

Mendoza, Tomás. 1867. *De lo vivo a lo pintado: comedia de costumbres en tres actos y en verso.* Santiago de Cuba: Imprenta de Espinal y Díaz.

———. 1868. *Los mocitos del día,* caricatura de costumbres, en un acto y en prosa. Havana: Imprenta de la viuda de Barcina y Compañía. [First performed 17 September 1868 by the Bufos Habaneros at the teatro Tacón.]

Monte, Laureano del. 1891. *La Tenoria, humorada bufa en dos actos divididos en cuatro cuadros, en verso.* [Published version missing title pages; possibly performed 1893]

———. 1894. *Con don y sin don, ayer y hoy; caricatura trágico-bufo-lírico-bailable, en un acto y cinco cuadros, en prosa.* Havana: Imprenta el Aerolito. Music by "M. F." [First performed 23 February 1894 at the teatro Alhambra.]

Morales Álvarez, Ramón. 1882. *El proceso del oso, ajiaco bufo-lírico-bailable.* Music by Enrique Guerrero. Manuscript. [First performed 28 January 1882 by the Bufos de Salas, under the direction of Eusebio Perales, at the teatro Torrecillas. Reprinted in *Teatro bufo, siglo XIX, antología, tomo 2,* 9–56, ed. Rine Leal. Havana: Editorial Arte y Literatura, 1975.]

Nuza, J. and Chacón. 1898. *Receta contra los celos, jugete cómico en un acto.* Manuscript.

Palacios, Don Santiago Infante de. 1887. *Las siete plagas de Cuba. Boceto fantástico de calamidades. cómico-lírico, en un acto y tres cuadros, en verso y original.* Havana April. Manuscript, ANC. Fondo: Gobierno General, Legajo. 584 number 28873.

Pardo Suárez, Vicente. 1896. *El sultán de Mayarí o el mono tiene rabia, zarzuela cómico-bufa en un acto y seis cuadros.* Havana: Imprenta la Republica. [First performed 25 July 1896 at the teatro Albisu.]

———. 1897. *Los príncipes del Congo, opereta cómica en un acto.* Music by Rafael Palau. Havana: Imprenta la República. [Performed 1 January 1897 at the teatro Irioja.]

Pequeño, Pedro N. 1872. *Músico, poeta y loco, jugete cómico en un acto y en verso.* Havana: Imprenta Militar de la viuda de Soler y Compañía, 1872. [Performed in the private theatre of "Don Agustín T. Muro de Calabazar" in 1870.]

———. 1885. *La africana, apropósito bufo en un acto.* Havana: Imprenta de Ferrocarriles. [Performed 1882.]

———. 1908. *Locura y sueño, un cuadro de los ocho en que está dividida la obra cómica-lírica-dramática.* Pinar del Río: Imprenta la Caridad, 1908. [Written in 1891.]

Piloto, Alfredo. 1893. *Un matrimonio en Haiti, zarzuela bufa en un acto, en prosa.* Cienfuegos: Imprenta Andreu y Comp.

Pitaluga y Delgado, Rafael. 1856. *Una viña en La Habana, episodio histórico en un acto y en verso.* Havana: "La Cubana."

Quintana, José María de. n.d. *La trichina, disparate bufo-crítico en un acto y en prosa.* Manuscript. [Reprinted in *Teatro bufo, siglo XIX, antología, tomo 2*, 57–82, ed. Rine Leal. Havana: Editorial Arte y Literatura, 1975.]

———. 1891. *Conflicto municipal, jugete cómico-lírico-bufo en un acto y en prosa.* Havana: Imprenta la Moderna. [Performed 20 July 1885 at the teatro Torrecillas.]

———. 1891. *Diputados a cortes, esperpento bufo-crítico en un acto y tres cuadros en prosa.* Manuscript, Havana, 1891.

———. 1891. *El demonio es la guaracha o Felipe Ginebrita, disparate bufo-lírico en un acto y en prosa.* Havana: Imprenta la Moderna, 1891. [Performed 12 November 1885 at the teatro Torrecillas.]

———. 1891. *El otro, jugete cómico en un acto, en prosa.* Manuscript. Also published: Havana: El Teatro Moderno, 1891. [Performed 14 July 1880, by the "Bufos Habaneros" at the Teatro Otero.]

———. 1891. *Juego prohibido, apropósito en un acto y en prosa.* Havana: Imprenta la Moderna. [Performed 17 December 1888 at the teatro Habana.]

———. 1891. *La mulata de rango, disparate cómico-lírico en dos actos, en prosa.* Havana: Imprenta la Moderna. Music by Raimundo Valenzuela. [First performed 3 October 1885 at the teatro Albisu.]

———. 1891. *Por una carbonería, o político, rey, nada, jugete cómico en un acto, en prosa.* Havana: Imprenta la Moderna. [Performed 21 October 1885 at the teatro Albisu]

———. 1891. *¿Quién quiere a mi mujer? o regalo mi mujer, pieza cómica en un acto, en prosa.* Havana: Imprenta la Moderna. [Performed 3 November 1885 at the teatro Albisu.]

———. 1891. *Trincheras contra el amor o la vieja y el andaluz, jugete cómico en un acto en prosa.* Havana: Imprenta la Moderna. [Performed by the Bufos Habaneros at the teatro Otero in Cárdenas.]

———. 1891. *¡Viva esta tierra! esperpento bufo-lírico-crítico-dramático, en un acto dividido en siete cuadros.* Havana: Imprenta la Moderna. [Performed 20 October 1885 at the teatro Albisu.]

———. 1892. *Adán y Eva, jugete cómico en dos actos y en prosa.* Havana: Imprenta la Moderna.

———. 1892. *Caneca torrero, esperpento cómico en dos actos y en prosa.* Havana: Imprenta la Moderna. [Performed 1 March 1887 at the teatro Albisu.]

———. 1892. *Llueven bufos, esperpento cómico-bufo en un acto y en prosa.* Manuscript. [Censored in 1886.]

Riquelme, Guillermo. 1887. *Encerrona política – Apropósito cómico-bufo-lírico, en un acto dividido en cinco cuadros.* February. Manuscript, ANC: Fondo: Gobierno General, Legajo 584 number 28870.

Riquelme, Guillermo, and Ramón Morales. 1887. *Tuti li mundi. Mamarracho cómico bufo-lírico, crítico fantástico en dos actos, en prosa y verso.* Havana. Manuscript, ANC: Fondo: Gobierno General Legajo 584 number 28872.

Salas, Miguel. 1887. *Trabajar para el inglés, jugete cómico, lírico, pantomímico, en un acto y tres cuadros.* Manuscript. [First performed 2 February 1887 by the Bufos de Salas at the teatro Albisu. Reprinted in *Teatro bufo, siglo XIX, antología, tomo 1*, 339–80, ed. Rine Leal. Havana: Editorial Arte y Literatura, 1975.]

Sánchez Maldonado, Benjamín. 1896. *La herencia de Canuto, zarzuela bufa en un acto, en cinco cuadros en verso y prosa.* Music by Antonio González. Manuscript: Havana. [Reprinted in *Teatro bufo, siete obras*, 83–120. Havana: Imprenta nacional, 1961.]

———. 1896. *Los hijos de Thalia o bufos de fin de siglo, desconcierto anti-literario, cómico-bufo-lírico-burlesco y mamarrachero, en verso y prosa, en un acto y tres cuadros.* Music by Rafael Palau. Manuscript: Havana. [Reprinted in *Teatro bufo, siete obras*, 215–55. Havana: Imprenta nacional, 1961.]

Saragacha, Ignacio. 1880. *Un baile por fuera, pieza bufa en un acto.* Manuscript. Also published: Havana: Imprenta de la Habana. [Written for the benefit performance of Miguel Salas, performed 29 August 1880 by the Bufos de Salas at the teatro Albisu. Reprinted in *Ignacio Saragacha, Teatro*, 7–32. Havana: Editorial Letras Cubanas, 1990.]

———. 1881. *En la cocina, jugete cómico-bufo en un acto y en prosa.* Manuscript. [Performed 5 July 1881 by the Bufos de Salas at the teatro Albisu. Reprinted in *Teatro bufo, siglo XIX, antología, tomo 2*, 229–75, ed. Rine Leal. Havana: Editorial Arte y Literatura, 1975.]

———. 1881. *Esta noche sí.* Manuscript.

———. 1881. *Lo que pasa en la cocina, cuadro de costumbres en un acto.* Manuscript: Havana. [Performed 5 July 1881 by the Bufos de Salas at the teatro Albisu. Reprinted in *Ignacio Saragacha, Teatro*, 79–104. Havana: Editorial Letras Cubanas, 1990.]

———. 1882. *Los bufos en África.* Manuscript.

———. 1888. *El doctor Machete, parodia de 'el médico a palos.'* Manuscript. [Performed at the Salon Trocha in 1888. Reprinted in *Ignacio Saragacha, Teatro*, 105–21. Havana: Editorial Letras Cubanas, 1990.]

———. 1900. *La padovani en Guanabacoa, o ¡Yo te daré el two-step!, jugete cómico en un acto.* Manuscript. [Reprinted in *Ignacio Saragacha, Teatro*, 167–86. Havana: Editorial Letras Cubanas, 1990.]

———. 1896. *Mefistófeles, parodia en un acto y seis cuadros.* Manuscript. [Performed

21 January 1896 at the teatro Irijoa. Reprinted in *Ignacio Saragacha, Teatro*, 143–66. Havana: Editorial Letras Cubanas, 1990.]

———. 1895. *Una plancha . . . fotográfica, jugete en un acto*. Manuscript. [Performed in October 1895; author is listed as "Narciso Agachagay," a pseudonym and acronym for Ingacio Saragacha. Reprinted in *Ignacio Saragacha, Teatro*, 121–42. Havana: Editorial Letras Cubanas, 1990.]

Saragacha, Ignacio, with José María de Quintana. 1892. *Habana y Almendares o Los efectos del base-ball, apropósito cómico-lírico en un acto y cinco cuadros, en prosa*. Music by Rafael Palau. Havana: Imprenta la Moderna. [Passed censors on 6 June 1887.]

Saragacha, Ignacio, in collaboration with Manuel Saladrigas. 1900. *¡Arriba con el himno! Revista política, joco-seria y bailable en un acto, cinco cuadros, y apoteósis final*. Manuscript: Havana. [Reprinted in *Teatro bufo, siglo XIX, antología, tomo 2*, 277–330, ed. Rine Leal. Havana: Editorial Arte y Literatura, 1975. Also in *Ignacio Saragacha, Teatro*, 187–219. Havana: Editorial Letras Cubanas, 1990.]

Tamayo, José, adapted by Miguel Salas. 1879. *Traviata o la morena de las clavelinas, parodia bufo catedrática en un acto y en prosa*. Manuscript. [First performed by the Tipos Provinciales in Santiago de Cuba, 1879. Reprinted in *Teatro bufo, siglo XIX, antología, tomo 1*, 305–338, ed. Rine Leal. Havana: Editorial Arte y Literatura, 1975.]

Tipos y costumbres de la isla de Cuba, por los mejores autores de este género. 1881. Illustration by Víctor Patrício de Landaluze. Introduction by Antonio Bachiller y Morales. Havana.

Torre y Sola, Enrique de la. 1877. *Un taco del día, jugete cómico en un acto, en verso*. Matanzas: Imprenta del Ferrocarril.

Torroella, Alfredo. 1868. *El ensayo de don Juan Tenorio, descarillamiento cómico escrito espresamente* [sic] *para esta compañía*. Manuscript.

———. 1868. *Un minué, disparate catedrático en un acto escrito espresamente* [sic] *para los bufos habaneros*. Havana: Imprenta el Comercio. [Perfomed 22 August 1868 at the Teatro de Variedades.]

———. 1870. *El mulato, drama en tres actos y en prosa*. Mexico: Imprenta del Comercio.

Valerio, Juan Francisco. n.d. *Cuadros sociales, colleción de articulos de costumbres*. Manuscript.

———. 1868. *Perro huevero aunque le quemen el hocico, cuadro de costumbres cubanas en un acto, en verso*. Havana, Imprenta Intrépida, 1868. [First performed 26 August 1868 by the Bufos Habaneros at the teatro Villanueva. Also performed 22 January 1869 by the Bufos Caricatos at the Villanueva; the line "¡Viva la tierra que produce la caña!" (Long live the land that produces the sugarcane!) precipitated the Sucesos de la Villanueva. Reprinted in *Teatro bufo, siglo XIX, antología, tomo 1*, 231–62, ed. Rine Leal. Havana: Editorial Arte y Literatura, 1975.]

Zafra, Antonio Enrique de. 1865. *Tres para dos, jugete cómico-lírico en un acto, en verso*. Havana. [Performed 1 Feburary 1865 at the teatro Tacón.]

———. 1868. *La fiesta del mayoral, jugete cómico de costumbres cubanas an un acto, en verso*. Havana: Imprenta y Librería el Iris. [Performed 30 July 1868 by the Bufos Habaneros at the teatro Variedades.]

Periodicals Consulted

All from Havana, Cuba, unless otherwise noted.

El Ajiaco, periódico crítico, satírico burlesco, con caricaturas (1866), BNJM

El Almendares (1881, 1882), ILL

Aurora del Yumurí (Matanzas), Biblioteca Gener y del Monte, Matanzas, Cuba

Boletín de la Sociedad Antropológica de la Isla de Cuba (1878/1885), BNJM; ANC

Boletín Oficial del Teatro de Villanueva (1864), ANC

Los Bufos, periódico bailable, con caricaturas á la diablesca y capaces de volver anacoreta al mismo mefistófeles (1 issue, 1872; illustrations by Víctor Patricio Landaluze), BNJM

Camafeos (1865), ANC

La Chamarretta, periódico que huele a mechete y sabe a horquetilla (1869), ANC

El Criollo, BNJM

Cuba y América (New York City, N.Y., 1898), BNJM

El Diablo Cojuelo (1869), ANC

Diario de la Habana, BNJM

Diario de la Marina, BNJM, CHC

Don Circunstancias (1879-1881), CHC

Don Junípero, BNJM

El Espectador, BNJM, ILL

El Fígaro, BNJM

La Fraternidad, BNJM, ANC (1888–1894)

Gaceta de la Habana, BNJM

La Igualdad (1894), ANC, CHC

Minerva: Revista quincenal dedicada a la mujer de color, ILL

El Negro Bueno (1869), BNJM

Patria (New York City, N.Y.), ANC

Periodiquin Ambulante-satírico-burlesco de la Danza (1854), ANC

El Plantel, BNJM

La Prensa, BNJM

Revista Musical, later *Cuba Musical* (1882), BNJM

Periodicals published in the brief but important period of the freedom of the press, or “libertad de imprenta,” in January and February 1869 are bound and catalogued together at the ILL, as follows:

El Alacrán Libre

El Amigo del Pueblo

La Bandera Roja

Las Bijiritas

El Catalan Liberal

La Centinela Voluntario

El Charlatan

Los Cimarrones

El Conciliador
La Concordia
Contestacion al "Riojano"
Contestacion al Riojano por Varios Cubanos
La Cotorra
El Cucharon Del Diablo
El Cubano Libre, o sea el Ex-Fosforito
El Dependiente Honrado
El Diablo Cojuelo
Eco de la Libertad
El Eco Ibero
El Ensayo
El Estudiante Republicano
La Exposicion
El Farol
Lo Fill de'l Pardal
El Fosforito
El Gato de Guanjay
El Gegen
El Gorrion
El Gorro
La Guillotina
La Idea Liberal
El Imposible
El Insurrecto
El Jejen
El Machete
La Managuilla
La Mentira
El Moscon
El Negro Bueno
Los Negros Catedráticos
La Opinion de Cuba, o El Poeta Liberal
La Pica-Pica
El Polizonte
El Pueblo
El Pueblo Libre
El Puñetazo
La Revolucion
El Riojano
El Sol del Trópico
El Sopimpero
La Sopimpa
La Tijera
El Título Borrado
La Tranca

La Tremenda
El Vómito Negro
La Voz de España
La Voz del Pueblo

Additional Works Cited

Alén Rodríguez, Olavo. 1994. *De lo afrocubano a la salsa.* Havana: Ediciones Artex.

Álvarez Ríos, Baldomero. 1995. *La inmigración china en la Cuba colonial: El Barrio Chino de la Habana.* Havana: Publicigraf.

Agüero y Barreras, Gaspar. 1946. "El Aporte Africano a la música popular Cubana." In *Estudios Afrocubanos.* Havana: La Sociedad de Estudios Afrocubanos. Volume 5.

Anderson, Benedict. 1991. *Imagined Communities: Reflections on the Origin and Spread of Nationalism.* 2nd ed., rev. and extended. London: Verso.

Aparicio, Frances R. and Susana Chávez-Silverman, eds. 1997. *Tropicalizatons: Transcultural Representations of Latinidad.* Hanover, N.H.: University Press of New England.

Appadurai, Arjun. 1993. "Disjuncture and Difference in the Global Cultural Economy" in *The Phantom Public Sphere,* 269–96, ed. Bruce Robbins. Minneapolis: University of Minnesota Press.

Aretz, Isabel. 1984. "Music and Dance in Continental Latin America, with the Exception of Brazil." In *Africa in Latin America: Essays on History, Culture, and Socialization,* 189–226, ed. Manuel Moreno Fraginals. Trans. Leonor Blum. New York: Holmes & Meier Publishers, Inc.

Arrom, José Juan. 1944. *Historia de la literatura dramática cubana.* New Haven, Conn.: Yale University Press.

Austin, J. L. 1962. *How to Do Things with Words.* Cambridge, Mass.: Harvard University Press.

Bacardí y Moreu, Emilio. 1973. *Crónicas de Santiago de Cuba.* 2nd ed. 10 vols. Madrid: Gráficas Breogán,

Baker, Houston. 2001. *Critical Memory: Public Spheres, African American Writing, and Black Fathers and Sons in America.* Athens: University of Georgia Press.

Baltar Rodriguez, José. 1997. *Los chinos de Cuba: apuntes etnográficos.* Havana: Fundación Fernando Ortiz.

"Bartolomé José Crespo y Borbón." 1975–77. In *La enciclopedia de Cuba: Poesía,* 378. San Juan, PR: Enciclopedia y Clasicos Cubanos.

Bartra, Roger. 1992. *The Cage of Melancholy: Identity and Metamorphosis in the Mexican Character.* Trans. Christopher J. Hall. New Brunswick, N.J.: Rutgers University Press.

Bean, Annemarie, James V. Hatch, and Brooks McNamara, eds. 1996. *Inside the Minstrel Mask: Readings in Nineteenth-Century Blackface Minstrelsy.* Hanover, N.H.: Wesleyan University Press.

Benítez Rojo, Antonio. 1986. "Azucar/Poder/Texto," *Cruz ansata,* 9, 93-117.

———. 1992. *The Repeating Island: The Caribbean and the Postmodern Perspective.* Trans. James Maraniss. Durham, N.C.: Duke University Press.

Bennett, Tony. 1995. *The Birth of the Museum: History, Theory, Politics.* New York: Routledge.

Bhabha, Homi K. 1990a. "DissemiNation: Time, Narrative, and the Margins of Modern Nation. In *Nation and Narration,* 290–322, ed. Homi K. Bhabha. London: Routledge.

———. 1990b. "Introduction: narrating the nation." In *Nation and Narration,* 1–7, ed. Homi K. Bhabha. London: Routledge.

———, ed. 1990c. *Nation and Narration.* London: Routledge.

———. 1994. *The Location of Culture.* London: Routledge.

Bonich, Juan. 1933. "Los Teatros de la Habana." *Almanaque el mundo,* 325–35.

Brennan, Timothy. 1990. "The national longing for form." In *Nation and Narration,* 44–70, ed. Homi K. Bhabha. London: Routledge.

Brock, Lisa and Bijan Bayne. 1998. "Not Just Black: African Americans, Cubans, and Baseball." In *Between Race and Empire: African Americans and Cubans before the Cuban Revolution,* 168–204, ed. Lisa Brock and Digna Castañeda Fuertes. Philadelphia: Temple University Press.

Bronfman, Alejandra. 2004. *Measures of Equality: Social Science, Citizenship, and Race in Cuba, 1902–1940.* Chapel Hill: University of North Carolina Press.

Browning, Barbara. 1998. *Infectious Rhythm: Metaphors of Contagion and the Spread of African Culture.* New York: Routledge.

Bueno, Salvador, ed. 1985. *Costumbristas cubanos del siglo XIX.* Caracas: Biblioteca Ayacucho.

Cabrera, Ramiro. 1919. "Los Teatros de Ayer." *Social* (October).

Cabrera Saqui, Mario. 1969. "Vida, pasión, y glória de Anselmo Suárez y Romero." Introduction to Anselmo Suárez y Romero, *Francisco, el ingenio o las delicias del campo,* 7–36. Miami: Mnemosyne Publishing.

Cantero, J. G. and Eduardo Laplante. 1984. *Los ingenios de Cuba.* Ed. Levi Marrero. Barcelona: Gráficas M. Pareja [La Moderna Poesía Inc.].

Carpentier, Alejo. 1946. *Ese músico que llevo dentro. La música en Cuba.* Mexico: Fondo de Cultura Económica.

———. 2001. *Music in Cuba.* Ed. Timothy Brennan. Trans. Alan West-Durán. Minneapolis: University of Minnesota Press.

Castillo Faílde, Osvaldo. 1964. *Miguel Faílde Pérez: creador del danzón.* Havana: Editora del consejo nacional de cultura.

Centón epistolario de Domingo Del Monte. 1923–1957. 7 vols. Havana: El Siglo XX.

Chatterjee, Partha. 1993. *The Nation and its Fragments: Colonial and Postcolonial Histories.* Princeton: Princeton University Press.

Clenninden, Inga. 1991. *Aztecs: an interpretation.* Cambridge: Cambridge University Press.

Cole, Catharine. 1996. "Reading Blackface in Africa: Wonders Taken for Signs." *Critical Inquiry* 23: 183–215.

Cruz, Mary. 1974. *Creto Gangá.* Havana: Contemporaneo.

Daniel, Yvonne. 1995. *Rumba: Dance and Social Change in Contemporary Cuba.* Bloomington: Indiana University Press.

Dash, J. Michael. 1998. *The Other America: Caribbean Literature in a New World Context.* Charlottesville: University of Virginia Press.

Delany, Martin Robinson. [1859–1862] 1970. *Blake, or, The Huts of America: a novel.* Boston: Beacon Press.

———. 2003. *Martin R. Delany: a documentary reader*, ed. Robert S. Levine. Chapel Hill: University of North Carolina Press.

Deloria, Philip J. 1998. *Playing Indian.* New Haven, Conn.: Yale University Press.

Deschamps Chapeaux, Pedro. 1963. *El negro en el periodismo cubano en el siglo XIX; ensayo bibliográfico.* Habana, Ediciones R[evolución].

———. 1971. *El negro en la economía habanera del siglo XIX.* Havana: UNEAC.

El otro Francisco. [Motion picture.] 1975. Directed by Sergio Giral. Havana: Instituto Cubano de Artes e Industrias Cinematográficas (ICAIC).

Feijoo, Samuel. 1984. "African Influence in Latin America: Oral and Written Literature." In *Africa in Latin America: Essays on History, Culture, and Socialization,* 145–69, ed. Manuel Moreno Fraginals. Trans. Leonor Blum. New York: Holmes & Meier Publishers, Inc.

Ferrer, Ada. 1999. *Insurgent Cuba: Race, Nation, and Revolution, 1868–1898.* Chapel Hill: University of North Carolina Press.

Flores, Juan. 1997. "The Latino Imaginary: Dimensions of Community and Identity." In *Tropicalizatons: Transcultural Representations of Latinidad*, 183–193, ed. Frances R. Aparicio and Susana Chávez-Silverman. Hanover, N.H.: University Press of New England.

Florescano, Enrique. 1994. *Memory, myth, and time in Mexico: From the Aztecs to Independence.* Trans. Albert G. Bork. Austin: University of Texas Press.

Fraginals, Manuel Moreno. 1984. "Cultural Contributions and Deculturation." In *Africa in Latin America: Essays on History, Culture, and Socialization*, 5–22, ed. Manuel Moreno Fraginals. Trans. Leonor Blum. New York: Holmes & Meier Publishers, Inc.

Franco, José L. 1937."Juan Francisco Manzano, el poeta esclavo y su tiempo." Introduction to Juan Francisco Manzano, *Autobiografía, cartas y versos*, 9–32, ed. José L. Franco. Havana.

Fraser, Nancy. 1993. "Rethinking the Public Sphere: A Contribution to the Critique of Actually Existing Democracy." In *The Phantom Public Sphere*, 1–32, ed. Bruce Robbins. Minneapolis: University of Minnesota Press.

Fusco, Coco. 1995. *English is Broken Here: Notes on Cultural Fusion in the Americas.* New York: New Press.

———. 2001. *The Bodies That Were Not Ours.* London: Routledge, 2001.

Gates, Jr., Henry Louis. 1988. *The Signifying Monkey: A Theory of African American Literary Criticism.* Oxford: Oxford University Press.

Gilroy, Paul. 1987. *'There Ain't No Black in Union Jack': The Cultural Politics of Race and Nation.* London: Hutchinson, 1987.

———. 1993. *The Black Atlantic: Modernity and Double Consciousness.* Cambridge, Mass.: Harvard University Press.

González Echevarría, Roberto. 1999. *The Pride of Havana: A history of Cuban Baseball.* New York: Oxford University Press.

Goodall, Jane. 2002. *Performance and Evolution in the Age of Darwin: Out of the Natural Order.* London: Routledge.

Gould, Steven J. 1993. "American Poligeny and Craniometry before Darwin: Blacks and Indians as Separate, Inferior Species." In *The "Racial" Economy of Science: Toward a Democratic Future*, ed. Sandra Harding, 84–115. Bloomington: Indiana University Press.

Graham, Richard, ed. 1900. *The Idea of Race in Latin America, 1870–1940.* Austin: University of Texas Press.

Guarachas cubanas: Curiosa recopilación desde las más antiguas hasta las más modernas. 1982. 2nd ed. Havana: Librería "La Principal."

Habermas, Jürgen. 1991. *The Structural Transformation of the Public Sphere: An Inquiry into a Category of Bourgeois Society.* Trans. Thomas Burger and Frederick Lawrence. Cambridge, Mass.: MIT Press.

Hartman, Saidiya. 1997. *Scenes of Subjection: Terror, Slavery, and Self-Making in Nineteenth Century America.* Oxford: Oxford University Press.

Hauranne, Ernest Duvergier de. [1864–1865] 1974. *A Frenchman in Lincoln's America [Huit mois en Amérique: lettres et notes de voyage, 1864–1865].* Trans. and ed. Ralph H. Bowen. Chicago: Donnelley.

Helg, Aline. 1995. *Our Rightful Share: The Afro-Cuban Struggle for Equality, 1886–1912.* Chapel Hill: University of North Carolina Press.

Holland, Norman. 1992. "Fashioning Cuba." In *Nationalisms and Sexualities*, 122–46, ed. Andrew Parker, Mary Russo, Doris Sommer, and Patrica Yaeger. New York: Routledge.

Howard, Philip A. 1998. *Changing History: Afro-Cuban Cabildos and Societies of Color in the Nineteenth Century.* Baton Rouge: Louisiana State University.

Ibarra, Jorge. 1967. *Ideología Mambisa.* Havana: Instituto Cubano del Libro.

Jensen, Larry K. 1988. *Children of Colonial Despotism: Press, Politics, and Culture in Cuba, 1790-1840.* Tampa: University of Florida Press.

Joseph, May. 1999. *Nomadic Identities: The Performance of Citizenship.* Minneapolis: University of Minnesota Press.

Kirshenblatt-Gimblett, Barbara. 1900. "Problems in the Early History of Jewish Folkloristics." *Offprint from the Tenth World Congress of Jewish Studies*, 21–30. Jerusalem: World Union of Jewish Studies.

———. 1998. *Destination Culture: Tourism, Museums, and Heritage.* Berkeley: University of California Press.

Kruger, Loren. 1992. *The National Stage: Theatre and Cultural Legitimation in England, France, and America.* Chicago: University of Chicago Press.

Kutzinski, Vera M. 1993. *Sugar's Secrets: Race and the Erotics of Cuban Nationalism.* Charlottesville: University Press of Virginia, 1993.

Lapique Becali, Zoila. 1979. *Música colonial cubana.* Havana: Editorial Letras Cubanas.

———. 1996. *La mujer en los habanos.* Havana: Visual América Ediciones.

———. 2002. *La memoria en las piedras.* Havana: Ediciones Boloña.

Leal, Rine. 1975a. "Prólogo: La chancleta y el coturno." In *Teatro bufo, siglo XIX antología. tomo 1*, 15–46, ed. Rine Leal. Havana: Editorial Arte y Literatura.

———. 1975b *La selva oscura, tomo 1: Historia del teatro cubano desde sus orígenes hasta 1868.* Havana: Editorial Arte y Literatura, 1975(a).

———. 1975c. *La selva oscura, tomo 2: De los bufos a la neocolonia (Historia del teatro cubano de 1868 a 1902).* Havana: Editorial Arte y Literatura.

———, ed. 1975. *Teatro bufo, siglo XIX antología.* 2 vols. Havana: Editorial Arte y Literatura.

———. 1980. *Breve historia del teatro cubano.* Havana: Editorial Letras Cubanas.

León, Argeliers. 1991. "Notes toward a Panorama of Popular and Folk Musics." In *Essays on Cuban Music: North American and Cuban Perspectives,* 3–23, ed. Peter Manuel. Lanham, Md.: University Press of America

Lezama Lima, José, ed. 1965. *Antología de la poesía cubana, tomo III, siglo XIX.* Havana: Consejo nacional de cultura.

Linares, Maria Teresa. 1991. "The Décima and Punto in Cuban Folklore." In *Essays on Cuban Music: North American and Cuban Perspectives,* 87–114, ed. Peter Manuel. Lanham, Md.: University Press of America.

Lipsitz, George. 1998. "Their America and Ours." In *José Martí's "Our America": From National to Hemispheric Cultural Studies,* 293–316, ed. Jeffrey Belnap and Raúl Fernández. Durham, N.C.: Duke University Press.

López, Anna M. 1997. "Of Rythyms and Borders." In *Everynight Life: Culture and Dance in Latin/o America,* 310–44, ed. Celeste Fraser Delgado and José Esteban Muñoz. Durham, N.C.: Duke University Press.

López Lemus, Virgilio. 1995. *La décima. Panorama breve de la décima cubana.* Havana: Editorial Academia.

Lott, Eric. 1993. *Love & Theft: Blackface Minstrelsy and the American Working Class.* New York: Oxford University Press.

Luis, William. 1990. *Literary Bondage: Slavery in Cuban Narrative.* Austin: University of Texas Press, 1990.

Mahar, William J. 1999. *Behind the Burnt Cork Mask: Early Blackface Minstrelsy and Antebellum American Popular Culture.* Chicago: University of Illinois Press.

Mañach, Jorge. 1969. *Indagación del Choteo.* Miami: Mnemosyne.

Manzano, Juan Francisco. 1937. *Autobiografía, cartas y versos.* Ed. José L. Franco. Havana.

———. 1981. *The Autobiography of a Slave/Autobiografía de un esclavo,* ed. Ivan A. Schulman, trans. Evelyn Picon Garfield. Detroit: Wayne State University Press.

Martí, José. 1963–66. *Obras Completas.* 27 Vols. Havana: Editorial Nacional de Cuba.

———. [1891] 1991. *Nuestra América.* Havana: Centro de Estudios Martianos, Casa de las Americas.

———. 1999. *José Martí Reader: Writings on the Americas.* New York: Ocean Press.

Martinez-Alier, Verena. 1989. *Marriage, Class, and Colour in Nineteenth Century Cuba.* 2nd ed. Ann Arbor: University of Michigan Press.

Martínez-Fernández, Luis. 1994. *Torn between Empires. Economy, Society and Patterns of Political Thought in the Hispanic Caribbean, 1840–1878.* Athens: University of Georgia Press.

Merrim, Stephanie. 1991. *Feminist perspectives on Sor Juana Inés de la Cruz.* Detroit: Wayne State University Press.

Molloy, Sylvia. 1991. *At Face Value: Autobiographical Writing in Spanish America.* Cambridge, Mass.: Cambridge University Press.

Montejo Arrechea, Carmen. 1998. "*Minerva*: A Magazine for Women (and Men) of Color." In *Between Race and Empire,* 33–48, ed. Lisa Brock and Digna Castañeda Fuertes. Philadelphia: Temple University Press.

Montes-Huidobro, Matías. 1987. *Teoría y práctica del catedratismo en Los negros catedráticos de Francisco Fernández.* Miami: Editorial Persona.

_____, ed. 1995. *El laúd del desterrado.* Houston: Arte Público Press.

Montesinos, José F. [1959] 1983. *Costumbrismo y novela: ensayo sobre el redescubrimiento de la realidad española.* Madrid: Editorial Castalia.

Moore, Robin D. 1997. *Nationalizing Blackness: Afrocubanismo and Artistic Revolution in Havana, 1920–1940.* Pittsburgh: Pittsburgh University Press.

Morejón, Nancy. 1982. *Nación y mestizaje en Nicolás Guillen.* Havana: UNEAC.

Moreno Fraginals, Manuel. 1978. *El ingenio. El complejo económico social cubano del azucar.* 3 vols. Havana: Editorial de Ciencias Sociales.

———. 1984. "Cultural Contributions and Deculturation." In *Africa in Latin America: Essays on History, Culture, and Socialization*, 189–226, ed. Manuel Moreno Fraginals, trans. Leonor Blum. New York: Holmes & Meier Publishers, Inc.

Moten, Fred. 2003. *In the Break: the Aesthetics of Black Radical Tradition.* Minneapolis: University of Minnesota Press.

Mullaney, Steven. 1988. *The Place of the Stage: License, Play, and Power in Renaissance England.* Ann Arbor: University of Michigan Press.

Mullen, Edward J., Ed. 1981. *The Life and Poems of a Cuban Slave: Juan Francisco Manzano, 1797–1854.* Hamden, Conn.: Archon Press.

Muñoz, José Estéban. 1999. *Disidentifications: Queers of Color and the Performance of Politics.* Minneapolis: University of Minnesota Press.

Negt, Oskar and Alexander Kluge. 1988. "*The Public Sphere and Experience:* Selections." Trans. Peter Labanyi. *October* 46 (Fall): 60–82.

Ngugi wa Thiong'o. 1986. *Decolonising the Mind: The Politics of Language in African Literature.* Portsmouth, N.H.: Heinemann Educational Books.

Omi, Michael and Howard Winant. 1986. *Racial Formation in the United States: From the 1960s to the 1980s.* New York : Routledge & Kegan Paul.

Ortiz, Fernando. [1906] 1917. *Hampa afro-cubano: los negros brujos (apuntes para un estudio de etnología criminal).* Miami: Ediciones Universal.

———. 1930. Introductory remarks to *Los novios catedráticos* by Ignacio Benítez del Cristo, in *Archivos del folklore cubano* 5:2 (April–June): 119.

———. 1953. *Martí y las razas.* Havana: Comisión nacional organizadora de los actos y ediciones del centenario y del monumento de Martí.

———. 1984. "Los negros curros." In Fernando Ortiz, *Ensayos Etnográficos*, 79–161, ed. Miguel Barnet and Angel L. Fernández. Havana: Editorial de ciencias sociales.

———. 1991. "Los factores humanos de la cubanidad." In Fernando Ortiz, *Estudios etnosociologicos*, 10–30, ed. Isaac Barreal Fernández. Havana: Editorial de ciencias sociales.

———. [1965] 1993a. *La africanía de la música folklórica de Cuba.* Havana: Editorial Letras Cubanas.

———. [1951] 1993b. *Los bailes y el teatro de los negros en el folklore de Cuba.* Havana: Editorial Letras Cubanas.

———. [1940] 1995. *Cuban Counterpoint. Tobacco and Sugar.* Trans. Harriet de Onís. Durham, N.C.: Duke University Press.

Palmié, Stephan. 2002. *Wizards and Scientists: Explorations in Afro-Cuban Modernity and Tradition.* Durham, N.C.: Duke University Press.

Paquette, Robert L. 1988. *Sugar is Made with Blood: The Conspiracy of La Escalera a... the Conflict between Empires over Slavery in Cuba.* Middletown, Conn.: University of Wesleyan Press.
Pereira, Joseph R. 1983. "The Black Presence in Cuban Theatre." *Afro-Hispanic Review* (January): 13–18.
Pérez Cabello, Rafael [Zerep]. 1898. *En escena; crónicas y retazos literarios.* Habana: El Fígaro.
Pérez, Louis A. Jr. 1983. *Cuba between Empires, 1878–1902.* Pittsburgh: University of Pittsburgh Press.
———. 1985. *Cuba: Between Reform and Revolution.* New York: Oxford University Press.
———. 1992, ed. *Slaves, Sugar, & Colonial Society: Travel Accounts of Cuba, 1801–1899.* Wilmington, Del.: Scholarly Resources Inc.
———. 1994. "Between Baseball and Bullfighting: The Quest for National Identity in Cuba, 1868–1898." *Journal of American History* 81 (Sept. 1994) 494–516.
Pérez Firmat, Gustavo. 1990. *The Cuban Condition: Translation and Identity in Modern Cuba.* Cambridge: Cambridge University Press.
Phelan, Peggy. 1993. *Unmarked: The Politics of Performance.* London: Routledge.
Piedra, José. 1997. "Hip Poetics." In *Everynight Life: Culture and Dance in Latin/o America*, 93–140, ed. Celeste Fraser Delgado and José Esteban Muñoz. Durham, N.C.: Duke University Press.
Portuondo, José Antonio.1974. "Prólogo." In Mary Cruz, *Creto Gangá*, 7–12. Havana: Contemporaneo.
Pratt, Mary Louise. 1999. "Arts of the Contact Zone." *Border Texts: Cultural Readings for Contemporary Writers*, 367–77, ed. Randall Bass. Boston: Houghton Mifflin.
Rama, Angel. 1984. *La ciudad letrada.* Hanover, N.H.: Ediciones del Norte, 1984.
———. 1996. *The Lettered City*, edited and translated by John Charles Chasteen. Durham, N.C.: Duke University Press.
Roach, Joseph. 1996. *Cities of the Dead: Circum-Atlantic Performance.* New York: Columbia University Press.
Robreño, Eduardo. 1961. *Historia del teatro popular cubano.* Havana: Oficina del Historiador de la ciudad de la Habana.
———, ed. 1979. *Teatro Alhambra: antología.* Havana: Editorial Letras Cubanas.
Rodríguez, Victoria Eli. 1994. "Cuban Music and Ethnicity: Historical Considerations." In *Music and Black Ethnicity: The Caribbean and South America*, 91–108, ed. Gerard H. Béhague. New Brunswick, N.J.: Transaction Publishers.
Rogin, Michael. 1996. *Blackface, White Noise: Jewish Immigrants in the Hollywood Melting Pot.* Berkeley: University of California Press.
Roig De Leuchsenring, Emilio. 1937. "La Trágica noche del Villanueva." *Carteles*, 10 (January): 44–45.
Rowe, William and Vivian Schelling. 1991. *Memory and Modernity: Popular Culture in Latin America.* London: Verso.
Saragacha, Ignacio. 1990. *Ignacio Saragacha: teatro.* Ed. Rine Leal. Havana: Editorial Letras Cubanas.
Saxton, Alexander. 1990. *The Rise and Fall of the White Republic: Class Politics and Mass Culture in Nineteenth Century America.* London: Verso.

Scott, Rebecca J. 1985. *Slave Emancipation in Cuba: The Transition to Free Labor, 1860–1899*. Princeton: Princeton University Press.

Siegel, Micol. 2000. "Cocoliche's Romp: Fun with Nationalism at Argentina's Turn of the Century Carnival." *TDR: The Journal of Performance Studies* 44, 2 (T166) (Summer): 56–83.

Soja, Edward. 1993. *Postmodern Geographies: The Reassertion of Space in Critical Social Theory*. New York: Verso.

Sommer, Doris. 1991. *Foundational Fictions: The National Romances of Latin America*. Berkeley: University of California Press.

———. 1998. "Amerícan Accents Syncopate the State." In *The Ends of Performance*, 169–77, ed. Jill Lane and Peggy Phelan. New York: New York University Press.

Spivak, Gayatri Chakravorty. 1990. *The Postcolonial Critic: Interviews, Strategies, Dialogues*, ed. Sarah Harasym. London: Routledge.

Suárez y Romero, Anselmo. *Francisco, el ingenio o las delicias del campo*. Miami: Mnemosyne Publishing, 1969.

Taussig, Michael. 1987. *Shamanism, Colonialism, and the Wild Man: A Study in Terror and Healing*. Chicago: University of Chicago Press.

———. 1993. *Mimesis and Alterity: A Particular History of the Senses*. London: Routledge.

Taylor, Diana. 2003. *The Archive and the Repertoire: Performing Cultural Memory in the Americas*. Durham: Duke University Press.

Tchen, John Kuo Wei. 1999. *New York before Chinatown: Orientalism and the Shaping of American Culture, 1776–1882*. Baltimore: Johns Hopkins University Press.

Teatro bufo, siete obras. 1961. Preface by Samuel Feijoo. Havana: Imprenta Nacional.

Trexler, Richard. 1984. "We Think, They Act: Clerical Readings of the Missionary Theatre in 16th Century New Spain." In *Understanding Popular Culture: Europe from the Middle Ages to the Nineteenth Century*, 189–227, ed. Steven Kaplan. Berlin, New York: Mouton.

Turner, Victor. 1974. *Dramas, Fields and Metaphors*. Ithaca: Cornell University Press.

Upton, Elizabeth Perry. 1987. *Juan de Zabaleta and the Origins of Spanish Costumbrismo*. Ph.D. diss., New York University.

Urfé, Odilio. 1984. "Music and Dance in Cuba." In *Africa in Latin America: Essays on History, Culture, and Socialization*, 170–88, ed. Manuel Moreno Fraginals. Trans. Leonor Blum. New York: Holmes & Meier Publishers, Inc.

Villaverde, Cirilio. [1839/1881] 1981. *Cecilia Valdés, o la loma del angel*. Caracas: Biblioteca Ayacucho.

Villoch, Federico. 1946. "Los Bufos de Salas." *Carteles* 27, 1 (September 29): 22–23.

Vitier, Cinto. 1973. "Dos poetas cubanos: Plácido y Manzano." *Bohemia* 65:50.

Warner, Michael. 1993. "The Mass Public and the Mass Subject." In *The Phantom Public Sphere*, 234–56, ed. Bruce Robbins. Minneapolis: University of Minnesota Press.

Weiss, Judith, et al. 1993. *Latin American Popular Theatre: The First Five Centuries*. Albuquerque: University of New Mexico Press.

Williams, Lorna V. 1994. *The Representation of Slavery in Cuban Fiction*. Columbia: University of Missouri Press.

Williams, Raymond. 1977. *Marxism and Literature*. Oxford: Oxford University Press.

———. 1985. *Keywords: A Vocabulary of Culture and Society.* New York: Oxford University Press.

Ybarra, Patricia. 2002. *Staging Tlaxcala: From Cite of Complicity to Site of Resistance.* Ph.D. diss., University of Minnesota.

Zanetti, Susana, ed. 1973. *Costumbristas de América Latina (antología).* Buenos Aires: Centro Editor de América Latina S.A.

Ziter, Edward. 2003. *The Orient on the Victorian Stage.* Cambridge: Cambridge University Press.

Žižek, Slavoj. 1997. *The Plague of Fantasies.* London: Verso, 1997.

Index

Acknowledgments

This book is but one outcome of the extraordinary mentorship I have been so privileged to enjoy over the years from Joseph Roach, Diana Taylor, José Muñoz, Spencer Golub, and the late Bert O. States. Each of them, in his or her own way, has modeled scholarship as a vast and joyous art of the possible, creating the luminous conceptual architectures through which so many of us now move. My admiration for and my debt to them are immeasurable: this book is for them.

This project would not have been possible without the assistance and camaraderie of Fernando Saez and the Ludwig Foundation in Havana; Yasmina Proveyer; and the archivists and librarians at the Archivo Nacional de Cuba, the Sala Cubana of the Biblioteca Nacional José Martí, the Instituto de Literatura y Linguistica, and the Biblioteca Gener y del Monte in Matanzas. Generous conversations with Vivian Tabares Martínez, Tomas Robaína, Ambrosio Fornet, and the late Eduardo Robreño, who lent me a long afternoon in 1997, have all left their imprint on this project.

Research for this project was funded in part by an American Society for Theatre Research fellowship and an Ohio State University faculty research grant. An early essay from this project appeared in *Theatre Journal* (50 [1998]: 21–38), where it received important feedback and editing from Loren Kruger and anonymous readers. The conclusion appeared in different form as "Cubans on the Moon, and Other Imagined Communities," in *Fantasy and Colonialism*, edited by Graeme Harper (Continuum, 2002, 73–88.) Other material appears in "Black/face Publics," forthcoming in the second edition of *Critical Theory and Performance*, edited by Joseph Roach and Janelle Reinelt (University of Michigan Press). I owe thanks to Eric Cheyfitz, Jerome Singerman, and Theodore Mann at the University of Pensylvania Press for their support of the project, and I thank Erica Ginsburg and Christine L. Sweeney for their meticulous preparation of the manuscript.

The scope and ambitions of this project were shaped in the three remarkable post-disciplinary environments in which it developed. The first was the program in Performance Studies at New York University, where I was so fortunate to learn from Peggy Phelan, Barbara Browning, May Joseph,

Barbara Kirshenblatt-Gimblett, Brooks McNamara, Fred Moten, Ada Ferrer, and James Hatch, along with those listed above. I also benefited from inspiring colleagues, including Branislav Jakovljevic, Andre Lepecki, Jon McKenzie, Amanda Barrett, James Peck, Anna Bean, and Bertha Palenzuela, among so many others.

The second was my time in the dynamic Department of Comparative Studies at Ohio State University, led by the incomparable David Horn. Our collective work toward a program in comparative ethnic and American studies was an invaluable education; I am indebted to and remain a great admirer of my former colleagues Barry Shank, Thuy Linh Tu, Luz Calvo, Catriona Esquibel, Maurice Stevens, and Ruby Tapia. So too am I grateful for generative conversation and camaraderie with other OSU colleagues, including Laura Podalsky, Brian Rotman, Leslie Ferris, Amy Shuman, Galey Modan, Angeles Romero, Ileana Rodriguez, Fernando Unzueta, Gene Holland, Jon Ericson, and Phillip Armstrong.

Finally, the Hemispheric Institute of Performance and Politics, led by Diana Taylor, has created an extraordinary context for collaborative learning and research. I am so grateful to have had such brilliant interlocutors, among them Agnes Lugo-Ortiz, Doris Sommer, Sylvia Spitta, Gisela Canepa Koch, Leda Martins, Mary Louise Pratt, Linda Kintz, Antonio Prieto Stambaugh, Roselyn Constantino, Lorie Novak, and Teresa Marrero. The tireless efforts of Julie Taylor, Karen Young, Ayanna Lee, and Marlène Ramírez Cancio at the Institute were and remain far more valuable than they know.

The book developed in conversation with many more friends and colleagues along the way, including Erin Hurley, Rebecca Schneider, Shannon Steen, Judith Williams, Catherine Cole, Andrew Sofer, Shannon Jackson, Harvey Young, Una Chaudhuri, Alex Vasquez, Kate Ramsey, Deborah Paredez, Henry Bial, Josh Kun, and Bob Vorlicky, among others. For inspiration, I thank Bill Talen and Ricardo Dominguez. For friendship in and after the Havana archives, I thank Adrian Pearce, Jose Ortega, and the indomitable Manuel Barcia.

I am so grateful for the editing talents of Sarah Lane. Finally, I thank Ted Ziter for endless support and love, from the very beginning, and I thank Hanan for the daily gift of being herself.